WATER RIGHTS

WATER RIGHTS

Scarce Resource Allocation, Bureaucracy, and the Environment

Editor
TERRY L. ANDERSON

Foreword by
JACK HIRSHLEIFER

Pacific Studies in Public Policy

PACIFIC INSTITUTE FOR PUBLIC POLICY RESEARCH
San Francisco, California

International Standard Book Number: 0-88410-389-7 (CL)
0-88410-390-0 (PB)

Library of Congress Catalog Card Number: 83-3855

Printed in the United States of America

Library of Congress Cataloging in Publication Data

Main entry under title:

Water rights.

(Pacific studies in public policy)
Includes bibliographies and index.
Contents: Appropriators versus expropriators / Alfred G. Cuzán – The federal reclamation program / Randal R. Rucker and Price V. Fishback – Water pricing and rent seeking in California agriculture / B. Delworth Gardner – [etc.]
1. Water-rights – United States – Addresses, essays, lectures.
I. Anderson, Terry Lee, 1946-
II. Pacific Institute for Public Policy Research. III. Series.
KF5569.A2W37 1983 346.7304'691 83-3855
ISBN 0-88410-389-7 347.3064691
ISBN 0-88410-390-0 (pbk.)

The Pacific Institute for Public Policy Research is an independent, tax-exempt research and educational organization. The Institute's program is designed to broaden public understanding of the nature and effects of market processes and government policy.

With the bureaucratization and politicization of modern society, scholars, business and civic leaders, the media, policymakers, and the general public have too often been isolated from meaningful solutions to critical public issues. To facilitate a more active and enlightened discussion of such issues, the Pacific Institute sponsors in-depth studies into the nature and possible solutions to major social, economic, and environmental problems. Undertaken regardless of the sanctity of any particular government program, or the customs, prejudices, or temper of the times, the Institute's studies aim to ensure that alternative approaches to currently problematic policy areas are fully evaluated, the best remedies discovered, and these findings made widely available. The results of this work are published as books and monographs, and form the basis for numerous conference and media programs.

Through this program of research and commentary, the Institute seeks to evaluate the premises and consequences of government policy, and provide the foundations necessary for constructive policy reform.

PACIFIC STUDIES IN PUBLIC POLICY

Forestlands
Public and Private
Edited by Robert T. Deacon and M. Bruce Johnson
Foreword by B. Delworth Gardner

Urban Transit
The Private Challenge to Public Transportation
Edited by Charles A. Lave
Foreword by John Meyer

Politics, Prices, and Petroleum
The Political Economy of Energy
By David Glasner
Foreword by Paul W. MacAvoy

Rights and Regulation
Ethical, Political, and Economic Issues
Edited by Tibor M. Machan and M. Bruce Johnson
Foreword by Aaron Wildavsky

Fugitive Industry
The Economics and Politics of Deindustrialization
By Richard B. McKenzie
Foreword by Finis Welch

Money in Crisis
The Federal Reserve, the Economy, and Monetary Reform
Edited by Barry N. Siegel
Foreword by Leland B. Yeager

Natural Resources
Bureaucratic Myths and Environmental Management
By Richard Stroup and John Baden
Foreword by William Niskanen

Firearms and Violence
Issues of Public Policy
Edited by Don B. Kates, Jr.
Foreword by John Kaplan

Locking Up the Range
Federal Land Controls and Grazing
By Gary D. Libecap
Foreword by Jonathan R. T. Hughes

The Public School Monopoly
A Critical Analysis of Education and the State in American Society
Edited by Robert B. Everhart
Foreword by Clarence J. Karier

Resolving the Housing Crisis
Government Policy, Decontrol, and the Public Interest
Edited with an Introduction by M. Bruce Johnson

FORTHCOMING

The American Family and the State

Stagflation and the Political Business Cycle

Rationing Health Care
Medical Licensing in the United States

Oil and Gas Leasing on the Outer Continental Shelf

Taxation and Capital Markets

Myth and Reality in the Welfare State

Electric Utility Regulation and the Energy Crisis

Crime, Police, and the Courts

Drugs in Society

For further information on the Pacific Institute's program and a catalog of publications, please contact:

PACIFIC INSTITUTE FOR PUBLIC POLICY RESEARCH
177 Post Street
San Francisco, California 94108

CONTENTS

LIST OF FIGURES

LIST OF TABLES

FOREWORD

The allocation of resources to productive purposes always involves both market and political considerations. Even the most unrestricted market economy cannot operate without calling upon state power to deter theft, coercion, and fraud, and to enforce contracts entered into freely. Even the most absolute polity cannot rely solely on force and threats, but to some extent "buys" the consent of the governed—by providing services such as law and order, and by reserving some private sphere, however limited, for individual action. The relations between market and state may take on any of an enormous variety of institutional forms. Some of these, such as Soviet communism, have had such evil consequences for both economic efficiency and individual liberty that only the willfully blind can fail to read the message of history. On the other side, the advent of laissez faire in Britain signalled by the 1846 abolition of the Corn Laws ushered in an age of unparalleled economic, cultural, and humanistic development—a record that contrasts sadly with the modern decline of the United Kingdom, which dates from its embrace of the welfare state after World War I.

The story of the allocation of agricultural and urban water supplies in the United States, reported and analyzed in this book, is full of extremely useful lessons: about what the market can and cannot do, and about how and why state intervention, capable in principle of making things better, is likely to make things much worse.

Urban water development in the United States has followed a regular political cycle. As the typical great city grows in population and activity, it begins to press upon the limits of current water sources, thus creating a "water shortage" — a problem with irresistible attractiveness for politicians. The classic response of the city fathers has been to present a dramatic proposal, a projected miracle of engineering that will tap some vast new water source. (The alternative of simply raising water prices to users, thus providing at least a temporary respite, is never considered.) Finally the happy day arrives. The huge new supply comes on stream, only to be discovered to be a white elephant: costs are far higher than foreseen, and customers are scarcer. Now the political situation dictates keeping prices low, to save face for all concerned by inducing a respectable minimum usage. As for costs, the general taxpayer's purse is always available to be raided, with some help from creative bookkeeping. With the passage of time, however, continuing growth may bail out the project. Eventually, another generation of politicians comes to power, perceives its opportunity in the form of an impending new "water shortage," and 'round we go again.

The viability of the political water cycle depends upon ability to form a coalition that will overcome citizen skepticism (less necessary, of course, in those jurisdictions where huge bond issues can be floated without voter approval). Politicians and bureaucrats naturally have every incentive to join in an alliance that will allow them to distribute lucrative contracts and expand staffs, while posing in the spotlight as farseeing civic planners. Vendor interests and construction unions contribute finances and influence for the public campaign to promote the project. City boosterism groups can always be relied on to participate, and the naive good-government set often can be successfully cajoled into joining the winning coalition.

Provision for *agricultural* water supply illustrates a somewhat different political syndrome, though to much the same end: premature development on an excessive scale, combined with underpricing to stimulate use. The process here is not so much a cycle as a continuing logroll. On the federal level (the state and local levels differ only in details), project-generating agencies such as the Bureau of Reclamation and the Army Corps of Engineers are always active, supported by local politicians, potential beneficiaries of subsidies, and the usual contractor and vendor interests. As for the executive and legislative branches, various forms of vote buying, some subtle, some blatant, determine which projects are to be undertaken, and when.

But the era of glorious free spending by the government is now drawing to a close. While it is not true that we are running out of water in any absolute sense, we are certainly running out of supplies that can be developed with some degree of economic efficiency. There's still plenty of water up there in Alaska, true. But however the Ralph M. Parsons Co. and other avid contractors beat the drums, it is unlikely that the California citizenry can be conned into a Nome-to-Los Angeles aqueduct, at least not in the foreseeable future.

The political situation also has changed. Unthinking boosterism, which once exerted considerable force on public opinion and government policy, is now countered by antidevelopment fanaticism. Once-cozy dealings of the bureaucrat-politician-contractor establishment are now subject to searching scrutiny by suspicious radicals operating out of the district attorney's office. In an "age of limits," even usually reliable allies such as the League of Women Voters have grown doubtful about gigantic projects, about miracles of engineering as solutions to economic problems. And, very importantly, the growing politicization of society, in particular the bold political activism of the judiciary, is capable of generating an unlimited number of hurdles in the form of environmental impact reviews, complaints, injunctions, writs, appeals, depositions, hearings, and the like. It may be a true miracle if any project, however sound, can negotiate all these obstacles.

This increasing pressure on resources combined with loss of faith in establishment project politics poses a great opportunity and a great danger. The great opportunity is that government and public are now open to arguments in favor of allocating resources in accordance with economic principles. During the great "water shortage" of the 1950s and 1960s, the city of New York never considered modifying water prices that had been revised only once (in 1932) from a schedule dating back to 1896. But now the idea that prices should reflect real scarcity and the alternative cost of new supplies is seen on occasion even in the populist-radical press. Similarly, the economic attack upon patterns of discriminatory prices designed to favor groups with political clout—agriculture in some jurisdictions, wasteful and intensive water users elsewhere—is receiving a hearing, though listeners are typically more receptive to "equity" rather than efficiency arguments.

More difficult to make, in view of the spirit of the times, will be the case for assigning and perfecting property rights in water. As the authors of this volume explain, water rights should be well-defined, exclusive, secure, and transferable if the market is to function effectively in redirecting the resource to its most valuable uses. But in a populist era the idea of anyone having exclusive rights seems like an offense against the public. And in an activist age, the solution to be feared is subjecting all uses to the whim of a supervisory agency rather than to the even-handed enforcement of carefully defined property rights. When commissions or courts license only temporary uses, with tenure contingent upon "good behavior" according to some ill-defined notion such as serving the public good, the result is a grossly inefficient allocation of water resources. The timely historical and theoretical analyses contained in this book may significantly influence how this issue is resolved.

I would like to call attention to two themes addressed in many of the papers herein—rent seeking and the design of markets. Each of these themes illustrates how economic and political factors interact in social processes.

Rent seeking, known more accurately as *appropriative activity*, is the diversion of potentially productive resources toward efforts to acquire or defend politically defined rights to property. Not all appropriative activity is counterefficient. The creation of new assets by exploration or intellectual discovery and the capture of unpossessed and useless resources from the wild have been enormously valuable to society. But appropriative activity directed at redistributing already developed resources from possessors to new claimants is essentially nothing but social waste.

The very foundation of the state rests upon the publicization—the shift from the private to the public sphere—of much of the costly patrolling and monitoring dictated by the need to protect productive assets from being redistributed to intruding claimants. Were it not for this state policing that we call the *law*, human systems of property never would have advanced beyond mere territorial sequesterings backed by local preponderance of power.

But all systems of law are corrupted by the old problem: Who is to guard the guardians? Delegation of the power to defend private property rights necessarily implies the power to define, sit in judgment upon, tax away, and even ultimately seize such rights. The power of the political system to confer valuable resources upon suitably selected private parties has caused American farmers to cultivate the Congress rather than the good earth, supported vast numbers of talented people in a lobbying industry, and led to a shift of almost all headquarters of trade associations to Washington. The government agencies possessing such power have flourished like the cedars of Lebanon. The U.S. Bureau of Reclamation, discussed in detail in the Rucker-Fishback article, has compiled an unparalleled record of incredible waste through construction of costly, near-useless projects, as evidenced by practically universal financial default on the part of their client-beneficiaries.

But the situation is not hopeless. The extension of government power responsible for diverting private productive energies toward appropriative activity is restrained by a number of forces. Among them are the spirit and letter of constitutional restrictions and the lingering appeal of an ideology of limited government inherited from the founding fathers. But most important is the fact that politicians and bureaucrats ultimately compete with one another for office. The competition is imperfect, as detailed in Terry Anderson's introduction and Rodney Smith's contribution, but nevertheless real. With the help of books such as this one, citizens will gradually become better informed as to the causes, conduct, and consequences of rent seeking. When and if rent seeking becomes as notorious to the thinking public as protective tariffs have become, we will see politicians coming forth with proposals to counter this social evil. Of course, just as the battle against protective tariffs is never permanently won, the battle against wasteful appropriative activity promises to be a tough and continuing struggle. But the first step clearly is to put the facts and analysis before the public, as this volume does.

The second theme I want to mention, design of markets, focuses on returning to the private sphere some of the classes of decisions whose unwarranted publicization provides politicians and bureaucrats with the discretionary power that leads to rent seeking. To some extent, markets in valuable resources emerge naturally from anarchic situations by a social consensus, a process that has indeed occurred to some degree in the arid West, as described for the earlier historical period in Cuzán's paper and for recent times in Gardner's contribution. But almost always the state assumes a role early on, and how it defines property—for example, whether the riparian or the prior-appropriation rule is followed—can make an enormous difference (see the Tregarthen paper on Colorado law). The reason is that some forms of property rights are intrinsically less marketable than others: for example, a riparian water right typically is tied to riparian land even when more productive if used elsewhere.

A number of papers in this volume expand this concept, discussing the deliberate design of markets to promote efficiency in the use of water resources. One traditional argument used in attacks upon the private enterprise system has been the likelihood of market failure due to externalities, effects upon third parties not taken into account in two-sided exchange transactions. Pointing out that government failure poses at least as severe a problem as market failure, the authors of this volume proceed to the more constructive challenge of structuring possible systems of rights and markets that make the span of individual decisions conform with the consequences of those decisions, thus circumventing the problem of externalities. In this spirit Johnson, Gisser, and Tregarthen examine the problem of distinguishing rights of water *diversion* (with return flow) from rights of *consumptive use* (without return flow); Anderson, Burt, and Fractor study the possibility of parcelling out rights to waters in common underground basins; Huffman describes ways of assigning instream water use rights; and Maloney and Yandle address the issue of markets for tradable rights to emit pollutants. While all of these proposals are described with due scholarly caution, they remain very attractive possibilities. Realizing the potential benefits of market innovations will require the design or redesign of laws now governing property rights in water, thus providing some useful scope of action for constructive political entrepreneurship.

Jack Hirshleifer
University of California
Los Angeles

ACKNOWLEDGMENTS

Editing a book is often frustrating because it takes the coordination of so many people. In this case, however, the task was made much easier by the authors and by the personnel and support of the Pacific Institute for Public Policy Research. In particular, David Theroux, President of the Institute, encouraged me to undertake the project and assisted me as it progressed. Colleen Gilbride has made my editorial responsibilities much easier by communicating with the authors and with the copyeditor, Linda Chase, who did an excellent job of editing the manuscripts.

My colleague, Ron Johnson, also deserves much credit for the completion of this book. He read all the manuscripts and ensured that they were technically sound. Discussion with Ron has certainly improved my understanding of water institutions and improved the quality of the chapters contained herein. Finally, I want to thank John Baden, Director of the Center for Political Economy and Natural Resources, who also assisted in sounding out many of the ideas presented in this book.

If my family had been unwilling to put up with my absences and frustrations, my editing efforts would never have been completed. My wife, Janet, is always understanding and always supportive.

Terry L. Anderson

ACKNOWLEDGMENTS

INTRODUCTION
The Water Crisis and the New Resource Economics

Terry L. Anderson

Dried-up water supplies, sink holes the size of football fields, rivers that catch fire, and huge sprinkler irrigation systems are all indicators of a growing water crisis in the West. With memories of the Dust Bowl fresh in our minds, and as water shortages become more common, we are forced to ask, Are we running out of water?[1] If the answer is yes, what can we do about it?

Certainly these are not new concerns for residents of the arid West. Even before John Wesley Powell published his *Report on the Lands of the Arid Region of the United States* in 1878, the settlers were aware that water would be a limiting resource. To pioneers entering the Great Plains, where annual rainfall averages between 15 and 20 inches, it was clear that access to water was a prime consideration in choosing a location. As a result, initial settlement patterns can be traced to river and stream bottoms. If settlers found that a stream location was taken, they simply moved on to another water supply. It was not until all of these locations were claimed that the scarcity problem began to manifest itself. Farmers, growers of cattle and sheep, and miners all vied for the use of streams and lakes. When the location of water did not suit the needs of the user, the water was relocated. Sluices were built for mining and irrigation canals for

1. Jerry Adler, "Are We Running Out of Water?" *Newsweek*, 23 February 1981, pp. 26–37.

farming. When the time of year that water was available did not coincide with time of use, storage reservoirs were built. Conflicts over water use existed, but the settlers tried to resolve them by changing the institutions that governed allocation.[2] The riparian water doctrine from English common law, which provided that all owners of land abutting on a stream have equal or correlative rights to the water, was replaced with the arid region doctrine from the mining regions. The new doctrine held that ownership and use of water depends on prior appropriation and development of the resource.

The institutions that evolved from the miners' rules and regulations were simple and worked well until population growth put additional pressure on the water resources. Since the scarcity was caused in part by the uneven flow and geographic distribution of water, efforts were made to store water and control the flow. Major Powell suggested that this be accomplished through local self-governments organized according to hydrographic basins, but it was not long before the federal government was allocating funds to build dams, canals, and reservoirs to increase the supply at specific locations where water was scarce. The Newlands Reclamations Act of 1902 set in motion a long succession of federal projects aimed at increasing the supply of water. These eventually included the Colorado River projects, the Columbia Basin project, the Central Valley project, and the Tennessee Valley project—all dominated by massive dams and tremendous efforts to move water to nonriparian lands. In the Colorado-Big Thompson project of 1937, water was even transferred across the Continental Divide. The heritage of interbasin transfers is reflected in the controversial Peripheral Canal issue in California, which threatens to divide the state over the reallocation of water from north to south.

It is becoming increasingly clear that there simply is not enough water available to meet existing demands. Some argue that the water problem will persist until we move from a policy of supply management to one of demand management. If additional water is not made available, however, the issue becomes how the existing water should be allocated. Water rationing and political allocation according to a hierarchy of uses are often proposed, but the effectiveness of these schemes is questionable. The effectiveness of higher prices is not; as

2. For a discussion of water rights in the west, see Terry L. Anderson and P. J. Hill, "The Evolution of Property Rights: A Study of the American West," *Journal of Law and Economics* 18 (April 1975): 163–79.

municipal water bills have increased, water use per person has leveled off and in some cases even declined. With most water prices set by political agencies, however, it is unlikely that necessary price increases will occur and that demand management will be any more effective than supply management. Existing institutions simply appear to be incapable of providing enough additional water or of curtailing the growing demand.

The solution to the water crisis, therefore, will require institutional changes. Since the conventional laws, regulations, and agencies are not solving the water crisis and are often making it worse, we must search for institutions capable of expanding the supply whenever it is technologically and economically feasible and capable of efficiently allocating the water among competing demands. The energy crisis suggests that freely functioning markets offer this possibility.[3] When prices were allowed to rise to market levels, energy supplies increased and demands decreased. Before this can happen with water, ownership of the resource will have to be specified and impediments to trade removed.

The purpose of this book is to suggest an agenda for making such changes. The inequity and inefficiency brought about by "pork-barrel" allocations can no longer be ignored. The papers that follow suggest how markets in conjunction with private ownership will yield a more efficient and equitable allocation of water in the context of a free society.

THE NEW RESOURCE ECONOMICS

To understand the papers in this volume, it is useful to recognize the emerging new resource economics paradigm.[4] During the past few years, economists, lawyers, and political scientists have begun to refocus their attention on the institutional environment in which decisions are made. A return to traditional political economics, the new resource approach is a blend of the economics of property rights, public choice, and entrepreneurship.

3. See Robert E. Hall and Robert S. Pindyck, "What To Do When Energy Prices Rise Again," *The Public Interest* 65 (Fall 1981): 59–70.

4. For a more complete discussion of the new resource economics, see the work by Richard Stroup and John Baden, *Natural Resources: Bureaucratic Myths and Environmental Management* (Cambridge, Mass.: Ballinger and Pacific Institute for Public Policy Research, 1983).

The economics of property rights shows how the rules of the game affect the benefits and costs received and borne by private decision makers.[5] Individuals, not large groups or societies, make decisions, but they do so in an institutional framework. The property rights paradigm provides important analytical insight into how individuals interact. In its simplest form, the economics of property rights tells us that decisions will be affected by the benefits and costs faced by decision makers. These benefits and costs, in turn, will depend on the extent to which property rights are defined, enforced, and transferable, elements that are crucial to a well-functioning market.[6]

When property rights are well defined, individuals have a clear idea of what actions they can take regarding resources. This is necessary for market trades, which depend on parties to the transaction knowing what is being traded. For market allocation of water, such things as units of measure must be specified and superiority of rights must be recorded.

Enforcement will determine the likelihood that an owner of rights can enjoy the benefits of that ownership. Since rights cannot be perfectly enforced, ownership will always be probabilistic. When the probability of capturing benefits from a particular use is low, there is less likelihood that the owner will devote the resource to that use. For example, if a water owner leaves water in a stream to improve fish habitat but cannot exclude fishermen from using the stream, he or she will have less incentive to provide water for this purpose. In this sense, enforcement is the ability to exclude other users.

Finally, if owners are to be fully aware of the opportunity costs of their actions, property rights must be transferable. If owners are unable to transfer a resource to another use, they will not consider the full opportunity cost of that use and many higher valued uses may be ignored. Laws forbidding the use of water in coal slurry pipelines, for example, tell the water owner to ignore the value of water in this use; even if water for coal slurry is more valuable than for irrigation, the owner cannot capture the value by transferring the water to its higher valued use. Restrictions on transferability are restrictions on efficiency.

5. For a survey of property rights economics, see Eirik G. Furubotn and Svetozar Pejovich, "Property Rights and Economic Theory: A Survey of Recent Literature," *Journal of Economic Literature* 10 (December 1972): 1137-62.

6. For a summary of property rights applied to water, see Timothy D. Tregarthen, "The Markets of Property Rights in Water," in Jed P. Manada, ed., *Water Needs for the Future* (Boulder, Colo.: Westview Press, 1977), pp. 141-51.

When property rights are well defined, enforced, and transferable, individuals will reap the benefits and bear the costs of their decisions and actions. Through this connection, property rights guide the invisible hand of the marketplace.

Building on property rights concepts, the economics of public choice describes how individuals act within government. This approach helps us to predict the consequences of political institutions and compare the likely outcomes of alternative arrangements. It has taught us that the absence of property rights can generate *market* failure but that incentive structures within government can generate *government* failure. This increased understanding is most opportune given the increasing pressure from larger populations and from technologies that enhance our access to and ability to process natural resources.

Individuals acting in the political system are as likely as those in the private sector to be motivated by self-interest. Building on this premise, the public choice paradigm has uncovered several reasons why collective (governmental) action has failed to achieve efficient resource allocation.[7]

1. *Voter ignorance and imperfect information.* Because good information is costly in terms of time and effort (if not money) and because voters cannot capture the full benefits of being well-informed, voters remain rationally ignorant. As a result, the political process has a tendency to concentrate benefits and diffuse costs, allowing political entrepreneurs to serve their constituency through quotas, regulations, and subsidies that promote economic inefficiency.

2. *Special-interest effect.* With benefits concentrated and costs diffused, well-informed and articulate interest groups dominate the policy arena, contributing to campaigns and receiving political favors. Again, there is no check on economic efficiency.

3. *Short-sightedness effect.* Politicians who must face the electorate every few years have a tendency to be more concerned with the short run than with the long run. Policies that are efficient but that take time to produce beneficial effects will be of little interest to such politicians.

7. For a more complete discussion, see James D. Gwartney and Richard L. Stroup, *Economics: Private and Public Choice*, 2nd ed. (New York: Academic Press, 1980), chaps. 30–32.

4. *Little entrepreneurial incentive for internal efficiency.* Politicians and bureaucrats are not rewarded for efficiency. Politicians gain votes by serving organized interests in their constituency and bureaucrats gain power by enlarging the size of their bureaucracy. Efficiency is not a by-product of either.

5. *Imprecise reflection of consumer preferences and the bundle purchase effect.* Voters cannot shop around for specific policies. They must compare a bundle of political goods offered by one candidate with the bundles offered by opposing candidates. These bundles tend to reflect the preferences of a majority coalition rather than the wishes of individual voters.

Given these characteristics of the political sector, the economics of public choice suggest that the information and incentive structure is likely to generate government failure. Efficiency in government is not apt to occur unless the incentive structure faced by governmental decision makers is altered to conform more closely to that described by the property rights paradigm.

The third component of the new resource economics deals with the role of the entrepreneur. While this aspect has been ignored in the neoclassical economic literature, Austrian economics recognizes that the entrepreneur is the driving force in the competitive process.[8] When property rights are well defined, enforced, and transferable, the entrepreneur receives a residual reward for moving resources from lower to higher valued uses.[9] In this way, the residual claimant/entrepreneur *creates* added value for the economy. With a well-functioning system of private property rights, individuals can only obtain a residual through such a creation of value. The value created becomes a return over and above opportunity cost and is known in economics as a rent. The pursuit of such rents is a positive-sum game that produces the only free lunch available to society. For example, when a water owner reallocates irrigation water from a low-valued to a high-valued crop, the rent he or she captures is the difference between the two values. Because this value did not exist before the reallocation, it is truly created. Under efficient property rights, water

8. For the economics of entrepreneurship, see Israel M. Kirzner, *Competition and Entrepreneurship* (Chicago: University of Chicago Press, 1973).

9. For a discussion of the residual claimant, see Armen A. Alchian and Harold Demsetz, "Production, Information Costs, and Economic Organization," *American Economic Review* 62 (December 1972): 777-95.

owners have the incentive to seek out and find (and profit from) better uses for their water.

Unfortunately, the entrepreneur can also obtain rents through negative-sum games. When private property rights are attenuated, costs can be externalized so that one person's gain becomes another's loss. Under these conditions, the entrepreneur can obtain rents through subsidies and the regulation of competitors. Suppose, for example, that a person paying $50 per acre-foot for water lobbies for a regulation that prohibits water from being used where it is valued at $75 per acre-foot. If the regulation is enacted, the individual is implicitly receiving a return of $25 per acre-foot because he or she does not have to compete. Similarly, if a group convinces a state authority to allocate water to it and does not have to pay the opportunity cost of that water, it will be receiving a rent at someone else's expense. This is exactly what is happening with the Peripheral Canal in California.

Under these circumstances, entrepreneurs obtain rents by investing effort, time, and other productive resources in influencing governmental decisions. The transfers themselves represent a zero-sum game, but the investment in obtaining the transfers involves resources that are diverted from the production of goods and services elsewhere in the economy. Because resources are consumed and nothing of net value is created, the game is negative sum. In such a world, entrepreneurial talents are diverted from rent creation (productive activity) to rent seeking (transfer activity).[10] Any analysis of water policy must consider which type of activity is being encouraged and what the cost is.

The papers in this volume fit into the new resource paradigm. The reader with a background in the economics of property rights, public choice, or entrepreneurship will recognize most of the arguments but will find their application to water allocation innovative. The reader with no such background will find the conceptual framework as innovative as the applications. An effort has been made to limit economic jargon and technical economic models. Certain terminology (such as rent seeking), however, enhances communication and aids in our understanding of water problems. Furthermore, technical

10. For the distinction between rent creation and rent seeking, see James M. Buchanan, "Rent Seeking and Profit Seeking," in James M. Buchanan, Robert D. Tollison, and Gordon Tullock, eds., *Toward a Theory of a Rent-Seeking Society* (College Station, Tex.: Texas A&M University Press, 1981), pp. 3–15.

models ensure a degree of rigor that is necessary if future water policy is to have a sound foundation.

The first three papers provide an overview and historical background for water policy. Alfred Cuzán conceives of actors in the water game as "appropriators versus expropriators," a distinction that enhances our understanding of rent creation and rent seeking. Certainly the Bureau of Reclamation policy described by Randal Rucker and Price Fishback clarifies the ways in which rent seeking has been encouraged. The inefficiency and waste inherent in rent seeking is further exacerbated by water pricing policy, as described by Delworth Gardner.

Eliminating this inefficiency and waste will necessitate restructuring the institutions that govern water allocation. Micha Gisser and Ronald Johnson and Timothy Tregarthen provide insights into how the prior appropriation doctrine could be improved. The removal of restrictions on transfers and the definition of consumption rather than diversion rights offer two improvements. Rodney Smith describes the difference between private and public ownership of local irrigation facilities and explains why one form of ownership might be chosen over another. Since public ownership has often encouraged rent seeking, his paper provides important policy implications. Terry Anderson, Oscar Burt, and David Fractor tackle the difficult problem of privatizing groundwater basins. Their model identifies important externalities and leads to institutional prescriptions that could improve groundwater allocation. Application to the Tehachapi Basin in California provides a benchmark for evaluating groundwater privatization.

Two of the most difficult water rights problems center on instream use and pollution. By comparing private and public alternatives, James Huffman shows that public ownership is not necessary to guarantee efficient instream allocation. Revisions of the current institutional structure could make private alternatives viable. According to Mike Maloney and Bruce Yandle, tradable pollution rights are evolving in accordance with economic principles. Just as rights to land have changed as land has become more scarce, so have rights to pollute water as that resource has become scarcer. Their analysis suggests that a trend toward tradable pollution rights has improved water allocation.

This volume is not meant to cover the entire waterfront, but to set the agenda for future research. Applications of the new resource economics paradigm are necessary if water policy is to move toward improved efficiency. Well-defined, enforced, and tradable property rights for water offer the potential for encouraging productive activity and discouraging transfer activity. Consideration of this approach offers an alternative to the conflict inherent in public ownership—a system of cooperation through gains from trade.

PART I

PROPERTY RIGHTS AND DECISIONMAKING

Chapter 1

APPROPRIATORS VERSUS EXPROPRIATORS
The Political Economy of Water in the West

Alfred G. Cuzán

A POLITICAL ARGUMENT FOR THE PRIVATIZATION OF WATER IN THE WEST

Economists and philosophers since Locke and Smith have explained the economic laws of property and exchange. A solid body of scholarship, both classical and modern, suggests that aside from enforcing property rights, reducing transaction costs and, in some instances, providing for so-called public goods that are difficult to charge for, government can do little to improve the efficiency of free markets. This relatively unrestrained system, what Oppenheimer called the economic means of appropriation and exchange, constitutes one of the most effective mechanisms for harnessing the energies of enterprising human beings to increase production and raise living standards the world over.[1]

The same cannot be said for the other type of social system identified by Oppenheimer—the political means of expropriation and taxation. The indiscriminate use of laws and regulations, even in democracies, generally results in a net loss in efficiency as rent-seek-

1. Franz Oppenheimer, *The State* (Indianapolis: The Bobbs-Merrill Company Publishers, 1914); Ludwig von Mises, *Human Action* (New Haven, Conn.: Yale University Press, 1949).

ing groups team up with the bureaucracy and politicians to reap most of the benefits from public policy. The social costs of acting with institutions that raise revenues through taxes, register popular preferences with infrequent acts of voting, allocate resources in political struggles among small groups and manage them through a centralized bureaucracy generally exceed whatever benefits are bestowed on the public or the small, active minorities who exercise the most influence or control over the government's actions.[2]

The contrasts between the economic and the political means in the field of water resources has been of interest to economists and lawyers for some time. In their path-breaking book, *Water Supply*, Hirshleifer, DeHaven, and Milliman noted the many failures of water policies at the local, state, and federal levels, arguing that a better method would be to treat water like any commodity, subject to appropriation and exchange in a market economy.[3] Water policy in the nineteenth century embodied this approach, so the authors' recommendation actually was a reversal of the policies that had accumulated since 1880. Other writers have arrived at similar conclusions.

My purpose in this paper is not to repeat the economic arguments against government controls, but rather to make a political case for privatization. By examining the machinery of government and the dynamics of politics, I will show that the internal laws that regulate the political means necessarily promote centralization and bureaucratization of the water industry, not in the interest of equity or efficiency, but as a consequence of organized efforts by a ruling class to expropriate income and wealth from the public. This constant relation, as Mosca calls it, is probably the most solidly established law in political science.[4] In order to escape its perverse power, society must choose the economic laws of the market instead.

I begin with a discussion of Locke's positive theory of property, which explains the way water in fact was appropriated under nearly anarchical conditions in the West during the mid-nineteenth century. I then examine the evolution of public water policies since 1860, demonstrating that they have consistently expanded and centralized

2. See William C. Mitchell, *The Anatomy of Public Failure: A Public Choice Perspective* (Los Angeles: International Institute for Economic Research, Original Paper 13, June 1978).

3. Jack Hirshleifer, James C. DeHaven, and Jerome W. Milliman, *Water Supply* (Chicago: University of Chicago Press, 1969).

4. Gaetano Mosca, *The Ruling Class* (New York: McGraw-Hill, 1939).

the power of those who influence, control, and benefit from the political means. This is followed by an analysis of the organizational instruments that have planned, promoted, and implemented these policies in a comparative study of the federal Bureau of Reclamation and the Water and Power Department of the city of Los Angeles. These two agencies are remarkably similar in their political origins, territorial growth strategies, and evolution toward centralized bureaucratic management. I conclude with a suggested rule for reappropriating water in the United States.

THE AMERICAN DOCTRINE OF PRIOR APPROPRIATION: A LOCKEAN EXPERIMENT IN NATURAL LAW

In *The Second Treatise of Government*, John Locke explains how increasingly scarce common-pool resources come to be appropriated in a State of Nature according to the principles of priority of right and beneficial use, a model that can readily be applied to the history of the American doctrine of prior appropriation.[5] Locke assumes that, in the beginning, the earth and its products constitute a great common to mankind while individuals have a property in their own persons. Nature compels individuals to apply their labor to take what they need from the commons in order to survive.

A person's right to anything in the commons is established by the simple act of taking it or enclosing it with his or her own labor. With respect to water, Locke observes, "Though the water running in the fountain be everyone's, who can doubt that in the pitcher is his only who drew it out? His labor has taken it out of the hands of nature where it was common and belonged equally to all her children and has thereby appropriated it to himself."[6] Note that the act of *removing* a portion of the commons establishes an individual's property over it, eliminating the ambiguity associated with the concept of "mixing" one's labor with the earth: "the *taking* of what is common

5. Compare Locke's *The Second Treatise of Government* (Indianapolis: Liberal Arts Press, 1952) with the following two articles: Armen A. Alchian and Harold Demsetz, "The Property Rights Paradigm," *Journal of Economic History* 33 (1973): 16–27; and Terry L. Anderson and P. J. Hill, "The Evolution of Property Rights: A Study of the American West," *Journal of Law and Economics* 18 (1975): 163–179.

6. Locke, *Second Treatise*, p. 18.

and removing it out of the state nature leaves it in which begins the property, without which the commons is of no use" (emphasis added).[7] Locke calls this principle the "original law of nature."

In some instances, the act of discovery, itself being an act of labor, is sufficient to establish a prior right even before actual enclosure. The hunter, for example, who pursues a hare "has thereby removed her from the state of nature wherein she was common, and has begun a property."[8] Thus, a man who first discovers a gold mine or a new source of water establishes a right to it by virtue of having found it.

Under conditions of unlimited supply or relative abundance the appropriation of any part of the commons harms no one, as Locke observes with respect to water: "Nobody could think himself injured by the drinking of another man, though he took a good draught, who had a whole river off the same water left him to quench his thirst; and the case of land and water, *where there is enough for both*, is perfectly the same."[9] (emphasis added). However, under the more usual condition of relative scarcity of either land or water, where each succeeding appropriation leaves fewer or less valuable resources in the commons, an individual's right is limited to only so much as he or she can use to any advantage before it spoils; additional resources exceed his or her share and belong to others. This rule applies not only to the products of the earth, such as wildlife and water, but also to land: "As much land as a man tills, plants, improves, cultivates, and can use the product of, so much is his property. He by his labor does, as it were, enclose it from the common. . . ."[10]

Individuals may give away, barter, or exchange for money anything that they appropriate. It is only if one allows resources or products of the earth to rot or remain unproductive that "this part of the earth, notwithstanding his enclosure, was still to be looked on as waste and might be the possession of any other. . . ."[11]

Therefore, in a modern economy, one need not work resources directly in order to retain title. All one need do is to ensure that what one owns does not go to waste, for example, the stockholder in a water company, the buyer of canal bonds, and the speculator in water rights. Locke would not have found the commercialization of

7. Ibid.
8. Locke, *Second Treatise*, p. 19.
9. Ibid., p. 20.
10. Ibid., p. 20.
11. Locke, *Second Treatise*, p. 23.

water irreverent or objectionable in any way; on the contrary, he would have heartily agreed with the authors of *Water Supply* on this point.

Like a modern economist, Locke argued that as resources that were once part of the great commons of mankind rise in value, individuals strive to appropriate them. Far from harming those who fail to acquire a portion of the shrinking commons, the process of appropriation benefits them as well by increasing the productivity of the resource:

> He that encloses land, and has a greater plenty of the conveniences of life from ten acres than he could have from a hundred left to nature, may truly be said to give ninety acres to mankind; for his labor now supplies him with provisions out of ten acres which were by the product of a hundred lying in common.[12]

It is not my purpose here to evaluate Locke's theory as a normative principle of justice. Rather, I want to use the positive aspect of the theory to explain the process by which the waters of the West were originally appropriated outside the established legal framework, or as Locke would say, "out of the bounds of society."

Locke's theory of property rests on a natural law of appropriation regulated by economic forces. As resources held in common become more scarce, the most enterprising members of the community–the industrious and rational–apply their labor to enclose and put them to use. In order to minimize the cost or inconvenience associated with disputes over title or the size of possession, the appropriators, by voluntary consent, reach agreement on two fundamental rules for dividing the commons: (1) first come, first served, or priority of right acquired by virtue of discovery or possession, and (2) a person's right is limited to what he or she puts to beneficial use.

It is precisely these two principles upon which the American doctrine of prior appropriation rests. This body of rules was developed by communities of California miners in mid-nineteenth century. Around 1850, thousands of men came from around the world to search for gold in what was then largely a wilderness. They became squatters on the federal public domain, outside the established legal order, with no government to impose order or settle their disputes. In effect, they found themselves in a "state of nature." As Locke

12. Locke, *Second Treatise*, p. 23.

would have predicted, a first come, first served principle was adopted in the establishment of rights over what had been held in common—minerals and water—along with limitations on what any one individual could own.

> Following a tradition of collective action on the mining frontiers of other continents, the miners formed districts, embracing from one to several of the existing 'camps' or 'diggings' and promulgated regulations for marking and recording claims. The miners universally adopted the priority principle, which simply recognized the superior claims of the first arrival. But the . . . miner's codes defined the maximum size of claims, set limits on the number of claims a single individual might work, and established regulations designing certain actions—long absence, lack of diligence, and the like—as equivalent to the forfeiture of rights. A similar body of district rules regulates the use of water flowing in the public domain.[13]

In order to ensure that no valuable mineral rights were wasted, local custom sanctioned claim jumping whenever "the prior claimant had abandoned his claim, had failed to diligently work it, had staked it without following local regulations, or held more claims than district rules permitted."[14]

These customs spread throughout the West as miners, irrigators, and cattlegrowers took possession of the most valuable portions of the public domain without legal authorization from territorial, state, or federal governments. The first person to work a mine, graze a herd on a meadow, or divert water from a stream acquired a prior right to what he or she took, and these appropriations were for the most part respected by subsequent settlers.

Elwood Mead describes how cattlegrowers on the public domain divided the grasslands among themselves:

> There was no law by which men could legally secure control of the land they occupied. All the land laws dealt with farming land. There was no provision for leasing or settling the grazing land in tracts large enough to be of any service. Hence the range stockmen simply took possession of the country. Each man chose a location which suited him, fixed in a rough way the boundaries of his domain, and helped to create a public sentiment which made it unpleasant, if not dangerous, for a late comer to attempt to share with him the terri-

13. Charles W. McCurdy, "Stephen J. Field and Public Land Law Development in California, 1850-1866: A Case Study of Judicial Resource Allocation in Nineteenth-Century America," *Law and Society* (Winter 1976): p. 236.

14. Ibid., p. 243.

tory he had so marked out. In this way range rights came to have the force of law.[15]

The custom originated by miners and cattlegrowers had the greatest impact with respect to water used for irrigation. The American doctrine of prior appropriation, or arid region doctrine, was adopted by state constitutions, legislation, and judicial rulings. It sanctioned the diversion of water for use on lands far from the natural watercourse on the basis of priority of right and wrought what Webb called "a revolution in the law of water" displacing the riparian doctrine partially or totally over most of the West.[16] The greater the relative scarcity of water, the more it was appropriated. Thus, the doctrine became most firmly established in the most arid portions of the region–Arizona, New Mexico, Utah, Nevada, Colorado, and Idaho.

The new body of law effectively separated rights to water from rights to land. Companies mobilized private capital to build irrigation works and transport water to where it was most productively used. Writing in 1903, Mead called corporate irrigation "the leading factor in promoting agricultural growth of the Western two-fifths of the United States."[17] Mead credited canal companies with promoting efficient irrigation practices through contractual arrangements, advising the state of Colorado to study canal companies' management of the water they appropriated.

By 1910, over 13 million acres of land were irrigated privately in the 17 western states.[18] In a very short time, thousands of farmers had multiplied by many times the productive value of this region. Mead, who found much to object to in private water development, nevertheless acknowledged that "in the last third of the nineteenth century the arid West became one of the greatest irrigated districts of the globe. In mileage of ditches and in acres of land irrigated it surpasses any country of Europe or Africa and is second only to India and China in Asia. . . ."[19]

15. Elwood Mead, *Irrigation Institutions* (New York: Macmillan Co., 1903), pp. 28–29.

16. Walter Prescott Webb, *The Great Frontier* (Austin, Tex.: University of Texas Press, 1951), pp. 254–259.

17. Mead, *Irrigation Institutions*, p. 57.

18. Alfred R. Golzé, *Reclamation in the United States* (Caldwell, Id.: Cayton Printers, 1961), p. 12.

19. Mead, *Irrigation Institutions*, p. 349.

By the turn of the century, this remarkable phase of private development of the West, a reflection of the laissez faire era of the late nineteenth century, was in its twilight. A wave of so-called reform was being mobilized by men such as Major Powell and his nephew Arthur P. Davis, Elwood Mead, F. H. Newell, William Stewart, Theodore Roosevelt, and others. They sought to regulate the water industry with the police power, expropriate rights with the navigation acts, develop the American desert with public funds while simultaneously promoting democracy west of the hundredth meridian with the land grants.

EXPROPRIATION OF WATER BY STATE AND FEDERAL GOVERNMENTS: A HISTORY OF WATER POLICIES IN THE ARID LANDS

The history of water policies since 1860 is one of expropriation of property rights by federal, state, and local governments. This trend is manifested in the transformation of the appropriation doctrine into administrative law at the state level; control over canal company water rates by state and county governments; state controls over underground water pumping; the takeover of private water companies by municipal governments; and the imposition of federal controls over rivers, dams, reservoirs, and irrigation works for reclamation and power development. In this section, the evolution of state and federal controls is reviewed in general terms. Part IV compares in detail Bureau of Reclamation policies with those of the city of Los Angeles.

From Rights to Permits: The Evolution of the Water Law at the State Level

In much of the arid West, the appropriation doctrine was being applied by irrigators and miners before state or even territorial governments were organized. A potent political force, appropriators were able to resist or overcome efforts by the newly organized governments to establish bureaucratic controls over them. However, over a number of decades, an accretion of state and judicial controls, promoted by reformers and the federal government, transformed the doctrine of appropriation into a system of administrative law.

In one of its first acts, the California legislature in 1851 sanctioned the local customs by which water and mineral rights had been established.[20] Over the next decade, a series of state supreme court decisions lent additional sanction to the appropriation doctrine, which took its place along if not above the riparian doctrine.

The initial victory of the appropriators was relatively short-lived, however. No sooner had their rights been recognized than the political means were organized to expropriate them. State constitutions and statutes universally adopted the principle of public ownership over water. Appropriators were granted the right to use the water (usufructury right) but ownership over the resource itself (the *corpus* of water) was declared state property. The inherent tension between these two principles eventually was resolved in favor of state controls over water.

The first impetus to state controls over water were water rights disputes. As the population and water demands in the West grew, the decision or transaction costs associated with the establishment and the adjudication of rights increased. In periods of drought, disagreements between senior and junior and upstream and downstream appropriators presented opportunities for judicial and administrative interventions. These were taken partly at the behest of irrigators themselves, who wanted the state to subsidize, at least partly, the settling of conflicting or competing claims. For example, following a series of conflicts over the Cache La Poudre River in 1874, Colorado irrigators "met in convention to demand legislation for public determination and establishment of rights of appropriation, and then state superintended distribution of water in accordance with the thus settled titles. . . ."[21] These recommendations were incorporated into law in 1879.

The transformation of the appropriation doctrine into administrative law, begun with judicial or administrative interventions to settle disputes, established the following requirements and restrictions:

1. Requirements for the filing of new claims, first at the county, then the state level

20. McCurdy, "Public Land Law Development," p. 239; Samuel C. Wiel, *Water Rights in the Western States* (San Francisco: Bancroft-Whitney Company, 1980), p. 12.

21. Moses Lasky, "From Prior Appropriation to Economic Distribution of Water by the State Via Irrigation Administration," *Rocky Mountain Law Review* I:3: 173. See also Golzé, *Reclamation in the United States*, p. 10.

2. Limitations on the size of excessive claims and legal specifications on the duty of water (the amount applied to an acre of crops)
3. Attachment of water rights to specific land tracts
4. The disallowal of ownership to water by canal companies that did not irrigate lands of their own
5. Regulation of canal company rates by states and counties
6. State encouragement of the formation of irrigation districts with the power to tax, condemn property, and sell bonds to finance construction of irrigation works and buy out water companies
7. Legislative determination of what constitutes beneficial use, along with the ranking of uses by classes
8. Prohibition on sale of water rights beyond state or irrigation district boundaries
9. Administrative allocation of water during periods of drought
10. The establishment of a centralized bureaucracy headed by a state engineer or water commissioner to administer policies and judicial decrees and, in some states, undertake irrigation projects.

Thus, rights established extralegally in a quasi-anarchistic setting gradually were transformed to the status of permits or licenses held at the sufferance of state officials. As early as the first decade of the twentieth century, Professor Moses Lasky, perhaps prematurely, declared in a three-part article in the *Rocky Mountain Law Review*, that the principle of appropriation had all but vanished.[22] In his view, Wyoming and Colorado were leading a new "revolution" in western water law. The thrust of these changes was *away* "from various forms of extreme individualism and vested property rights of substance in water to the same goal, the economic distribution of state-owned water by a state administrative machinery through state-oriented conditional privileges of user. . . . The transition has been via administration, and in administration is most clearly noted."[23] Fifty years later this trend was confirmed by Milliman.[24]

22. Lasky, "From Prior Appropriation," p. 269.
23. Ibid., p. 162.
24. J. W. Milliman, "Water Law and Private Decision-Making: A Critique," *Journal of Law and Economics* II (1959): 41-63. See also Hirshleifer, De Haven, and Milliman, *Water Supply*, chap. IX.

The transformation of a system of water rights acquired independently of the government into one of permits secured from a state bureaucracy undermined the security of titles, making it difficult to transfer water to its most productive uses. This system increased the unreliability of water supply, prevented the integration of irrigation works and river systems, and led to a cumbersome structure of regulations and decrees. In a description of the distribution system of a California irrigation district, Mason Gaffney noted:

> The Kaweah water distribution system has had to grow in a manner analogous to the law itself, with one principle hanging on another back to the ancient and ultimate fountainheads of authority. It is questionable whether circuitous transfers of this sort are desirable at all, even if each individual operation shows a net gain. For as one ditch is latched on to another, more and more interests become vested in an increasingly absurd tangle and the hope of rationalization recedes even further into the realm of inattentive visions.[25]

Moreover, vesting property rights over water in irrigation districts and mutual water companies rather than in individuals had resulted in practical prohibition of its sale. Thus, much water "is effectively withdrawn from commerce in a mortmain grip as deadly as that fastened on the lands of medieval Europe."[26]

The cumbersome and antiquated system of controls described by Gaffney has made it difficult for much of the water to be transferred privately through marginal adjustments made by continuous sales. Instead, the system generates pressures for a step-wise program of monumental water schemes by state and federal agencies, which subsidize low-value crops such as alfalfa and pasture with a policy that produces "too much water, too late."[27]

Also contributing to political pressures for large projects has been the tendency of state governments to grant permits to a volume of water that is greater than what is, in fact, available. Because the water rights of the most junior appropriators are worthless unless additional volume is made available, support is generated for dams and water transfer projects, which raise the value of junior rights.[28]

25. Mason Gaffney, "Diseconomies Inherent in Western Water Laws: A California Case Study," *Western Resources and Economics Development*, Report #9, Western Agricultural Economics Research Council, 1961, p. 71.

26. Ibid., p. 74.

27. Ibid., p. 78.

28. See Elco Greenshields, *Journal of Farm Economics* (December 1955): 900.

Ironically, one of Mead's criticisms of the appropriation doctrine was that it sanctioned excessive claims, often amounting to several times the known river flow. Yet the imposition of state controls did not end the practice; it simply made the results far more costly. Individual overappropriations were checked by their resources to invest in diversion works. State overappropriations are constrained only by the amount of money the federal government is willing to spend augmenting local supplies.

Reclamation and Navigation: The Imposition of Federal Controls

As indicated in the previous section, state legislatures and courts had begun to legalize private claims on the basis of the appropriation doctrine. At the initiative of Nevada Senator William Stewart, Congress in 1866 followed suit and gave its consent to the state laws and local customs on which private claims to minerals and water rested.[29] From then on, however, public entrepreneurs such as Major John Wesley Powell and future commissioners of the Bureau of Reclamation such as F. H. Newell, Arthur P. Davis, and Elwood Mead seemed to be engaged in a race with appropriators for the control of water and irrigable lands in the region. They claimed that federal control would promote scientific conservation and development of land and water resources; prevent the monopolization of water by corporations and speculators; streamline the system for establishing and enforcing water rights; and encourage the development of rural democracy by war veterans and other deserving pioneers. These policies received the strong backing of at least three presidents, including the two Roosevelts and Herbert Hoover.

In 1878, Major Powell, director of the U.S. Geological Survey, presented to Congress his *Report on the Lands of the Arid Region* in which he urged the federal government to assert vigorous control over its western holdings in cooperation with locally organized districts. While welcoming the impetus given to western development by private efforts, he warned that the separation of water rights from land titles would lead to concentration of ownership. "Monopolies of water will be secured, and the whole agriculture of the country

29. Wiel, *Water Rights in the Western States*, p. 26.

will be tributary thereto—a condition of affairs which an American citizen having in view the interests of the largest number of people cannot contemplate with favor."[30]

During the next decade Powell single-mindedly pursued what can only be characterized as a massive land grab of the West, withdrawing from entry 850 million acres of the public domain. He designed large-scale plans for their orderly surveying, irrigation, and development under federal guidance. His budget grew from $50,000 in 1878 to $156,000 in 1881, reaching over $750,000 in 1890.[31]

Powell's policies elicited a mixed response from irrigation interests. As chairman of the Senate Committee on Irrigation, Senator Stewart managed to increase Powell's budget and support his plans for federal surveys of irrigable lands and reservoir sites. The senator was particularly interested in the development of the waters of the Carson, Walker, and Truckee Rivers in Nevada, which in his view were being allowed to go to waste. In 1889, the two men, along with other members of the Senate Irrigation Committee, toured the arid region seeking support for a federal role in irrigation. Two years later irrigation congresses began to meet to promote federal reclamation policies.

But soon after the trip the friendship between Stewart and Powell cooled as their personalities and ideas clashed. Stewart simply wanted federal subsidies with few strings attached to water rights or land uses. Powell, on the other hand, wanted greater federal control preceded by years of study and planning. As the latter continued to withdraw additional millions of acres from entry, opposition in the Congress grew, led by Stewart and another Nevadan, Congressman Francis G. Newlands, an owner of land and reservoir sites along the Truckee and Carson Rivers. Newlands, who later became a U.S. senator, opposed Powell's long-term planning schemes because they obstructed "practical" federal irrigation projects such as the one that now bears his name. Powell was forced to resign in 1894 and Congress loosened the controls he had imposed.

30. J.W. Powell, *Report on the Lands of the Arid Region of the United States*, House of Representatives Ex. Doc. No. 73, 45th Cong., 2nd sess., April 1878, p. 43.

31. Wallace Stegner, *Beyond the Hundredth Meridian: John Wesley Powell and the Second Opening of the West* (Boston: Houghton Mifflin Company, 1954), pp. 233, 273, 337, 341. For a less romantic view of Powell and others associated with reclamation see Stanley Roland Davison, "The Leadership of the Reclamation Movement, 1875-1902" (Doctoral diss., University of California, 1951).

Eight years later, the Reclamation or National Irrigation Act was enacted, initiating a new era of federal subsidies and controls. It began as a relatively modest effort designed to win the support from the West without generating too much opposition from the East. The government would sell public lands and put the proceeds into a separate reclamation fund out of which projects would be financed to irrigate new lands. Capital costs would be repaid within ten years and no interest would be charged. Expenditures among the western states would be proportional to the amount of revenues generated by sales of public lands within their borders. Farms would not exceed 160 acres, which would promote rural democracy. Irrigation works and the acquisition of water rights would conform with state laws, provided that the water rights be made appurtenant to the land. Finally, no "Mongolian" labor (a statutory reference to Oriental immigrants seeking work) was to be employed in the construction of irrigation works.

Hibbard summarizes what in retrospect turned out to be remarkably accurate predictions by the opponents of the act:

> A New York Congressman estimated that the plan would ultimately cost the country billions of dollars. Dalzell of Pennsylvania believed it a plan to "unlock the doors of the treasury." Mr. Cannon of Illinois dubbed the bill a "direct grant in an indirect way." Payne of New York was of a like mind, while Hepburn of Iowa insisted . . . "that this is a thinly veneered and thinly disguised attempt to make the government, from its general fund, pay for this great work—great in extent, great in expenditure, but not great in results."[32]

As it turned out, the critics were right. Within a few years, the federal treasury had to funnel tens of millions of dollars into the fund; repayment periods were extended first to twenty, then forty, then over fifty years as most projects failed financially.

In his seminal study of the relative costs and benefits of land reclamation in the Southeast and West, Rudolph Ulrich estimated that the costs of bringing desert land into agricultural production were from five to fourteen times as great as the costs of clearing, fertilizing, and controlling water inputs to lands in the Southeast.[33]

32. Benjamin H. Hibbard, *A History of the Public Land Policies* (Madison, Wisc.: University of Wisconsin Press, 1965), p. 442.

33. Rudolph Ulrich, "Relative Costs and Benefits of Land Reclamation in the Humid Southeast and the Semi-arid West," *Journal of Farm Economics* 35 (1953): 62–73.

Thus, federal efforts to make marginal desert lands bloom made no economic sense. Yet the more resources were spent for this purpose, the fewer remained to invest in the South, as Hibbard observed:

> In passing the Reclamation Act in 1902 as a nation we clearly forgot those things which were behind, the millions of unoccupied acres of the Mississippi Valley, consisting mostly of fertile, well-watered land needing only to be drained or cleared. Had we really been concerned over the future food supply as we pretended to be, or, being so concerned, had we calmly asked how to increase it in the cheapest and easiest manner, certain of the Reclamation projects would still be undeveloped.[34]

While support for reclamation projects was being harnessed, the federal government used the navigation acts to prevent private parties from developing reservoir sites or rivers it had already selected for itself. These acts asserted federal control over navigable rivers and all their tributaries on the basis of the commerce clause of the Constitution. They gave the government the power to expropriate property so that private concerns could not impede navigation without making any compensation. In several instances, such as in the Rio Grande and Colorado rivers, this power was invoked in order to block private irrigation projects that the Bureau of Reclamation later built itself, bringing ruin to the private developers.[35]

In his critique of the much-abused navigation doctrine, Charles E. Corker noted that it has proved to be a useful judicial device even when it was evident that the river was not navigable.

> Both the Congress and the courts have been content to treat the word "navigation" as an open sesame to constitutionality. So long as Congress uses the word in statute and the case relates to something moist, the Court takes at face value the declaration that the legislation is in furtherance of navigation. Moreover, the test of what constitutes a navigable stream has been stretched to embrace most of the waters of the United States.[36]

34. Hibbard, *History of Public Land Policies*, p. 449. Hibbard quotes a former director of the Reclamation Service as saying, "The fundamental object was to 'make men, not money'," a project in human or social engineering that socialist dictatorships favor in their attempts to build a "new socialist man."

35. Stegner, *Beyond the Hundredth Meridian*, pp. 310–312; Charles E. Corker, "Water Rights and Federalism – The Western Water Rights Settlement Bill of 1957," *California Law Review* 45 (1957): 604–637; Morris Hundley, Jr., *Water and the West* (Berkeley: University of California Press, 1975), pp. 19–26.

36. Corker, "Water Rights and Federalism," pp. 616–617.

It is evident that the long-term trend of federal policy has been to mobilize financial, administrative, political, constitutional, and judicial resources at its disposal to gain—or, perhaps more accurately, regain—control of western waters. It is as if, having been presented with a fait accompli in 1867, federal officials entered a race against time to gain control of the land and waters that were left unappropriated and recoup their previous losses. This was accomplished with a combination of subsidies designed to persuade irrigators and state governments to surrender or compromise their rights and open-ended constitutional claims to federal powers.

Note that federal and state policies have pursued similar strategies. The appropriation doctrine has been undermined, water rights have been virtually expropriated and converted into licenses or permits, and control over western waters has been centralized in state and federal governments. The tools may have been different, but the results have been the same.

THE IRON LAWS OF POLITICAL SCIENCE: A COMPARATIVE STUDY OF THE BUREAU OF RECLAMATION AND THE CITY OF LOS ANGELES

The long-run trend of public policies to expropriate water rights and centralize control over the resource in federal and state bureaucracies can be explained by two natural laws of politics: *the iron law of political redistribution* and *the law of hierarchical centralization.* Here I present a model of government in which a ruling class of bureaucrats, politicians, and interest groups—Lowi's "iron triangles"[37]—use political means to transfer wealth from the mass of the public to themselves. Such transfers are more efficiently carried out the greater the centralization of the government. I illustrate the model with a comparative study of the federal Bureau of Reclamation and the city of Los Angeles.

37. Theodore Lowi, *American Government: Incomplete Conquest* (New York: Holt, Rinehart and Winston, 1976).

A Political Model[38]

In government, individuals act in order to maximize their own utility with the political means of taxation, expropriation, and control or influence over so-called public resources. Those who specialize in exerting control or influence over specific policies constitute what Mosca calls a ruling class. Since the costs of public policy are borne, directly or indirectly, by the entire society, the ruling class in every policy area succeeds in transferring wealth or income from the mass of the public to itself. I call this phenomenon the *iron law of political redistribution.*

Political actors include the following:

1. *Bureaucrats.* The managers of public enterprises, they are control-maximizing actors who strive to secure as many resources—land, water, budgets, employees, or regulatory power—as possible. The more they control, the greater their utility.

2. *Politicians.* These influence-maximizing actors secure votes and consent from the public and its leaders. Politicians run for offices that are constitutionally or legally authorized to make the fundamental policy decisions on behalf of the public. They are the ultimate legitimators of what government does by enacting its laws and approving its budgets. With these decisions they influence the behavior of the bureaucrats. Politicians tend to specialize at influencing those agencies most relevant to their interests, sometimes to the extent that they actually control the agencies. For example, western congresspersons and senators tend to dominate congressional committees that authorize reclamation projects.[39]

38. This model is part of a theory of politics I have presented in "Political Profit: Taxing and Spending in the Hierarchical State," *American Journal of Economics and Sociology* 40 (1981): 265–275. Among the many contemporary scholarly works that have influenced my thinking, three are of special significance: Anthony Downs, *An Economic Theory of Democracy* (New York: Harper & Row, 1957); Gordon Tullock, *The Politics of Bureaucracy* (Washington, D.C.: Public Affairs Press, 1965); and Randall Bartlett, *Economic Foundations of Political Power* (New York: Free Press, 1973).

39. Helen Ingram, "Patterns of Politics in Water Resources Development," *Natural Resources Journal* 2 (1971): 110. See also Arthur A. Maass, "Congress and Water Resources," *American Political Science Review* 64 (1950): 576–593, and Aaron Wildavsky, *The Politics of the Budgetary Process* (Boston: Little, Brown, 1964).

3. *The Bureaucracy.* This consists of the public employees who carry out public policy under the direction of bureaucrats, who make personnel decisions such as job assignments, hiring and firing, salary, promotions, and so on. In the Bureau of Reclamation, engineers constitute the most important professional group.

4. *Clientele.* This is a collection of individuals each of whom has a substantial stake in the material or symbolic outcomes of public policy, making it economical for them to organize into interest groups. Irrigators, construction companies, real estate developers, banks, suppliers of agricultural inputs, chambers of commerce, naturalists, environmentalists, and others who stand to gain or lose from the bureau's projects make up the clientele of reclamation policies at the federal level. They form national, regional, and local associations on a temporary or permanent basis to press for their preferences and interests. The intensity of their support or opposition is proportional to the expected gains or losses. Group success is in large part a function of their numbers and their density, that is, the degree to which they present a united front. The greater the density and size of the group, the greater its influencc. Within limits, these two characteristics serve as substitutes for each other. Examples of interest groups formed to influence reclamation policy are the League of the Southwest, which lobbied for federal projects on the Colorado River during the 1920s, and the National Reclamation Association, formed to protect the bureau from eastern interests opposed to federal subsidies toward irrigation about the same time.[40]

The clientele is organized around the supply of inputs to or outputs from particular agencies. Rents are created whenever an agency increases its purchases from factor owners or expands its supply of goods or services to customers at a price below opportunity costs. The owners of scarce factors, such as land, construction materials, or labor, and the recipients of subsidies, such as irrigators, make windfall gains that are quickly capitalized as property, licenses, or privileges and marketed legally or illegally. In the Westlands Irrigation District of California, for example, windfall gains accruing from the sale of "excess land" (acreage beyond Bureau of Reclamation limitations) have been estimated to average approximately $1.45 million

40. The origins of the National Reclamation Association are discussed in Golzé, *Reclamation in the United States*; for an account of the League of the Southwest, see Hundley, *Water and the West*, ch. 3.

per owner, while sales of nonexcess land have resulted in average gains of $49,000 per owner.[41] Naturally, those who paid the market price for this land or made "windfall" gains oppose any change in federal policy that will result in a capital loss for them.

Since support is generated in the process of rent creation, and since rents are quickly capitalized, it pays politicians and bureaucrats to spread the effect of the policy over time. Thus, many projects are started simultaneously and funded intermittently over a period of time longer than is necessary to complete the project economically. While bureaucratic inertia and rigidities were probably partly responsible for Reclamation Bureau projects taking so long to be completed, the incentive to spread benefits of the project over the careers of key bureaucrats and politicians also pointed in the same direction. As of 1973, the bureau had a backlog of construction projects valued at about $7 billion.[42]

5. *The Public.* This is the large mass of the population who pay the taxes and bear the cost of public water policies. They are the relatively passive "consumers" of reclamation projects, dams, and state water laws. Their political acts rarely go beyond voting for the politicians who influence these decisions, attending an occasional citizens' meeting, writing a letter to a newspaper, or making a small contribution to a party or candidate. In a study of public participation in water policies in the state of Washington, it was found that only 18 percent of respondents had acted politically to influence water policy. This figure may be exaggerated, since only 61 percent of the questionnaires were returned to the investigators, suggesting that activists were overrepresented in the sample.[43]

The public's attention is divided over innumerable policies, each of which receives relatively little attention. Due to high information costs, the votes of the public are largely ideological, cast in response to symbols such as "more water," "develop the desert," and "save the farmers," and rhetoric about water "shortages" and "droughts."

41. E. Phillip Le Veen and George E. Goldman, "Reclamation Policy and the Water Subsidy: An Analysis of Emerging Policy Choices," *American Journal of Agricultural Economics* 60 (1978): 929–934.

42. Statement by Gilbert Stamm, Commissioner of the Bureau of Reclamation, 1973–1977, quoted in *Reclamation Era*, Spring 1973.

43. See John C. Pierce, Kathleen M. Beatty, and Harvey R. Doerksen, "Rational Participation and Public Involvement in Water Resource Politics," in *Water Politics and Public Involvement*, ed. John C. Pierce and Harvey R. Doerksen (Ann Arbor, Mich.: Ann Arbor Science Publishers, 1976), p. 172.

Hence their influence over policy is marginal and diffuse, setting limits on the general level of taxation or signalling gross changes in opinions, attitudes, and the popularity of a particular politician, bureaucrat, or policy. It does not specify in any detail programs, organizational structure, budgets, or personnel.

Politicians and bureaucrats are the public entrepreneurs who make and implement government decisions, initiating new programs and agencies, carrying out administrative reorganizations, making policy proposals, planning projects, and deciding on budgets. Major Powell, Arthur Powell Davis, F.H. Newell, Elwood Mead, Senators Stewart and Newlands, President Theodore Roosevelt, and Secretary of Commerce and later President Herbert Hoover were the principal entrepreneurs of federal irrigation policies. They mobilized support for federal controls over western waters, designed and implemented large-scale reclamation and power-generation projects, and organized and defended the Bureau of Reclamation during its formative years. As we shall see, Ezra F. Scattergood, founder and builder of the Bureau of Power and Light, William Mulholland, chief engineer of the municipal aqueduct, and Mayor George E. Cyer performed similar functions in the city of Los Angeles.

Bureaucrats are usually responsible for the creation and growth of public agencies, while politicians provide the necessary support or unwelcome opposition.[44] Major Powell was the "father" and director for fourteen years of the U.S. Geological Survey, where federal irrigation policies and projects were planned for two decades before the passage of the National Reclamation Act of 1902. F.H. Newell and A.P. Davis, both of whom began their careers under Powell, were the first and second commissioners of the Bureau of Reclamation. The first served twelve years as director and the second nine years.

The entrepreneurs exercise control or influence by accumulating power. Power is net support, or the difference between the support and opposition generated with public policy from other entrepreneurs, the bureaucracy, the clientele, and the public. In government, entrepreneurs allocate and reallocate resources so as to generate maximum support over opposition, which strengthens and expands their

44. A similar argument is presented in J.T. Bennett and M.H. Johnson, *The Political Economy of Federal Growth: 1959-1979* (College Station, Tex.: Texas A&M University, 1980).

control or influence over public resources. As support for or opposition to specific agencies, policies, and individual bureaucrats or politicians shifts, so do the fortunes of organizations, programs, and individuals. Policy and administrative initiatives and changes are taken in the direction that yields an excess of support over opposition and in direct proportion to this difference. If the difference is small, the new agency or program is limited in authority, size or resources. For example, in his discussion of the political struggles that took place in Arizona during the 1940s and 1950s over groundwater pumping, Mann shows that near-equality in the forces supporting and opposing such controls resulted in a relatively weak policy, which was just as weakly enforced.[45]

Water policies at the local, state, and federal levels tend to redistribute income and wealth from the mass of the public to the ruling class of politicians, bureaucrats, and interest groups. Political struggles take place largely within this class as the various actors and entrepreneurs maneuver for position and power. Conflicts are often precipitated by the formation or increase in the power of interest groups that seek to change, initiate, or stop programs, elect, appoint, or remove politicians and bureaucrats, and otherwise change public policy. Though struggles take place within this class and though new groups and individuals may join it, the general tendency is for the class to benefit at the expense of the public, who subsidize the programs, projects, and policies with their taxes. The greater the inefficiency of the projects, the greater the public burden.

The redistributive nature of politics leads to the centralization of the government. Income and wealth are more efficiently redistributed the larger the jurisdiction of the government and the higher the level of decision. The larger the jurisdiction, the bigger the resource base, the smaller the per capita burden of taxes and hence the more passive the public. The higher the level of decision, the fewer the number of decisionmakers and hence the lower the costs of reaching agreement. The implication that federal subsidies to water projects should be greater than state projects, such as those undertaken by the California state government, is supported by fact.[46]

45. Dean E. Mann, *The Politics of Water in Arizona* (Tucson: University of Arizona Press, 1963), pp. 51–61.

46. Gardner Brown, "The Economics of Agricultural Water Use," in Thomas H. Campbell and Robert O. Sylvester, *Water Resources and Economic Development of the West*, no. 3 (Tucson, Ariz.: Western Agricultural Economics Research Council, 1955), p. 17.

The histories of the Bureau of Reclamation and the Water and Power Department of the city of Los Angeles can be interpreted and explained with the use of the theory developed here.

The Bureau of Reclamation

The Bureau of Reclamation is a direct descendent of Major Powell's plans and projects, even though it was established as a service within the U.S. Geological Survey in 1902, eight years after his resignation. Between 1898 and 1900 the Survey examined 147 reservoir sites, many of which no doubt had been selected by Powell during his tenure as director. Within five years, the bureau had secured congressional authorization for twenty-four projects, with at least one in every western state. Most of the projects were begun in great haste with little attention paid to "economics, climate, soil, production, transportation and markets."[47] It appears that the bureau was more concerned with establishing a political base in the West than in designing economical projects. In this respect, its strategy resembled that of an imperial power securing territorial control with the establishment of "missions" or "forts" over its domain.

It soon became apparent that the reclamation fund as originally established—revenues from the sale of public lands and repayments by irrigators—would not suffice to finance these projects. The costs of the projects turned out to be greater than originally estimated and the ability or willingness of irrigators to repay costs below what had been anticipated. In 1910, President Taft recommended and the Congress approved the issuance of $20 million in certificates payable out of the reclamation fund. In 1914, the repayment period was extended from ten to twenty years. These were the first in a long series of alterations of the original act designed to broaden the tax base with which to finance the projects and reduce the financial obligations of the irrigators.[48]

After two decades of reclamation, the bureau found itself facing increasing opposition in Congress, particularly from eastern interests who did not want to subsidize increased agricultural production in the West. Also, many of the bureau's project recipients were dissatis-

47. Raymond Moley, *What Price Reclamation?* (Washington, D.C.: American Enterprise Association, 1955).

48. Ibid., p. 7.

fied with the agency's long delays in construction and with the results of the projects. In 1932, western governors formed the National Reclamation Association in support of bureau policies and projects.

President Hoover came to the rescue of the bureau, which was faced with extinction, with the Boulder Canyon project. This massive undertaking, which included Boulder (now Hoover) Dam and the "all-American canal" to transport water from the Colorado to Southern California, expanded the bureau's jurisdiction to include hydroelectric power as a major source of revenue and political support. As Secretary of Commerce, Hoover served as federal representative on a commission made up of representatives of Colorado River states that drafted an interstate compact to divide the waters of the rivers between upper- and lower-basin states.[49] The agreement made it possible for the federal government to undertake the Boulder Canyon project. The bill was passed under the administration of President Coolidge but it followed Hoover's financial recommendations. Construction and contracts were implemented during Hoover's tenure as president. The city of Los Angeles became one of the operators of the dam's power facilities.

The Great Depression was a "boom" period for the bureau. President Franklin Roosevelt gave the bureau vigorous support. Between 1935 and 1937, $800 million of projects were authorized, mostly from the general fund. In 1939, a new act was passed relaxing repayment provisions and extending the repayment period up to forty years or more at the discretion of the Secretary of the Interior.

During World War II, new reclamation projects were postponed as resources were shifted to the war effort. But plans for postwar construction efforts continued apace. It was during this period, in fact, that the bureau became embroiled in long and costly struggles with the U.S. Corps of Engineers for control of water resources in the Central Valley of California and in the Missouri basin.[50] These represent the boundaries of the bureau's territory, which is limited to

49. Hundley, *Water in the West*, pp. 138–214.

50. For a discussion of struggles between the two agencies in California see Arthur Maass, *The Kings River Project* (Indianapolis: Bobbs-Merrill Company, 1952) and Maass, "Congress and Water Resources," *American Political Science Review* 64 (1950): 576–593. On the division of functional responsibilities in the Missouri Basin see Marian E. Ridgeway, *The Missouri Basin's Pick-Sloan Plan: A Case Study in the Congressional Policy Determination* (Urbana, Ill.: University of Illinois Press, 1955), and Carlos Davis Stern, "A Critique of Federal Water Resources Policies: Hydroelectric Power Versus Wilderness Waterway on the Upper Missouri River" (Ph.D. dissertation, Cornell University, 1971), ch. II.

Table 1-1. U.S. Presidents and Bureau of Reclamation Commissioners, 1902-1982.

President	*Commissioner*	*Year Appointed*	*Tenure in Office*	*Mean Tenure in Office*
T. Roosevelt	F.H. Newell	1902	12	
H. Taft				
W. Wilson	A.P. Davis	1914	10	8.75
C. Coolidge				
W. Harding	D.W. Davis	1923	1	
	E. Mead	1924	12	
H. Hoover				
F. Roosevelt	J.C. Page	1936	7	
	H.W. Bashore	1943	2	
H. Truman	M.S. Strauss	1945	8	6.8
D. Eisenhower	W. Dexheimer	1953	6	
J. Kennedy	F. Dominy	1959	11	
L. Johnson				
R. Nixon	E. Armstrong	1970	3	
G. Ford	G. Stamm	1973	4	3.7
J. Carter	R.K. Higginson	1977	4	
R. Reagan	R. Broadbent	1981		
				$\bar{x}$ = 6.7

the western states. The struggles resulted in a division of functions in which the bureau was given control over irrigation projects and the corps over flood control projects. This agreement paved the way for a major expansion in the acreage supplied by the bureau, which doubled between 1945 and 1965 from 4 to 8 million acres.

Today the acreage irrigated partly or totally with bureau-supplied water is roughly 11 million acres, or about 25 percent of the total. But the number of farms directly benefiting from federal water projects is only about 150,000. Thus, "the per farmer stakes can be high indeed. . . . Even a modest farm operation of 160 acres in California may receive a subsidy on water costs, the capitalized value of which is in excess of $100,000."[51] Yet, roughly two-thirds of the lands supplied with bureau water are devoted to relatively low-value crops such as grains and forage.[52] Thus a small minority organized around irrigation has managed to redistribute income and wealth from the taxpayers to itself while misallocating water resources to relatively inefficient uses.

Table 1-1 shows that the bureau has evolved from a relatively autonomous agency controlled by bureaucrats who founded it to one under increased presidential control. For over three decades, the bureau was run by three men who had been active in promoting federal intervention in western irrigation before 1900: F.H. Newell, A.P. Davis, and Elwood Mead. This era of relative autonomy ended with Franklin Roosevelt, who appointed two commissioners. Since then, every new occupant of the White House except Lyndon Johnson has changed commissioners. Note that the mean tenure in office has declined steadily. Thus, the level of decisionmaking in the bureau has been raised to the maximum, a trend in keeping with the law of hierarchical centralization.

Water and Power in the City of Los Angeles: 1890-1950

The political history of water and power in the city of Los Angeles bears a striking resemblance to that of the bureau, at least on those aspects that are relevant to the theory presented in this paper. What follows is a necessarily brief description based on Vincent Ostrom's *Water and Politics.*[53]

Before 1900, the city of Los Angeles was served by privately owned water and power companies. The water company had a contract to supply the city with water from the Los Angeles River, which the municipal government owned in its entirety on the basis of judicial interpretations of Spanish and Mexican pueblo rights.

51. David Sechler and Robert A. Young, "Economic and Policy Implications of the 160-Acre Limitation in Federal Reclamation Law," *American Journal of Agricultural Economics* 60 (1978): 575.

52. William E. Martin, "Economies of Size and the 160-Acre Limitation: Fact and Fancy," *American Journal of Agricultural Economics* 60 (1978): 923-928.

53. Vincent Ostrom, *Water and Politics: A Study of Water Policies and Administration in the Development of Los Angeles* (Los Angeles: Haynes Foundation, 1953).

Toward the end of the nineteenth century, various reform groups argued that the city should develop its own water. After a long period of agitation, the Los Angeles City Water Company was forced to sell the properties it had developed under a thirty-year lease to supply the city with water. William Mulholland, superintendent of water works for the private company, became the chief water engineer for the city, a position he held for twenty-six years. He came to play the dominant role in the city's water policies.

Shortly after it acquired the local waterworks the city embarked on a vast new project, supported by the Bureau of Reclamation, to bring water to the city from Owens Valley, over 200 miles away beyond the mountains to the north. Valley residents opposed the acquisition of water and land by the city, waging a war against what became the Los Angeles Aqueduct.

This project was begun even though the Los Angeles River could have supplied additional water to serve the urban population at less cost. It was subsequently learned that a syndicate composed of several of the leading civic leaders behind the project had bought large tracts of land in the San Fernando Valley that were later irrigated with water from the aqueduct. In fact, for many years most of the new water was used for irrigation. The owners of the San Fernando properties were able to capitalize a very substantial increase in the value of their property as a result, another instance of the iron law of political redistribution.

Control over water in the Los Angeles River and Owens Valley provided the city with a weapon with which to expand territorially. An aggressive annexation campaign multiplied by many times the original tax base. Also, the city's bureaucrats were one of the leading entrepreneurial forces behind the Boulder Canyon project, the Colorado River project, and the Metropolitan Water District (MWD). An independent agency with taxing powers over an area of more than 3,000 square miles in Southern California, the MWD acts as a water wholesaler to cities and districts of the region. Its biggest project is the Colorado River Aqueduct, which brings water from Lake Davis over 240 miles away. The aqueduct has been relatively inefficient, supplying high-cost water while operating at less than half of capacity between 1940 and 1960.[54] However, it heavily subsidizes agricultural uses by taxing the urban populations, particularly Los Angeles

54. Hirshleifer, DeHaven, and Milliman, *Water Supply* p. 294.

residents. As late as 1951, 15 percent of the water used by the city, most of it imported from Owens Valley and the Colorado River, was sold to irrigators at a price less than half of what it cost the city to buy water from the district.[55] Thus, like the Bureau of Reclamation, Los Angeles City pursued a policy of territorial expansion implemented with inefficient projects paid for by the general taxpayer with the support of organized minorities, including irrigation interests.

The Los Angeles Aqueduct also became a source of electric power for the city. Its engineers took advantage of the drops in elevation from Owens Valley to the coast in order to generate hydroelectric power. In 1922, the city forced the private utility companies to sell their properties to the department, subsequently contracting with the Bureau of Reclamation to generate power from Hoover Dam.

As in the Bureau of Reclamation, policy decisions on water and power in Los Angeles were for decades dominated by the men who built the two systems. For twenty-six years Superintendent Mulholland was the most powerful voice on water policy. In 1929, he was succeeded by van Norman, who had been with the department since the construction of the Los Angeles Aqueduct. Van Norman served as director for thirteen years. Ezra F. Scattergood, founder and builder of the Bureau of Power and Light, served as its director for over thirty years and came to rule a veritable political machine. In 1940, a local newspaper observed that Scattergood's bureau "through its many ramifications, its advertising in many small community newspapers and throwaways, and its influence over the thousands of employees, virtually has constituted the balance of power in municipal elections."[56]

Politicians were unable to gain control over the water and power bureaucrats despite several spirited attempts. It proved more advantageous for politicians to support the bureau than to oppose it, as Mayor George E. Cyer discovered. During the 1920s, Cyer "unquestionably made the greatest contribution of any Los Angeles mayor to the development of the program of the Department of Water and Power; but his contribution was in providing political leadership for the policies formulated within the department."[57]

With the passing of Mulholland, van Norman, and Scattergood, who was forced to resign and given a lucrative consulting contract

55. Ibid., p. 308.
56. Ostrom, *Water and Politics*, p. 75.
57. Ibid., p. 108.

that took him away from Los Angeles, the water and power sections of the department were consolidated and centralized. Ostrom, writing in the 1950s, noted that those reorganizations "have tended to raise the level of decision about many of the operational and policy problems that were formerly resolved at the bureau or system level. The office of the General Manager and Chief Engineer has become a vital center of decision-making and leadership for the entire Department of Water and Power."[58]

Summary

This brief comparative study of the political histories of the Bureau of Reclamation and the Department of Water and Power of the City of Los Angeles has generated a number of parallels between the two agencies:

1. Bureaucratic entrepreneurship and dominance of policy occur during the first thirty to forty years of the agency's life.
2. Entrepreneurship by politicians is limited largely to providing support for the bureau's policies and plans; it is unprofitable for politicians to oppose the bureau consistently.
3. Evolution toward centralization or "raising the level of decision" occurs once the bureau founders pass away.
4. Territorial expansion is brought about with the construction of inefficient projects.
5. Costs of projects shifted to the general taxpayer over as large an area as possible, while benefits were concentrated on small minorities.
6. Finally, it is worth noting the role which economic or meteorological "crises" have played in expanding the power of these two agencies. The drought and depression of the 1890s over much of the West generated significant support for federal reclamation legislation, as did the severe winter of 1886 and the slump in agricultural prices between 1880 and 1900.[59] The Great Depression brought an infusion of public works money into the bureau.

58. Ibid., p. 103.

59. See Stegner, *Beyond the Hundredth Meridian*, pp. 294–304, and Glass, *Water for Nevada*, ch. II.

Ostrom notes the similar effect of drought on the support for public water projects in Los Angeles:

> Every major development in water resources programs and water administration has been closely correlated with drought cycles in Southern California. The drought of 1893-1904 produced the Los Angeles Aqueduct; the drought of the 1920s initiated the Boulder Canyon project, the Colorado River Aqueduct, and the organization of the Metropolitan Water District; and the drought of the 1940s produced the "dry cycle harvest" of annexations to the Metropolitan Water District.[60]

TOWARD THE REAPPROPRIATION OF WATER

The history of water policies in the West over the last hundred years shows very clearly the objectives, methods, and results of the political means in action. Irrigators and other beneficiaries of reclamation have capitalized rents created with public policy at all levels of government. Federal and big-city bureaucrats have built impressive monuments to their engineering skills, breaking world records for size and capacity of various dams. And the political entrepreneurs who made it all possible achieved a type of immortality for their efforts: Lake Powell, Lake Mead, Hoover Dam, Lake Roosevelt, and Lake Davis are now part of the political archeology of the Colorado River, the largest in the Southwest. The economic burden of these policies and projects has been borne by the mass of the taxpaying public, who have had to forego the income that western waters would have yielded in uses other than those dictated by the reclamation ruling class.

Currently, federal and state governments are under pressure to engage in ever larger projects or extend bureaucratic controls further. While economists demonstrate the inefficiencies of large-scale water transfers within California, engineers are now making plans for the transfer of tens of millions of acre-feet from the Pacific Northwest, Canada, and even Alaska. It is currently estimated that the most ambitious of these plans would cost $200 billion and take thirty years to build.[61] At the state level, new or tighter controls are being imposed on underground pumping, sometimes at the insistence of

60. Ostrom, *Water and Politics*, p. 234.

61. Arthur F. Pillsbury, "The Salinity of Rivers," *Scientific American* 245 (July 1981): 64.

the Bureau of Reclamation. For example, state control over underground pumping has been made a condition for the Central Arizona Project.[62]

Needless to say, continental water transfers and federally influenced controls over underground pumping would vastly increase the power that the bureau (now the U.S. Water and Power Resources Service) already exercises over the West. In light of the results of the bureau's projects and policies, this policy cannot be to the advantage of the region or the nation, even if a minority in the West and in Washington will undoubtedly continue to benefit.

Today, however, the political means appear to command less enthusiasm and support in the United States than scarcely a decade ago. The ideas of classical liberalism seem to be undergoing a revival in universities and other centers of learning. Perhaps it is only fitting that the American doctrine of prior appropriation be reconsidered as an institution for dealing with the problems of water shortages and conflicting interests over water allocation and use.

In principle, private property over surface and underground water could be reestablished with relatively simple rules of appropriation. The first step would be to establish the physical boundaries of rivers, streams, lakes, and aquifers. In the latter case they could reflect variations in pumping lifts. Next, each basin or watershed would be declared the corporate property of those who currently divert or pump water out of it and of those private or public organizations that manage bodies of water for instream uses. Each individual or organizational share of the basin would be proportional to the capacity of its water-using facilities, including diversion works, pumps, and volume reserved for instream uses. These shares would be bought and sold in an open market. State, federal, and private parks, municipalities, recreational associations, and others interested in nonconsumptive or instream uses of water would be free to purchase as many shares as they wanted. Water would thus be divided among uses and users according to its marginal value to each.

Shareholders would elect a set of officers who would appoint corporate managers. Each corporation would be free to decide whether to conserve, mine, export, or import water. All federal and state irrigation works would be sold or given to these corporations. The only role for government would be to enforce contracts among corpora-

62. Mann, *Politics of Water in Arizona*, pp. 50–60.

tions and ensure that water is not transferred among owners or corporations without the consent of the participants.

Such an arrangement is not without precedent. Interstate compacts now divide the water of rivers among states. Mead himself described how Utah streams were incorporated by existing appropriators: "All parties having used water from the stream come to an agreement as to their rights, usually on an acreage basis; then form a corporation and issue to each farmer or to each ditch company stock in proportion to their rights. The stream is then controlled by the water master, who is elected by the members of the corporation."[63] Mead thought that this solution would be practical only on smaller streams but did not explain how he reached this conclusion. There is no reason why this ingenious device cannot be applied not only to streams, rivers, and lakes, but to underground water as well.

63. Mead, *Irrigation Institutions*, p. 233.

Chapter 2

THE FEDERAL RECLAMATION PROGRAM
An Analysis of Rent-Seeking Behavior

Randal R. Rucker
Price V. Fishback

INTRODUCTION

In many regions of the western United States, nature has not been kind enough to provide abundant riparian land. Thus farmers in these regions have been forced to develop methods for bringing water to the land. The earliest efforts of this sort were made by enterprising individuals and groups acting without direct aid from the federal government. At the turn of the century western leaders and farmers sought direct assistance from federal authorities for irrigation works. Congress responded by providing interest-free loans and directing the Department of Interior to administer the projects and subsidies and to enforce certain restrictions. To carry out these directives, the Reclamation Service (later renamed the Bureau of Reclamation) was formed and has since played an important part in development of irrigation in the West.

The policies of the Bureau of Reclamation recently have been reviewed by the courts. A statutory interpretation that had exempted

In addition to the Pacific Institute, which has provided funding, both authors would like to thank the Economics Department of the University of Washington for general support. The authors would also like to thank Lee Alston, Terry Anderson, Robert Higgs, Ron Johnson, Mark Plummer, and George Sheldon for their comments and suggestions on earlier drafts of this paper. We owe a special debt to Sharie Olson for her diligent efforts in typing this paper. The responsibility for any errors remains with the authors.

irrigators in the Imperial Valley from acreage limitations since 1933 was overturned by a 1977 circuit court ruling (*United States* v. *Imperial Irrigation District*), which was reversed by the Supreme Court in 1980 (*Bryant* v. *Yellen*, 100 Supreme Court, 2232, 1980). In *National Lands for the People Inc.* v. *Bureau of Reclamation*, the bureau was ordered to propose new policy rules for the enforcement of acreage limitations and other legislative restrictions regarding residency on and disposal of lands receiving federal irrigation water.[1] Changes in the optimal size of farms have led to questions concerning the need for and proper size of acreage limits. Analysis of the effects of policy changes in earlier periods is useful for understanding the possible effects of recent changes in the bureau's policies.

In this paper we will use a model of rent-seeking behavior to analyze earlier actions of the irrigators and bureaucrats who attempted to increase the size of the subsidy and to alter its distribution. Two dimensions of federal policy will be discussed in detail: (1) the provisions established for repayment of construction costs by the settlers (which determined the size of the subsidy), and (2) the limitations on the amount of land eligible to receive irrigation water from federal projects (which determined the distribution of the subsidy). Since these policies have undergone important changes during this century, we will examine the form, effects, and possible explanations of these changes.

In the next section a rent-seeking model that outlines the incentives of irrigators and bureaucrats is described. The following section discusses the nature of the subsidy provided for federal irrigation projects and how irrigators and bureaucrats gained from changes in the rules that determined its size. Constraints placed by Congress on the subsidy's distribution among irrigators and the efforts of irrigators and bureaucrats to capture the rents are then discussed, followed by a brief summary and conclusion.

THE ANALYTICAL FRAMEWORK: A RENT-SEEKING MODEL

Economists define rents as the returns to an owner of a resource in excess of the opportunity costs of that resource. When rents exist,

1. Nancy Jones, "Proposed Rules for Administering the Acreage Limitation of Reclamation Law," in *Natural Resources Journal* 18 (October 1978): 936–937.

profit-maximizing individuals will compete to capture them by diverting the resources they command into those activities. This rent-seeking behavior will be observed both when resource movements are guided by the invisible hand of the market system and when those movements are restricted by political barriers.[2] Interest groups will also seek to create rents through the establishment of political barriers. Under any institutional setting, competition by rent seekers dissipates the rents to the marginal firm or individual if property rights to them cannot be established and enforced.[3] In this paper the efforts of irrigators and bureaucrats to capture the rents created by the federal irrigation program, which was initiated by Congress in response to pressure from special interest groups, are analyzed within this simple rent-seeking framework. The actions of the members of Congress, the judiciary, and the executive branch are treated as exogenous constraints on the behavior of bureau members.

The forms of the rent-seeking behavior of irrigators and agents of the bureaucracy in charge of federal reclamation policy were largely determined by two important cornerstones of that policy. The first of these was the repayment system established for federal irrigation projects in which irrigators were provided with interest-free loans for construction costs. The fact that this repayment scheme later proved to be extremely flexible encouraged rent-seeking activities designed to increase the value of the rents from federal reclamation. The second cornerstone was the limitation placed on the amount of federally supplied water that an individual landowner was eligible to receive. This excess-land law or acreage limitation was crucial in determining the distribution of the benefits from the federal irrigation program. These limitations and the regulations for their implementation, the most controversial aspects of reclamation policy, have been important in determining the nature of activities designed to increase the share of the rents going to the owners of excess lands.

2. James M. Buchanan's "Rent-Seeking and Profit Seeking" in *Toward a Theory of the Rent-Seeking Society*, ed. James M. Buchanan, Robert D. Tollison, and Gordon Tullock (College Station, Tex.: Texas A&M University Press, 1980) distinguishes between profit-seeking under a market structure and rent-seeking under government actions that interfere with the market adjustment process. Use of the term "rent-seeking" in this paper is consistent with this definition.

3. For a discussion of the various methods of dissipating rents through nonprice adjustments, see Steven N. S. Cheung, "The Theory of Price Controls," *Journal of Law and Economics* 17 (April 1974): 53–71. Cheung emphasizes that complete dissipation of rents occurs only if property rights to those rents cannot be established and enforced.

Irrigators on a project included individuals who owned land before the project was initiated as well as settlers who wanted to homestead public lands or buy the excess private lands. Both of these groups received the subsidy from federal involvement in irrigation, dissipating the rents from the subsidy by expending resources in various ways to increase the size of the subsidy or their share of it. For example, settlers homesteaded public lands before federal project water made them irrigable, while large landowners often spent considerable resources devising methods to avoid the acreage limitation.

Members of the Bureau of Reclamation and the Department of Interior were charged with enforcing and administering the reclamation policy. They are not treated as passive respondents to either the directives of Congress or the pressures from irrigators but rather as rational maximizers who developed objectives and policies of their own within the constraints imposed by Congress. Since bureaucrats cannot directly receive the subsidy on federal irrigation projects, the bureaucratic rent-seeking model suggests that their primary goals were to increase their salaries, job security, and power within the political system. These goals might be attained through increased legislative demand for the bureau's output, expanded administrative control and discretionary power over allocation of irrigation water, enlarged staffs, and increased budgets. For example, more political power and higher salaries are often correlated with larger staffs and increased budgets, while increased discretionary power over the budget gives the bureaucrat more freedom to fund pet projects.[4]

That tradeoffs between complying with congressional constraints and achieving these goals occur is indicated by the wide variety of administrative and enforcement policies adopted for different reclamation projects. Our model suggests that bureaucratic actors attempted to capture a portion of the rents from federal reclamation

4. See Roger L. Faith, "Rent-Seeking Aspects of Bureaucratic Competition," in Buchanan, Tollison, Tullock, *Rent-Seeking Society*, pp. 332-345; and Terry Anderson and P.J. Hill, "Establishing Property Rights in Energy Efficient vs. Inefficient Processes," *Cato Journal* 1, no. 1 (Spring 1981): 87-105. An alternative to the rent-seeking model, if attempts to increase the bureau's discretionary control are seen as a means of increasing the demand for the bureau's budget, is a budget-maximizing model such as that of William A. Niskanen in *Bureaucracy and Representative Government* (Chicago: Aldine-Atherton, 1971), and "Bureaucrats and Politicians," *Journal of Law and Economics* 18 (December 1975): 617-643. This model has been applied to the Department of Interior's policies on land disposal for grazing lands by Gary Libecap in "Bureaucratic Opposition to the Assignment of Property Rights: Overgrazing on the Western Range," *Journal of Economic History* 41 (March 1981): 151-158.

with these policies. The process through which the irrigation rents were created, the constraints within which rents were sought, and the actual forms of the rent-seeking activities are discussed in detail in the following sections.

REPAYMENT OF CONSTRUCTION COSTS: ESTABLISHING THE SUBSIDY AND INCREASING ITS VALUE

The congressional policy of providing direct subsidies to irrigators on federal reclamation projects was established in response to pressures from western interest groups with the passage of the Reclamation Act of 1902. The initial subsidy took the form of a ten-year interest-free loan for construction costs of federal projects. Over time, the value of this subsidy to irrigators was increased significantly by such modifications as extensions in the term of the repayment period, allowances for development periods during which no payments are required, and the adoption of the policy of using power revenues from multiple-purpose projects to repay irrigation costs in excess of irrigators' ability to pay. This section describes the events leading to the establishment of this subsidy and the efforts by irrigators and members of the Bureau of Reclamation to increase its value.

Irrigation of arid lands in the West began before American settlement of the frontier. Indians were irrigating their lands when the Spanish first explored California. As early as 1776, the Spanish padres at Mission San Diego de Alcalca irrigated their grapes and gardens. The first efforts to use irrigation methods by American settlers were made by the Mormons upon their arrival in Utah in 1847. By 1890, settlers in California, Wyoming, and Colorado had irrigated over 3 million acres.[5]

Most of the early private irrigation projects involved little more than the construction of ditches and canals for diverting waters from the rivers onto adjacent farmlands. Opportunities for building projects of this type at low cost were soon exhausted. New projects involved the construction of canals for carrying water to lands further

5. Frederick Merk, *History of the Westward Movement* (New York: Knopf, 1978), p. 507.

from the streams and rivers, and of dams and reservoirs for storing water. Western leaders and landowners sought federal aid for these expensive undertakings arguing that further successful settlement of the public lands of the West required that they be irrigated, and that this irrigation would require direct government assistance.

Congress had previously tried to encourage irrigation with the Desert Lands Act of 1877 and the Carey Act of 1894, which offered tracts of land at low prices to those settlers who irrigated the land. Neither of these acts, which are discussed in detail in the next section, had significant effects on irrigation in the West. The movement calling for direct assistance from the federal government gathered momentum. A series of "Irrigation Congresses" were called to press for federal aid and to develop an irrigation policy for promoting the successful settlement of the West that would be acceptable to representatives from all the western states. Additional support came from an 1897 report prepared by Captain Hiram H. Chittenden of the Army Corps of Engineers, which stated that "a comprehensive reservoir system in the arid regions of the United States is absolutely essential" and that "it is not possible to secure the development of such a system except through the agency of the General Government."[6]

Western leaders were encouraged by the responses to their efforts. By 1900 the Geological Survey and the Department of Agriculture were receiving regular appropriations from Congress for investigating different aspects of the irrigation problem.[7] In the 1900 presidential election the platforms of the major parties included planks favoring the reclamation of arid lands. Despite this early success, a federal reclamation bill introduced early in 1901 failed to obtain congressional approval.

Theodore Roosevelt provided the support that finally resulted in the passage of a federal reclamation bill. In his first presidential message to Congress, he declared himself to be strongly in favor of federal construction of western irrigation projects.[8] A compromise reclamation bill was quickly drawn up, passed by a comfortable margin, and signed into law as the Reclamation Act of 1902. Defenders

6. Quoted in Norris Hundley, *Water and the West* (Berkeley, Calif.: University of California Press, 1975), p. 10.

7. For a description of these appropriations, see Alfred R. Golzé, *Reclamation in the United States* (New York: McGraw-Hill, 1952), pp. 21–23.

8. For this portion of Roosevelt's message, see Frederick H. Newell, *Irrigation* (New York: Thomas Y. Crowell and Co., 1906), pp. 393–396.

of the act declared that federal involvement in irrigation was constitutional since it promoted the general welfare by providing a release for overpopulated areas of the East and by conserving the nation's natural resources. To the argument that output produced using the water from federal projects would provide competition detrimental to farmers in the Midwest and East, defenders responded that most of the produce grown in the West would also be consumed there, and that any surplus could be exported to the Orient. It was also noted that even though 112 million acres of federal land had been disposed of in the 1890s, the prices of agricultural goods were about the same at the end of the decade as at the beginning.

Opponents of the act also argued that the benefits from these projects would not justify the expenses, which would be borne by the nation's taxpayers. To allay these objections, the authors of the act established a revolving Reclamation Fund through which the federal projects would pay for themselves and provide funds for additional projects. The funds that would provide the base for the Reclamation Fund were to be revenues from the sale of public lands in the western states. Later acts supplemented the Reclamation Fund with other sources of funds, including proceeds from sales of oil leases and from potassium royalties, as well as revenues from federal power licences, public power revenues, and the sale of town lots on the projects. According to the 1902 act, the settlers in a given project area were to agree to repay the construction costs within ten years.

The subsidy given to irrigators took the form of an exemption from interest charges on the loan for construction costs.[9] Apparently, this feature received little attention during the discussion of the bill. It was obvious that western interests wanted a subsidy, but why Congress opted for this particular form and not a direct payment is unclear. Since an interest subsidy is more subtle than a direct subsidy, it is possible that this form was chosen to make the subsidy more acceptable to nonwestern congressmen, whose constituents were subsidizing irrigation projects.

The value of the subsidy initially obtained by irrigators was significant. To get an idea of this value, imagine a project where the irrigation works have been completed and the cost of the project was $10,000. If the settlers paid the costs immediately, the present value

9. Another subsidy—the difference between the price charged to cover costs and the market price of the water—would have been received by settlers even if they had been required to repay construction costs with interest (assuming, of course, that the market value of the water was greater than the price required to recover costs).

of the payment would be the full value of construction costs, $10,000. The Reclamation Act of 1902 allowed the settlers to repay construction costs over a period of ten years in equal annual installments. The present value of this stream of payments depends on the discount rate used. A minimum measure of the value of the subsidy would be obtained by using the interest rate for risk-free investments. At a rate of 3 percent (which was the approximate rate of interest on risk-free government bonds at that time), the present value of the payments would have been about $8,530, implying a subsidy of about 14.7 percent of construction costs. However, a more accurate appraisal of the size of the subsidy would take into account the risky nature of investment on irrigation projects. Table 2-1 demonstrates that at a discount rate of 10 percent (which probably is a better approximation of the rate of interest faced by settlers), the value of the initial interest subsidy was almost 39 percent.

After the passage of the Reclamation Act, no time was wasted in allocating responsibilities and initiating projects. Frederick H. Newell, former chief hydrographer for the Geological Survey, was appointed chief engineer in charge of the service. Eleven days after the act was passed, land for six projects and surveys was withdrawn from disposal under other federal acts for use in reclamation projects. The construction of four projects was authorized by the end of 1903, and in 1904 and 1905 sixteen more projects received authorization.

It was not long before the Reclamation Service encountered financial problems and settlers began seeking increases in the size of the subsidy. The revenues from public land sales proved to be inadequate for financing the construction of the service's proposed projects, necessitating a congressional loan to the Reclamation Service in 1910. Settlers on reclamation projects complained that costs had been underestimated—Newell's estimate of $5 per acre was well short of the actual cost of $50 to $100 per acre. Settlers also objected that construction was not being completed on schedule. Settlers seeking to capture rents from federal irrigation water were homesteading land before the projects were completed. They were expected to be residents of the land to maintain title, but much of the land was virtually useless without irrigation water. When projects were not completed on schedule as expected by the settlers, many were faced with the choice of starving or relinquishing their rights.

Defaults on repayments were often attributed to the settler's inexperience and lack of the substantial capital needed to prepare arid

Table 2-1. The Interest Subsidy: Subsidized Proportion of Costs.

Payment Plan	Rate of Discount[a] 3	6 (percent)	10
10-year repayment period; equal installments	14.7	26.4	38.6
20-year repayment period; equal installments	25.5	42.5	57.5
20-year repayment period; graduated installments[b]	28.9	47.8	64.0
20-year repayment period; graduated installments with grace period and down payment[c]	30.7	50.3	66.7
40-year repayment period; equal installments	42.3	62.5	75.5
40-year repayment period; equal installments with 10-year grace period	57.0	79.0	91.0

a. These subsidies were calculated by subtracting the present value of the payments (for any given schedule) from the construction costs, dividing that difference by the construction costs, and multiplying by 100.

b. Repayment schedule (outlined in the act of August 13, 1914) was 2 percent of construction costs for the first four years, 4 percent for the next two years, and 6 percent for the final fourteen years.

c. Repayment schedule (outlined in the act of August 13, 1914) was 5 percent of construction cost down, followed by a five-year development period, then annual payments of 5 percent for five years and 7 percent for the final ten years.

lands for irrigation. The Reclamation Service described this capital problem on early projects:

> Many of the settlers are attempting what is for them practically an impossibility; they are trying to start a farm-business which requires when fully developed as a "going concern" a capital or investment frequently of from $8,000 to $10,000 or more. They are attempting to do this usually with a capital of perhaps only a fourth as much. A 40-acre irrigated farm in best condition represents practically the investment in time and labor as above stated, of from $100 to $200 per acre or more in improvements, in subduing the soil, and in stocking the farm.[10]

10. U.S. Department of Interior, *Thirteenth Annual Report of the Reclamation Service 1913-1914* (Washington, D.C.: Government Printing Office), p. 14.

Agricultural depressions and bad harvests sometimes left settlers starving on their lands. In other areas organized resistance to the repayment of construction charges emerged, even though agricultural conditions were favorable. As a result, defaults on repayment contracts were common during the first three and a half decades of the Reclamation Service's existence—as of 1923, less than $16 million of the $143 million expended on federal irrigation projects had been repayed.[11] In a letter to Compton I. White, chairman of the House Committee on Irrigation and Reclamation in 1937, Charles West, the Acting Secretary of Interior, described the repayment problem of the Bureau of Reclamation:

> The revolving feature of the fund has been seriously retarded and there are projects where water has been available for 29 years and only six annual construction installments have been paid. There has often been organized resistance to the repayment of these charges, which is still being continued, and this notwithstanding the fact that nearly all of the projects have just passed through a successful year and in some cases the most successful year in their entire history.[12]

During this period water users sought and received increases in the size of the subsidy from Congress in five forms: (1) extension of the repayment period, (2) graduation of the scheduled payments, (3) postponement of the date when the first payment was due, (4) increased flexibility in the repayment schedule, and (5) moratoria on repayments during periods of crop failure. The first increase in the interest subsidy was granted in the Reclamation Extension Act of 13 August 1914, which authorized repayment contracts with twenty-year terms, graduated payment schedules, and five-year grace periods on new projects. The grace period and graduated payments were justified on the grounds that the burden on settlers during the years when they were establishing themselves would be reduced if smaller payments were required at the beginning of the repayment period.

The effects of these changes on the value of the interest subsidy are shown in Table 2-1. The extension of the repayment period to twenty years accounted for most of the increase in the subsidy's

11. U.S. Congress, Senate, "Federal Reclamation by Irrigation," Senate Document 92, 68th Cong., 1st sess., p. xi.

12. Quoted in U.S. Congress, House of Representatives, "Relief to Water Users on Federal Reclamation and Irrigation Projects," House of Representatives Report No. 1440, 75th Cong., 1st sess., pp. 3-4.

value. At a 3 percent discount rate, which provides a minimum estimate of the value of the subsidy, an increase in the term of a contract (calling for equal annual payments) from ten to twenty years increased the value of the subsidy from 14.7 percent to 25.5 percent of construction costs. For existing contracts that were renegotiated as a result of the 1914 act, the new repayment schedule required payments of 2 percent of the remaining construction costs for four years, followed by payments of 4 percent for two years, and 6 percent for the final fourteen years. This graduated scheme increased the value of the subsidy to 28.9 percent of construction costs. The formula for new contracts required a down payment of 5 percent, followed by a five-year grace period, then five annual payments of 5 percent and ten payments of 7 percent. This repayment scheme increased the subsidy's value on new projects to more than 30 percent of construction costs.

Defaults on repayment continued to be a problem. On some projects, these defaults could be attributed to the distress in several agricultural areas in the early 1920s. However, there were other projects "where powerful influences [sought] on various pretexts to evade paying. On one project the water users organization in an appeal for blanket deferment said: 'Not one irrigator on this project can pay anything.' "[13] The Bureau of Reclamation denied the blanket deferment but said that they would listen to individual requests for deferral on that project. Their belief that most of the settlers were able to pay appears to have been confirmed when "thousands of dollars came at once into the reclamation treasury" from individuals who could not give firm reasons for not paying their debt.[14] Urged by representatives from projects with large delinquencies to grant moratoria on past due debts, Congress granted this relief in 1921, 1922, and 1924.[15]

In 1923 a fact-finders' committee was appointed to investigate the reclamation program. In response to their recommendations, a new repayment scheme that allowed payments to vary with the productivity of the land was authorized in the Fact Finders Act of 1924. The annual charge for farms in a given district was to be 5 percent

13. U.S. Department of Interior, *Twenty-Fourth Annual Report of the Bureau of Reclamation for the Fiscal Year Ended June 30, 1925* (Washington, D.C.: Government Printing Office), p. 6.

14. Ibid., p. 6.

15. Ibid., p. 8.

of the average gross crop value for the preceding ten years. In practice payments based on this scheme were so small that repayment periods occasionally extended beyond seventy or eighty years. Authority to negotiate repayment contracts under this plan was quickly repealed in the Omnibus Adjustment Act of 1926.

The crop value repayment schemes were replaced by repayment contracts with forty-year terms in the act of 1926. Many of the contracts written under this act called for repayment on a graduated scale, which increased the value of the subsidy beyond the 42.3 percent subsidy that would have resulted under a schedule with equal installments (see Table 2-1). This rearrangement of payments was designed to relieve settlers during a period of low agricultural prices from 1926 to 1930. Unfortunately, crop incomes continued to decline after 1930 and payment stopped completely on some projects. At the request of the settlers, Congress again granted moratoria on payments from 1931 to 1936. Once again it should be noted that water users were engaging in rent-seeking behavior. Although some farmers were starving, others were less affected by the depression and simply refused to pay the construction charges.

The default problem appears to have been solved with the Reclamation Project Act of 1939, which empowered the bureau to enter into more flexible repayment contracts. There were no defaults on contracts negotiated under this act.[16] It is not clear whether the default record has improved as a result of the longer repayment periods and graduated payment schemes per se, or whether these improvements resulted from the increased subsidy that accompanied these modifications.[16a] Contracts negotiated under section 9(d) of the act were permitted repayment periods of forty years with development periods of up to ten years. The contracts could be written to allow for charges that varied with the productivity of different classes of land within the project area and for annual charges that depended on gross crop values. Table 2-1 shows that the grace period increased the subsidy's discounted value to 57 percent of construction charges. The flexibility of the payments under these con-

16. Frederick Warne, *The Bureau of Reclamation* (New York: Praeger, 1971), p. 63.

16a. That is, the repayment period could have been extended and payments shifted beyond the difficult transitional years of a project without increasing the value of the subsidy, simply by levying appropriate interest charges. Since relief measures have generally been accompanied by implicit increases in the value of the subsidies, it would be extremely difficult to empirically identify these separate effects.

tracts increased the subsidy's value even more by reducing the burden of the risk borne by irrigators. Under Section 9 (e) of the act, authority was granted to negotiate contracts that did not require complete repayment of construction costs within forty years. In these contracts, water recipients were charged rates sufficient to cover an appropriate share of annual operation and maintenance costs and fixed construction costs. From the viewpoint of irrigators, the problem with these contracts was that the contracted water rights did not become attached to their land when the contract ended. Later legislation assured irrigators of their rights to renew these contracts and provided that payments above and beyond operation and maintenance costs would be credited towards repayment of construction costs if they decided to switch to 9 (d) contracts.

Later acts made minor changes in the general rules for repayment and authorized more flexible repayment schemes for specific projects. The Small Reclamation Projects Act of 6 August 1956 authorized interest-free loans for small projects (overall cost of less than $10 million) with a repayment period of up to fifty years. Increased flexibility in repayment contracts was provided by the Variable Plan Amendment of 1958, which permitted adjustments in the installment payments (with the constraint that charges must still be repaid within forty years). Several of the special congressional acts authorizing specific projects have specified repayment periods considerably longer than forty years, including the Kennewick division of the Yakima project (sixty-six years), the Mancos project in Colorado (sixty years), and the Paonia project, also in Colorado (sixty-eight years).[17] However, the Reclamation Project Act of 1939 was the last act in which major modifications in the general rules for repayment of construction costs were made.

A rent-seeking model suggests that since members of the Bureau of Reclamation and the Department of Interior were unable to directly capture the gains from the provision of irrigation water, they would have attempted to appropriate the rents obtainable from administering the program. By winning congressional approval that would lead to increased appropriations and administrative power, the bureaucrats could have increased the potential size of the administrative rents. Where possible, the members would have sought to increase the part of their budget that was not part of the common pool

17. Golzé, *Reclamation*, p. 248.

of federal revenues. This portion of the budget provides a budgetary base that is not subject to direct congressional appropriations and therefore is not shared with other agencies.[18]

One important part of the bureau's budget was the repayment of construction charges into the Reclamation Fund. Increasing the stream of repayments into the fund was in the bureau's interest for three reasons. First, successful repayment could be pointed to as an indication that the bureau was successfully carrying out its congressional mandate. Repayment demonstrated that a particular project had been successfully irrigated and that the bureau was "paying its own way." Second, these funds did not go into the common pool of federal revenues to be reassigned by Congress. Instead, the funds were automatically allocated to the Department of Interior for new reclamation projects chosen by the bureau and approved by Congress. Third, the fact that settlers on a project were able to make their scheduled payments indicated that they were maintaining a reasonable standard of living. Keeping water users happy benefited the members of the bureau, since complaints from unhappy irrigators caused Congress to view the bureau's activities with disfavor. Moreover, discontented settlers could make a local agent's job unpleasant.

Given that the bureau wanted successful settlement and repayment of costs, it was clearly in their interest to have qualified applicants settling on their projects. The writer in the bureau's annual reports in its first twenty years consistently pointed to the settlers' lack of capital, experience, and perseverance as primary reasons for failures to repay charges. At the suggestion of a fact-finders' committee on reclamation appointed by the Secretary of Interior in 1923, the bureau received the authority to require settlers to meet specified qualifications in the Fact Finders Act of 1924. The value of this authority was enhanced by the fact that the guidelines established in the act were general, allowing the bureau extensive leeway in establishing the qualifications. The secretary was authorized "under regulations to be promulgated by him, to require of each entry to public lands on a project, such qualifications as to industry, experience, character, and capital, as in his opinion are necessary to give reasonable assurance of success by the prospective settler."[19]

18. For a similar argument in a different context, see Anderson and Hill, "Establishing Property Rights," p. 91.

19. Subsection C of the Second Deficiency Act (Fact Finder's Act), 1924, (43 Stat. 702, 43 U.S.C. 433).

Another method of achieving the objectives of successful settlement and repayment was to extend the term of the repayment period. These extensions generally reduced the annual payments assessed against the settlers, thereby increasing the likelihood that payments would be made and improving repayment records. Until the bureau began funding larger multipurpose projects, the administrative control was taken over by water users after a certain percentage of the construction costs were repaid.[20] This gave the bureau additional incentive to lengthen the repayment period and maintain control over these projects. However, extensions of the repayment period were not entirely in the bureau's interest, since they reduced both the present value of the payment stream to be received from settlers and the flow of revenues into the Reclamation Fund.

Because most of the repayment extensions were legislated, it is difficult to directly observe the bureau's desired tradeoffs. The fact that the Department of Interior did not take a general stand against extensions is some indication that at the margin, the bureau preferred contented settlers and impressive repayment records to rapid payment. As the scope of the bureau's undertakings broadened to include huge multipurpose projects, increasing the relative importance of special congressional appropriations, it might be expected that the bureau would be relatively less concerned with maintaining the flow of repayment revenues into the Reclamation Fund and more concerned with presenting a rosy picture of their operations to Congress.

Two specific instances show the nature of the bureau's interest in an impressive repayment record: (1) the bureau's opposition to blanket repayment moratoria in the 1920s and 1930s, and (2) their support of the fact-finders' committee's suggestion to write off construction costs on some projects. In 1924 the bureau opposed repayment moratoria, arguing that many irrigators who were able to make payments were using the agricultural depression as an excuse to postpone repayment. Many settlers who were suffering on project lands had "sacrificed" and made their payments, providing a limited flow of revenue into the Reclamation Fund. Blanket moratoria were expected to encourage the settlers to join "the repudiation ranks," which would temporarily cut off the entire flow of revenues into the fund without increasing the probability of repayment by those settlers. Members of the bureau were in favor of granting moratoria for repayments only on projects of their choice during the 1920s and

20. Warne, *Bureau of Reclamation*, p. 68.

1930s, an additional discretionary power that would have allowed the bureau to avoid problems of nonpayment by successful water users.[21]

Several of the early projects were failures. Irrigation water had not improved the lands' productivity enough to support farming; consequently the bureau did not expect the construction costs ever to be repaid. Faced with increasing objections to the financial failure of their projects, the bureau sought a way to exclude these projects from the Reclamation Fund and improve their collection record. Settlers on the projects and the bureau supported the recommendation of the fact-finders' committee of 1923 that $27 million in construction costs on early projects be written off as nonrecoverable losses. Congress responded in 1926 by passing the Omnibus Adjustment Act, which allowed costs on specific projects to be written off.

In the early 1920s the Bureau of Reclamation was confronted with calls for the end of the reclamation program from other federal agencies.[22] The Department of Agriculture led this opposition to continued construction of irrigation projects, arguing that subsidies given to irrigation farmers worsened conditions for all farmers by creating an "oversupply" of farm goods in an already depressed market, and furthermore that many of the projects had been financial failures. The Department of Interior replied that the lands on the reclamation projects were used primarily for growing specialty crops that were not in oversupply. They also maintained that publicly reclaimed land was providing the basis for a society of independent farmers in the arid regions of the West, a nonfinancial benefit that must be considered when evaluating the federal reclamation program.

This crisis was averted with the passage of the Boulder Canyon Act in 1928, which marked the beginning of the bureau's involvement in the development of multipurpose projects. The benefits of such projects as Hoover Dam in the Boulder Canyon project and Grand Coulee Dam in the Columbia River basin included the provision of public power, delivery of municipal water, flood control, and improved river navigation in addition to irrigation. The movement into

21. See *Twenty-Fourth Annual Report*, p. 9, and Charles West's letter to Compton White cited in note 12.

22. Often members of agencies dissipate rents while competing with other agencies to maintain or increase the legislative demand for their services. For a discussion of this form of competition, see Faith, "Rent-Seeking Aspects," pp. 332-345.

multipurpose projects eventually provided irrigators with additional subsidies.

The bureau competed with the Army Corps of Engineers for the rights to build several flood-control projects, including the Central Valley and Missouri River basin projects. The Army Corps had a slight advantage until 1944, when irrigation on flood-control projects was placed under reclamation law. The two agencies actually combined forces on the Missouri River basin project to prevent the creation of a new competitor similar to the TVA.[23]

The Reclamation Project Act of 1939 authorized the allocation of costs among different classes of project beneficiaries. Revenues from power and municipal water users were to be applied to their respective shares of the total costs. Portions of the costs were also to be charged to flood control and navigation on a nonreimbursable basis (see Section 9 [b]). Costs allocable to the preservation of fish and wildlife and to construction of recreation facilities have also been exempted either partly or wholly from reimbursement.[24] This policy eased the repayment burden on irrigators but did not furnish them with a direct subsidy. The major irrigation subsidy generated by the new allocation of costs was derived from the policy of using revenues from municipal and industrial power users to pay the portion of irrigation costs judged to be beyond their irrigators' ability to pay. The bureau gained from this practice, since the lower charges to irrigators enhanced the probability of repayment of their remaining share of the construction costs. This arrangement, while not authorized in the general reclamation law, was expressly authorized for a number of individual projects and has been practiced on most other federal projects.[25]

23. Merk, *History of Westward Movement*, p. 543, and Mary Montgomery and Marion Clawson, *History of Legislation and Policy Formation of the Central Valley Project* (Berkeley, Calif.: Bureau of Agricultural Economics, 1946), pp. 228-238.

24. For discussions of acts relating to the reimbursement policies for these uses, see Charles Meyers and A. Dan Tarlock, *A Coursebook in Law and Public Policy* (Mineola, N.Y.: Foundation Press, 1971), p. 539, and Robert E. Clark, *Water and Water Rights*, vol. 2 (Indianapolis: Allen and Smith Company, 1967), pp. 147-153.

25. See Clark, *Water Rights*, p. 272, for examples of projects where this policy has been authorized. A second subsidy to irrigators may exist if costs are not allocated "correctly" among the project beneficiaries. Meyers and Tarlock (*Coursebook in Law*, p. 545) believe that costs apportioned to nonreimbursable uses are overestimated, which has the effect of increasing the subsidy to irrigation users by reducing the portion of total costs assigned to them. Whether this type of overestimation actually occurs is difficult to determine, since values of the nonreimbursable benefits are not generally determined through market transactions.

Table 2-2. The Power Subsidy.[a]

Project	Costs Allocated to Irrigation	Costs to be Repaid by Irrigators	Percentage of Irrigation Costs Subsidized
Central Valley California	687,152,000	606,646,000	11.1
Chief Joseph Dam[b] Washington	11,083,200	6,050,000	45.4
Collbran Colorado	6,105,000	1,089,101	82.2
Columbia Basin Washington	745,111,398	135,916,400	81.8
Fryingpan-Arkansas Colorado	69,946,000	50,512,300	27.8
Rouge River Oregon	18,064,000	9,066,500	49.8
San Angelo Texas	8,853,904	4,000,000	54.8
The Dalles Oregon	5,994,000	2,550,000	57.5
Venturia River California	18,273,128	10,746,300	41.2
Washita Basin Oklahoma[c]	10,403,011	8,221,000	21.0

a. On some of these projects, a portion of the subsidy to irrigators came from industrial and municipal users.

b. Includes costs and repayments from Foster Creek and Greater Wenatchee Divisions.

c. Includes costs and payments from Fort Cobb and Fass Divisions.

Source: Reclamation Payments and Payout Schedule, Department of Interior, Bureau of Reclamation (Government Printing Office, 1965).

An indication of the value of this subsidy is given in Table 2-2 for several projects. The third column shows the percentage of the total costs allocated to irrigation that has been subsidized by other project beneficiaries. These figures, which range from 11 percent to over 82 percent, demonstrate that this subsidy has been extremely valuable to irrigators on a number of federal reclamation projects.

By seeking legislation making repayment schedules longer and more flexible, irrigators were able to increase the value of the rents accruing to them from the interest-free loan on construction costs. The rents were increased further as the Bureau of Reclamation expanded its administrative role to provision of multipurpose projects.

The total value of the cost and interest subsidies shown in Tables 2-1 and 2-2 can be calculated for specific projects. For example, the repayment contract for the San Angelo project called for "forty successive equal annual installments commencing with the first year following the last year of a development period which is not to exceed ten years following completion of construction."[26] Assuming that the full ten-year development period was allowed and using a 6 percent discount rate, the irrigators on this project received a subsidy of nearly 90 percent of the construction costs allocated to irrigation. With subsidies of this magnitude it is not surprising that extensive efforts were made to increase the size of the rents.

ACREAGE LIMITATIONS–THE DISTRIBUTION OF THE SUBSIDY

Congress set acreage limits and guidelines for land disposal to promote irrigation of arid lands by small-scale family farmers. The members of the Bureau of Reclamation administered these policies, which determined the distribution of rents from federal water to two groups of water users–settlers on public lands and private landowners. In this section the efforts of the irrigators and bureaucrats to appropriate these rents within the constraints imposed by Congress are described in the context of three aspects of reclamation policy: the rules for settling public lands, the restrictions on the sale of excess lands, and exemptions from the acreage limitation.

Before specific types of rent-seeking behavior can be properly analyzed, the precise nature and intent of the congressional constraints must be examined. A recent court ruling (*United States* v. *Tulare Lake Canal Co.*, 9th Circuit Court, 1976) concluded that "the goals of the reclamation laws were to create family sized farms in areas irrigated by federal projects, to break up and redistribute large private land holdings, to have wide distribution of the subsidy involved and to limit speculative gains."[27] To accomplish these ends, section 8 of the Reclamation Act of 1902 limited the land to which irrigation water would be distributed to a maximum of 160 acres in a single ownership. The nature of this limitation differed from previous

26. U.S. Department of Interior, Bureau of Reclamation, *Reclamation Payments* (Washington, D.C.: Government Printing Office, 1965), p. 343.

27. Jones, *Rules for Acreage Limitation*, p. 936.

federal policies insofar as it limited water rights rather than the amount of land that an individual could own. Once obtained, the water right was tied to the land, not to the individual, and limited to the amount that could be put to "beneficial use." Since the projects were expected to provide water primarily for previously unsettled public lands, the law also established basic requirements for land use that had to be satisfied before ownership of the land would be transferred.

These constraints on the size of holdings and their use were similar to the provisions in nineteenth-century public land laws, which had been designed to combat land monopoly and speculation. The Homestead Act of 1862 limited land ownership to 160 acres and required continuous residency on the land for a five-year period. The Desert Lands Act of 1877, an attempt at stimulating settlement of arid lands, allowed settlers to obtain title for up to 640 acres of land each if they irrigated the land within three years after filing. This act was later amended to reduce the maximum acreage to 320 acres and to establish a more stringent set of requirements to ensure the sincerity of settlers on public lands.[28] The Carey Act of 1894 ceded up to 1,000,000 acres of federal lands to any state where those lands were settled, irrigated, and at least partly cultivated. Ownership of these lands was restricted to 160 acres per person.

These rules proved ineffective in promoting irrigation and preventing large landholdings. Even though over 500,000 acres of land were entered annually between 1877 and 1884, only a minute portion were actually irrigated and patented. Ranchers devised a variety of methods, some of them fraudulent, for skirting the acreage limitations of this act and secured large tracts for grazing.[29] Despite the failure of these earlier restrictions to control land monopoly and speculation, the authors of the Reclamation Act expressed confidence that the stipulations they devised would successfully limit land monopolies. Frank Mondell of Arizona stated:

> It is a step in advance of any legislation we have ever had in guarding against the possibility of speculative land holdings and in providing for small farms and homes on the public lands, while it will also compel the division into

28. For a description of the changes contained in the acts of 1890 and 1891, see Benjamin Hibbard, *History of the Public Land Policies* (New York: Macmillan Co., 1974), p. 431.

29. Several of these methods are described in Hibbard, *History of Land Policies*, pp. 428-434, and Clark, *Water Rights*, p. 15. These sources support the view that the acts of

small holdings of any large areas . . . in private ownership which may be irrigated under its provisions.[30]

In retrospect this confidence seems to have been unfounded, largely because basic provisions for settlement and establishment of water rights were no more specific that those of earlier acts, and because implementation of the provisions again relied heavily on administrative interpretations by the Department of Interior.

The acreage limitations and rules for securing the property rights to irrigation water led to different forms of rent-seeking activities on lands in public and private ownership. These differences are demonstrated by analyzing public and private ownership separately.

The guidelines established in section 3 of the 1902 act for settlement of public lands authorized the Secretary of Interior to withdraw from entry (except under the provisions of the Homestead Law) any public land he believed to be "susceptible" to irrigation by government works. If and when construction of the project began, the secretary was to announce the construction charges and the maximum irrigable acreage per entry, which was to be that "reasonably required for the support of a family upon the lands in question" and was not to exceed 160 acres or be less than 40 acres. All public lands were to be settled under the Homestead Law on a first come, first served basis. Settlers filing entry between the time the secretary withdrew the land and the time he decided whether a project would be undertaken were required to establish residency within six months of filing, regardless of whether water was available. Before settlers could receive title to the land, they were required to live on (or in the neighborhood of) the land for five years, to reclaim at least half of the irrigable acreage on their claims for agricultural purposes, and to pay off the construction costs levied on their tracts. Claims to federally irrigated lands under the commutation clause of the Homestead Laws, under which settlers obtained patent to federal lands by making a cash payment before the residency period expired, were disallowed so that large land empires could not be amassed.

1877 and 1894 failed in promoting the goals of Congress. Fraudulent activities used to obtain federal timber lands in the Northwest are described in Gary Libecap and Ronald Johnson, "Property Rights, Nineteenth-Century Federal Timber Policy, and the Conservation Movement," *Journal of Economic History* 39 (March 1979): 129–142.

30. Quoted in Paul S. Taylor, "The Excess Land Law: Execution of Public Policy," *Yale Law Journal* 64 (February 1955): 484.

These settlement guidelines were important determinants of the distribution of and competition for the subsidy benefits among settlers. The acreage limits restricted the size of the entries and therefore the rents available to each settler, while the residency requirements and the first come, first served rule determined the form of the competition for those benefits.

This set of rules led to the dissipation of the rents from public lands at the margin through early settlement.[31] The present value of expected net returns on unhomesteaded public lands prior to irrigation was probably negative. In most cases the expected value of the lands increased dramatically when irrigation water was provided. If settlers had been able to obtain land when water was first provided they would have earned rents on their entries. But under the act of 1902, initial rights to the land went to the settlers who first filed their claims. To keep those rights, they had to establish residence on the land within six months of filing, remain there, and cultivate it for the next five years. They competed for the irrigated lands by settling prior to the completion of the projects. Between settlement and completion of the project, settlers earned negative returns on their lands, which were not profitable to homestead without subsidized irrigation works. When faced with competition, people settled earlier and earlier as long as the present value of the negative costs associated with settling before the project was completed was less than the positive present value of the irrigated homestead.

Early settlement on federal projects was widespread. In 1911 the Reclamation Service reported that considerable numbers of settlers were homesteading "adjacent to every area on which surveys had been made by the Government," whether a project was actually being built or not.[32] Evidence of early settlement on specific projects is found in the following statements from annual reports of the Reclamation Service:

> The Public land under this project (the Payette-Boise Project in Idaho) has been filed on rapidly since its withdrawal on March 5, 1903, for reclamation purposes. At the present time practically every tract that can be irrigated

31. Intramarginal settlers received rents from federally irrigated public lands even in the presence of competition.

32. U.S. Department of Interior, *Eleventh Annual Report of the Reclamation Service* (Washington, D.C.: Government Printing Office, 1912), pp. 9–10.

> under the project has been entered, even though it is well known that in some parts of the project it will be several years before water can be delivered.[33]

> The lands (on the Minidoka Project in Idaho) were rapidly settled when it became known that the Reclamation Service had undertaken the construction of the project and most of the irrigable areas had been entered under the homestead act before the farm units had been determined and considerably in advance of the delivery of water.[34]

> Many homestead entries were made (on the Lower Yellowstone Project in Montana and North Dakota) at about the time of the withdrawal of lands for the irrigation project on August 23, 1903.[35]

Construction on the Yellowstone project was not authorized until 10 May 1904, and project water was not actually delivered until 1909. On this project settlers homesteaded the lands not only before construction was completed, but before it was even decided whether the project would actually be constructed.

In the discussions prior to the 1902 act, early settlement had been anticipated and "an attempt was made at that time to exclude settlement until the works were built. This was opposed on the grounds that no intelligent man would think of attempting to make settlement in a desert until the water was actually in sight."[36] After discovering that intelligence was less widespread than previously believed, that many settlers were starving and that projects were failing as settlers used up their savings prior to delivery of water, the law was amended in 1910. Settlement of all lands withdrawn by the Secretary of Interior was prohibited under section 5 of the 1910 act until the secretary announced the unit of acreage established, and fixed the water charges and the date of delivery of the water. Section 10 of the Reclamation Extention Act of 1914 prohibited entry prior to the time water was actually ready to be delivered. Dissipation though early settlement appears to have been effectively stopped but the bureau complained of the poor quality of some settlers who obtained land under the homestead rules. The Fact Finders Act of 1924 (subsection 4) gave the bureau more direct control of the distribu-

33. U.S. Department of Interior, *Seventh Annual Report of the Reclamation Service* (Washington, D.C.: Government Printing Office, 1908), pp. 89–90.

34. U.S. Department of Interior, *Ninth Annual Report of the Reclamation Service* (Washington, D.C.: Government Printing Office, 1910), p. 105.

35. Ibid., p. 174.

36. U.S. Department of Interior, *Eleventh Annual Report of the Reclamation Service* (Washington, D.C.: Government Printing Office, 1912), p. 10.

tion of lands when minimum requirements for capital and experience were added to the criteria for entrymen.

It was initially thought that most of the land reclaimed by projects constructed under the act of 1902 would be federal lands and that most of the water from these projects would be delivered to settlers on these lands. However, the Reclamation Service quickly discovered that much of the land on the most promising project sites was already privately owned. As a result it soon became apparent that a large portion of the federally provided water would serve private lands. The distribution of the subsidy benefits on these lands was determined by the acreage limitation and the policies governing the sale of excess lands. The reluctance of landowners to voluntarily sell their excess lands indicated that incentives to dispose of their excess lands were not adequate. To understand why these and other policies failed and why the policies were altered as they were, one must look more closely at the incentives faced by large landowners and members of the Bureau of Reclamation.

Insight into the incentives of landowners can be gained from considering the following expression. Let $V_{\hat{d}}$ be the average dry land (or preproject) value to the landowner of an acre of land, $V_{\hat{w}}$ the average value to the landowner of an acre of land receiving federally subsidized irrigation water, $P_{\hat{d}}$ the dry-land market price, and $P_{\hat{w}}$ the market price of federally irrigated land. Assume that we are looking at the options of a landowner who owns 1000 acres of land and who is allowed to sell excess land at its full market value after the federal irrigation project is completed. The landowner will be able to receive water for 160 acres of land. If the irrigation subsidy has positive value to this individual, the value placed on an acre of land will increase from $V_{\hat{d}}$ to $V_{\hat{w}}$. By selling the other 840 acres of land the individual will receive the "with-water" market price for them, and the total gains from the project will be:

$$G_{sell} = (V_{\hat{w}} - V_{\hat{d}}) \times 160 + (P_{\hat{w}} - V_{\hat{d}}) \times 840$$

Several useful observations can be made from this simple expression. First, if the subsidy has positive value to this landowner (and if the irrigated value of the land is greater than the market price of the irrigated land, that is, if $V_{\hat{w}} > P_{\hat{w}}$), the owner will have the incentive to devise methods for avoiding the acreage limitation provisions. Such methods might include pressing for special legislation to exempt the project from the acreage limitation and encouraging the Bureau of Reclamation to adopt policies whose effect is to relax these restrictions (such as allowing a married couple to own 320 acres). Second, if there are economies of scale to irrigation farming for lots larger than 160 acres, this landowner will have additional incentives to avoid the acreage limitation, since $V_{\hat{w}}$ will be larger the more land is irrigated. Third, if $P_{\hat{w}} < V_{\hat{d}}$, which might occur if this individual is extremely efficient at farming without project water, it will not be in the owner's interest to sell the excess lands, even at the irrigated market value.[37] Finally, this landowner has incentives to delay selling excess land if there is a possibility that $P_{\hat{w}}$ will rise in the future, provided the expected rate of return from holding the land is greater than the return from selling now and reinvesting the proceeds. There are indications that landowners did engage in this type of speculation.[38]

These incentives change when we assume that the landowner is required to sell excess lands at a price that does *not* include the value of the subsidy ($P_{\hat{d}}$). Consider again the landowner who owns 1000 acres of land prior to the reclamation project. According to the law, this individual is eligible to receive federal project water for a maximum of 160 acres, leaving 840 acres for which water is not received. The fact that the owner held excess land before the project was begun indicated the value of that land ($V_{\hat{d}}$) was at least as great as its market value ($P_{\hat{d}}$). Since the owner is restricted to receiving $P_{\hat{d}}$ in a sale of excess acreage, there would be losses from the sale equal to $(V_{\hat{d}} - P_{\hat{d}})$ 840. The owner has no incentive to sell the lands at the preproject market price. The landowner will not be able to get subsidized water on excess lands and will not be willing to sell them to potential buyers who would be able to receive the water. If the owner refuses to sell, nobody receives the subsidy on the excess lands. In this situation both large landowners and potential buyers have incentives to break the law so they can capture the subsidy.

37. One way in which the landowner can farm efficiently without project water is by pumping groundwater for his lands. Opponents of acreage limitations in California's Central Valley argued that large landowners would gain from the project by pumping groundwater replenished by water from irrigated lands. It appears that their arguments were unfounded, as most large landowners chose to join the project. See Warne, *Bureau of Reclamation*, pp. 76-83.

38. For references to these types of activities, see Montgomery and Clawson, *History of Central Valley Project*, p. 138; "Reclamation by Irrigation," pp. 113-114; and Clark, *Water Rights*, p. 211.

Numerous bureau policies allow the subsidy to be obtained and shared by excess-land holders and buyers. One is to permit large landholders to sign a contract that allows them to receive water on their excess lands for a limited time period but forces them to sell those lands at the preproject value (P_d^*) at the end of the period. If the period is long enough, the landowners have incentives to sign the contract and sell their lands at the specified time. The buyers of these lands will pay the preproject value of the lands and will receive subsidized federal water on the project when they obtain the land. Under this policy it is in the interest of the large landowners to delay the actual sale of their lands as long as they can, while the buyers will push for shortened contract periods.

This policy leads to a division of the irrigation subsidy benefits (to lands that are initially privately owned) between the large landowners and the buyers. The landowners get the full benefits of the subsidy on 160 acres of their land, plus the benefits from receiving water for their excess lands until those lands are sold. Settlers who bought the excess land at its preproject price receive the remainder of the subsidy benefits.[39]

The actual division of the benefits is determined by the political power of the two groups. Large landowners would be expected to have the advantage in political competition since they are a smaller, more concentrated group with established ownership (implying that they face lower organization costs) than the group of potential buyers. Under all of the policies for sales of excess lands, the costs of the subsidy are borne by the taxpayers on pure irrigation projects. On later multipurpose projects, power users also paid for a share of the irrigation subsidy.

The incentives of bureaucratic actors associated with federal reclamation were also extremely important in determining the actual distribution of the subsidy when federal projects served privately owned lands. Because their interests often conflicted with those of Congress, these actors made tradeoffs between legislative and constituent pressures in an effort to capture a portion of the rents from the federal reclamation program.

39. One possible method of reducing high rates of returns on those lands—settlers paying "above-market" prices for improvements and structures owned by the landlord that were sold with the excess land—was excluded in contracts from the Central Valley project in California, which included provisions that nonland assets also be sold at assessed prices. U.S. Congress, House of Representatives, *Central Valley Project Documents*, House Document No. 246 (Washington, D.C.: Government Printing Office, 1957), pp. 84–139.

The members of the Bureau of Reclamation and the Department of Interior were expected to administer the acreage limits and land resale policies and ensure that the subsidy was widely distributed by promoting the development of family farms. It therefore appears to have been in the interest of the bureau to enforce the acreage limitation laws established by Congress, since without congressional approval the bureau would be unable to undertake new projects. The bureau also was pressured *not* to enforce these excess-land laws. The most obvious source of pressure for nonenforcement came from large landholders on reclamation projects who were willing to incur considerable expense in their efforts to find methods of avoiding these acreage limitations.

In addition to these pressures, the bureau had other incentives to adopt policies of nonenforcement. There are at least three reasons why nonenforcement of acreage restrictions might have increased the flow of repayment on a particular project, which was strongly correlated with project success desired by both Congress and landowners. First, if there were economies of scale in irrigation for farms larger than the acreage limitation on a particular project, the prospects for repayment were enhanced by allowing large landholders to receive (and pay for) water for their excess lands. In the presence of scale economies, the net income available for payment of construction costs from one 320-acre farm was greater than that available from two 160-acre farms. Second, the Bureau of Reclamation generally had more complete, reliable information on the abilities of current landholders to repay construction costs than on the abilities of prospective settlers, particularly on projects that supplied supplemental water to irrigation farmers. Third, if excess lands were not allowed to receive water and large landowners chose not to sell these lands, the construction charges for the project would have been divided among fewer acres, increasing the construction charges on participating acreage and reducing the probability of successful repayment.

It is apparent that the bureau had to make tradeoffs between its goals of ensuring the repayment of construction costs and promoting the development of family farms through the enforcement of acreage restrictions. It is also apparent that enforcement was not an all-or-nothing activity. There was a wide range of policy options available between the extremes of absolute enforcement, where no excess land received water under any circumstances, and total nonenforcement, where no efforts whatsoever were made to encourage landowners to comply with the acreage limitation laws. The actual enforcement policies of the Bureau of Reclamation were determined by a variety of factors, including: (1) the visibility of the decision makers and (2) the intensities of opposing pressures from large landowners on one side, and Congress, the president, and the courts on the other. The intensity of pressure from owners of excess lands in their efforts to increase the rents they received from the federal water subsidy was a function of the net value of the subsidy, the proportion of lands held in excess, and the probability (as perceived by the large landholders) of successfully avoiding the acreage limitations. The pressures applied by the different branches of the government varied over time with the convictions of the individuals in office.

The visibility of the decisionmaker was important in determining the different responses of members of the Bureau of Reclamation and the Department of Interior to political and constituent pressures. Since it was costly for the lawmakers to monitor the actions of the administrators of the program, the agents were more likely to enforce the laws the more visible their position.[40] For example, the Secretary of Interior and commissioner of the bureau, whose actions were easily observed by the Congress and the president, were relatively more responsive to pressures from political and judicial sources. On the other hand, it was difficult for the president to observe the actions of local bureau representatives, who therefore were relatively less responsive to pressure from Washington to enforce acreage limitations, especially when large landowners demanded nonenforcement. enforcement.

The preceding discussion lays the groundwork for the analysis of actions taken by large landowners and the Bureau of Reclamation in response to the legislation concerning the disposal of excess lands and enforcement of the acreage limitation. The authors of the Reclamation of 1902 clearly wanted to break up land monopolies, but their attitudes toward the distribution of the subsidy from federal water were unclear. In the initial act there was no limitation placed on the sale price of excess lands. Senator Francis G. Newlands explained the relationship of the acreage limitation of 160 acres to the large landowner's incentives:

40. The lawmaker's problems with monitoring bureaucratic agents is a central theme in Douglass North's "A Framework for Analyzing the State in Economic History," in *Explorations in Economic History* 16: 249-259, and *Structure and Change in Economic History* (New York: W. W. Norton and Co., 1981), pp. 20-32.

The fact that waters from the irrigation project can be brought within the reach of [a] large holding raises its value. Purchasers of that holding in tracts of 160 acres can secure water rights under this Act. The large landed proprietor is benefited by having the water brought within reach. He has the opportunity of making sales of lands hitherto unsalable and a purchaser can unite the water with the land by buying a water right from the government and thus dedicate the land to future productiveness and so that act not only guarantees against monopoly in the state but will gradually destroy existing monopoly and disintegrate these holdings in the country without injury to any and benefit to all.[41]

Since no limitation was placed on the price at which the excess lands were to be sold, the expected future net gains from the receipt of federally subsidized irrigation water would be capitalized into the sale price of that land. In other words, all of the windfall benefits from the project would be received by the large landowners, assuming estimates of the value of future subsidies were on average correct.[42] Apparently, the original reason for breaking up large landholdings was *not* to ensure that the project benefits were widely distributed among the settlers on the resulting family-sized farms, but simply to break up the large holdings.

By 1914 it was apparent that large landholders would not willingly sell their excess holdings under the rules established by the act of 1902. Large landowners were holding their excess lands out of production while they waited for the prices to rise, which delayed the flow of repayment revenues into the Reclamation Fund. To remedy this, the Reclamation Extension Act of 1914 required the owners of excess lands to agree to dispose of those lands at prices specified by the Secretary of Interior before any construction work was done, or they would not receive project water. As written, the act gave no indication as to whether the price established by the secretary was to include the capitalized value of the federal subsidy. This omission increased the discretionary control of the Department of Interior

41. Quoted in Montgomery and Clawson, *History of Central Valley Project*, p. 134.

42. To the extent that federal estimates of construction costs were used to calculate these subsidy values, the benefits received by a large landowner when the land was sold would be greater than the true windfall gains from the project, since federal estimates of construction costs were consistently lower than actual costs.

over the distribution of the subsidy to buyers and sellers of excess lands.

Ten years later the Fact Finders Report of 1924 concluded that these antimonopoly measures were ineffective. Its authors objected to the distribution of the subsidy established by the bureaucrats administering the law. Some of the prices established for the sale of excess lands included the value of project water, thereby giving all of the subsidy from federal water to the large landholder.[43] In other instances, part of the subsidy was going to so-called speculators, since there were no limits on the activities of middlemen who purchased the land at the secretary's price and resold it at the market price. The authors also objected that the Reclamation Service was allowing large landholders to receive water on their excess lands, which was contrary to the clearly stated intent of Congress. The landowners would agree to sell their lands but the actual sale was often delayed indefinitely. In the interim the service interpreted the law to allow delivery of water to the excess lands.

To correct these shortcomings, Congress passed the Omnibus Adjustment Act of 1926. Section 46 of the act required the following to be included in all repayment contracts between the secretary and organizations: (1) all irrigated land held by a single owner in excess of 160 acres was to be appraised in a manner prescribed by the secretary; (2) the appraised price would reflect the value of the land without the value added by the reclamation project; (3) no excess land was to receive water from a federal project if the owner refused to execute a recordable contract agreeing to sell those lands at a price not to exceed the appraised price; (4) until half the construction charges were paid, the purchase price of any sale of excess land had to be approved by the secretary before that land would be eligible to receive project water; and (5) if it was found that the purchase price of excess lands had been falsely reported, the secretary could cancel the water rights attached to that land.[44]

The apparent purpose of these provisions was to ensure that excess lands would be sold and that the selling price would be limited, thereby achieving a wider distribution of the subsidy. Although the members of the bureau and the Department of Interior were constrained to setting dry land prices, the act contained loopholes that

43. "Reclamation by Irrigation," pp. 113–114.
44. Clark, *Water Rights*, p. 212.

still allowed them to control the subsidy's distribution. As in the 1914 act, landowners were only required to *agree* to sell their excess lands; no requirement that these lands actually be sold within a given period of time was imposed. The secretary established the distribution of the rents by requiring landowners to agree to sell their excess lands within ten years and by interpreting the law to allow the delivery of water to excess lands during that period.[45] Another dimension of water contracts that was not specified in Section 46 was the penalties for selling lands at "speculative" prices. These penalties were determined by negotiations between the bureau and the irrigation districts. The contract with the Kittitas Division of the Yakima project in Washington provided that half of the difference between the sale price and the appraised price go to the irrigation district and be credited against the construction costs of the project; the other half to be retained by the seller of the excess lands.[46] Under this type of an arrangement, the incentives of the landowner-speculator would still be to sell excess land at the market price. If the objectives of the irrigation district and the Bureau of Reclamation include early repayment of construction costs, it may also be to their advantage if excess land is sold at a price above the appraised price.

Several acts passed after 1926 contained provisions relating to specific projects or classifications of projects. For example, the Small Reclamation Projects Act of 1956 provided that the repayment plan on qualifying projects would require the payment of interest "on that portion of the loan which is attributable to furnishing irrigation benefits in each particular year to land held in private ownership by Because the Department of Interior has interpreted this passage as a repeal of the excess-land law for small projects, large landowners involved in projects falling under the jurisdiction of this act can receive water for their excess lands by foregoing the interest subsidy and are not required to sign recordable contracts for the disposal of

45. Ibid., pp. 213-214. It is interesting to note that the loopholes allowing the delivery of water to excess lands under the acts of 1914 and 1926 were the same. If Congress really had wanted to prevent the monopoly of federal irrigation water, it seems reasonable to assume that it would have required the actual sale of the land.

46. Warne, *Bureau of Reclamation*, p. 73. Under the Columbia Basin Anti-Speculation Act of 1937, the maximum that could be kept by the participants in the sale–50 percent of the price differential if the penalty was paid immediately–was to fall by 1 percent for every month that the penalty payment was delinquent. If the penalty payment was not made within fifty months, the government was to receive all of the price differential.

those lands.[47] Efforts to obtain this exemption for all reclamation projects have failed. The Omnibus Adjustment Act was the last act containing general provisions for acreage limitations and sales of excess lands.

Most of the controversy over reclamation policy has stemmed from the bureau's enforcement or lack of enforcement of the acreage limit. The enforcement policies adopted by the bureau on different projects have different implications for (1) the nature of the distribution of rents among irrigators and (2) the net benefits accruing to different members of the bureau. The key factors determining these differences in policies have been the intensity of pressure for nonenforcement from constituent landowners, vacillations in congressional pressure to enforce the law, and the visibility of the decisionmakers' actions to the legislative and executive branches.

From the bureau's perspective, the most desirable method of avoiding enforcement of acreage limitations was legislative exemptions, which gave congressional sanction to nonenforcement policies. Large landowners on such projects were appeased by this guaranteed exemption, and the probability of successful repayment from these established farmers was increased. Administrative exemptions by the Secretary of Interior or the head of the Reclamation Bureau for specific projects were less desirable to both the bureau and large landowners. These exemptions were easily monitored by Congress and the president and could have been politically costly to the bureau if these groups desired enforcement. On the other hand, administrative exemptions enhanced the likelihood of successful repayment and relieved bureau representatives at the local level of pressures from large landowners. From the landowners' viewpoint this type of exemption was less attractive than legislative exemptions, since it was less permanent and its legality less certain. The probability of a new Secretary of Interior changing the policy was greater than the probability of Congress retracting a legislated exemption. Exemption through nonenforcement at the local level, the least visible form, was the least costly to the bureau in the face of congressional pressure to enforce the law. Landowners were even less enamored with this type of an exemption, since it was illegal and less permanent than the others. Each of these methods of avoiding acreage limitations

47. Clark, *Water Rights*, p. 289.

has been employed during the history of the federal reclamation program.

One of the most important general relaxations of the acreage limits was the policy of allowing a husband and wife to receive federal water for 320 acres of land. Administrative rulings supporting this policy were made as early as 1904 and have since been applied to virtually all federal reclamation projects.[48] Nearly 16 percent of all acres irrigated on projects built prior to 1944 were freed from the acreage limitation by this exemption. In the 1946 landownership survey 704,410 acres in 3,187 land holdings were freed from the acreage limit by the husband-wife exemption.[49] This policy increased the likelihood of successful repayment in areas where economies of scale existed and where the land was originally in private ownership. This policy, though visible and therefore potentially costly in political terms, seems to have avoided widespread controversy.

Political pressure to enforce the acreage limits appears to have been relatively low in the 1930s. A 1933 statutory interpretation by Interior Secretary Ray Wilbur exempting landowners in the Imperial Valley of California from acreage limits, was overturned in *United States* v. *Imperial Irrigation District*, but was finally upheld by the Supreme Court in 1980 in *Bryant* v. *Yellen.*[50] Legislative exemption granted to the Colorado-Big Thompson project in 1938 had the support of the bureau and was passed by Congress with no opposition. The justification for exempting both of these projects was that federal water was only supplemental to privately supplied irrigation water. The Truckee River and Humboldt projects in Nevada received this rare congressional exemption because the climate and elevation in these regions made the land so unproductive that 160 acres would not support a family.[51] Under these conditions, it seemed unreasonable to disrupt the regional economies by breaking up the large landholdings.

This attitude toward enforcement contrasts sharply with that adopted during the negotiations with California's Central Valley

48. One exception to this was enacted in the Columbia Basin Project Act of 1943, which expressly stated that a family could only receive water sufficient for one unit of land, the size of which was to be established by the Secretary of the Interior.

49. Bureau of Reclamation, *Landownership Survey on Federal Reclamation Projects* (Washington, D.C.: Government Printing Office, 1946), pp. 16–17.

50. For a discussion of the 1977 case see Jones, *Rules for Acreage Limitation*, p. 936.

51. See Montgomery and Clawson, *History of Central Valley Project*, p. 144.

water users, which began during the late 1930s. Local bureau representatives on the Kings River project (and apparently on other projects in the Central Valley) initially assured irrigators that their lands would be exempted from acreage limitations. This policy was supported by Secretary of Interior Ickes and seemed consistent with policies of the previous decade, since most of the land in the Central Valley was already receiving water from private projects.[52] In 1943, after a policy review with the Department of Interior, the bureau was reorganized. Soon afterward Ickes issued a statement, apparently at the request of President Roosevelt, ruling that Central Valley projects would not be exempted from the excess-land laws.

Surprised by this reversal of policy, the landholders in the Central Valley regrouped and began to pressure Congress for a legislative exemption of their lands. They managed to push a rider to the Rivers and Harbors Bill through the House of Representatives in 1944, but it was defeated in the Senate because of strong opposition from Roosevelt. The landowners also attempted to have their projects placed under the authority of the Army Corps of Engineers to be built under flood-control law, but they were stymied in 1944 when Congress made corps projects subject to the excess-land provisions of reclamation law.

After a bill to exempt projects in California, Colorado, and Texas died in committee in 1947, the landowners increased the pressure on members of the bureau to exempt their lands. In 1948 a rider was successfully attached to a bill passed by Congress that effectively removed two influential supporters of enforcement from the payroll of the Bureau of Reclamation.[53] Despite this pressure, water rights in the Central Valley were eventually administered under the acreage limits and large landowners were forced to sign recordable contracts to sell their excess lands before they could receive water.[54]

During the debates over the Central Valley project, the landowners on the Kings River project negotiated with local bureau representatives over the inclusion of a provision allowing for exemption from acreage limits by prepayment of construction costs. Prior to 1946, less than 1 percent of project lands were exempted under this

52. See Arthur Maass and Raymond Anderson, . . . *and the Desert Shall Rejoice* (Cambridge, Mass.: MIT Press, 1978), pp. 264-265.

53. For descriptions of this incident, see Taylor, *Excess Land Law*, pp. 504-505. President Truman later restored these men to the payroll.

54. See Warne, *Bureau of Reclamation*, pp. 80-81.

clause.[55] Throughout the 1950s contracts containing various forms of this provision were negotiated and approved at the local level, but several Interior secretaries hesitated to commit themselves on the question of the legality of the exemption.[56] Eventually, the issue was left up to the courts, where the provision was ruled illegal in 1977.[57]

One less visible type of nonenforcement occurred on the Kings River project during the negotiations over prepayment of construction charges. Throughout the decade of debate over the legality of the prepayment extension, water from Pine Flat Dam was delivered to excess lands and none of the water users on the project were required to comply with the acreage limitation.[58]

By nature, evidence of the extent of nonenforcement is difficult to obtain. However, a landownership survey published by the Bureau of Reclamation in 1946 indicated that such practices had important effects on several projects at that time. On each of the following projects more than 10 percent of the total irrigable acreage was known to be in violation of acreage limitations: Klamath (18.6 percent), Salt River (12.5 percent), Yuma (14.3 percent), Carlsbad (12.9 percent), Rio Grande (15.1 percent) and North Platte (10.3 percent).[59] On the other hand, the survey also indicated that on 28 out of 52 projects, less than 1 percent of the lands was known to be held in violation of the excess-land laws. This result may imply that some local bureau officials were more effective enforcers of the acreage limit or that the optimal farm size was less than the acreage limit on the projects where the law appears to have been enforced. In the latter case there would be less pressure from landowners to not enforce the acreage limit.

55. Estimated from *Landownership Survey*, pp. 16–17.

56. See Maass and Anderson, *Desert Shall Rejoice*, pp. 267–269.

57. For a detailed history of the legislation and administrative decisions concerning prepayment see Taylor, *Excess Land Law*, pp. 490–512. A description of the 1977 court case can be found in Jones, *Rules for Acreage Limitation*, p. 935.

58. See Maass and Anderson, *Desert Shall Rejoice*, p. 271.

59. See *Landownership Survey*, pp. 16–17. These excess lands did not include lands for which recordable contracts had been signed nor for which construction costs had been repaid.

SUMMARY AND CONCLUSION

In this paper we have analyzed the actions of irrigators and bureaucrats who competed to obtain rents from federal water projects within constraints imposed by Congress. In the Reclamation Act of 1902, potential water users successfully obtained federal subsidies in the form of interest-free loans for the construction costs of irrigation works. Congress established rules to control the distribution of these subsidies, the value of which increased over the next forty years as water users successfully obtained more flexibility and longer extensions in their repayment contracts. Often their efforts were consistent with the interest of members of the Bureau of Reclamation, who were seeking to increase the congressional demand for their output by providing an image of successful settlement and repayment on their projects.

The distribution of rents among landowners was determined by acreage limitations and rules for the disposal of public and private lands. According to the 1902 act settlers could obtain the rent on public lands by settling those lands under the Homestead Act on a first come, first served basis. These rents were dissipated by the settlement of project lands prior to the delivery of irrigation water. To reduce dissipation and increase the financial success of projects, Congress passed legislation to restrict early settlement and eventually gave the Bureau of Reclamation increased discretionary power over who settled the public lands.

Under the 1902 act Congress tried to ensure the dissolution of large landholdings by allowing private landowners to sell their excess lands at market prices. It was soon discovered that rather than selling, landowners were holding land until the prices rose further. To remedy this, Congress gave the Secretary of Interior discretionary power to set the selling price of excess lands. In 1926 Congress tried to restrict the secretary's discretionary power and limit the subsidy to large landowners, but the bureau found new ways to control the susbidy's distribution.

Large landowners continually applied pressure for exemptions to the acreage limitation law, while congressional pressure for enforcement of the law varied over time. Enforcement of the acreage limit was expected by Congress, but success on projects (which was desired by Congress, the water users, and the bureau itself) would have been enhanced by nonenforcement. The more visible decisions made by the heads of the Department of Interior and the bureau to exempt large landowners from restrictions were made when congressional pressures to enforce the law were low. When enforcement pressure increased, the bureau toughened its visible policy stance but pursued less visible exemptions of large landholders through nonenforcement of the acreage limit at the local level. We do not know the timing of this nonenforcement, but we do know that it existed.

This description of the first five decades of the federal reclamation program has demonstrated how efforts were made to influence the magnitude and distribution of the subsidies from this particular government program. The nature of these efforts, as well as their effects, are not unique to the reclamation program. Whenever rents are created by government programs and distributed on the basis of nonmarket criteria, competition will lead to dissipation of those rents. As in the reclamation program, attempts to reduce this dissipation by controlling competition along certain margins will generally lead individuals to direct their energies along other, uncontrolled margins in an effort to appropriate available rents.

Chapter 3

WATER PRICING AND RENT SEEKING IN CALIFORNIA AGRICULTURE

B. Delworth Gardner

INTRODUCTION

Without irrigation water, agriculture in California would be little more than limited livestock grazing and some dryland farming of cereal crops. With irrigation water, California produces over 200 crops and is the leading agricultural state with nearly $4 billion in sales in 1980. The state's gross cash receipts from farm sales have consistently approached 10 percent of the national total every year since 1960.

Of course, water is only one of several crucial inputs utilized in agricultural production—others are land; capital in form of machinery, tools, and implements; energy; chemicals for fertilizer and pest control; and perhaps most important, human effort. If production is profitable, all factors must be paid at least their opportunity costs if they are to be used on a continuing basis. Those existing in relatively fixed (inelastic) supply will earn *economic rents*—the difference between a productive factor's worth in use and its costs—if there are revenues left after the variable factors have been paid. If a factor of production is priced far below its economic value and, relatively constraining in determining the quantity, quality, and location of output, economic rents will tend to be large and persistent through time.

The author is indebted to Carole F. Nuckton and Ray G. Huffacker for analytical and editorial assistance.

In the irrigation economy of the West, water, probably more than any other factor of production, is a constraining input frequently priced below its value in use. The control of water, therefore, provides access to enormous magnitudes of economic rent and is for this reason a hot political issue in the West. Institutional arrangements in the form of water law, water pricing policies, acreage ownership limitations on land receiving subsidized federal water, lobbying for new water development, and land allocation rules all have played their roles in determining the distribution as well as the size of these economic rents. It is the thesis of this paper that some of these institutional arrangements have seriously misallocated water by diminishing the value of the economic product yielded by water and its complementary inputs far below what would have been attainable under optimal water allocation.

Pricing policy is a critical issue that encompasses many other water-related problems. If water is not price rationed to where it is most valuable, then some other rationing schemes must be employed to allocate it. What efficiency losses may result if nonprice allocation criteria are used? For example, without market prices to reveal the value of water, how shall it be determined whether or not new water development is economically feasible?[1]

This paper will first demonstrate by citing estimates of elasticity of demand that farmers are price responsive in their use of irrigation water, followed by an empirical analysis of the main types of responses to higher water prices: (1) use less water on a given crop, (2) change irrigation technology, (3) shift water applications to more water-efficient crops, and (4) change crop mix to higher valued crops. A final major section discusses the water-allocating institutions in California, how their pricing and allocating rules misallocate water, and the implications for the distribution of economic rents.

WATER PRICES AND USE RATES IN CALIFORNIA AGRICULTURE

Water often has been considered to be different from marketable commodities that are directed to their highest and best uses by the

1. B. Delworth Gardner, "The Water Management Crunch: An Economic Perspective," in *Economics, Ethics, Ecology: Costs of Productive Conservation*, ed. Walter E. Jeske (Ankeny, Iowa: Soil Conservation Society of America, 1981), pp. 67–77.

price system. Historically, water's seeming abundance contributed to its allocation at prices reflecting the costs of capture and distribution rather than its economic value. Legal criteria such as "beneficial use" determined eligible user groups.

To most water planners "demand" for water frequently means projected "requirements" or "needs" for people and plants. In agriculture, water planners and engineers tend to think of irrigation water in terms of per-acre "needs" or "requirements" of the crops in an area—for example, an acre of barley in Kern County, California, requires 1.5 acre-feet of water in a growing season; an acre of alfalfa, 4.5 acre-feet.

The California Department of Water Resources (DWR), the state agency responsible for supplying water to farmers and city dwellers through its State Water Project, bases its estimates of water demand on the apparent ability of farmers to put it to profitable use, figured as the per-acre agricultural receipts for a crop minus its nonwater costs divided by the number of acre-feet needed to grow that particular crop. Crops for which the calculated ability to pay exceeds the water cost involved enter the projections; those with lower capacities do not. The demand for water, then, according to DWR, is computed by summing the products of water requirements and acreages of those crops "able to pay" for the water.[2] The quantity of water utilized per acre is assumed to be fixed for a given profitable crop. Such prescriptions for water use are designed to maximize yield, not profit.[3] Only with a zero water price are the two objectives one and the same. Generally, farmers stop using water at the profit-maximizing point (where the value of the marginal product equals the water price), which is *short* of the yield-maximizing point (where the marginal product of water is zero).

Partly because of the prevalence of the "water-is-different" syndrome, the solution to water shortages that occur through time as need grows has been to develop new water supplies rather than to raise prices—to increase the supply to meet the fixed demand.[4] The

2. Cleve Edward Willis, "An Application of Water Resource Planning with Emphasis on Desalting" (Ph.D. dissertation, Department of Agricultural Economics, University of California, Davis, 1972).

3. Harry W. Ayer and Paul G. Hoyt, *Crop-Water Production Functions: Economic Implications for Arizona*, Arizona Agricultural Experiment Station, Technical Bulletin no. 242, September 1981.

4. M.M. Kelso, *The Water is Different Syndrome, or What is Wrong with the Water Industry?* (Paper presented at the Third American Water Resource Conference, American Water Resource Association, San Francisco, California, 1967).

economist would find this policy unobjectionable so long as it could be shown that the "new" water was worth more in use than its development and distribution costs. This aspect is too often overlooked in water development decisionmaking, however.

It is easy to demonstrate that water users are responsive to price. During a critical water shortage in 1949–1950, residents of New York City, which has unmetered water, reduced per capita consumption from 85 to 60 gallons a day in response to a vigorous water conservation campaign. Meanwhile, water consumers in Detroit, which has universal metering, consumed only 49.5 gallons per capita per day without any nonprice pressures to conserve despite their similarity to New York users in other respects.[5]

A number of studies have attempted to estimate farmers' responsiveness to the price of irrigation water. Studies done in different areas of California with varying cropping patterns over a period of more than a decade all indicated considerable farmer response to changes in water price. Although the findings differ as to the *degree* of price responsiveness, together they contradict a widespread view that farmers are *insensitive* to water price changes in their production decisions.

Linear programming models were constructed by Moore for farms of different sizes on the eastern side of the San Joaquin Valley in Tulare County, California.[6] Optimum crop programs were calculated for each model as irrigation water prices were raised from zero to about $30 per acre-foot. A given crop mix and its associated water requirements remained optimum over a small range in price, creating a stepped demand schedule for water. The schedules were aggregated over the size groups, a linear regression fitted, and elasticities computed. Elasticities ranged from quite inelastic (–0.14) at a low water price ($5.00 per acre-foot) through quite elastic (–1.58) at $25.00 per acre-foot.[7] For the entire range of prices considered (zero to

5. Melvin H. Chiogioji and Eleanor N. Chiogioji, *Evaluation of the Use of Water Pricing as a Tool for Conserving Water*, Washington Technical Institute, Water Resources Research Institute, Report no. 2, November 1973.

6. Charles V. Moore, "Economics of Water Demand in Commercialized Agriculture," *American Water Works Association Journal* 54 (August 1962): 913–920.

7. An elastic demand (greater than 1.0 in absolute terms) means that for a 1 percent change in price, a greater than 1 percent change in quantity demanded would be expected. While an inelastic demand (less than 1.0 in absolute terms) means less than a 1 percent change in quantity for the 1 percent price change, some responsiveness is nevertheless in evidence. It is only when the elasticity reaches zero that complete insensitivity to price is indicated.

$30 per acre-foot), elasticity was -0.65—that is, for a 10 percent increase in price, about a 6.5 percent decrease in quantity could be expected.

Moore and Hedges fit two quadratic regression equations to two distinct price segments of the same aggregate demand schedule. The resulting elasticities were -0.188 for the lower segment and -0.702 for the upper, with the overall elasticity again being -0.65. In a cross-sectional analysis of thirty-four California water districts, Bain, Caves, and Margolis also found a price elasticity of -0.64.[8]

In a 3,220-equation, 5,426-variable linear programming model, a group of researchers tested for the impacts of alternative futures on the demand for water for agriculture in seventeen western states.[9] As water price increased from an average of $7 per acre-foot to $30, irrigated acreage was reduced an estimated 14.8 million acres, and dryland farming increased about 15 million acres, about a one-for-one substitution. Of course, the crop mix was correspondingly altered. Carson computed the elasticities implied by the Heady model for four incremental water price changes.[10] As price was raised from $7 to $30 per acre-foot the elasticity estimates increased from -0.17 to -0.56 with an overall average of -0.37.

Moore, Snyder, and Sun, using shadow prices from linear programming solutions to a water quality–crop production model for Imperial County, California, found that for quantities greater than 1 million acre-feet, demand is quite elastic.[11] At the then current low price of $2.35 per acre-foot, however, and with much smaller quantities of water, demand was relatively inelastic even though the water cost was less than its value in use.

In evaluating regional resource use for agricultural production in California in 1961–1965 and in 1980 (projected), a spatial linear pro-

8. Charles V. Moore and Trimble R. Hedges, *Economics of On-Farm Irrigation Water Availability and Costs, and Related Farm Adjustments*, pt. 3, University of California, Giannini Foundation Research Report no. 261, March 1963; Joe S. Bain, Richard E. Caves, and Julius Margolis, *Northern California's Water Industry*, Resources for the Future (Baltimore: Johns Hopkins Press, 1966).

9. Earl O. Heady, Howard C. Madsen, Kenneth J. Nicol, and Stanley H. Hargrove, "National and Interregional Models of Water Demand, Land Use, and Agricultural Policies," *Water Resources Research* 9 (August 1973): 777–791.

10. Janet Raudenbush Carson, "The Price Elasticity of Demand for Water" (M.S. thesis, Engineering, University of California, Los Angeles, 1979).

11. Charles V. Moore, J. H. Snyder, and Peter Sun, "Effects of Colorado River Water Quality and Supply on Irrigated Agriculture," *Water Resources Research* 10 (April 1974): 137–144.

gramming location model was constructed by Shumway, King, Carter, and Dean.[12] Particular attention was directed in this study to water pricing on the west side of the San Joaquin Valley in two of the model's ninety-five assumed homogeneous production areas (HPA). Two demand functions were estimated using the parametric program observations for each HPA; Shumway fitted a single equation to the data points for each.[13] In contrast to the several studies reviewed above, these estimates indicate quite an elastic water price response. In the two-equation model, five out of six point estimates had an absolute value greater than one. The exception was -0.56 in one HPA at a very low water price of $4.70 per acre-foot. At a water price of $19.36 in the other HPA, the estimate was -2.32. In the single-equation model, at a deflated water price (1965 dollars) of $4 per acre-foot, the elasticity estimate was -0.48, becoming unitary (-1.0) at a price of about $8.50, and elastic at higher prices. At $17.00, the elasticity estimate was -2.03.

What do these high elasticities mean? Shumway, King, Carter, and Dean concluded that farmers in these two HPAs would not be using all the water DWR was planning to send them at the price it was planning to charge. According to their study results, the marginal cost of water to the farmer would have to be reduced between $4 and $6 per acre-foot (from a contractual price of $14.70 per acre-foot in one HPA and $19.36 in the other) before DWR's projected half million acres would be brought into production.

Howitt, Watson, and Adams recently demonstrated that the various linear-programming (LP) approaches reported above may seriously underestimate price elasticities.[14] They show that the quadratic-programming (QP) method, which incorporates product demand functions into the objective function, will yield higher elasticities for water than will the LP method for the same data. As an example, a statewide model of nine California field crops and twenty-eight vegetable crops was estimated using both the LP and QP ap-

12. C. Richard Shumway, Gordon A. King, Harold O. Carter, and Gerald W. Dean, *Regional Resource Use for Agricultural Production in California, 1961-65 and 1980*, University of California, Giannini Foundation Monograph no. 25, September 1970.

13. C. Richard Shumway, "Derived Demand for Irrigation Water: The California Aqueduct," *Southern Journal of Agricultural Economics* 5 (December 1973): 195-200.

14. Richard E. Howitt, William D. Watson, and Richard M. Adams, "A Reevaluation of Price Elasticities for Irrigation Water," *Water Resources Research* 16 (August 1980): 623-628.

proaches, the latter indeed yielding more elastic estimates. (Perennial crops, were afforded full water allocations and were not included in the model.) In the water price range from $25 to $35, the LP-derived elasticity was -0.97; the QP estimate was -1.50.

There are extremely important implications for policy in these elasticity numbers. For example, as Howitt, Watson, and Adams suggest, if demand for irrigation water is as elastic in the $25-to-$35 price range as the numbers presented indicate, farmers may reduce their water use by a far greater amount than expected by the water planners in the next few years as State Water Project prices are renegotiated. Such a reduction could "offset the current predictions of severe supply shortfalls calculated under the assumption of inelastic 'needs' for agriculture."[15]

In fact, if the demand for irrigation water is elastic (greater than 1.0 in absolute terms) the reductions in quantities demanded in response to price increases will reduce the total water bill. Districts selling water will receive smaller total revenues and probably will have to alter the way water is paid for.

Generations of economists have been taught that elasticity increases as the firm moves from the short to the long run. Johnston pointed out that agricultural demand for water in the short run is almost always more inelastic than in the long run.[16] If the technological base of production in agriculture is in place (for example, the orchard is planted), demand for irrigation water may not be very price responsive. In the long run, however, changes can (and will) be made in this base if water is priced at a higher level.

The same point was made by Shumway in comparing his more elastic estimates with Moore and Hedges's inelastic ones.[17] The study area for the latter was fully developed for agricultural production with the existing water distribution system well in place, whereas the west side of the San Joaquin Valley used in Shumway's model was "predominantly barren of agricultural production. Consequently, water distribution facilities must be constructed . . . and would not be constructed if the price of water appeared too high."[18] This

15. Ibid., p. 627.

16. W. E. Johnston, *The Economist's Role in Water Pricing* (Paper presented at the Water Pricing Conference, University of California, Los Angeles, March 1968, University of California Water Resources Center Report no. 13, 1968), pp. 28–40.

17. Shumway, "Derived Demand."

18. Ibid., p. 199.

means that demand for irrigation water for undeveloped land is especially price responsive.

The conclusion that has emerged from this literature review of agricultural water use in California is clear: demand for irrigation water is more price responsive than is generally believed. Underestimating this responsiveness can result in serious resource misallocations—of scarce and valuable nonwater resources in unwarranted and premature water development.

It has been shown that farmers respond to water price increases by cutting back in water use. The next section of the paper indicates more precisely how their production decisions accommodate this action.

FARMERS' RESPONSES TO INCREASES IN WATER PRICE

Suppose that irrigation water became very expensive (say, $75 per acre-foot) but farmers could have all they might want at that price. Three responses by the farmers seem likely: (1) they might apply less water to a given crop (possibly putting it under stress), (2) they might utilize a different (more efficient) irrigation technology and water application practice, and (3) they might choose a different cropping pattern. These issues will be discussed in turn.

Water Price and Application Rates

Plant growth is determined largely by the amount of water available through precipitation and irrigation to the plant in the root zone during the growing season. The capacity of the soil to retain water is an important factor. The plant uses some water in the process of photosynthesis, but most is transpired from the plant's leaves. Other water is lost through evaporation from the soil surface. Table 3-1 shows seasonal and annual rates of potential evapotranspiration (ET) for various regions in California. The numbers in the table are maximum amounts of water that plants will use if adequate soil moisture is available and if foliage covers all or nearly all of the ground surface. Under these conditions, approximately 90 percent of the water loss is by transpiration. Other factors determining ET rates are solar

Table 3-1. Seasonal and Annual Potential Evapotranspiration Rates in California.[a]

	Season		
	November–March	*April–October*	*Annual*
	Inches		
Northwestern mountain valleys	5.1	37.1	42.2
North coast – coastal valleys and plains	5.3	20.8	26.1
North coast – interior valleys	6.3	34.9	41.2
Sacramento Valley	8.5	40.7	49.2
San Joaquin Valley	7.9	40.7	48.6
Central coast – coastal valleys and plains	10.7	30.6	41.3
Central coast – interior valleys	10.8	37.5	48.3
South coast – coastal valleys and plains	12.1	32.3	44.4
South coast – interior valleys	11.5	37.9	49.4
Southern California desert	17.7	65.1	82.8

a. These are the rates of water loss one would observe from a well-watered lawn.

Source: Vegetative Water Use in California, 1974, Bulletin no. 113-3, Department of Water Resources (Sacramento, Calif.: Resources Agency, 1975).

radiation, air moisture, temperature, wind speed, reflectiveness of the ground surface, and the way and time interval over which water is delivered to the land. The numbers in Table 3-1 reveal great differences in potential ET rates in the various regions of California, the largest being in the southern desert.

While little can be done to change basic ET, there are adaptive strategies for maximizing production with limited supplies of water or for higher cost water. For example, crops can be moved toward the cool season when ET is lower. Table 3-2 lists the seasonal ET requirements of the major crops in the San Joaquin Valley. It is pos-

Table 3-2. Evapotranspiration of Major Field Crops in the San Joaquin Valley.

Crop	*Season*	*Days*	*Total ET (in.)*
Annual Crops			
Small grains	November through May 15	200	13
	December through May	180	16
	January through June	180	21
Beans (pinto)	April through July	120	21
	May to August 15	110	20
	June 15 through September	110	18
Grain sorghum	May through September	150	24
	June 15 through October	140	18
Corn	March 15 to August 15	150	27
	April 15 to September 15	150	28
	May 15 through September	140	24
	June to October 15	140	23
Cotton	March through September	180	31
	March 15 to October 15	180	31
	May through October	180	32
Sugar beets	February through August	210	36
	March 15 to September 15	180	35
	May through January	280	36
	June 15 to March 15	300	29
Rice	April through August	150	39
	May through September	150	39
Perennial Crops			
Alfalfa	All year, but with winter dormant period		48
Pasture	All year, but slower growth in winter		49
Grapes	March through mid-November		
	Wine, raisin		30
	Table		40
Deciduous orchards	February-March through November		
Clean cultivated			36
with cover crop			up to 48

Source: David C. Davenport and Robert M. Hagan, "Assessing Potentials for Agricultural Water Conservation," *Western Water*, November-December 1979, pp. 6-11.

sible to change total water use by varying the types of crops grown, changing the acreages in the various crops, and shortening the growth duration of crops.

Of primary interest is the relationship between water applied and yield; the former largely influencing the marginal water cost and the latter, the marginal benefits from incremental applications of water. Research at the University of California indicates that water applications 10 percent below that producing maximum yields would reduce alfalfa yields by 10 percent; cotton, 12.5 percent; corn, 12.5 percent; grain sorghum, 10 percent; pinto beans, 23.5 percent; and pink beans, 21 percent.[19] Some preliminary results of continuing research suggest that stress irrigation (that is, water application less than that considered adequate for full plant growth) might be used with perennial crops such as raisin and wine grapes and almonds, but only in areas where sufficient water is available during the winter to satisfy leaching requirements. Unfortunately, the economics of putting the plant under some stress in order to save costly water have not been worked out. Income may be higher or lower depending on costs and returns. The important point, however, is the acknowledgment that rational farmers might very well apply less irrigation water to their crops at higher water prices than at lower ones.

Water Price and Irrigation Practice

As argued earlier, the price of water may have a significant influence on the rational farmer's choice of irrigation practice and technology. If water is cheap, the irrigation technique and the frequency of application may be relatively inefficient in water use but quite efficient in economizing on other scarce inputs, such as labor and capital. Farmers might choose irrigation methods that use more water but are more convenient. They may not find it profitable to keep their irrigation systems in good repair so as to avoid leaks and seepage losses. They may have little incentive to invest in the control of thirsty phreatophytes or to switch to expensive but water-saving irrigation systems such as sprinkler or drip.

The water supply agencies (generally, water districts as established by law and described more fully later in the paper) use pricing prac-

19. J. Ian Stewart, "Conservation Irrigation of Field Crops: A Drought Year Strategy," *California Agriculture* 31 (April 1977): 6–9.

Table 3-3. Variable and Total Water Costs and Irrigation Efficiency Kern County, 1975.

	Surface Water		*Ground Water*		*Irrigation Efficiency*
	A	*B*	*C*	*D*	*Y*
	Variable Cost	*Total Cost*	*Variable Cost*	*Total Cost*	
	Per Acre-Foot				*Percent*
Arvin-Edison	14.93	20.83	22.88	30.51	69
Bellridge	25.18	25.18	–	–	71
Berrenda Mesa	12.53	33.51	–	–	75
Buena Vista	5.67	8.68	10.60	16.05	65
Buttonwillow	19.62	20.75	15.73	21.23	65
Cawelo	46.00	51.07	22.80	30.60	83
Delano-Earlimart	3.47	6.68	19.54	25.47	65
Henry Miller	15.83	28.20	9.93	16.60	61
Kern Delta	8.22	11.67	12.03	17.32	64
Kern-Tulare	–	–	31.31	40.03	77
Lost Hills	11.87	20.04	16.80	24.55	67
North Kern	10.27	11.94	16.25	22.44	65
Pond Poso	–	–	14.46	20.32	65
Rag Gulch	35.60	35.60	20.64	26.75	67
Rosedale-Rio Bravo	–	–	13.94	19.12	64
Semitropic	–	–	14.19	19.77	65
Shafter-Wasco	4.01	8.15	19.08	26.79	65
Southern San Joaquin	6.00	7.43	21.87	28.27	66
West Kern County	–	–	18.24	24.48	65
Wheeler Ridge-Maricopa	44.92	46.96	23.35	31.70	71

Source: William D. Watson, Carole Frank Nuckton, and Richard E. Howitt, *Crop Production and Water Supply Characteristics of Kern County*, Giannini Foundation Information Series no. 80-1, Division of Agricultural Sciences Bulletin no. 1895, University of California, April 1980.

tices that cause the water costs to farmers to vary widely. In 1975, in Kern County, California, total surface water costs per acre-foot varied between $6.68 in the Delano-Earlimart district and $51.07 in the Cawelo district (Table 3-3 and Figure 3-1). The disparity in groundwater costs was somewhat less—$16.05 in Buena Vista to $40.03 in the Kern-Tulare district.[20]

20. William D. Watson, Carole Frank Nuckton, and Richard E. Howitt, *Crop Production and Water Supply Characteristics of Kern County*, University of California, Division of Agricultural Sciences, Bulletin no. 1895, Giannini Foundation Information Series no. 80-1, April 1980.

Figure 3-1. Kern County Water Districts.

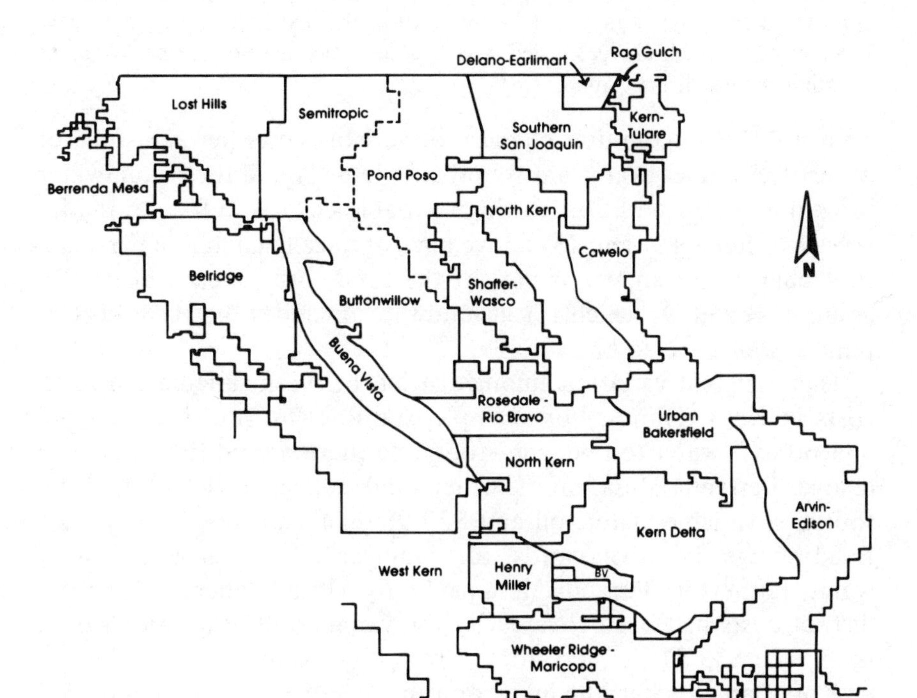

The farmer's total water costs, of course, can be broken down into component parts, only some of which are generally relevant to the decision as to the quantity of water demanded. It is the outlay associated with an incremental unit of water (marginal cost) that must be compared with its value.

Water districts vary somewhat in pricing practices utilized to recover their costs of supplying water. In most instances, three components make up the total water bill:

(1) A water toll charge–'user charge'–is commonly levied directly by the water district as a variable cost based on the number of acre-feet drawn.

> (2) A water availability and general service charge is imposed, usually on a per-acre or per-value basis. This is a fixed cost not related to the amount of water delivered and is used to service district debts . . . and pay operating, maintenance, and salary costs. (3) Finally, there are a number of indirect costs which may or may not be included in the district's quoted farm gate water costs. Such charges levied by the county tax assessor are paid as taxes rather than as direct water costs.[21]

In Table 3-3, the user charges, or variable costs per acre-foot of water, for surface water are found in column A and for groundwater in column C. In addition to these variable costs, the fixed costs involved in items (2) and (3) above have been calculated as a per-acre-foot charge and appear as part of the total cost for each district in columns B and D, which for groundwater includes the fixed cost in pumps, wells, and so on.

There is great variation among districts between variable and fixed costs in Kern County. For example, the Rag Gulch district charged $35.60 as a water toll per acre-foot, and there was no fixed per-acre charge. Berrenda Mesa, on the other hand, collected $12.53 per acre-foot as a variable water toll and $20.98 on a per acre-foot basis as a fixed charge. In other words, to obtain an additional acre-foot of water, farmers in Berrenda Mesa paid only $12.53, whereas if the full district costs had been covered by the variable toll, the price would have been $33.51 per acre-foot. Given the elasticity of demand figures presented earlier, the impact on the quantity of water demanded would be very substantial had $33.51 rather than $12.53 been charged for the marginal acre-foot of water.

To test the hypothesis that farmers change irrigation practice and technology to conserve water when water prices are high, water costs were correlated with irrigation efficiency for the Kern County water districts. Irrigation efficiency was calculated as a ratio of the average per-acre consumptive use of water in the district to the amount of water delivered to the district. Since irrigation efficiencies are measured at the district and not at the farm level, some of the water losses resulting in reduced irrigation efficiency may have occurred before water was delivered at the farm gate. If so, on-farm irrigation efficiency may have been higher than those reported in Table 3-3.

21. Ibid., pp. 47-48.

A correlation coefficient value of one would indicate a perfect relationship between water cost and irrigation efficiency; a coefficient of zero would indicate no relationship. For both groundwater and surface water the correlation coefficients—.732 and .642, respectively—are positive and closer to one than to zero, indicating that higher irrigation efficiencies are associated with higher costs.

One must be careful not to infer too much from the relationship between water price and irrigation efficiency. It might be a temptation to argue, for example, that large quantities of water could be saved in agriculture simply by raising the price. Water could be moved to other uses, thus forestalling costly new water development. The problem with this line of reasoning is that not all water saved on an individual farm or even in an irrigation district is a net water saving for the basin as a whole. Much of the water lost, causing low irrigation efficiencies, returns to the water system in the form of aquifer replenishment or surface return flows. It is thus recoverable in a physical sense. Nearly all irrigated system leakage as well as tailwater—the irrigation water that accumulates on the surface at the lower end of the field—returns to the system and is available for future use. Of course, it is important to recognize that recovering used water is not costless, since pumping is required for groundwater reuse and water quality is almost always reduced in the process of irrigation. The water picks up salts and other contaminants as it is used again and again. For these reasons farmers may find it profitable to invest in reducing water losses, even if the water is recoverable.

Recoverable losses may be reduced by:

- Improved irrigation scheduling, which helps in applying water in the right amounts at the right time
- Better drainage and salinity management, which will reduce water needs
- Automation of systems to increase application efficiency
- Shorter irrigation runs (at the expense of more labor)
- Use of lined ditches or pipelines
- Use of tailwater recovery systems

Water lost to evapotranspiration is lost to the entire water system and is thus nonrecoverable. If these losses can be reduced, the system's supply will be augmented. Much research is being directed toward finding ways of reducing evapotranspiration within existing cropping patterns by controlling weeds and aquatic plants and by limiting or eliminating cover crops.[22] Economists have important work to do in evaluating the economic feasibility of reducing water losses, both recoverable and nonrecoverable.

Water Price and Cropping Patterns

It has already been shown that the water districts in Kern County with the highest water prices to farmers tend to have the highest irrigation efficiencies. Another response to higher water prices might be a shift in cropping patterns to more water efficient or higher valued crops.

As water costs rise, farmers may plant more water efficient crops. If farmers can only grow field crops such as sugar beets, wheat, feed grains, and cotton because of climatic, soil, or market conditions, they may switch to those that have lower ET requirements.

In a linear programming model of two typical 640-acre Yolo County, California farms—one with high-grade soil, the other with medium grade—Hedges showed how cropping patterns in the optimal mix would shift as water prices rise.[23] The optimum cropping pattern for the high-grade soil farm at a zero water price calls for 150 acres each of tomatoes, sugar beets, and wheat plus 47 acres of alfalfa, 65 of beans, and 38 of safflower. As water prices are raised, alfalfa acreage is the first to be reduced, gradually dropping out entirely at $13.50 an acre-foot.[24] Safflower, a low water-using crop, expanded in acreage as did barley, which replaced sugar beets at the highest water price, $22.50. Similar results were obtained for the farm with medium-grade soil.

22. B. Delworth Gardner, Raymond H. Coppock, Curtis D. Lynn, D. Williams Rains, J. Herbert Snyder, and Robert S. Loomis, "Agriculture," in *Competition for California Water: Alternative Solutions*, eds. Ernest A. Engelbert and Ann Foley Scheuring (Berkeley and Los Angeles: University of California Press, 1982), pp. 11-36.

23. Trimble R. Hedges, *Water Supplies and Costs in Relation to Farm Resource Decisions and Profits on Sacramento Valley Farms*, University of California, Giannini Foundation Research Report No. 322, June 1977.

24. One of the indirect impacts of cropping pattern shifts not accounted for in this analysis is the effect on prices. For example, reduced production of alfalfa could be expected to increase alfalfa prices depending on the elasticity of demand for alfalfa facing affected farmers. If the price rose in response to decreasing supplies, less acreage would have to shift to other crops in the process of reaching a new optimum. These price effects are usually accounted for by employing a quadratic programming rather than a linear programming model.

Seasonal evapotranspiration also may be reduced by shifting to a variety of an existing crop that requires a shorter growing season. Or, if climatic conditions permit, farmers may plant earlier to avoid the hot season when high evapotranspiration occurs. At the limit, after all these adjustments have been made, if the water is not available or if it costs too much, acreage may have to come out of crop production.

Another response that farmers might make to higher water prices is to shift to higher (per-acre) value crops. Since water has become more expensive relative to other inputs, the tendency is to use more of the latter to the extent that they are substitutable. Using labor, land, and capital more intensively could bring on a crop-mix change away from field crops toward high-value (and high-cost) orchards, vineyards, and vegetables.

Another reason for shifting to high-value crops as water prices rise involves risk management. High-value crops also tend to be high-risk crops, in terms of both yields and prices.[25] Higher water prices may induce farmers to abandon the low-risk crops with low average profits in favor of high-value, high-risk crops.

To test the hypothesis that high water costs are associated with higher valued crops, a cross-sectional analysis was made of twenty Kern County water districts using 1975 data.[26] Recall that surface-water costs among the districts ranged from a high of $51.07 per acre-foot in Cawelo to $6.68 in Delano-Earlimart; groundwater from a high of $40.03 in Kern-Tulare to a low of $16.05 in Buena Vista (see Table 3-3). A weighted groundwater and surface-water cost average was constructed and used as an explanatory variable in two linear equations fitted by ordinary least squares.

The dependent variable in the first equation was the percent of the district's acreage in orchards, vineyards, or vegetables (high per-acre revenues and costs); in the second equation, the dependent variable was the percent of the acreage in field crops (low-value crops). Rice was excluded from the analysis because of its high water require-

25. William Lin, G.W. Dean, and C.V. Moore, "An Empirical Test of Utility vs. Profit Maximization in Agricultural Production," *American Journal of Agricultural Economics* 56 (August 1974): 497-508.

26. Watson, Nuckton, and Howitt, *Crop Production and Water Supply.* West Kern Water District was excluded from the group of districts analyzed because in 1975 only 633 acres were planted and it was therefore an insignificant part of the total acreage.

ments and because its cultivation in the area is determined primarily by soil and drainage conditions.

In the regression equations, a positive sign on the water price coefficient would be expected in the first and a negative sign in the second. Obviously, water price is not the only explanatory variable affecting cropping patterns. Others are soil and drainage, possibilities of frost, and available markets. The Kern County water districts cover areas in the foothills on the east side of the valley, older production areas on the east side, areas on the newer west side, and areas in the valley trough where soils are very heavy and drainage is a serious problem. In the regression, a soil variable was included representing the percentage of the district's land with better soil (scores of 60 and above on the Storie Index). The expected sign of this variable would be positive in the first equation and negative in the second. Dummy variables were used to represent the combined influence of all variables associated with location.

Equation 3-1: Orchards, Vineyards, and Vegetables

$$OVV = -16.936 + \underset{(2.16)}{0.927\,WWC} + \underset{(1.62)}{0.242\,SOIL} + \underset{(3.75)}{37.59\,D_1},$$

$$+ \underset{(0.32)}{3.182\,D_2} - \underset{(-0.55)}{7.985\,D_3}$$

Numbers in parentheses are t values.

$R^2 = .72$

Equation 3-2: Field Crops

$$FC = 102.03 - \underset{(-2.13)}{0.988\,WWC} - \underset{(-0.53)}{0.085\,SOIL} - \underset{(-3.91)}{42.39\,D_1},$$

$$- \underset{(-.001)}{0.014\,D_2} + \underset{(1.06)}{16.565\,D_3}$$

$R^2 = .72$

where

OVV = percentage of district acreage in orchards, vineyards, or vegetables

FC = percentage of district acreage in field crops, excluding rice

WWC = weighted groundwater and surface-water cost per acre-foot

SOIL = percentage of district acreage above 60 on the Storie Index

D_1 = 1 if district is in the foothills, 0 otherwise

D_2 = 1 if district is on the west side, 0 otherwise

D_3 = 1 if district is in the valley trough, 0 otherwise

The two equations explain the variation in the respective dependent variables equally well (R^2 = .72), and both water-cost coefficients have the expected signs and are statistically different from zero at the 97.5 percent confidence level, using a one-tailed *t*-test (the first in the positive direction; the second, negative). The soil variable had the expected signs but was not statistically significant. The foothill dummy explained some of the difference in cropping patterns among districts. The statistically significant coefficient reflects the fact that many of the county's orchards and vineyards flourish in the gently sloping terrain of a nearly frost-free thermal belt.

The conclusions of this section on the impacts of water price are quite clear. The elasticity of demand for irrigation water is high for very good reasons. Water price really matters because farmers can and do adjust by: (1) using less water on a given crop, (2) undertaking investment that increases irrigation efficiency, (3) substituting water-efficient crops for those less efficient, and (4) shifting to crops that have higher nonwater costs, higher risk, *and* a higher per-acre value. Evidence has been presented supporting all these conclusions. Are we to assume, therefore, that water allocation in agriculture is optimal? Unfortunately, we cannot. The reason is to be found in the institutional framework that determines water pricing and allocation. In California, that framework centers on the water districts and their management practices.

INSTITUTIONS GOVERNING WATER ALLOCATION IN CALIFORNIA

An astonishing array of private and public institutions exist in California for the purpose of developing and allocating water resources. Numbering in the thousands, they employ operating rules established broadly by enabling legislation. These rules largely determine the distribution of economic rents connected with water use and influence the efficiency of water development and use.

The important private institutions are long-standing commercial water companies and mutual water agencies numbering in the hundreds. Their principal purposes are to establish rights to water use and to sell and deliver water to users. The mutual agencies sell water to members at supply costs and are thus nonprofit. The water companies sell water to customers within their service areas at whatever prices the market will bear, and the profits are distributed to stockholders as with any other private company.[27] It is not known how much water is allocated by these private entities, but the mutual companies are more frequently utilized in irrigation, whereas the commercial companies are more heavily involved in serving urban customers.

The public water districts that supply most of the water to agriculture in California are the reclamation districts, authorized by legislation in 1867; the irrigation districts, authorized in 1897; the water districts, authorized in 1913; and the water storage districts, authorized in 1921. Some of these districts and the quantities of water handled are listed in Table 3–4. Their primary purposes are to reclaim and protect lands from overflow and to irrigate lands both inside and outside the district.[28] Irrigation districts supply, distribute, and salvage water for beneficial use. Water districts and water storage districts may produce, store, and distribute irrigation water to individual farmers.

Each of these public districts becomes in essence a nonprofit wholesaler of water to farmers. They may have water supply sources (including rights) of their own, both surface water and groundwater, or they may be contractors for water developed by the federal government through its Central Valley Project or by the state of California through its State Water Project. They are governed by boards of directors, may have powers of eminent domain, and have the power to sell general obligation bonds, levy water charges, and impose ad valorem taxes on landowners within the district.

As argued in the introduction, economic rents are captured when the costs of obtaining and using a resource are lower than its value in use. Let us suppose that a farmer has an annual entitlement of water of three acre-feet per acre. The average per-acre-foot cost is $20, and its value in use is $30 per acre-foot. As defined above, annual

27. L. T. Wallace and T. B. O'Connell, *Survey of California Water Service Organizations*, University of California, Giannini Foundation Information Series no. 66–4, July 1966.

28. Ibid.

Table 3-4. California's Fifteen Largest Federal and State Water Contractors, Volume Delivered from October 1974 through September 1975.

Contractor	*Volume Delivered*	*Principal Source*[a]
	Acre-Feet	
Westlands Water District	1,250,279	CVP
Kern County Water Agency	788,409	SWP
Central California Irrigation District	527,894	CVP
Municipal Water District–Southern California	479,565	SWP
Orland Water User Association	252,788	CVP
Lower Tule River	223,000	CVP
Tulare Lake Water Storage District	201,202	SWP
Arvin Edison Water Storage District	191,200	CVP
Madera Irrigation District	188,888	CVP
Tulare Irrigation District	186,000	CVP
San Luis Canal Company	169,711	CVP
Delano-Earlimart Irrigation District	168,100	CVP
Southern San Joaquin Municipal Utility District	138,700	CVP
Chowchilla Water District	129,867	CVP
Panoche Water District	113,745	CVP
San Luis Water District	104,291	CVP
Santa Clara Valley Water District	103,745	SWP
Dudley Ridge Water District	80,356	SWP
Firebaugh Canal Company	79,162	CVP

a. CVP = the Federal Central Valley Project
SWP = the State Water Project.

Source: State of California, *The California Water Atlas* (prepared by the Governor's Office of Planning and Research in cooperation with the California Department of Water Resources, 1979).

economic rent captured by the farmer is $10 per acre-foot, or $30 per acre of irrigated land. Total water rent could be calculated by multiplying the per-acre rent by the number of irrigated acres operated by the farmer. From our discussion thus far it must be obvious that the annual income of our farmer is materially influenced by the magnitude of the water rent.

The farmer's asset wealth position may likewise be affected by rent. If the water entitlement were an appropriative right that could be separated from any particular parcel of land, the water right itself would be worth the discounted present value of the flow of economic rents. If the entitlement were a riparian water right attached to riparian land, the flow of economic rents would become capitalized in the value of the land itself. If the entitlement were a twenty-year water contract with a public water agency, the contract would take on a value reflecting the present value of the discounted flow of rents over the contract period. It follows that the wealth value of the annual water rents is influenced by the type of property right incorporated in the entitlement. The conclusion is that income and wealth effects on farmers resulting from water use are a function of the magnitude of economic rent and the nature of the property right in the use entitlement. The pricing and allocation policies of the water districts are crucial elements in determining the cost and value of water.

ALLOCATIVE AND DISTRIBUTIVE EFFECTS OF DISTRICT PRICING POLICIES

Allocative efficiency requires that the marginal values of water consumptively used be equal in each employment, net of the costs of transport and assuming that marginal values include both private and social benefits and costs. In the development of new water, economic efficiency requires that discounted benefits from the proposed project exceed discounted costs and that development is permitted to proceed only so long as the marginal benefits received from water supply exceed the marginal opportunity cost of the resources needed to bring forth the new supply. District and agency policies prevent the users of water from determining the relevant cost or value, and therefore the user decisions in water allocation are not economically efficient. Given the elasticities of demand for irrigation water presented earlier and the derived use values, a low marginal cost for water means that farmers will want to use more of it. In fact, if water were free to move among prospective users without restriction and prices were free to seek equilibrium levels, water prices should vary among users only by the cost of moving it from one user to another, which is how the market works for more mobile inputs such as machinery, energy, and fertilizer. Those users who can earn high economic rents in its use will bid it away from lower rent users by offering a price higher than the rent earned in the less valuable use. Thus, one way of judging whether or not water misallocation is occurring is to look at the distribution of water prices among water districts net of transport costs.

Recall once more the substantial differences in water price among water districts in Kern County (Table 3-3). There appear to be two important reasons for the variance in these pricing policies, both related to the sources of water supply available to a given district and what they cost: (1) Since a district is nonprofit, it must capture sufficient revenues to meet its total financial obligations (most of which are tied up in water costs that it incurs as a wholesaler) and at the same time sell the water available; and (2) in order to create distribution facilities many of the districts have sold bonds, which are easier to sell if the financial backing is in the form of fixed charges that are not dependent on direct water sales.

Most districts, which may sell water only to farmers inside the district boundaries, expect future use to be greater than present use. Since running out of water is costly, the districts tend to contract for large surface supplies, especially if they are cheaper than expected costs of pumping groundwater. If the district has a large supply compared to its demand, the marginal cost (the variable water toll) must be kept low so that the quantity available can be sold. If the resulting low toll does not generate sufficient resources to meet repayment obligations, the fixed charge or the land tax will need to be relatively higher. Of course, the reverse situation would call for high variable tolls (marginal costs) if surface supplies were short and the district was faced with the need to pump expensive groundwater. Since the districts' expectations of future demand, groundwater alternatives, and financial obligations differ, the mix of fixed charges and variable tolls are highly variable among districts.

This relationship between revenues generated and variable water tolls can create financial problems for the district. If demand for water were highly inelastic, an increase in the variable toll would not significantly reduce the quantity demanded, and the toll would be an effective instrument in raising revenues for the district. If, however, demand elasticity approaches unity and may sometimes even exceed it, as indicated in the previous section, increasing the water toll may not increase revenues at all. The increase in price would be more than offset by reductions in the quantity demanded. No wonder several of the districts rely heavily on a fixed charge, which would seem to be their only alternative if they must increase revenues to cover their costs.

The water costs to the district also are crucial in determining the variable toll charged the farmers; if the costs are low the water toll will be low. The Kern County districts with the low tolls—Buena Vista, Delano-Earlimart, Kern Delta, North Kern, Shafter-Wasco, and Southern San Joaquin—either get the bulk of their supplies from old rights to the Kern River at very low costs or from the Central Valley Project (CVP), where ability-to-pay pricing has produced low contracted rates for very long periods of up to forty years. Those districts charging high rates generally receive higher cost state water or are heavily dependent on expensive groundwater.

It would appear that the economic rents captured by the water users are highly variable, given this evidence from Kern County. Even though demand studies that would reveal the use value of water for each district have not been made, similarities in cropping patterns would suggest that use values are not as disparate as water costs. If economic rent is defined as the difference between per-unit water value and cost, the upshot is that high-cost districts would be capturing lower rents than low-cost districts.

Of course, over the longer run if higher annual economic rents are secure, they would tend to be capitalized into higher land values. Wealth gains would be captured by landowners. If the land were sold to new owners, the favorable economic rents attributable to water procurements would be offset by higher land costs, *ceteris paribus.* Thus the original landowner would capture the bulk of the benefits of the higher water rents. Unfortunately, no systematic studies have been made of the land market in Kern County that would establish empirically the relationship between water rents and land prices.

This policy of combining variable tolls with fixed charges may be perfectly sensible as viewed by the district's management as a means of raising revenues to cover cost. It may not be socially optimal if efficient water allocation is a significant policy goal. If quantities demanded were free to adjust so that the marginal value of water would be equal to the variable water toll, then great variation in the toll implies great variation in the marginal value of water among users. This, in turn, suggests that water reallocation from uses and users of low value to high value would increase water's economic productivity.

There is substantial empirical evidence that water values are highly disparate, even within agriculture. Noel, Gardner, and Moore's study of conjunctive use of groundwater and surface water allocated by several water agencies in Yolo County used an economic-hydrologic linear quadratic control model to estimate the marginal values of irrigation water in the aquifer's six basins, which differed in pumping and surface-water costs.[29] The range was large—from $2.44 per acre-foot in an area near the Sacramento River, where surface water is plentiful and cheap and the pumping lift was less than 20 feet, to $61.13 in another area scarcely 25 miles away, where water is pumped from more than 100 feet. This disparity in values suggests that large economic gains could be captured by water transfers from areas of low value to areas of high value. These transfers do not occur because of institutional impediments resulting from district, state, and federal water policies, the most significant of which will be discussed in the following sections.

Fixed Charges

A common pricing policy, particularly by districts in the Sacramento Valley, is to impose a fixed per-acre water charge that varies by crop. As a typical example, one irrigation district that sells large quantities of water to rice farmers announced water rates effective 7 February 1980 as: $17.25 per acre flooded for rice; $12.10 per acre irrigated for sugar beets and tomatoes; $10.35 per acre irrigated for pasture, clover, ear corn, alfalfa, and orchard; and $6.90 per acre irrigated for general crops (barley, vine crops, wheat, milo, other cereal grains, and silage corn). The announcement also specified that the regular rates will apply to three irrigations (except for rice). Water

29. Jay E. Noel, B. Delworth Gardner, and Charles V. Moore, "Optimal Regional Conjunctive Water Management," *American Journal of Agricultural Economics* 62 (August 1980): 489–498.

quantities delivered are not measured. Lands outside the district may be supplied with water if a prior agreement has been made with the irrigation district's board of directors, but per-acre water charges outside will be twice the announced per-acre inside charges.

Such a policy violates the requirements of economic efficiency. Since the water charge is not related to the quantity applied or consumptively used, at the margin the water cost is zero. A sugar beet grower would pay the same flat rate to apply 45 inches of water as for 35 inches per acre, a rice grower could get 10 acre-feet for the same total cost as 6 acre-feet. (Of course, other costs involved in irrigation, such as the irrigator's wage, may constrain water use.) Under this pricing policy there is little incentive for conserving water by careful irrigation practice.

Another problem with the fixed per-acre charge is that some crops bear higher water costs than others per acre-foot used consumptively. Alfalfa and pasture in the area consumptively use about 48 inches of water annually, rice about 56 inches on average. Most of the other crops use much less. In the example cited above, it is apparent that growers of alfalfa, pasture, and probably rice are receiving economic rents much higher than they would if water were priced at equal per-acre-foot rates for all crops. Tomato and sugar beet growers appear to be capturing smaller water rents than if per-acre-foot prices were equal. If the fixed per-acre charge were replaced with an economically efficient per-acre-foot toll that was the same for all crops, it is likely that substantial shifts in cropping patterns would ensue. This question should be researched to determine the extent of the current misallocation.

One of the reasons commonly given for pricing water on a per-acre basis is the difficulty and cost of determining how much is delivered to a given farmer, especially for surface-water diversions and for riparian users of water courses. Meters, weirs, and other measuring devices are available, however, and there is little doubt that their implementation would permit a more efficient pricing policy.

Taxes

Land or water taxes, imposed on all landowners in a district to raise district revenues, are even farther removed from direct water use than per-acre charges. Many California water districts, especially those selling urban water, exercise their legislative authorization to levy taxes. In an efficiency sense, it makes little difference to water-use decisions whether these taxes are used to pay off fixed indebtedness or to cover current operations and maintenance costs. In either case the amount of the tax is divorced from the quantity of water used and thus has no impact on water allocation at the margin. High-cost water that may not be economically justified in that costs exceed benefits may be paid for by spreading the costs among district taxpayers, some of whom may use little or no water. The tax may be an effective instrument for raising district revenues, but it is inefficient as a mechanism for producing efficient new-water development, allocating water to its highest valued uses, and providing incentives to economize on the amount of water used.

Price Averaging

In its allocative effects, perhaps the most pernicious of all pricing practices commonly utilized in the water districts and by the water agencies is so-called price averaging. Suppose an existing supply of water delivers 3 acre-feet per acre to the district's farmers and the average cost to the farmers is $10 per acre-foot. Suppose the average value of this water is $20 per acre-foot, which means the farmers are capturing a rent of $10 per acre-foot. Let us assume a new supply source could be made available to the district that would double the water supply and would cost $25 per acre-foot. If the average value of existing water can be taken as the marginal value, it is apparent that the farmers would not want the additional supply if they had to pay $25 per acre-foot. This would be the end of it and the new water would not be developed. What the district commonly does, however, is average the old and the new water costs; in our example, this average is $17.50. Because this is still below the average value of water, there is demand for the new supply. The effect of this price blending is to distort the true supply price of the new water. The upshot is that uneconomic supplies are developed and per-acre-foot rents are diminished.

Should the district use this practice to expand its acreage, there would be a transfer of rent from the farmers on the original acreage to those on the new land. Uneconomic water is developed and allocated to new land that otherwise would not be producing crops. Empirical analysis is also needed to quantify this type of misallocation.

A vivid example of price averaging and its effects on water rents is provided by a proposal by the Bureau of Reclamation.[30] The separable costs assigned to irrigation for new agricultural water supplies forthcoming from the proposed Auburn Dam in the Sierra foothills near Sacramento have been estimated at approximately $63 per acre-foot. (Agricultural water users do not pay interest charges on the capital costs of constructing new projects.) For the sake of argument, let us assume that this figure is a true representation of the marginal supply costs of the new irrigation water. Only if water is worth $63 per acre-foot is it economically efficient to develop it. Repayment-capability budgets of the bureau suggest that in general farmers could not afford such high water prices. Current bureau prices in California are far lower–generally from $2.50 to $15 per acre-foot.

The bureau proposes spreading the costs of the new water over all users of federal water, existing as well as new users. Some of the existing users are far removed from Auburn Dam and the area of intended use. By averaging the cost in this fashion, the water rates to all existing users would rise by $3.25 per acre-foot, reducing economic rents by the same amount. Short of a lawsuit, existing users would have no say in the matter; the new rates would simply be imposed.

The efficiency implications are indeed ominous: (1) almost any project, regardless of water costs, could be justified and paid for by this mechanism; and (2) the increase in price to all users may drive water costs above the resource's worth and cause previously economic production to be uneconomic, resulting in misallocation. The equity implications–the imposition of the equivalent of a water tax without the consent of the affected irrigators–are no less objectionable.

30. Information given in an address by Dave Schuster, Assistant Director, Mid-Pacific Region, U.S. Bureau of Reclamation, "What's Ahead in Water Pricing," to the Association of California Water Agencies, 1981 Fall Workshop Conference, Monterey, 19 November 1981.

Entitlement and Surplus Water

Policies of both the Department of Water Resources of California, which administers the State Water Project, and the Bureau of Reclamation, which administers the federal Central Valley Project, differentiate between contracted (entitlement) water and surplus water. Entitlement water is contracted for long periods and usually well in advance of delivery, and the supply agency must plan to meet the requirements of these contracts. Because of random climatic variables and the need to provide a firm supply of entitlement water, the quantity in the entitlement is less than is available in all but the dry years. The rules specify that the price for state entitlement water must cover the pro-rata share of the fixed capital costs of the project as well as the variable costs of delivery. In the federal case, the water price on contracted water is usually determined by an ability-to-pay rule.

In the early years of the long-term agreement the contractors often are unable or unwilling to take all the water available, particularly if supplies are augmented by precipitation. The resulting surplus water is sold at the variable costs of delivery, which depend on how far the water must be transported and how much it costs to pump it through the system. Federal surplus water also is sold below contracted prices and has been used to replenish groundwater aquifers in years of plentiful supply.

An interesting example of surplus water allocation is provided in Kern County. The Kern County Water Agency, a water broker for several of the water districts discussed earlier, has been receiving large quantities of state surplus water in the last decade because the Metropolitan Water District in Southern California has not been using its full entitlement.[31] The price averaging process among districts is a mechanism whereby the agency distributes this cheap surplus water among users, who thereby capture economic rents.

The water law in California presents some obstacles to developing markets to efficiently allocate water. Individual water users do not themselves own the water rights—the water companies or districts do. In California, the Bureau of Reclamation and the Depart-

31. Perhaps it soon will, as 650,000 acre-feet of Colorado River water now flowing to Southern California might be lost to Arizona beginning in the mid-1980s.

ment of Water Resources are permittees of the State Water Resource Control Board, which has ultimate jurisdiction over water rights. Contractors of these agencies technically do not hold any permanent water rights beyond their contracts. They are given options to purchase water from the districts on terms specified in the contract. The district, which is bound by contract to supply water, isn't really free to negotiate the sales of water rights or even water rentals unless it has surplus available. In the case of State Project water, any changes in contracts or in points of diversion must be approved by the director of the Department of Water Resources. This type of administrative approval is likely to be difficult to obtain. The ultimate water users are powerless to make any transfers at all. The most they can do is simply forfeit their use of water, but usually they are committed by contract to take a certain amount. The result is an inflexible and inefficient water-allocating system.

This complicated milieu of water allocation by the water districts in California is no doubt what led researchers of the Rand Corporation to argue that the treatment of water rights is one of the most crucial factors in achieving efficiency of water use and that title to water should be passed from the water district to the water user, thus providing full economic incentives to transfer water to parties valuing its use more highly.[32]

CONCLUSION

One might interpret the foregoing discussion as being pessimistic regarding prospects for improving the efficiency of water allocation in California. That would be an erroneous interpretation. Water policy is dynamic and responsive to economic pressures, and the next decade is likely to bring many changes in the rules of water pricing and allocation. These changes will probably have a significant impact on the economic rents captured by water users.

Water users themselves are taking significant steps to improve water mobility in time and space. Marketlike arrangements are developing in many water districts where conditions are conducive. Some

32. Charles E. Phelps, Morlie H. Granbard, David L. Jaquette, Albert J. Lipson, Nancy Y. Moore, Robert Shishko, and Bruce Wetzel, *Efficient Water Use in California: Executive Summary*, Rand Corporation, Santa Monica, R-2385-CSA/RF, November 1978.

districts that have capacity are storing water for other districts, both above and below the ground, at mutually acceptable terms. Within districts, some farmers with relatively inexpensive groundwater are selling their surface water to other farmers who have either expensive groundwater or none, at prices that benefit both parties. These immensely encouraging developments should be supported by effective legislation and administrative policies.

At the federal level the 1902 Reclamation Act, which restricts the acreage receiving federal water under one owner to 160 acres, is likely to be replaced by more liberal legislation. Bills being considered by Congress would expand the restriction to 960 acres of owned land. The question of whether additional acreage may be leased is being hotly debated, as is the issue of whether to require owner residency on or near the land. Some versions of the proposed legislation would require irrigators to pay the full supply cost of federal water utilized on acreages over 960 acres, including an interest charge on the capital stock. The impact on the economic rent earned by water could be substantial. The worth of water per acre-foot is related to the size of the farm if economies of size exist. Rents no doubt will be less if water prices are increased more than the value of water increases in use. When land receiving subsidized water is rented, it is not clear a priori whether the lessor or the lessee captures the water rent. It would depend on the characteristics of the land rental market and who has market power.

Costly state water projects must be funded by water sales, which affect water prices and thus water rents. Even if no new water is developed, water prices will be much higher as new contracts are negotiated in 1984 due to increases in energy costs. Water prices set by administrative fiat should increase faster than the value of water and therefore economic rents will decline. Also, the quantity of water demanded will decline substantially as farmers adjust by using less water on a given crop, employing more water-efficient technology, and shifting to more water-efficient and higher valued crops. As a result, the state probably will encounter greater difficulties in finding contracting buyers of irrigation water. Those irrigators who have either riparian private water sources with firm rights or can obtain water cheaply will continue to capture large water rents and their land prices will continue to escalate relative to those irrigators who must pay the higher water prices.

SELECTED BIBLIOGRAPHY (PART I)

Bain, Joe S.; Caves, Richard E.; and Margolis, Julius. *Northern California's Water Industry*. Baltimore: Johns Hopkins University Press, 1966.

Buchanan, James M. "Rentseeking and Profit Seeking." In James M. Buchanan, Robert D. Tollison, and Gordon Tullock, eds., *Toward a Theory of the Rent-Seeking Society*. College Station: Texas A&M University Press, 1980.

Davison, S. R. "The Leadership of the Reclamation Movement, 1885-1902." Ph.D. dissertation, University of California, 1951.

Engelbert, Ernest A., ed. *Competition for California Water*. Berkeley: University of California Press, 1982.

Gardner, B. Delworth, and Fullerton, Herbert H. "Transfer Restrictions and Misallocation of Irrigation Water." *American Journal of Agricultural Economics* 50 (3) (August 1968): 556-71.

Jones, Nancy. "Proposed Rules for Administering the Acreage Limitation of Reclamation Law." *Natural Resources Journal* (October 1978): 936-37.

Libecap, Gary. "Bureaucratic Opposition to the Assignment of Property Rights: Overgrazing on the Western Range." *Journal of Economic History* 41 (1) (March 1981): 151-58.

Locke, John. *Second Treatise of Civil Government*. Indianapolis: Liberal Arts Press of the Bobbs-Merrill Company, 1952.

Maass, Arthur, and Anderson, Raymond L. *And the Desert Shall Rejoice: Conflict, Growth, and Justice in Arid Environments*. Cambridge, Mass.: MIT Press, 1978, pp. 317-18.

Mead, Elwood. *Irrigation Institutions*. New York: Macmillan, 1903.

Merk, Frederick. *History of the Westward Movement*. New York: Knopf, 1978, p. 507.

Meyers, Charles, and Tarlock, A. Dan. *A Coursebook in Law and Public Policy*, vol. 2. Mineola, N.Y.: Foundation Press, 1971.

Oppenheimer, Franz. *The State.* Indianapolis: Bobbs-Merrill, 1914.

Ostrom, Vincent. *Water and Politics: A Study of Water Policies and Administration in the Development of Los Angeles.* Los Angeles: Haynes Foundation, 1953.

Phelps, Charles E.; Graubard, Morlie H.; Jaquette, David L.; Lipson, Albert J.; Moore, Nancy Y.; Shishko, Robert; and Wetzel, Bruce. *Efficient Water Use in California: Executive Summary.* Santa Monica, Calif.: Rand Corporation, R-2385-CSA/RF, November 1968.

Seckler, David, and Young, Robert A. "Economic and Policy Implications of the 160-Acre Limitation in Federal Reclamation." *American Journal of Agricultural Economics* 60 (4) (November 1978): 575-88.

Warne, Frederick. *The Bureau of Reclamation.* New York: Praeger, 1971.

PART II

INSTITUTIONS AND INSTITUTIONAL REFORM

Chapter 4

WATER IN COLORADO
Fear and Loathing of the Marketplace

Timothy D. Tregarthen

There seems to be general agreement among economists that the private market is perfectly capable of allocating water rights.[1] Indeed, an economist might be defined as someone who doesn't see anything special about water. Given this belief in the virtues of the marketplace, economists have looked with favor on the doctrine of prior appropriation, a system in which rights in water are more or less clearly defined and are transferable. Colorado, as the first state to adopt explicitly the doctrine of prior appropriation and having the purest form of this doctrine, should therefore enjoy a special measure of approbation.[2] But in Colorado, as in other states whose waters are allocated under prior appropriation doctrine, the courts act as referees to enforce the rules of the market and, to a large degree, as policymakers who establish those rules. As an unfettered market does not seem to be nearly as congenial an institution to the jurist as to the economist, the result is a market constrained by rules that limit its efficiency. This chapter examines public policies that

1. For general statements of this view, see Jerome Milliman, "Water Law and Private Decision-Making: A Critique," *Journal of Law and Economics* 2 (October 1959): 41–63; and Jack Hirshleifer, James DeHaven, and Jerome Milliman, *Water Supply* (Chicago: University of Chicago Press, 1969).

2. Phillip O. Foss, "Institutional Arrangements for Effective Water Management in Colorado" (Fort Collins, Colo.: Colorado State University, Completion Report No. 88, November 1978), p. 129.

affect the market for water in Colorado and explores possible changes that might improve its efficiency. Before reviewing these issues of public policy, however, it will be useful to examine characteristics of water that pose special problems for such policy.

WATER AS AN ECONOMIC GOOD

Perhaps the two features of water that distinguish it most clearly in public opinion from other goods are its necessity and its scarcity. Water is requisite to life, and there is not enough of it; hence, it often seems to take on almost mystical qualities, particularly in the West. But water's essentiality hardly makes it unique. Life would also be awkward without food, clothing, and shelter, none of which present particular problems for the market. Furthermore, while it is certainly true there is not enough water, it is also true there is not enough of nearly everything—this is the commonplace problem of economic scarcity, the subject of all of economic analysis. Indeed, a world of plenty in which there was enough of a significant number of things would raise the terrible possibility of having enough economists. Neither water's great usefulness nor its scarcity pose problems that distinguish it from other economic goods.

Water, however, does have characteristics that create difficulties in its allocation. The total amount available in any one year fluctuates significantly with the vagaries of the weather. More importantly, the nature of the relationship of surface and underground flows is enormously complex and not well understood. This will be a consideration of increasing importance as continuing growth in demand forces the exploitation of more costly, but far more abundant, underground resources. Colorado has about 16 million acre-feet of surface water per year, of which only a third is available for use within the state, but it has some 2 billion acre-feet of underground water.[3] Fluctuations in supply and the complexity of hydrological characteristics introduce considerable uncertainty into the allocative function of the market for water. Nonetheless, just as usefulness and scarcity are not unique to water, uncertainty is hardly limited to this one market. Given this pervasive phenomenon and differences in the degree of

3. Harold F. Morgan, "Appropriation and Colorado's Ground Water: A Continuing Dilemma?" *University of Colorado Law Review* 40 (1967): 133.

risk aversion among individual agents, one would expect to see market adjustments that permit the reallocation of risk, just as one sees adjustments in forms such as insurance, guaranties, and contingent contracts in other markets.

Like many other goods, water is characterized by significant economies of scale in storage and delivery systems. The economic theory of clubs—groups of individuals united to achieve economic gain—examines the wide range of market arrangements through which such economies of scale may be exploited.[4] The market arrangements discussed below for enhanced water consumption are an impressive example of the power of the concept of clubs.

Water does present a significant potential for externality problems. Its use as a waste dump by one agent affects others; the large number of affected agents may preclude private arrangements to deal with the problem. In cases where such externalities exist, public sector intervention to improve water quality may be desirable.[5] The focus of this paper, however, is the allocation of quantities of water; the problem of pollution will not be considered.

Another significant aspect of water allocation is consumptive use. Many uses of water do not significantly reduce the amount of water available in the system. The use of a stream to run a turbine, for example, takes little from downstream uses. Growing soybeans uses up less water than growing corn. While the amount of water used or diverted is of interest to the consuming agent, the amount used up affects the efficient use of the entire stream. The ability of the market to deal with this problem is a crucial test of its efficacy in allocating water.

No characteristic of water precludes its allocation by the market. But the market for water is clearly different from the market for other goods. For the most part, these differences must be ascribed to features of the market for water that are the result of peculiarities of public policy toward water, rather than water itself. In the next sections, the economic considerations important to an efficient market will be examined in conjunction with the institutional constraints im-

4. While water rights-consuming groups have not been analyzed within the structure of club theory, they represent an important example of the phenomenon. See Todd Sundler and John T. Tschirhart, "The Economic Theory of Clubs: An Evaluative Survey," *Journal of Economic Literature* 18 (December 1980): 1481-1521.

5. See, for example, A. Myrick Freeman III, Robert H. Haveman, and Allen V. Kneese, *The Economics of Environmental Policy* (New York: Wiley,1973).

posed by public sector intervention in this market in Colorado, where significant policy features frustrate the efficient use of water.

WATER AS PROPERTY

The first condition necessary for any market is that property rights be well defined and exclusive to the agent owning them. The doctrine of appropriation has the potential to serve this condition well. Appropriation doctrine grants exclusive use of a well-specified quantity of water to a single agent. This agent may be an individual or a collection of individuals.

Two factors made the use of appropriation doctrine a logical choice in Colorado. First, the state's relatively dry climate created a demand for irrigation, which consumes a significant fraction of the water diverted. Given this fact and the limited quantity of water available for diversion, it was clear from the outset that water was scarce in the economic sense. The diversion of water for one use, at least under some conditions, would represent an alternative to some other use. Appropriation thus was clearly superior to the riparian doctrine that grew out of the British tradition of implicitly assuming water to be a scarce, free good.[6] The Colorado Supreme Court recognized the desirability of private rights in water in 1872[7] and explicitly rejected the riparian alternative in 1882:

> But we think the [prior appropriation] doctrine has existed from the date of the earliest appropriations of water within the boundaries of the state. The climate is dry, and the soil, when moistened only by the usual rainfall, is arid and unproductive; except in a few favored sections, artificial irrigation is an absolute necessity. Water in the various streams thus acquires a value unknown in moister climates. Instead of being a mere incident to the soil, it arises when appropriated to dignity of a distinct usufructuary estate or right of property.[8]

The second factor in Colorado that suggested the superiority of appropriation doctrine was the fact that much Colorado land was in

6. G. E. Radosevich, K. C. Nobe, D. Allandice, and C. Kirkwood, *Evolution and Administration of Colorado Water Law: 1876-1976* (Fort Collins, Colo.: Water Resources Publications, 1976), p. 16.

7. *Yunker* v. *Nichols*, 1 Colo. 551 (1872).

8. *Coffin* v. *Left Hand Ditch Co.*, 6 Colo. 443 (1882).

the public domain, prohibiting private use of water if ownership of water were linked to ownership of land, as was the case under riparian doctrine:

> Water rights acquired by appropriation for purpose of irrigation in this state cannot be held to be inseparable and next to the land in connection with which such rights were acquired. Even though under certain circumstances such rights may be considered appurtenant to the land, they may undoubtedly be severed from the land and be sold and conveyed separate and apart therefrom, and where such severance, sale and conveyance have taken place as by the assignment and sale of stock representing water rights in an incorporated ditch company, a subsequent sale and conveyance of the land does not pass the title to such water rights.[9]

The first successful appropriation of water in Colorado occurred in 1851 with the adoption of the state constitution:

> The water of every natural stream, not heretofore appropriated, within the State of Colorado, is hereby declared to be the property of the public, and the same is dedicated to the use of the people of the state, subject to appropriation as hereinafter provided.[10]

Thus, the rights to water in Colorado are vested in the people but subject to appropriation by private agents. The private right remains usufructuary, permitting the appropriator to use the water and to derive all returns from it.[11]

BENEFICIAL USES

The usufructuary nature of rights in water and the vesting of rights with the state are technicalities that have yielded some mischief. To obtain and maintain title to water, an appropriator must put the water to a "beneficial use," that is, use the water in a useful industry or supply a well-recognized want.[12] This provision that water must be in beneficial use if it is to be owned grew our of a common worry that the private market might otherwise waste it.[13] The present state

9. *Oppenlander* v. *Left Hand Ditch Co.*, 18 Colo. 142, 32 P. 854 (1892).
10. Colorado Constitution, Article 16, §5.
11. *Wyatt et al.* v. *Larimer et al.*, 18 Colo. 298, 33 P. 144 (1893).
12. *Hammond* v. *Rose*, 11 Colo. 524, 19 P. 466.
13. James G. Felt, "Overview of Water Law: General Principles, Appropriation v. Riparian," mimeographed (Continuing Legal Education in Colorado, Inc., 1979).

law continues to reflect this odd concern, defining a beneficial use as one that is "reasonable and appropriate under reasonably efficient practices to accomplish without waste the purpose for which the diversion is lawfully made."[14] One can thus "own" a right to water and lose it as a result of a failure to put it to a beneficial use. Such a loss could result, for example, from nonuse over a very long period, together with a showing of an intent to abandon the right.[15] The beneficial use restriction also creates problems in the acquisition and transfer of water rights. The doctrine gives the courts a role in arbitrarily deciding whether a use is beneficial, a judgment for which one might expect the market to be better equipped. In a recent decision denying an application for water rights, for example, the water judge ruled that using water for dust control or land reclamation would not be beneficial, using it for cooling might be, and using it for slurry pipelines would be.[16] One wonders how other markets would function if such judicial determinations of usefulness were required.

A related curiosity in the treatment of water rights is the notion of preferential use, as stated in the Colorado constitution:

> Where the waters of any natural stream are not sufficient for the service of all those desiring the use of the same, those using the water for domestic purposes shall have the preference over those claiming for any other purpose, and those using the water for agricultural purposes shall have the preference over those using the same for manufacturing purposes.[17]

Given that the purpose of all economic activity is consumption, this preferential use concept seems a bit silly. Its chief practical consequence is that it forms the basis for condemnation of water by preferred users, especially cities, a practice for which there is no apparent justification.

The doctrines of beneficial and preferential use permit the injection of judicial whim into decisions in the marketplace for water. They create uncertainty in the title to and nature of water rights. It is instructive to note that no title company in Colorado has insured

14. Colorado Revised Statutes §37-92-103 (4).

15. *Orr* v. *Denver*, Colo. 572 P. 2d 805 (1977).

16. *Southeastern Colorado Water Conservancy District* v. *Huston,* 79-CW-1 (Arapahoe, Colorado, 1981).

17. Colorado Constitution, Article 16, §6.

legal title to water rights, a result of the high degree of uncertainty attached to them.[18]

TRANSFERABILITY AND THE PROBLEM OF CONSUMPTIVE USE

A water right, once defined, must be transferable. The inability to transfer a right shields the holder of the right from recognition of its opportunity cost, the value another agent places on it. An important virtue of the appropriation system is the enhanced ability to transfer rights, given their severability from land. But a problem in any transfer is the determination of what the seller actually owns. This question is of particular importance in transfers between uses, as when a city seeks to buy irrigation water. This section distinguishes rights to divert water from rights to consume it or to use it up. The distinction is a crucial one. It is argued below that the method for making the distinction and applying it in the market in Colorado creates unnecessary uncertainty, high transaction costs, and perverse incentives.

In Colorado, the right that can be transferred is not the amount of water appropriated to the agricultural use but the "duty of water" at the decreed point of use, which has been defined by the Supreme Court as:

> that measure of water, which, by careful management and use, without wastage, is reasonably required to be applied to any given tract of land for such period of time as may be adequate to produce therefrom a maximum amount of such crops as ordinarily are grown thereon. It is not a hard and fast unit of measurement, but is variable according to conditions . . . every element that concerns or affects the consumption of water in the particular case before the Court is to be considered.[19]

This doctrine of the duty of water thus limits transfers of water rights, based on the consumptive use by the seller and the prospective consumptive use by the buyer. From 1925 to 1934, for example,

18. Ward H. Fischer, "Water Title Examination," *The Colorado Lawyer* 9 (October 1980): 2042–57. In an interview on 29 December 1981, Fischer noted the possibility of insuring title to water rights has been considered by the Attorneys Title Guarantee Fund, but that no decision has been made.

19. *Farmers Highline Canal and Reservoir Co.* v. *City of Golden,* Colo., 272 P. 2d 629 (1954).

the city of Denver sought to purchase rights the appropriated total of which was 396.80 cubic feet per second (cfs) of water; the courts agreed to transfer only 77.39 cfs.[20] The purpose of such restrictions, of course, is to protect downstream users from a loss of water. When rights are transferred, the use of the water may change, and with it the amount of water consumed. The result would be a change in the amount of water available to downstream appropriators. The courts have sought to prevent such losses by limiting transfers so that the amount of water consumed is not changed. An appropriator thus owns the right to *divert* a given quantity of water per unit of time but can transfer this right only according to the amount *consumed.*

Suppose an appropriator owns a right to divert 100 cfs from a stream, and that the appropriator's consumptive use is 60 percent of that amount, that is, the appropriator is using up 60 cfs. Suppose further that a potential purchaser of this right would use this water in such a way that 75 percent of the water diverted would be consumed. To assure protection of downstream appropriators, the court might then award the purchaser the right to divert 80 cfs, thus maintaining consumptive use at 60 cfs.

At first glance, this system of limiting transfers based on previous and prospective consumptive use seems efficient. As decisionmakers, appropriators should be faced with the costs as well as the benefits of their decisions. The cost of an appropriator's use of water is the value of the best alternative use of the water. The relevant measure of such use must be in terms of the appropriator's consumptive use. In the example above, the first appropriator's consumptive use of 60 cfs represented a cost to society; the 40 cfs returned to the stream represented, in effect, a costless use by that appropriator.[21] By focusing on consumptive use, the courts have changed the effective status of a right to divert to a right to consume. But there are two features of the application of this idea that interfere with the achievement of an efficient allocation.

First, recall that appropriators are assigned a right to divert, not to consume. This right is then limited by the tests of beneficial use and the duty of water but still is defined according to a quantity to be diverted. When an appropriator seeks to transfer such a right,

20. L. M. Hartman and Don Seastone, *Water Transfers: Economic Efficiency and Alternative Institutions* (Baltimore: Johns Hopkins Press, 1970), pp. 23–24.

21. The added issue of possible changes in the point of return of the unconsumed water is ignored here.

application is made to a water court. Downstream appropriators are given the opportunity to object to the transfer, based on possible changes in the degree of consumptive use resulting from the change. The result is an adversarial proceeding in which the court determines the amount of water consumed by the existing and prospective uses and thus the amount of water that can be sold.[22] In the earlier example, estimates would have been presented by various parties of the amounts of water consumed by the two uses. From these estimates, the court would have determined the 60 and 75 percent figures and awarded the transfer of 80 cfs. Estimates presented to the court may vary widely. Hartman and Seastone cite estimates of the fraction of consumptive use ranging from 35 to 71.2 percent in a case involving a transfer of water to Fort Collins, Colorado.[23]

Because rights are defined in terms of amounts diverted, neither appropriators nor potential buyers know in advance how much water can be transferred when a change in use is involved. The result is considerable uncertainty and expensive information. The determination of how much water is effectively available with a certain right whose purchaser intends a change of use requires costly court proceedings, the outcome of which is highly uncertain.[24]

A more important problem with the courts' policy toward consumptive use is the refusal to allow appropriators to capture rights to any increase in the quantity of water they return to the stream. Returning to the example, if the first appropriator were to reduce the fraction of consumptive use to 30 percent from 60 percent, that individual would be unable to claim the additional 30 cfs returned to the stream. Indeed, this effort at conservation would not only fail to achieve a benefit for the first appropriator, it would result in harm. Once consumptive use was established at 30 percent, the amount of water that could be sold to the buyer whose consumptive use was 75 percent would fall to 40 from 80 cfs, in order to maintain the lower consumptive use of 30 cfs.

Three cases illustrate the refusal of the Colorado courts to allow appropriators any claim to an increase in returned water. The city of

22. Hartman and Seastone's *Water Transfers* provides a description of the adversarial proceedings involved in several transfers of water in Colorado.

23. Ibid., p. 30.

24. In an interview on 9 September 1981, Assistant Water Division Engineer Kenneth Cooper estimated legal costs at water hearings at $100,000 per inch of submitted briefs; such hearings are often "several inches thick."

Trinidad, Colorado, built purification plants and attempted to sell the treated water for irrigation. In a 1922 ruling, the Colorado Supreme Court held that this treated water could not be sold. While the court recognized the water thus treated would have been otherwise unavailable, it did not constitute new water. Only water brought in from another watershed could be resold.[25]

More recently, an appropriator sought to increase the amount of water in Monument Creek, Colorado, by clearing phreatocytes (in this case, cottonwoods) along the creek to reduce water loss from transpiration. A claim made for a senior priority for the water thus saved was rejected by the court, again on grounds it was merely salvaged water.[26] The rejection of claims from phreatocyte clearance is significant: Longenbaugh and Wymore have estimated annual consumptive use in the White River basin of Colorado as 55,280 acre-feet from irrigation and roughly 10,000 acre-feet from phreatocytes.[27]

The legal barriers to a market in rights to water returned to the stream are further illustrated in a recent ruling on the point of return. Denver built a new sewage treatment plant downstream from a user who had a decreed right to the water flow from the original plant. The court held that while a point of diversion cannot be changed in a way that injures other appropriators, the point of return can be. Denver could use its water as it wanted and return it where it wanted, the court argued, provided only that the change not be arbitrary or unreasonable.[28]

In effect, Colorado appropriators are permitted no interest in nor responsibility for water returned to the stream. This results in a perverse set of incentives. For a Colorado appropriator, it is better to consume than to return. The incentives for a wide range of conservation alternatives are thus reduced. The choice of crop, as well as the lining and covering of ditches and the removal of phreatocytes, can affect the degree of consumptive use, as shown in Table 4-1. All other things equal, one would expect appropriators to choose crops

25. *Pulaski Irrigation Ditch Co.* v. *City of Trinidad,* 70 Colo., 565, 203 P. 681 (1922). It is interesting to note the courts in New Mexico have permitted such claims.

26. *Southeastern Colorado Water Conservancy District* v. *Shelton Farms, Inc.,* Colo. 529 P. 2d 1321 (1974).

27. R. A. Longenbaugh and Ivan F. Wymore, "Analysis of Methods for the Determination of Water Availability for Energy Development," Federal Energy Administration Project CA-05-50041-00, May 1977.

28. *Metropolitan Denver Sewage* v. *Farmers Reservoir and Irrigation Co.,* Colo., 499 P. 2d 1190 (1972).

Table 4-1. Seasonal Consumptive Use Crop Coefficients for Irrigation.

Crop	*Consumptive-Use Coefficient*[a]
Alfalfa	0.80 to 0.90
Bananas	.80 to 1.00
Beans	.60 to .70
Cocoa	.70 to .80
Coffee	.70 to .80
Corn (Maize)	.75 to .85
Cotton	.60 to .70
Dates	.65 to .80
Flax	.70 to .80
Grains, small	.75 to .85
Grain, sorghums	.70 to .80
Oilseeds	.65 to .75
Orchard crops:	
Avocado	.50 to .55
Grapefruit	.55 to .65
Orange and lemon	.45 to .55
Walnuts	.60 to .70
Deciduous	.60 to .70
Pasture crops:	
Grass	.75 to .85
Ladino whiteclover	.80 to .85
Potatoes	.65 to .75
Rice	1.00 to 1.10
Soybeans	.65 to .70
Sugar beet	.65 to .75
Sugarcane	.80 to .90
Tobacco	.70 to .80
Tomatoes	.65 to .70
Truck crops, small	.60 to .70
Vineyard	.50 to .60

a. The lower values are for the more humid areas, and the higher values are for the more arid climates.

Source: U.S. Department of Agriculture, "Irrigation Water Requirements" (Washington, D.C.: Government Printing Office, 1971), p. 11.

and production methods that increase the degree of consumptive use, in order to increase the amount of water they can sell. The problem is a significant one; if agricultural users of water in Colorado were to reduce their consumptive use by 5 percent, the amount available for municipal and industrial use would be nearly doubled.[29]

29. Based on total use figures provided by Foss, *Effective Water Management.*

The present system for establishing rights based on consumptive use thus leaves a great deal to be desired. Rights to divert are clearly defined, but it is the right to consumptive use that is important from an allocative standpoint. For rights remaining in agricultural use, the present system does not provide an incentive to reduce the fraction of consumptive use; indeed, it encourages an increase. Because the determination of what can be transferred is left to the courts, neither appropriators nor prospective purchasers know who owns what and who can purchase what when a change in use is contemplated.

A simple reform that would preserve the spirit of the existing system while eliminating these defects is to define rights in terms of consumptive use rather than according to amounts diverted. Agents in the water market would then know who owned what; transfers would not require costly litigation to make the determination. Further, appropriators would gain an incentive to conserve; a reduction in consumptive use would create water that could be sold to downstream users.

WATER, PROFITS, AND RISK

Once water rights are defined, their owners are subject to further uncertainty and risk, a significant source of which is the variation in the amount of precipitation. Because the quantity of surface water available varies over time, the property rights system must provide a basis for determining how the rights are to be allocated. The system that developed in Colorado, and in much of the West, was the priority, or first-in-time, first-in-rights system, which had been developed for gold claims in California.[30] Rights to divert water for beneficial use are dated at the time of the claim; this date establishes a priority date. If the flow of a river on any one day is sufficient to provide for only two-thirds of the amount actually appropriated, a call on the river will shut off the diversions of the lowest priority rights to one-third of the water. This lexicographical allocative system fulfills all the demands of appropriators in order of decreasing priority until the available water is exhausted, at which point the remaining appropriators get none.

The priority system has the virtue of clarity. It provides a clear indication of how rights will be allocated if the quantity of water

30. *Irwin* v. *Phillips*, 5 Cal. 140 (1855).

available is reduced. The priority system, however, should be viewed as providing an initial basis for exchange rather than as a final solution to the problem of fluctuating water supplies.

An appropriator with a relatively senior priority date is exposed to less risk than a more junior appropriator. Given diminishing returns, however, one would expect senior appropriators receiving their full appropriations to place a lower value on the last unit of water diverted than would junior appropriators receiving nothing. Thus, even though juniors might be cut off completely under the priority system, one would expect further exchange to occur, with senior users selling or leasing water to junior users. These informal, unrecorded exchanges are common according to people active in the water market.[31] They reduce the exposure to risk of junior appropriators; the opportunity to purchase water in the face of an exhausted supply is certainly superior to having no opportunity to obtain water at all.

An important accommodation to the need to share risks is the mutual water companies, which dominate the water market in Colorado. Of the 20,000 decreed rights on the Arkansas River basin, for example, nearly all of the roughly 100 rights with priorities dated 1907 or sooner are owned by mutual companies.[32] Users own shares in a company, which in turn owns water rights under the priority system. Ownership of shares entitles one to a proportion of the company's water equal to the proportion of shares owned. Within the company, shares may be given priorities or they may be prorationed. Whatever the arrangement, trading or renting of water is common among members and does not require a court decree. Mutual companies thus serve to economize on transaction costs as well as to facilitate risk sharing.[33] The shares of these mutual companies are traded in the market, just as shares of stock in companies are traded. The

31. Interviews in September 1981 with Paul Murphy and Sandy MacDougall, attorneys; Kenneth J. Cooper, Assistant Division Engineer, Colorado Water Division 2; and Jack McCoullough, former president, Twin Lakes Reservoir and Canal Co.

32. Because no record is kept of who owns water rights (only initial court decrees are recorded), it is necessary to rely on the estimates of active observers of the market. This estimate by Kenneth Cooper was confirmed by other observers. In the summer of 1981, a year of above-normal precipitation, no right decreed more recently than 1906 received water from the Arkansas.

33. For a discussion, see Wells A. Hutchins, *Water Rights Laws in the Nineteen Western States*, vol. 1, Department of Agriculture Miscellaneous Publication 1206 (Washington, D.C.: Government Printing Office, 1971).

purchase of shares in mutual companies is an important source of water for municipalities as well as for farmers.[34]

It is in the preclusion of private speculation that the courts have most clearly demonstrated their aversion to the free play of the marketplace and to the possibility of individuals and firms profiting in it. Unless they are made by farmers, profits appear unseemly to the judicial mind: "Our Constitution guarantees a right to appropriate, not a right to speculate. The right to appropriate is for *use,* not merely for profit."[35] This muddled statement was issued in stripping a private company of water storage rights it had acquired in anticipation of selling them to municipal and other users. The company could have acquired the rights if purchasers were already under contract, but could not purchase the rights otherwise. This policy gives an advantage to mutual companies in the development of water projects, since the members are purchasers, but it makes it difficult for a nonconsumer to bear the burden, and receive potential profits, of investing in water projects. The storage of water is common but not without risk. The value of water stored for summer use, for example, will depend on precipitation amounts and demands that summer. By barring the company from the opportunity to speculate by storing water, the courts have placed the burden of storage costs directly on consumers.

In a recent ruling, the special water judge appointed by the Colorado Supreme Court cited a test by which other jurists could detect the evil of speculative intent:

> The application itself, without other evidence, can indicate by the size of the quantity claimed and the uses listed and the general purposes *only* being stated, that it is pure speculation for monetary or pecuniary benefit and that the decree is sought for profit, rather than actual beneficial use by the applicant.[36]

Again, one wonders about the court's logic. Should developers be barred from the purchase of large quantities of land if they can state only some "general" use, perhaps residential development, because the obvious intent is profit? Should law firms be barred from tying

34. McCoullough interview.

35. *Colorado River Water Conservancy District* v. *Vidler Tunnel Water Company*, Colo., 594 p. 2d 566.

36. *Southeastern Colorado Water Conservancy District* v. *Huston,* 79-CW-1 (Arapahoe, Colorado, 1981).

up large quantities of office space if they can state only some vague intent such as serving more clients, on grounds this reveals a clear desire to earn profit? The refusal by the courts to permit firms to acquire rights in water for speculative purposes deprives the market of an important specialized function—the acceptance of risk for the possibility of profit. A further difficulty with the limitation is the problem it creates for efficient groundwater allocation.

GROUNDWATER

Colorado law recognizes two kinds of groundwater, tributary and nontributary. Tributary groundwater, which flows into surface streams, is allocated under the normal appropriation system. Nontributary groundwater, however, is not allocated under the appropriation system in its usual form.[37]

One difficulty involved in tributary groundwater is that the receiving surface water typically is appropriated to senior users, so that wells tapping underground flows may be shut off in the face of calls on the stream. This problem may be overcome by efforts of the junior well owners to augment the water in the system so they can continue pumping without injury to senior appropriators. The augmentation may take the form of a purchase of shares from a mutual water company. A developer, for example, might acquire the right to drill wells for a subdivision by buying shares of a mutual water company and turning them over to the state engineer, who acts as manager of the stream. These shares can then be used to augment stream flows. Another kind of water club, an association of well users, may form to facilitate augmentation schemes. The Groundwater Appropriators of the South Platte (GASP), for example, has acquired junior surface rights, which yield water during periods of abundant flow that can be pumped back into the aquifer to augment it. The process is cheap and obviates interbasin diversions.[38]

37. H. J. Morel-Seytoux, R. A. Young, and G. E. Radosevich, "Systematic Design of Legal Regulations for Optimal Surface-Groundwater Usage, Phase I," Completion Report No. 53 (Fort Collins, Colo.: Colorado State University, August 1973).

38. Chin Y. Lee, A. Razig Qazi, and Jerris A. Daniels, "A Digital Model Applied to Ground Water Recharge and Management," *Water Resources Bulletin* 16 (June 1980): 514–521.

Nontributary aquifers are those whose water does not flow into a surface water system.[39] Waters designated as nontributary are administered by the state's Ground Water Commission, which is directed by the state engineer. Alternatively, a local district may be formed to administer the resource. In allocating water from a nontributary deposit, the law provides for a significant departure from the priority system:

> While the doctrine of prior appropriation is recognized, such doctrine should be modified to permit the full economic development of designated ground water resources. Prior appropriations of ground water should be protected and reasonable ground water pumping levels maintained, but not to include the maintenance of historical water levels.[40]

The state engineer and Ground Water Commission have adopted a variety of formulae for allocating water under this provision. In the Northern High Plains, the commission developed a 3-mile–40 percent–25-year rule. The state engineer checks to see whether the present use by wells within a three-mile radius of a prospective pumping site would use up 40 percent of the available water within twenty-five years. If not, a right to divert a given amount of water through pumping is granted.[41] This procedure, modified to adjust for the overappropriation that emerges from overlapping three-mile circles, requires that the water thus appropriated be put to a beneficial use.[42] In other basins, net withdrawals in any one year are limited to one percent of the basin's estimated initial capacity, so that the basin can be expected to be depleted in 100 years.

All these measures are responses to the common property problem of nontributary aquifers; given a large number of users of the aquifer, no one user will have a significant interest in maintaining water levels in the aquifer. The result is generally thought to be excessive use of the resource.[43]

39. In a finding reminiscent of Learned Hand's definition of monopoly, the court has held that groundwater whose removal would affect surface flows within forty years is tributary, while if the effect is likely to take 100 years or more, it is not. The status of intermediate cases has not been determined. *District 10 Water Users Association* v. *Barnett,* Colo., 599 P. 2d 894 (1979).

40. C. R. S. §37-90-102.

41. *Fundingsland* v. *Colorado Ground Water Commission,* Colo., 468 P. 2d 835 (1970); *Berens* v. *Colorado Ground Water Commission,* Colo., 614 P. 2d 352 (1980).

42. *Thompson* v. *Colorado Ground Water Commission,* Colo., 575 P. 2d 372 (1978).

43. The classic statement of the problem is found in Anthony Scott, "The Fishery: The Objectives of Sole Ownership," *Journal of Political Economy* 63 (August 1955): 116–124.

One way of dealing with the common property problem is to unify its ownership under a single agent who would then have an economic interest in efficiently allocating use of the aquifer over time. But this interest results from the opportunity to profit from wise use, an interest not viewed with favor by the courts. Indeed, a recent attempt to acquire underground water was rejected on grounds it might achieve precisely what one would expect from unified ownership:

> If a claim for water in an application for adjudication is phrased in pure general language for extreme magnitudes of amount . . . and is thereby attempting to tie up . . . vast quantities of underground water and, thus, antedate those who later might have a real need and uses, and force them to deal with the owner of the conditional decree, such claim is not within the principle of the maximum use policy or in line with case law.[44]

An attempt at unified ownership thus would be thwarted by the courts. Note that the problem of monopoly implied in the ruling above ignores the alternative of purchasing other water rights. Once again, the principal objection seems to be that firms acquiring such rights might profit from them. But it is the opportunity to earn profits that moves firms in the direction of efficient allocations. Water is too valuable a resource not to be left to profit-seeking firms.

SUMMARY

Prior appropriation doctrine provides for a system of property rights that could form the basis for a reasonably efficient allocation of water. But, as applied in Colorado, several difficulties exist. Defining rights as rights to divert but permitting transfers based on adversarial proceedings to determine consumptive use increases transactions and information costs and creates a perverse set of incentives against conservation. The doctrine of beneficial use creates unnecessary uncertainty in the title to rights. The judicial distaste for profit reduces the opportunity for profit-seeking firms to assume risks in developing water and seek to unify ownership of common property resources.

Colorado's prior appropriation doctrine, the central feature of which is a private market for rights in water, thus poses an intriguing dilemma. The courts that regulate this market have exhibited, in

44. *Southeastern Colorado Water Conservancy District* v. *Huston,* 79-CW-1 (Arapahoe, Colorado, 1981).

ruling after ruling, a fundamental lack of confidence in the efficacy of private-market solutions. The result is a needlessly costly and uncertain system in which innovation is difficult. The fear and loathing of the private market under prior appropriation doctrine, of course, does have one other significant result—a greatly expanded role for the judicial system that administers it. The relatively simple steps of defining and recording existing rights in terms of consumptive use, leaving to the market the issue of what sorts of uses are beneficial, would significantly enhance the ability of the private market to serve the interests of consumers of water in Colorado.

Chapter 5

INSTITUTIONAL RESTRICTIONS ON THE TRANSFER OF WATER RIGHTS AND THE SURVIVAL OF AN AGENCY

Micha Gisser
Ronald N. Johnson

> *"Restrictions upon the transfer of water rights, just as those upon the transfer of any property, should be viewed with suspicion."*[1]

Throughout the United States, conservancy districts frequently place broad restrictions on the transfer of water rights. The Northern Colorado Water Conservancy District, for example, explicitly prohibits the sale of water allotments outside district boundaries, and New Mexico's Middle Rio Grande Conservancy District (MRGCD) has refused to approve the transfer of water rights from within the district to points outside its boundaries.[2] The restrictions themselves, while indicative of inefficiencies, are not sufficient to conclude that an inefficient allocation of the water resource necessarily results. For example, to the extent that rights are not well defined, the most frequently raised argument in discussions of water transfers, transfer can result in a net loss of economic wealth.[3] Opposition to transfer

1. J.W. Milliman, "Water Law and Private Decision-Making: A Critique," *Journal of Law and Economics* 2 (October 1959): 54.

2. See Raymond L. Anderson, "Windfall Gains from Transfer of Water Allotments within the Colorado–Big Thompson Project," *Land Economics* 43 (August 1967): 265–73; Joseph L. Sax, *Water Law: Cases and Commentary* (Boulder, Colo.: Pruett Press, 1965); and Walter R. Parr, "Water Law: Legal Impediments to Transfers of Water Rights," *Natural Resources Journal* 7 (July 1967): 439.

3. See L.M. Hartman and Don Seastone, *Water Transfers: Economic Efficiency and Alternative Institutions* (Baltimore: Johns Hopkins University Press, 1970), pp. 6–33;

can then be justified where the property rights structure lacks the precision and enforcement to prevent negative externalities or uncompensated third-party effects. Furthermore, restrictions on transfer may be imposed to ensure payment of capital and maintenance costs. With changing conditions one can anticipate that some water users will want to sell their water rights outside the system. In the absence of a prior restrictive agreement, the departure of some water users means that remaining users will have to shoulder a greater share of the fixed capital and maintenance costs. The possibility of this departure can be expected to reduce the initial incentives for membership in the organization and to make it more costly to obtain financing. Thus, formal restrictions on the transfer of water rights may be required to reduce the incentive for opportunistic behavior.

In this paper we consider the general objections to transfer as well as those specific to the MRGCD. The first section presents a conceptual framework for analyzing externalities in water transfers. The justification of restrictions on transfers on the basis of ill-defined rights is shown to depend on whether rights are defined on the basis of consumptive use and whether there are ample checks against potential third-party impairments. We then compare the derived criteria for a well-defined property rights system to the rules and regulations pertaining to transfer in the state of New Mexico, where it appears that the necessary conditions for a well-defined system have been met.

The third section of this paper proposes an explanation of why the MRGCD restricts transfer. Water users within the district boundaries have historically been viewed by the conservancy as having the right to use water but not to transfer it. Findings indicate that the behavior of the MRGCD cannot be justified on the grounds of the internalization of externalities nor by an obligation to repay incurred debts. Rather, the district's behavior is more likely that of a political entity attempting to survive in a changing environment.

The transfer of water is a major concern in the western states. Institutions such as conservancy districts provide a form of collective action but appear to have their own set of costs. As this paper hopes to demonstrate, restrictions on transfer can be expected to reduce

Charles L. Meyers and Richard A. Posner, *Market Transfers of Water Rights: Toward an Improved Market in Water Resources* (Arlington, Va.: National Water Commission, 1971), pp. 27–32; and H.S. Burness and J.P. Quirk, "Water Law, Water Transfers and Economic Efficiency: The Colorado River," *Journal of Law and Economics* 23 (April 1980): 111–34.

allocative efficiency and increase the cost of development while members of the agency become the prime beneficiaries.

WATER RIGHTS AND EXTERNALITIES

The rules used to define the rights to a resource affect the allocation of that resource. Most property rights definitions clearly specify the right to use, exclude, and transfer, which normally facilitates market allocation and fosters the achievement of an efficient outcome.[4] But concomitant with the hypothesized efficient outcome is the criteria that the definition of water rights consider third-party impairment. To the extent that property rights are well defined, the contention that prohibition on transfers can be justified on the basis of negative externalities loses credibility. This section offers a simplified model of water allocation that should convey the basic principles of a well-defined property rights system. This model suggests that the maximum quantity of water an individual can transfer to another party without impairment to others is the amount to which the seller has a consumptive-use right.

At the heart of the problem of water allocation is the fact that the same water is used and reused along a river basin. A farmer diverting water from a river will decrease flow at the point of diversion by the amount diverted. But not all water diverted will be consumed. Some water will be absorbed by plants and some will be lost to the system by evaporation. The remaining portion of the diverted water will usually return via underground seepage to the river system. The return flow then becomes available to downstream users. Clearly, actions of upstream users that affect return flows can affect downstream users.

To illustrate the potential for problems when rights are ill-defined, consider the following example. There are three users along a river, and flow at the head of the stream is 1,000 acre-feet per unit of time (per year). Farmer A, at the head of the stream, diverts 1,000 acre-feet, consumes 500, and returns 500 to the stream. Downstream, farmer B diverts 500 acre-feet and returns 250, and farmer C diverts

4. For a discussion of the structure of property rights and how they affect subsequent contracting, see Steven N.S. Cheung, "The Structure of a Contract and the Theory of a Non-Exclusive Resource," *Journal of Law and Economics* 13 (April 1970): 49–70.

250 acre-feet and returns 125. The three users divert a total of 1,750 acre-feet, a greater amount than the initial stream flow. Now assume that for each of the three users, an acre-foot of water has a net value of $1. If a buyer of water rights who planned to consume all the water he or she diverts was to offer farmer A $1,100 for the right to divert 1,000 acre-feet, farmer A would gain $100 by selling but farmers B and C would be subjected to a combined loss of $750. There would be a net loss for the entire system of $650.

With property rights based on diversion, third-party impairment is likely to follow whenever transfers alter the ratio between consumptive use and diversion. If, however, it were stipulated that consumptive use rather than diversion was the measure of the water right, then farmer A could sell no more than 500 acre-feet. Because the transfer would be equivalent to farmer A's current act of consuming 500 acre-feet, there would be no third-party impairment. Basing water rights on consumptive use rather than on diversion offers a check against third-party impairment. Furthermore, consumptive-use rights can be shown to be consistent with the criteria for an efficient allocation of water resources.

To further demonstrate and to provide additional examples and qualifications, let us assume there are only two users along a stream and that stream flow is large relative to diversion at any point along the river.[5] The relatively large size of stream flow may result from a regional agreement among states that calls for a certain flow of water at a particular point downstream, such as the one that exists between Texas and New Mexico regarding the Rio Grande. The total amount of consumptive water appropriated by the two users leaves a flow that precisely satisfies the compact agreement. Provided that water rights are based on consumptive use, are transferable, and have relatively low transaction costs, an efficient allocation that results in the maximization of the water resources–use value will be obtained.[6] Maximization in this example is characterized by the value of the marginal physical product (*VMP*) of consumptive use being equal for all users.

5. This model ignores evaporation and seepage problems, but even if these factors were incorporated into the model, the general conclusion would remain intact.

6. Our statement concerning the achievement of an efficient allocation does ignore problems associated with changing water quality as a result of a change in use. Although real, that problem is not an issue that can be related to conservancy districts' restrictions on transfer. At no time that we are aware of has the issue of water quality been utilized by the districts as a reason for opposing transfer.

The *VMP* of water is the dollar value of the addition to total output from an incremental increase in the amount of water applied. For example, if by applying one additional unit of water during the season a farmer can obtain two additional units of output and sell them in a competitive market for $2, the *VMP* is $4. The *VMP* depends not only on the market value of the output but also on the levels of other factors used in the production process; hence different users (for example, farmers with different land qualities) will have different *VMP* schedules. For our purpose here, the *VMP* schedules are the derived demand functions for water and accordingly are negatively sloped in the relevant range. Note that the *VMP* of water can be measured in units of consumptive use (VMP_C) or in units of diverted water (VMP_D). As we will show, however, maximization of the aggregate use value of water is achieved when all users equate the VMP_C of consumptive use rather than their VMP_D of water diverted.

To demonstrate the validity of the above statement, we return to the example of two users, each of whom owns a certain amount of consumptive-use rights to water. Let the value of the marginal physical product of diverted water be denoted by VMP_D^1 for water diverted by user 1 and VMP_D^2 water diverted by user 2, who is located downstream from user 1. Let R denote the return-flow coefficient (the fraction of diverted water not consumed). Assume that $R_1 = 0.75$ and $R_2 = 0.5$; that is, user 1 returns to the stream 0.75 of the diverted water, and user 2 returns 0.5 of the diverted water.

Initially each user is consuming the full allotment of water and $VMP_D^1 = VMP_D^2 = \$2$. With the VMP_D s equal but the users having different return-flow coefficients, it can be shown that gains from trade exist. By purchasing one acre-foot of consumptive-use rights from user 2, user 1 could increase diversion by more than one acre-foot. The reasoning here is that a consumptive-use right is proportional to the amount diverted. If we denote C as the consumptive-use right and S as diversion, then $C \equiv (1-R)S$. This relationship is in fact an identity. Accordingly, a purchase of one acre-foot of consumptive-use rights by user 1 permits an increase in diversion by four acre-feet [$4 = 1/(1-0.75)$]. The transfer will increase the value of user 1's output by approximately $8 [$2 × 4]. User 2 in selling one-acre foot will now have to decrease diversion by two acre-feet [$2 = 1/(1-0.5)$] and the value of user 2's output will then fall by approximately $4. Trade between the two users results in a net gain of $4. As additional amounts are traded, diminishing returns will cause

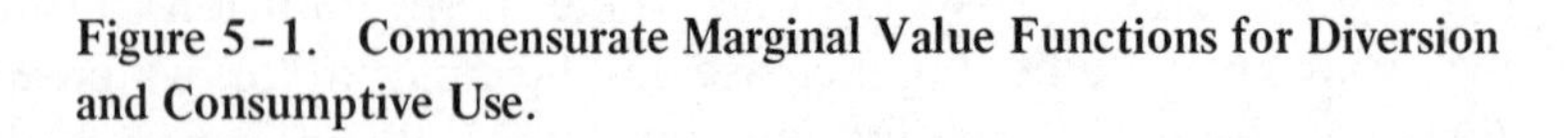

Figure 5-1. Commensurate Marginal Value Functions for Diversion and Consumptive Use.

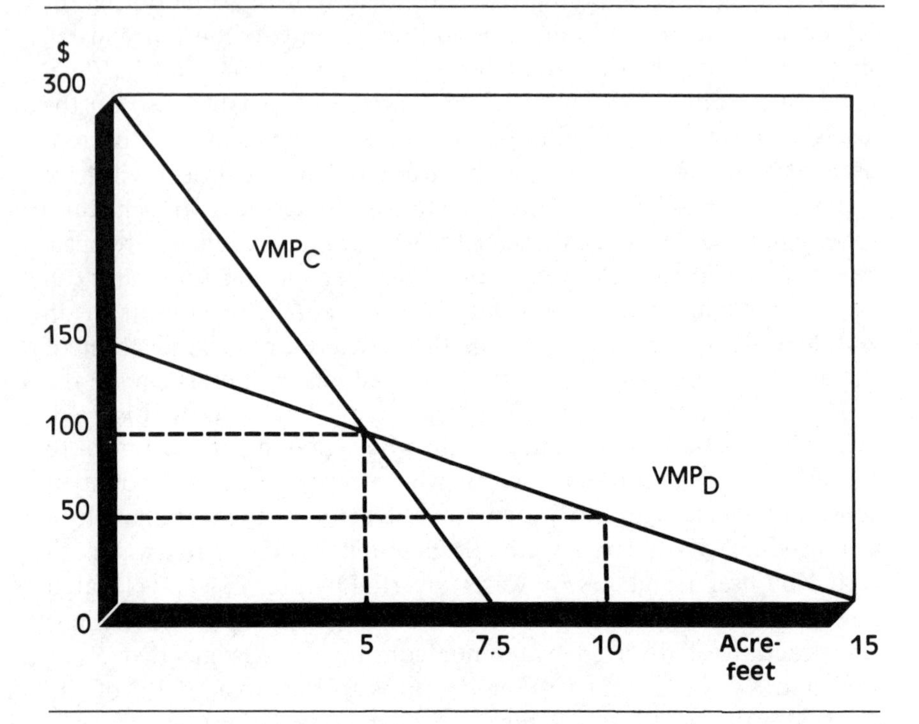

VMP_D^1 to fall and VMP_D^2 to rise. Eventually, an equilibrium will be established when $VMP_D^1/(1-R_1) = VMP_D^2/(1-R_2)$, at which point the aggregate-use value for the given stock of water will have reached a maximum. By definition, there are no further gains to be had from trade. The equilibrium condition indicates that unless return-flow coefficients are the same for all users, simply equating the marginal values of diverted water across all users does not lead to a maximum.

Furthermore, dividing the *VMP* of diverted water by $(1-R)$ yields the marginal value of consumptive use at the equilibrium point. This follows directly from the identity $C \equiv (1-R)S$ and can be simply illustrated with Figure 5-1. Let the value of the marginal product of diverted water have the explicit form of $VMP_D = 150-10\,S$. If the return-flow coefficient is equal to 0.5, then it follows that the value of the marginal product function for consumptive use must take the form $VMP_C = 300 - 40\,C$. The two functions must be commensurate. In other words, if the user in question were allowed to divert 10 acre-feet, the total use value would be equal to $1,000. This is the area underneath the VMP_D function in Figure 4–1 up to 10 units of diversion(s). Given that R is equal to 0.5, the area under the VMP_C function out to 5 acre-feet is also equal to $1,000. Note that when the user diverts 10 acre-feet, VMP_D is equal to $50. Dividing VMP_D by $(1-R)$ yields $100, which is exactly equal to the commensurate VMP_C amount for 5 acre-feet of consumptive use.

The intuitive argument presented above can be stated more formally and easily applied to a case where there are n users along the stream. To demonstrate, consider a stream with a headwater flow of $\hat{S}$ acre-feet and a compact agreement calling for a flow downstream amounting to $\bar{S}$ acre-feet per unit of time. Assume that there is no augmentation to flow and no evaporation along the stream. Since water is fully appropriated, the n users are constrained by the following equation:

$$\sum_{i=1}^{n} (1-R_i)S_i = \hat{S} - \bar{S} = S^* \qquad (5\text{-}1)$$

Here, S_i is the amount diverted by user i, R_i is i's return-flow coefficient, which of course can vary across users, and S^* is the total consumption constraint. The i's can also be thought of as representing location along the water course with user 1 at the head of the stream. We make no presumption about the size and related location of various users. Rather, demand for water at a given location depends, in part, on the attributes of the site. For example, the demand for water in a mining operation is site specific. We do assume, however, that stream flow at any given point i is sufficient to satisfy the diversion requirements that emerge from the maximization problem. Later in the analysis we will impose flow constraints.

Denoting the value of the marginal physical product of diverted water for the ith user as VMP_i and assuming the cost of diverting is zero, the optimization problem becomes one of maximizing,

$$\sum_{i=1}^{n} \int_0^{Si} f_i'(\alpha_i)\, d\alpha_i \qquad (5\text{-}2)$$

subject to Equation (5–1). Here, f_i' is the mathematical notation for VMP_i, and α_i is the dummy variable of integration. Setting the proper Lagrange equation, differentiating and equating to zero yields the following solution:

$$\frac{f_1'}{1-R_1} = \frac{f_2'}{1-R_2} = \ldots = \frac{f_n'}{1-R_n} = \lambda \qquad (5\text{-}3)$$

where λ is the Lagrange multiplier. Since f_i' is the value of the *VMP* for diverted water, dividing it by $(1-R_i)$ converts it to the value of the *VMP* of consumptive use. Equation 5-3 tells us that in order to maximize total value along a stream, the value of the *VMP* of consumptive use must be the same for all users. By applying similar procedures it can be shown that if the marginal cost of diverting water (maintaining ditches, for example) is K_i' for the ith user, then the term $f_i'/(1-R_i)$ in Equation 4-3 should be replaced by $(f_i' - K_i')/(1-R_i)$.

The above results suggest that with rights based on consumptive use, individual rightholders can transfer those rights by simple two-party arrangements, resulting in the constrained maximization depicted by Equation 5-3. Indeed, once rights are defined on the consumptive-use basis, water becomes like any other private good. Should, for example, a new user purchase water rights from any of the existing users, that transaction need not affect the amount of water utilized by others who are not a part of the transaction. The sale of a consumptive-use right protects against third-party impairment because the total amount of water available to all other users is unaffected. This result holds regardless of whether the seller and purchaser have similar return-flow coefficients. The stock of water is depleted not by diversion but rather by consumption. The sale of 20 acre-feet of consumptive-use rights bv a party with a return-flow coefficient of 0.75 to a party who had a return coefficient of 0.5 would alter diversion amounts but not consumption. While the seller had previously diverted 80 acre-feet in order to consume 20, the new user could only divert 40 acre-feet. Any amount of diversion greater than 40 acre-feet would exceed the new user's consumptive right and third-party impairment would result. Defining and enforcing rights on the basis of consumptive use alleviates the need to explicitly protect returns flows that are utilized by downstream users. The appendix to this paper offers a more formal presentation of the effects of transferring rights by providing some numerical examples.

To this point we have been assuming that stream flows are ample at each point of diversion. Essentially, this amounts to arguing that there are no additional constraints on the system other than those contained in Equation 5-1. On large streams and rivers, any given user's diversion is likely to be substantially less than stream flow at the point of diversion. Our assumption, then, that there are no binding flow constraints does not appear to constitute a significant omission. On smaller creeks and streams, however, the possibility of binding flow constraints cannot be readily dismissed. When binding flow constraints are present, we can no longer be assured that transfer is a one-to-one operation. That is, third-party impairment can result even when consumptive use is the measure of the water right that can be transferred.

For example, the transfer of a water right upstream with consumptive use and diversion remaining the same will necessarily reduce stream flow between the old point of diversion and the new point. There is no guarantee that stream flow between the new and the old points will be sufficient to satisfy existing rightholders located in that region. Accordingly, third-party impairment can result. Although third-party impairments can result even when consumptive use is the measure of the right, the results shown in the appendix indicate that maximization does not call for a total ban on transfer. Rather, optimization requires that the volume to be transferred be reduced below that which would occur if only two parties, buyer and seller, were involved.[7]

While we have argued that defining rights in terms of consumptive use and allowing transfer will lead to a constrained maximization it does not automatically follow that water rights should be defined on that basis. Returning to our identity statement, $C \equiv (1-R)S$, it is clear that measuring actual consumptive use requires kmowledge of both return-flow coefficients and diversion. The cost of monitoring and enforcing rights based on consumptive use demands greater information than if rights were simply defined on the amount diverted. Where water is abundant and hence its scarcity value is low, defining rights on the basis of consumptive use may not be economical, which may well explain why the eastern states have adhered to the riparian doctrine while states in the arid West have defined rights based on the appropriative doctrine.[8]

7. For a more detailed discussion of the problems associated with binding flow constraints, see R. N. Johnson, M. Gisser, and M. Werner, "The Definition of a Surface Water Right and Transferability," *Journal of Law and Economics* 24 (October 1981): 273-88.

8. See J. W. Milliman, "Water Law and Private Decision-Making."

Even under the appropriative doctrine, however, rights are not always clearly defined in terms of consumptive use. Diversion still appears to be the measure of the right in some areas. For example, under California's mixed system of riparian, correlative, and appropriative doctrine it is difficult to make any statement about the degree of precision in defining water rights and the effects on efficiency if transfer were freely allowed. Where rights are not clearly defined, proposals such as those for water banking may offer an improvement.[9] Restrictions on transfer in such cases may be justified, for as we have shown, third-party impairment can result when only diversion is measured.

Even where consumptive use is the measure of the right transferable, problems can arise. Estimates of return flows are subject to error, which can result in third-party impairment. Accordingly, even where water laws are based on consumptive use and transfer is allowed, constraints on certain actions may exist. For example, a farmer who changes to a new method of irrigation and claims an increase in return flow may not be able to convince the state water authorities that for the same diversion he is now consuming less and should be allowed therefore to sell the excess consumptive rights. Legal impediments on the sale of salvaged or conserved water do appear to exist in some states.[10] However, in New Mexico, an irrigator who reduces consumptive use can sell the excess or apply it to additional acreage. Because the New Mexico state engineer requires that such "water spreading" be accompanied by special metering, the cost of which is to be paid by the irrigator, few irrigators have elected to do so. Rules of thumb that specify standard water use for specific crops, while inflexible and in need of change, can reflect monitoring costs, which will be a factor in deciding alterations in the law.

It must be emphasized that the measure of any right is always a matter of degree. Because of the prohibitive cost, no contract is likely to specify all relevant margins or possible contingencies. But as

9. See Sotirios Angelides and Eugene Bardach, *Water Banking: How To Stop Wasting Agricultural Water* (San Francisco: Institute for Contemporary Studies, 1978). On the subject of water right transfers in California, see Clifford T. Lee, *The Transfer of Water Rights in California*, Staff Paper no. 5 (Governor's Commission to Review California Water Rights Law, December 1977).

10. See Lee Brown, et al. *Water Reallocation, Market Proficiency, and Conflicting Social Values* (Albuquerque, N.M.: Bureau of Business and Economics Research, University of New Mexico, 1980).

the value of water rises, we would expect rights to become more precisely defined. Indeed, greater precision in measurement and definition of rights is occurring. For example, in 1973 the Wyoming legislature replaced its archaic rules that held that water rights could not be detached from the land with a new law permitting transfer and relating quantification to consumptive use. (Wyo. Stat. 41–3–104, 1977). Similar changes have been made in Montana and other western states.

This exercise indicates that a well-defined property rights system for water will specify that consumptive use is the measure of the right's transferability. Given that third-party impairment can still occur where stream flow is low or because of measurement error, we anticipate that even in a well-defined system grievances will occur and procedural checks will be designed to detect third-party impairments. Transfer of water rights under a well-defined system will allow the resource to be employed by the highest valued users and the efficiency conditions derived here will be achieved. On the other hand, institutional restrictions on transfer where rights are well defined would appear to be contrary to efficiency criteria and result in a lower aggregate-use value for the resource. The MRGCD of New Mexico provides an example of restrictions on transfer that lower aggregate-use value even though water rights in that state are well defined.

THE TRANSFER OF WATER RIGHTS IN NEW MEXICO

New Mexico has a broad statutory framework and administrative procedures that allow for the transfer of water rights. Section 72–5–24 of the New Mexico Statutes Annotated, 1978, permits appropriators, with the approval of the state engineer, to change the purpose of use or change the point of diversion of their water rights. The water right may be sold in whole or in part and may also be sold apart from the land. A person desiring to transfer a water right must make formal application and provide maps and a detailed description of the proposed change to the state engineer, who will approve the application for transfer if it is not to the detriment of existing rights and subject to certain rules. Detrimental effects are the only real basis the state engineer has for denying the transfer.

If the application is in proper form the state engineer issues a Notice for Publication, which is published for three consecutive weeks in a general-circulation newspaper in the stream system in which the transfer is to take place. Any individual or group may protest the transfer on the grounds that it would be truly detrimental to their valid and existing rights in the waters of the stream system in question. The state engineer then sets a date and place for a hearing at which both sides of the question are fully presented. Upon reaching a final decision on a protested application, the state engineer issues a Findings and Order. Either party may appeal the decision of the state engineer by filing in the district court of the proper jurisdiction.

An investigation of applications to transfer a water right and dedications of water rights reveals that a measure of the consumptive use and diversion requirements are stated.[11] For particularly complicated transfers involving a change from agricultural to industrial use and surface water to groundwater use the forms and data collection process are detailed. Simple transfers may require only a few pages of the necessary forms. In addition to specifying the quantity of water to be transferred and locations involved, the state engineer may also specify the flow rate of diversion if not implicit in the application itself. Transfers that change the purpose of use are likely to affect the rate at which a given quantity of water is diverted and consumed. In order to avoid impairment during the dry season, flow rates may be restricted. As a case in point, the application of Kaiser Steel Corporation to change a point of diversion and to change place and purpose of use from agricultural to industrial was amended by the state engineer. Pursuant to the findings of a hearing examiner the flow rate of diversion was explicitly reformulated so that the transfer would not cause impairment.[12] The applicant may be requested to alter the transfer amount or the manner in which the water will be applied.

In the area of transaction costs involving transfers, the New Mexico system compares favorably. In their comparison of the administrative procedures utilized in New Mexico with the judicial method employed in Colorado, Seastone and Hartman concluded that the New

11. For additional details and examples of water rights transfers in New Mexico, see Johnson, Gisser, and Werner, "Definition of Surface Water Right."

12. File no.'s 71-B, 0804-D, and 02560, State Engineer's Office, Santa Fe, New Mexico.

Mexico system is superior both in terms of cost and consistency in handling cases.[13] In New Mexico filing fees for an application to change a point of diversion or change a place or purpose of use is only $5.00.[14] Based on recent survey data the average transaction cost per acre-foot transferred is around $4.36, which when compared to the market value of an acre-foot of consumptive use ranging between $300 and $3,000 does not appear extravagant.[15] Should there be a protest hearing the cost of that hearing generally is under $300.[16] In the last few years the state engineer's office has averaged around 275 applications for transfer per year with only around 10 of those applications resulting in a formal hearing.[17] Of course, should one of the parties decide to appeal the ruling of the state engineer by filing in the district court, litigation costs can increase significantly. It is perhaps indicative of the procedures utilized by the state engineer that between 1956 and June 1979, there have been only fifty-eight appeals to the courts. Of the appeals made, the courts have concurred with the findings of the state engineer in 86 percent of those cases.[18]

In recent years, the annual budget for the state engineer's office has hovered around $3 million.[19] The budget includes expenditures for surveys as well as administrating transfers both for surface-water and groundwater rights. Total consumptive use in New Mexico is estimated to be around 2.3 million acre-feet per annum.[20] The cost of protecting rights on the basis of consumptive use amounts to about $1.30 per acre-foot per annum, which is not excessive considering

13. D.A. Seastone and L.M. Hartman, "Alternative Institutions for Water Transfers: The Experience in Colorado and New Mexico," *Land Economics* 39 (February 1963): 31–43.

14. New Mexico State Engineer, *Surface Water Rules and Regulations* (Santa Fe, N.M.: State Engineer's Office, 1953), p. 16.

15. Rahman Khoshakhlagh, "Forecasting the Value of Water Rights: A Case Study of New Mexico" (Ph.D. dissertation, University of New Mexico, 1977), p. 60.

16. Interviews with personnel of the State Engineer's Office, October 1980.

17. The figure in the text includes only applications to change place and/or purpose of use. The state engineer's office processed over 22,000 water-use-related instruments in the period 1 July 1976 to 30 June 1978. State Engineer, *Thirty-Third Biennial Report of the State Engineer* (Santa Fe, N.M.: State Engineer's Office, 1978).

18. D.E. Gray, "New Mexico View of Ground Water Law" (Santa Fe, N.M.: State Engineer's Office, 1979), p. 7.

19. State Engineer, *Biennial Report.*

20. Earl F. Sorenson, *Water Use by Categories in New Mexico Counties and River Basins, and Irrigated and Dry Cropland Acreage in 1975* (Santa Fe, N.M.: State Engineer's Office, 1977).

that the value of a water right typically approaches the $2,000 range. Of course, even if rights were defined solely on the basis of diversion, administrative cost would not be zero. Furthermore, given the increased possibilities of third-party impairment under a simple diversion rule, the value of water rights would likely fall.

The evidence present in this section leads us to conclude that water rights in New Mexico are well defined and consistent with the optimality conditions described in the previous section. With the existence of safeguards against third-party impairment, attempts to restrict the transfer of water rights by the MRGCD appear suspect. In the following section we consider the objections of the MRGCD to transfers of water rights.

TRANSFER RESTRICTIONS: THE CASE OF THE MIDDLE RIO GRANDE CONSERVANCY DISTRICT

A History of Transfer Restrictions

The Middle Rio Grand Conservancy District was conceived in the early 1920s when farmers in the Middle Rio Grande Valley were being subjected to serious flooding and a rising water table. The latter condition led to a salinity problem, and some agricultural lands became unsuited for growing crops. The farmers organized, and the state legislature officially recognized the MRGCD with passage of the Conservancy Act of 1925.[21] The conservancy proceeded to issue bonds and finance the repair of ditches and levies and the construction of a dam. Repayment of the loans and operation and maintenance expenditures were to come from a tax levied on property owners within the district. At the present time, the MRGCD jurisdiction covers approximately 227,760 acres along the Rio Grande River. The district's boundaries stretch 150 miles in length, vary in width from one to five miles, and fall within the most populous area of the state.

As a result of the district's projects, the salinity problem was reduced and flood protection was increased. In 1951 the district

21. For details of New Mexico's Conservancy Act, see New Mexico Statutes Annotated, 73-14-1, 1978.

entered into a contract with the U.S. Bureau of Reclamation. Under the terms of the contract, the Bureau of Reclamation assumed the bonded indebtedness of the district and contracted to perform maintenance and operations on many of the irrigation canals and ditches. The district agreed to pay operation and maintenance charges and to repay the bonded indebtedness assumed by the bureau at a zero interest rate.[22]

In constructing dams and participating in diversion projects, the district has accumulated a block of water rights. The state's Conservancy Act explicitly allows the district to be a legal holder of water rights, but the amount of water rights over which the district actually has control presents a legal problem. Persons who are currently located within the district's boundaries but whose rights predate the organization of the district are holders of a vested right.

> The rights of persons or public corporations and of other users of water, to the waters in and of the District for irrigation, water supply, industrial purposes, water power, or for any other purpose, shall extend only to such rights as were owned by them or their predecessors prior to their inclusion in the District; and to such use as could be made of such waters if the improvements of the District had not been made.[23]

The state engineer has taken the position that holders of individual rights that predate the organization may transfer rights within or outside the district's boundaries without the conservancy's approval.[24] Although the Rio Grande basin has not been fully adjudicated, the state engineer has estimated that 46 percent of the approximately 140,000 irrigated acre-feet within the district boundaries are appurtenant with water rights that predate the organization.[25]

The state engineer also clearly recognizes that the optimality conditions expressed in the first section of this paper can be violated by restrictions on transfers.

> The district's policy prevents the free economic competition for water which is necessary if our water resources are to find their way into the most eco-

22. Middle Rio Grande Conservancy District, "A Brief History of the Middle Rio Grande Conservancy District," (Albuquerque, N.M.: MRGCD, n.d.), p. 9.

23. New Mexico Statutes Annotated, 73-14-47(c), 1978.

24. Steve E. Reynolds, State Engineer of New Mexico, "Statement of Policy," 24 August 1959.

25. Steve E. Reynolds, State Engineer of New Mexico, "Affidavit Concerning Availability of Water for Rio Rancho Estates," 14 February 1975, p. 4.

nomic uses. New enterprises needing water in the Middle Valley outside the district boundaries are forced to pay inflated prices for water rights because, under the district's policy a large block of existing rights are made unavailable for such use at any price.[26]

The district's board of directors has asserted that even the transfer of vested water rights violates district laws.

> The District does object to any application for transfer of water rights out of the benefited area of the District for reasons that such transfers are in violation of law, not within the jurisdiction of the State Engineer, in violation of the assessment and lien rights of the District, and in violation of the lien rights and contract rights of the United States. Further, the District objects to such transfers outside the District for the reason that the same impair District water rights and water rights of property owners within the District.[27]

An examination of records in the state engineer's office indicates that since 1960 there has been a total of nineteen transfers of water rights from within to outside the district boundaries, all of which involved water rights that predate the organization of the district.

Until recently, the conservancy did not formally challenge the jurisdiction of the state engineer in such cases but instead routinely filed letters objecting to the transfers. However, in 1975 William and Nancy Cox made formal application to the state engineer for a change in the point of diversion and in place and purpose of use and for a change from surface right to a groundwater right.[28] The original use was agricultural on lands lying within the district. The intended purchaser was a real estate developer, and the new location was northwest of Albuquerque outside the district boundaries. Based on survey maps and sworn affidavits, the state engineer determined the existence of a water right predating the organization of the district. The conservancy formally protested the transfer by questioning the jurisdiction of the state engineer in a clear attempt to block the individual transfer of any water rights lying within the district.[29]

The conservancy's contention that water rights transfer would impair existing rightholders has not been substantiated by any hard

26. Steve Reynolds, State Engineer of New Mexico, "Memorandum," 24 August 1958, p. 1.

27. Letter from G.W. Hannett, Attorney, MRGCD, to James T. Everheart, State Engineer's Office, New Mexico (22 July 1971).

28. File no. 02327-A, RG-10591, and RG-6745, State Engineer's Office, Santa Fe, N.M.

29. File no. 02327-A, State Engineer's Office, District 1, Albuquerque, N.M.

evidence. Indeed, in the Cox case, the MRGCD did not object on the grounds of third-party impairment, but on jurisdictional grounds.[30] The state engineer in New Mexico is charged with approving transfers provided they do not result in third-party impairment. In the Cox case and in the other nineteen transfers, the state engineer did not detect a serious potential for third-party impairment. Furthermore, the conservancy has issued a blanket objection to transfer, making no attempt to specify why and how a particular transfer would cause impairment to existing rights.

As of 1981, the transfer requested by the Coxes in 1975 had not been undertaken. Conversations with the attorneys involved indicate that the applicant may have become frustrated by the lengthy legal maneuvering and the cost involved. The Cox case appears to have affected other rightholders, attempts to transfer, as the following statement from an internal memo obtained from the state engineer's office indicates.

> The Middle Rio Grande Conservancy District has protested all applications to transfer water rights from inside to outside the District since the Cox application was filed. A number of users listed have not filed applications to transfer because of the known policy of the District and are waiting the outcome of the Cox case.[31]

The MRGCD's policy of vigorously protesting transfers, by raising the costs of transactions, appears to have been effective.

In defense of its policy of opposing transfers the MRGCD has argued that repayment obligations to the federal government require restrictions. Essentially, the water right is viewed as collateral, a common stance taken by conservancy districts throughout the United States.[32] The frequency with which the argument is used does not, of course, imply validity. Repayment of financial obligations does not require blanket restrictions on the sale of goods. The actions taken by privately owned and managed water projects can provide some insight on this issue.

Collective effort has frequently been involved in the development of water resources in the arid western United States. The construction of irrigation ditches, canals, and reservoirs has permitted the

30. *Middle Rio Grande Conservancy District* v. *Cox*, N.M. 13th JDC, 7147, filed 4 August 1977.

31. Memo from J.L. Williams, Supervisor, District 1, to Don Klein, Legal Division, 13 January 1978.

32. See Meyers and Posner, *Market Transfers of Water Rights*, pp. 18–25.

realization of economies of scale in water delivery systems. But not all water projects are the work of governmental agencies. To facilitate contracting among various water users for the financing, construction, and maintenance of jointly used water works, a number of privately owned organizational entities have evolved. The *acequias* of northern New Mexico, community ditches constructed when the region was under Spanish and Mexican rule, offer an example of small, privately managed systems wherein individuals who own transferable water rights share the cost of ditch maintenance.[33] The ditches of the *acequias* are generally small, requiring no major capital outlays. Much larger projects, however, have been undertaken by mutual ditch companies. The mutual companies and stockholders hold a contract that charges the corporation with managing the business in the interest of the stockholders.[34] The corporation has the right to assess stockholders for capital and maintenance costs. Although the mutual ditch company may own the naked legal title to water rights, the stockholders are the actual owners of the water rights.

In Colorado, where mutual companies represent large blocks of water rights, stock certificates represent title to water rights, and stockholders may sell their water rights or change their places of diversion or use.[35] Shares are treated as vested water rights, much as a right obtained via direct appropriation. However, corporation bylaws may occasionally restrict transfer or sale of stock to avoid uneconomical deliveries and defaults on assessment charges.[36] Moreover, Denver attorney John P. Akolt III, who is familiar with transfers originating from mutual companies, suggests that "so long as any type of injury, be it economic or otherwise, would be prevented by a

33. For a discussion of the *acequias* and their bylaws, see Phil Lovato, *Las Acequias del Norte* (Taos, N.M.: Kit Carson Memorial Foundation, 1974).

34. For a discussion of mutual ditch companies, see R.J. Moses, "Irrigation Corporations," *Rocky Mountain Law Review* 32 (1960): 527–33. For an analysis of the legal structure of mutual ditch companies and the rights of shareholders in Colorado, see Gary L. Greer, "A Review of Recent Activity in Colorado Water Law," *Denver Law Journal* 47 (1970): 259–62.

35. For estimates of the amount of water rights held by some of the mutual companies in the Denver area, see R.L. Anderson, N.I. Wengert, and R.D. Heil, *The Physical and Economic Effect on the Local Agricultural Economy of Water Transfer from Irrigation Companies to Cities in the Northern Denver Metropolitan Area*, Report. no. 75 (Fort Collins, Colo.: Environmental Resource Center, Colorado State University, 1976). See also Greer, "Recent Activity in Colorado Water Law," p. 261.

36. Moses, "Irrigation Corporations," p. 529.

reasonable restriction on transfer, that such restriction would be upheld if challenged."[37] Similar restrictions, however, could be applied under Colorado law to a petition for transfer filed by a direct appropriator. Restrictions exist, but it seems apparent from the numerous transfers that have taken place that they cannot be applied in an arbitrary and capricious manner.

In Colorado mutual companies have provided large blocks of water rights for urban and industrial development. Transfer has been allowed as long as it did not impair existing rightholders, and the courts long ago resolved the issue of liability for corporate obligations and maintenance expenditures when a water right is transferred.

> In a 1907 Colorado case, the court found that the only particular in which the company or other stockholders could be injured was that the expense of maintaining the ditch would not be decreased by the proposed change, which, we take it, means that the expense of maintaining the ditch would be as great after, as before, the change. The decree therefore expressly provided that the proposed change should not be held in any manner to impair or affect the relative rights of the stockholders of the Wadsworth company as between themselves, and that the shares of capital stock of the petitioner should still be liable to assessment for maintaining the ditch the same as if the proposed change were not made. It further reserved to the corporation the same control to enforce its assessments which it always had exercised, and expressly saved to it the right to enforce its by-laws in all cases against the petitioner.[38]

The right to continue assessment after the transfer offers a seemingly simple solution to meeting the repayment obligation to the federal government. In the case of sale and transfer of water rights, new owners continue to be liable for assessments whether or not they utilize the delivery system of the ditch company. Of course, it would also be feasible after a transfer to continue taxing the land at the old point of use. That liens can be continued and obligations fulfilled is borne out by actual practice. In the Santa Cruz Irrigation District, a political subdivision under the laws of the state of New Mexico, transfers to locations outside district boundaries have been approved on the condition that land from which the water is to be transferred would continue to be liable to assessment by the district as irrigated land whether or not it is irrigated.[39] Irrigation districts

37. Communication to authors, 15 May 1981.
38. *Wadsworth Ditch Co.* v. *Brown*, 39 Colo. 57: 58 (1907).
39. See File no. 1659 and RG-23043, State Engineer's Office, Santa Fe, New Mexico.

operate more like mutual ditch companies than conservancy districts. Their tax base is restricted to water users, and often they are not engaged in contracting with the Bureau of Reclamation.[40]

While the argument that assessments can continue either at the new or old site offers a rebuttal to transfer objections, there are potential problems. First, if the lien is not transferred with the water right there is a possibility that the value of the old site will, in the absence of water, be reduced and increase the risk of default. However, just the opposite affect could also hold. Land values could rise as farm land is dried up and converted to urban and industrial use.

Second, the payment of operation and maintenance expenditures contains an element of subsidy and could lead to inefficiencies. With a share of total operation and maintenance expenditures being paid by nonusers and with the total volume of water delivered through the system declining, there is no guarantee that the remaining use values exceed total variable costs. Even though the rule of continuing assessments if rights are transferred preserves the financial integrity of the system, it removes incentives for remaining users to shut down when actual variable costs exceed remaining use value. Of course, contracting among remaining users and those who have sold rights outside the system could solve this problem. We would argue that such contracting is more likely where water rights are privately owned then where a public agency controls water allocation and depends on delivery for justification of its existence, as was the case in Utah. In 1981 the Intermountain Power Agency (IPA) purchased a large block of water from the shareholders of five water companies located near Delta, Utah. The transfer was from agriculture to industrial usage. The joint venture agreement between the IPA and the shareholders specified the amount of stock each shareholder could sell and provided for the elimination of water delivery to certain areas.[41]

In any event, this does not constitute an argument against transfer. If transfer is allowed, total use value for a given stock of water will be higher than if transfer were not allowed. This statement holds even when the delayed shutdown problem is taken into consideration.

40. See Sax, *Water Law*, pp. 270, 281–83.

41. *Article II General Provisions Joint Venture Agreement*, Consolidated Water Users. (Supplied by Thorpe A. Waddingham, Attorney at Law, Delta, Utah). Also see Victor F. Zonana, "Land vs. Energy: Quandry Over Water–To Sell It or Not–Faces Utah Farmers at Power-Plant Town" *Wall Street Journal*, 27 February 1981, p. 40.

In addition to the potential for continuing assessments either at the new site or the old, the MRGCD is well situated and is capable of remaining solvent. The ability to tax land and improvements within the district whether or not irrigation water is received is explicitly stated in the statutes governing the district.[42] The removal of water does not mean that the right to tax has vanished. Indeed, under the current tax scheme, three-fourths of the tax revenue collected comes from assessments on residential and industrial property that does not benefit directly from the use of irrigation water.[43] There are two basic forms of property classification: Class A properties are irrigable lands of a unit operation containing five acres or more; Class B properties are all other lands, urban and suburban. Class A properties are charged on a per-acre basis, while class B is assessed on an ad valorem basis using the county assessor's valuation of land and improvements. The amount of taxes levied on class A lands in 1978 was $714,663.66 and $1,971,948 on class B lands. Approximately $11,500,000 remains due to the United States for reimbursable construction costs. Annual repayments are in the neighborhood of $400,000.

Property values in the Middle Valley have risen dramatically in the last ten years because of inflation and a population influx. The indebtedness to the Secretary of Interior is, of course, stated in nominal dollars. The tax base, then, does appear sufficient, and it is worth noting that the Bureau of Reclamation has not joined the conservancy district in objecting to the transfers that have taken place since 1960.

The conservancy's opposition to the transfer of water rights outside the district cannot be justified on the basis of spillover effects or third-party impairment. Rather, the issue has been the control of water rights.

The Survival of an Agency

Having rejected the argument that the conservancy has restricted transfer because of its obligations to the Secretary of Interior or because of significant, unaccounted third-party effects, we propose another hypothesis to explain the reasons behind the conservancy's

42. New Mexico Statutes Annotated, 73-18-16, 1978.

43. *Annual Report of the Board of Directors of the Middle Rio Grande Conservancy District*, 1978, p. 21.

actions: the MRGCD seeks to survive and expand as a political entity in a changing environment.

Much of the recent research on the study of bureaucracy and representative government has pointed to the tendency of those who manage public entities to encourage the growth of their agencies and expand their budgets.[44] In this regard, the MRGCD budget is consistent with patterns expected when bureaucrats attempt to maximize their own self-interest by fostering the growth of their agency. From 1961 to 1971, total disbursements made by the MRGCD grew by 65 percent in nominal terms while the number of acres actually irrigated remained fairly constant and the consumer price index rose 37 percent. Operation and maintenance charges per acre irrigated went from $16.79 in 1961 to $33.90 in 1971.[45] In fiscal 1971 total disbursements were over $2 million. "Comparative cost trends both from public and private entities indicate that recent increases in components of O&M costs in the Middle Rio Grande Project Irrigation Division has been abnormally high, not only from a local standpoint, but when compared to national figures as well."[46] Such figures, however, are merely suggestive, and our hypothesis does not rest on them alone.

In recent years the conservancy has been losing the support of some of its main constituents–irrigators.[47] With a rising value of water in nonagricultural use, irrigators with water rights have sought to transfer those rights outside the district. The loss in the volume of water managed by the district will make it increasingly difficult to justify the existing budget, let alone its expansion. At the same time, the rising conservancy budget has brought increasing opposition from nonirrigators, who contribute three-fourths of the district's tax revenue.

44. The performance of public entities has been critically analyzed in William A. Niskanen, *Bureaucracy and Representative Government* (Chicago: Aldine-Atherton, 1971); Cotton M. Lindsay, "A Theory of Government Enterprise," *Journal of Political Economy* 84 (October 1976):1061–76; and Thomas E. Borcherding, ed., *Budgets and Bureaucrats: The Sources of Government Growth* (Durham, N.C.: Duke University Press, 1977).

45. Gordon Herkenhoff and Associates, Inc., *Middle Rio Grande Conservancy District, Management and Policy Study, Statistical Supplement*, (Albuquerque, N.M.: Gordon Herkenhoff and Associates), tables 1 and 2.

46. Ibid., p. 8.

47. See Sam Peltzman, "Toward a More General Theory of Regulation," *Journal of Law and Economics* 19 (August 1976): 211–40, for a general discussion of regulation and the effect of opposing group votes on the behavior of regulations as conditions change.

From its inception in the 1920s until 1975 the district was managed by a board of directors appointed by the court of the judicial district where the petition for the creation of the conservancy district was filed. The directors were to have derived at least 75 percent of their individual incomes from irrigation.[48] Since 1975, as a result of opposition from nonirrigators, board members are to be elected by voters residing within the district boundaries.[49] Over the last few years, millage rates applied to nonirrigator's property have fallen and budgetary growth has eased. But opposition by the board to transfer, as evidenced by the Cox case, has actually increased.

Conventional wisdom is that once governmental agencies are created it is next to impossible to dismantle them. The MRGCD is no exception. If the district can maintain control over water rights it will remain a strong political entity. The district's objective is apparent in the following statement by R.R. Nannings, the district general manager:

> Anyone who is aware of the water problems in the arid Southwest knows that we do not have an unlimited supply of water. However, priorities for the use of our water begin first with domestic use, moves next to industrial use with agriculture relegated to a lesser position. The needs of people predominate; the economics of the use of water dictate that industry has a higher position than agriculture. Leasing water to accommodate new development fits in with the surveillance of the ground water. It fits the State Engineer's program and the District has an opportunity to spread its tax base.[50]

Some leases, which by law cannot exceed fifty years, already have been made to users outside the district boundaries, indicating that the district is not opposed to transfer outside the boundaries provided it receives the revenue.[51] The potential revenues also explain why elected officials would oppose transfer by individuals. Conversations with district personnel indicate that revenue from leasing water will be used to reduce the tax rate of nonirrigators. Of course, since the conservancy is not a profit maximizer, such revenues are to be

48. New Mexico Statutes Annotated, 73-14-17, 1978.

49. Laws of New Mexico, 1975, chapter 262.

50. R.S. Nannings, General Manager, MRGCD, "Memorandum to the Board of Directors MRGCD," 24 May 1976. There are, in fact, no priorities attached to type of use of water in New Mexico. Regarding the last statement that "it fits the State Engineer's program," one can only note that the State Engineer supports transfer.

51. See *Annual Report of the Board of Directors of the Middle Rio Grande Conservancy District*, 1978, p. 30.

expended. With a growing urban population and a declining agricultural base, the conservancy is considering more elaborate channelization projects and other services to the community.

> With so much of the present development in our community occurring outside the boundaries of the district, new problems are developing. The future may provide the catalyst that will provide the solution to these problems. This could very possibly be one of a completely opposite nature to the one which led to the creation of the Middle Rio Grande Conservancy District. . . . It could evolve as one centering on the salvaging of all water available for its maximum and best use.[52]

It is conceivable that should the MRGCD lease water at a competitive rate and without regard to district boundaries, the argument against the district being the holder of water rights is largely one of distribution, not efficiency. But there remain two opposing points. First, the district's behavior has been consistent with the rent-seeking objectives outlined by Anderson and Hill, and the district can be expected to continue to expend resources to establish rights whenever there is conflict with users who predate the organization.[53] The Cox case and other sources of objections to the transfer of vested rights have caused a misallocation of resources, at least in the interim. Second, there is no reason to expect leasing revenue to be used on projects based on some measure of the willingness to pay. We must await further evidence on the second point, but the history of the conservancy does not support a prognostication of an efficient outcome.

CONCLUSIONS AND POLICY RECOMMENDATIONS

In considering the restrictions on transfers, we have discussed several facets of water rights and allocative efficiency. We have argued that where rights are well defined and there is protection against third-party impairments, economic efficiency requires that transfers be permitted. Furthermore, if rights are well defined we see no reason why water rights need be held by public agencies, such as conserv-

52. Middle Rio Grande Conservancy District, *A Brief History of the Middle Rio Grande Conservancy District* (Albuquerque, N.M.: MRGCD, n.d.), p. 12.

53. Terry L. Anderson and Peter J. Hill, *The Birth of a Transfer Society* (Stanford: Hoover Institution Press, 1980).

ancy districts. As we have noted, individual shareholders in mutual ditch companies are considered to be holders of vested rights. These companies seem to provide water delivery systems and, indirectly, flood protection much like conservancies without necessarily holding the water rights. While the Cox case may eventually provide the legal basis for the transfer of vested rights that predate the conservancy, litigation costs have undoubtedly hampered recent attempts to transfer. Even then, the conservancy would remain the holder of approximately 54 percent of the water rights presently managed by the district. If water allotments received through participation in reclamation projects were converted into private rights and transfer allowed, the allocative efficiency we have outlined would more likely be achieved.

It can be inferred from our argument that governmental agencies will seek to protect their tax base by controlling a resource, such as water, and that such attempts can lead to misallocation of that resource. Of course, there may be many conservancy districts where attempts to control water rights have not led to a misallocation of resources. This condition, however, may be the result of a lack of opportunity rather than a case of enlightened sacrifice. In the case of the MRGCD, the issue of transfer has come to a head only as demand outside the district increased. Thus, the behavior exhibited by the MRGCD is likely to occur elsewhere, particularly in the West, as the conditions of scarcity and growth collide with districts' dedication to political survival. Privatization of water rights and defining those rights on the basis of consumptive use would significantly reduce the influence of rent-seeking agencies.

APPENDIX

In this appendix we illustrate transferability and maximization with some simple numerical examples. Assume initially that stream flow ($\hat{S}$) is 26 acre-feet per unit of time and there is compact agreement ($\bar{S}$) calling for 14.5 acre-feet. Also, initially, there are two users on the stream diverting, S_2 and S_3 (here again, the subscripts refer to order of location on the stream). The *VMP* (demand for diverted water) curves of the users are given by

$$VMP_2 = 150 - 10S_2$$

$$VMP_3 = 18 - 1.2S_3$$

In addition, both users have the same return flow coefficients: $R_2 = R_3 = 0.5$. Applying Equation 5-3 plus the constraint yields the solution to the optimizing problem and calls for user 2 to divert 14.25 acre-feet (consumption = 7.125) and user 3 to divert 8.75 acre-feet (consumption = 4.375). This situation is illustrated in panel (a) of Table 5-1.

Next, allow for user 1 to arrive on the scene and express a desire to purchase water rights and commence operation above user 2. For simplicity, assume that user 1 and user 2 have identical *VMP* functions and return-flow coefficients. User 1 purchases 4.375 acre-feet of consumptive-use rights from user 3 and 1.375 acre-feet from user 2. The value of the water resource is maximized when users 1 and 2 each divert 11.50 acre-feet and user 3 diverts none. This is illustrated in panel (b) of Table 5-1.

The above example calls for both users 2 and 3 to sell water rights to user 1. However, waiving the question of optimality for the moment, it is clear that users 2 and 3 could sell consumptive-use rights independent of one another with no third-party impairment. In other words, provided that there is ample flow at each point of diversion, Equation 5-3 indicates that water rights are like any other private good. Transfer is one to one, and there are no negative impacts on third parties. This is best illustrated by the example in panel (c) of Table 5-1.

User 1, who exports two acre-feet of consumptive-use rights in panel (c), adjusts by decreasing consumptive use at the stream by two acre-feet, which is equivalent to decreasing diversion by four acre-feet. This does not affect downstream users. (We ignore the fact that it would now behoove user 1 to purchase some water rights from user 2.)

Panel (d) of Table 5-1, illustrates a situation in which a fourth user ($R_4 = 0.5$) imports 1.25 acre-feet above user 2 but diverts the associated 2.5 acre-feet below user 2. Again, this type of transaction does not affect the welfare of the current water users.

To illustrate the problem of binding flow constraints, we will use the data in Table 5-1 with the following modifications: (1) stream flow ($\hat{S}$) is reduced from 26 acre-feet to 16 acre-feet and (2) the compact agreement is reduced from 14.5 acre-feet to 4.5 acre-feet. This situation is illustrated in Table 5-2.

Panel (a) of Table 5-2 is identical to panel (a) of Table 5-1. However, if user 1 were to purchase 4.375 acre-feet of consumptive-use

Table 5-1. Optimizing Stream Value.

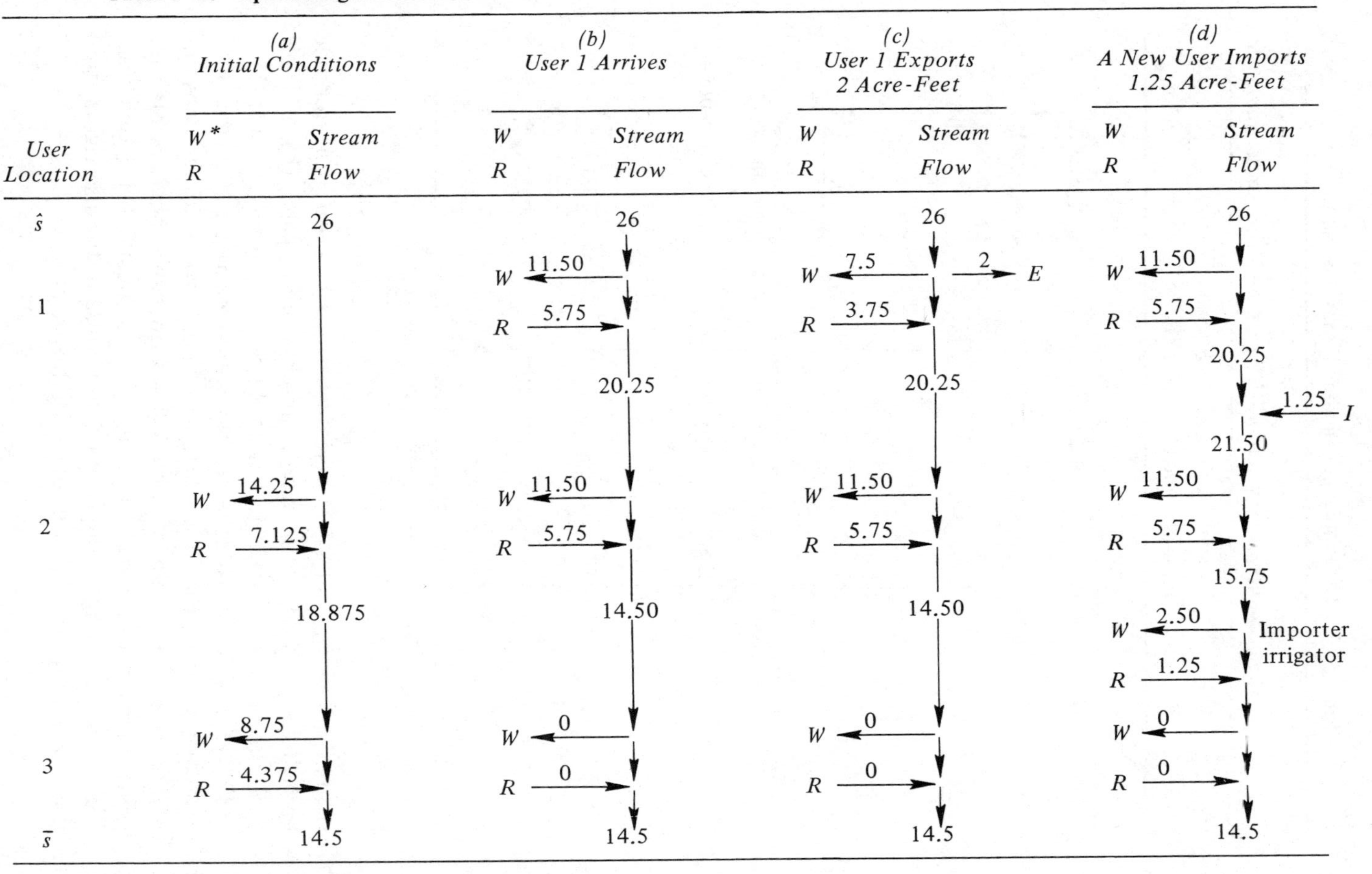

User Location	(a) Initial Conditions W* R	(a) Stream Flow	(b) User 1 Arrives W R	(b) Stream Flow	(c) User 1 Exports 2 Acre-Feet W R	(c) Stream Flow	(d) A New User Imports 1.25 Acre-Feet W R	(d) Stream Flow
$\hat{s}$		26		26		26		26
1			W 11.50		W 7.5	2 → E	W 11.50	
			R 5.75		R 3.75		R 5.75	
				20.25		20.25		20.25
								1.25 ← I
								21.50
2	W 14.25		W 11.50		W 11.50		W 11.50	
	R 7.125		R 5.75		R 5.75		R 5.75	
		18.875		14.50		14.50		15.75
Importer irrigator							W 2.50	
							R 1.25	
3	W 8.75		W 0		W 0		W 0	
	R 4.375		R 0		R 0		R 0	
$\bar{s}$		14.5		14.5		14.5		14.5

* *W* and *R* stand for withdrawal and return flow, respectively.

Table 5-2. The Problem of Binding Flow Constraint.

User Location	(a) Initial Conditions: W* / R	(a) Stream Flow	(b) Solution: Using Eq. 5-3: W / R	(b) Stream Flow	(c) Solution: Nonlinear: W / R	(c) Stream Flow
$\hat{s}$		16		16		16
1			W 11.50		W 11.7344	
			R 5.75		R 5.8672	
				10.25		10.1328
2	W 14.25		W 11.50**		W 10.1328	
	R 7.125		R 5.75**		R 5.0664	
		8.875				5.0664
3	W 8.75		W 0		W 1.1328	
	R 4.375		R 0		R 0.5664	
$\bar{s}$		4.5		4.5		4.5

* W and R stand for withdrawal and return flow, respectively.

** Not feasible.

rights from user 3 and 1.375 acre-feet from user 2 on a one-for-one basis, user 2 would be impaired. Simply note in panel (b) of Table 5-2 that if user 1 were to divert 11.50 acre-feet [= 2(4.375 + 1.375)], a flow of 10.25 acre-feet would be left for user 2, 1.25 acre-feet short of the flow needed for user 2 to be able to consume 5.75 acre-feet per unit of time. When flow constraints are binding, transactions can no longer be assumed to be on a one-for-one basis. User 1 can no longer simply purchase consumptive-use rights from user 3 and move the point of diversion upstream.

A solution yielding maximum total value for users is now neither simple nor can it be based on Equation 5–3. As the reader might suspect, maximization must now involve flow constraints guaranteeing that users will have water flows that are at least as large as their diversions. Basically, this is translated into a nonlinear programming model in which the objective function requires maximizing the areas under the three users' *VMP* functions subject to three flow constraints and one compact restraint:

$$\max_{S_1, S_2, S_3} \int_0^{S_1} (-10\alpha_1 + 150)\, d\alpha_1 + \int_0^{S_2} (-10\alpha_2 + 150)\, d\alpha_2 + \int_0^{S_3} (-1.2\alpha_3 + 18)\, d\alpha_3 \tag{5-4}$$

subject to

$$\begin{aligned} S_1 &\leq 16 \\ .5S_1 + S_2 &\leq 16 \\ .5S_1 + .5S_2 + S_3 &\leq 16 \\ .5S_1 + .5S_2 + .5S_3 &\leq 11.5 \\ S_1 \geq 0, S_2 \geq 0, S_3 &\geq 0 \end{aligned}$$

The first three constraints are the flow conditions that must be satisfied, and the fourth constraint is due to the compact agreement. Without getting involved in the optimization procedures, the solution to this problem is $S_1 = 11.7344, S_2 = 10.1328$, and $S_3 = 1.1328$ acre-feet. Note that $\lambda_1 = 0$, $\lambda_2 = 32.0312$, $\lambda_3 = 0$, and $\lambda_4 = 33.2813$; thus, the Kuhn Tucker conditions are satisfied. The result is illustrated in panel (c) of Table 5–2. The arrival of user 1 along the stream calls for a transfer of consumptive-use rights from users 2 and 3 to user 1. However, the amount that user 3 can transfer is no longer independent of effects on user 2. With the flow constraint binding, user 1 must compensate user 2 for any decrease in stream flow that causes impairment.

We conclude by noting that binding flow constraints do not call for a complete prohibition on transfer. Rather, they call for a modification of the usual simple trading rules.

Chapter 6

THE ECONOMIC DETERMINANTS AND CONSEQUENCES OF PRIVATE AND PUBLIC OWNERSHIP OF LOCAL IRRIGATION FACILITIES

Rodney T. Smith

The history of irrigation in the western United States shows a coexistence between private and public ownership of facilities used in capturing and transporting water between the locations of natural water supply to fertile agricultural lands. The nineteenth century was dominated by private ownership, which almost exclusively financed and operated the irrigation facilities, primarily through private mutual companies and partnerships. Public ownership arose during the twentieth century, as local governments exerted financial and operating control over many irrigation facilities. Yet by 1970, barely one-fourth of the irrigated acreage in the western United States was contained in public irrigation districts.[1]

According to traditional regulatory economics, the development and distribution of water for agricultural purposes is riddled with potential for market failure, which supposedly can be overcome only by public ownership.[2] Irrigation projects require relatively large initial capital outlays years prior to operation; local areas are presumed

1. See Table 1 in Rodney T. Smith, "Private and Public Ownership of Agricultural Water Districts" (unpublished manuscript, Center For the Study of The Economy and The State, University of Chicago, May 1980).

2. A sample of this line of reasoning can be found in Michael F. Brewer, *Water Pricing and Allocation with Particular Reference to California Irrigation Districts* (Berkeley, Calif.: California Agricultural Experiment Station, Giannini Foundation of Agricultural Economics, October 1960).

to have experienced difficulties acquiring financing under private ownership. Once in place a project becomes the sole source of imported water into the area; the potential for monopoly pricing is expected to deter irrigation. Finally, private ownership is believed to be crippled by the variable nature of the water supply. Thus public ownership is presumed to be superior for efficiently allocating economic risk.

This traditional perspective of irrigation history suffers from two fundamental problems. First, the predominance of private ownership belies the alleged frequency of institutional failure. Second, public ownership has not proved to be a paragon of correcting market failures. Economic analyses of public districts have consistently found a systematic misallocation of resources.[3] A different theory of the determinants of the choice between private and public ownership, and the consequences of that choice, is required.

The alternative theory is based upon economic analysis of decisionmaking under private and public ownership. The ensuing discussion will clarify the likely outcomes under the ownership rules and identify the reasons why the different institutions have been adopted. Under the competitive forces described in this chapter, the rules of private ownership promote an economically efficient allocation of resources and avoid monopoly pricing problems. In contrast, the rules of public ownership have a predictable tendency for the economic inefficiency commonly criticized by prior studies. Yet economic efficiency for the group as a whole does not portend that private ownership would be selected under specific circumstances. The theory relates that institutional decision to the rules of choice about form of ownership outlined in state laws.

This chapter adopts the assumption that the selection of private or public ownership reflects a conscious choice by individuals to achieve specific economic effects. Under private ownership, a set of rules governs the nature of contracts that parties may enter into for constructing irrigation facilities, allocating the water supply, and defraying costs. Within that set of rules, however, mutual consent among parties governs the relations among contracting individuals. In contrast, public ownership involves group decisionmaking under public choice. The results of that process do not require full mutual

3. Jack Hirshleifer, James C. DeHaven, and Jerome Milliman, *Water Supply: Economics, Technology, and Policy* (Chicago: University of Chicago Press, 1960).

consent of all affected parties but bind all individuals to follow the actions prescribed by the dominant political coalition. The resulting theories of private and public ownership concentrate on identifying how these alternative decision-making procedures influence the distribution of benefits and costs of irrigation and the utilization of irrigation water.

Under either form of ownership, the decisions confronting the allocation of water rights and the distribution of irrigation costs are made within a competitive environment. Farmers are geographically mobile, so in the long run the policies set by either a private or public irrigation enterprise could not affect the income earned by the area's farmers in their role as residual claimants in farming. The policies of the irrigation organization, however, could influence the prevailing level and pattern of land values. The theoretical analysis focuses on how land-holding interests are affected by the form of ownership of irrigation facilities. The choice of organizational form revolves around whether the requisite fraction of landowners (dictated by state government enabling acts for the formation of public irrigation districts) are better off under private or public ownership.

This theory is developed for the purpose of testing its empirical implications in two important areas. First, how is the use of irrigation water affected by the payment schemes instituted by the various forms of ownership? Second, is an area's choice of organizational form influenced by the economic factors that create the differences in resource allocation and the distribution of the gains from irrigation under the two forms of ownership?

The development of this analysis begins with a brief description of the key rules under private and public ownership, followed by a theory of resource allocation under private ownership. Particular emphasis is placed on the efficiency of the resulting allocation of risk bearing and contractual solutions to the alleged monopoly problem. A majority-rule, voting model for determining water pricing policy under public ownership then is developed. The key issue is how heterogeneity in the distribution in water demand per acre influences the political viability of water subsidization financed by property taxation. An econometric analysis of water usage and choice of ownership form in California during 1929 is then presented. The empirical evidence contradicts the traditional regulatory economics explanation of public ownership and supports the theory emphasizing the economic effects on land-holding interests. The discussion concludes with a brief introduction to possible institutional reforms that would increase the role of private ownership in irrigation.

IRRIGATION INSTITUTIONS: A HISTORICAL BACKGROUND

Early investment in and operation of the transportation facilities for water used in irrigation were organized almost exclusively as private enterprises.[4] In the most common form of private ownership, the company constructed the canal facilities, turning over ownership of the canal to an irrigation company once a specified fraction of the designated capacity was sold. The terms of this transfer of ownership were specified prior to construction.

The private irrigation companies themselves were formed along the lines of a mutual corporation with six important rules:

1. The company was formed according to the same rules governing the formation of any privately owned corporation.
2. Each share of stock was to be treated identically, with the total number of shares outstanding equaling the capacity of the canal system. Available water in any year was prorated in accordance to stock ownership.
3. The shares of stock were tradable at prices negotiated between buyer and seller. Members could also rent any or all of their water rights.
4. The expenses associated with operation, maintenance, and servicing or retiring of the company's debt were also prorated in accordance to stock ownership.
5. Stockholders' liability was not limited as in other corporate enterprises. The land of the stockholder could be used as a lien against any financial obligations originating from stock ownership.
6. Private irrigation companies possessed the power to condemn land for right-of-way, provided they paid just compensation.

4. The historical information concerning the rules of decisionmaking under private ownership is taken from Elwood Mead, *Irrigation Institutions* (New York: Macmillan Co., 1907), and Wiles A. Hutchins, *Mutual Irrigation Companies in California and Utah* (Washington, D.C.: U.S. Farm Credit Administration, Cooperative Division, October 1936).

By the late 1880s, state legislatures had formulated mechanisms for developing and operating irrigation facilities under public ownership. Procedures were developed for the creation of a local government whose sole responsibilities involved the operation and financing of irrigation facilities.

The statutory impetus for public ownership began in 1887 when California passed the Wright Act.[5] A procedure of petitioning and voting was created for the political determination of whether public or private ownership should control irrigation activities. Half of the landowners owning 50 percent or more of the affected land could file a petition seeking the creation of a public irrigation district. The county commissioners in that jurisdiction then had to call a special election to establish a district if two-thirds of the voters approved.

The district's board of directors, elected by majority rule, was empowered to administer the obligations of the district. The board's key decisions involved the distribution of the cost burden of irrigation between direct water charges and property taxes. Water rights were assigned according to acreage. The issuing of bonds to finance any board-initiated development plan had to be directly approved by a two-thirds majority of votes cast in a special election. In contrast, if a development plan was initiated by petitioning farmers, then the bonds could be approved by only a simple majority of votes cast in the special election. All sixteen other western states passed similar legislation within the next few decades, though some differed as to specific provisions.[6] California itself issued a new statute that effectively replaced the Wright Act but left unchanged the basic provisions that concern the subsequent analysis.

In comparing the rules of private and public ownership, two differences are important to this discussion. First, water rights in mutual companies could be traded separately from the land, while the implicit water rights of public districts could not. The freedom of trade in water rights separate from land effectively generated an

5. The historical interpretations and description of rules under public ownership can be found in Joseph Long, *A Treatise on the Law of Irrigation: Covering All States and Territories*, 2nd ed. (Denver: W. H. Courtright Publishing Co., 1916).

6. Ten states required the district to use "just and equitable" allocation schemes; five required greater pluralities than a simple majority for approving the issuance of bonds; and eight placed explicit constraints on the district taxation powers, requiring an equal tax be levied on all acreage in the district. For a fuller description and discussion of the economic implications of differences in these state rules, see Smith, "Water Districts."

equity market capable of efficiently allocating among farmers the risk associated with the variable supply of water. Second, unlike public districts, mutual irrigation companies could not use property taxation for financing their expenses. The districts' ability to tax land for cross-subsidizing water use created income redistribution powers for the local government, the exercise of which proved to be an important incentive for some landholders preferring public ownership.

Table 6-1 provides some background information on the relative importance of and growth in private and public ownership in California from 1920 to 1950. The single farm enterprise showed the greatest growth during this period, increasing its share of total irrigated acreage from 36 percent in 1920 to 58 percent by 1950. Mutual and commercial enterprises, on the other hand, were declining in their relative importance. Starting from a low level, public irrigation districts displayed sustained growth over this period.

As indicated by Figure 6-1, the bulk of irrigation district formation occurred between 1918 and 1925. Interestingly, irrigation district formations barely exceeded dissolutions during the so-called decade of euphoria following the passage of the model Wright Act (1887).

Two observations can be drawn from the data summarized in Table 6-1 and Figure 6-1. First, the predominant competition between private and public ownership of irrigation facilities (involving more than a few farmers) was between public irrigation districts and the mutual companies described above. Second, in California at least,

Table 6-1. California Irrigated Acreage by Type of Enterprise, 1920-1950.

	Irrigated Land (thousands of acres)			
Type of Enterprise	*1920*[a]	*1930*[a]	*1940*[b]	*1950*[b]
Single farm	1503	1735	2353	4260
Mutual irrigation	1216	854	898	889
Commercial	813	312	392	296
Public irrigation district	577	1599	1779	1821

a. U.S. Department of Agriculture, *Irrigation of Agricultural Lands* (Washington, D.C.: Government Printing Office, 1930), p. 87.

b. U.S. Department of Agriculture, *Census of Irrigation* (Washington, D.C.: Government Printing Office, 1950), p. 85.

Figure 6–1. California Irrigation Districts Organized and Dissolved and Gross District Acreage, 1887–1956.

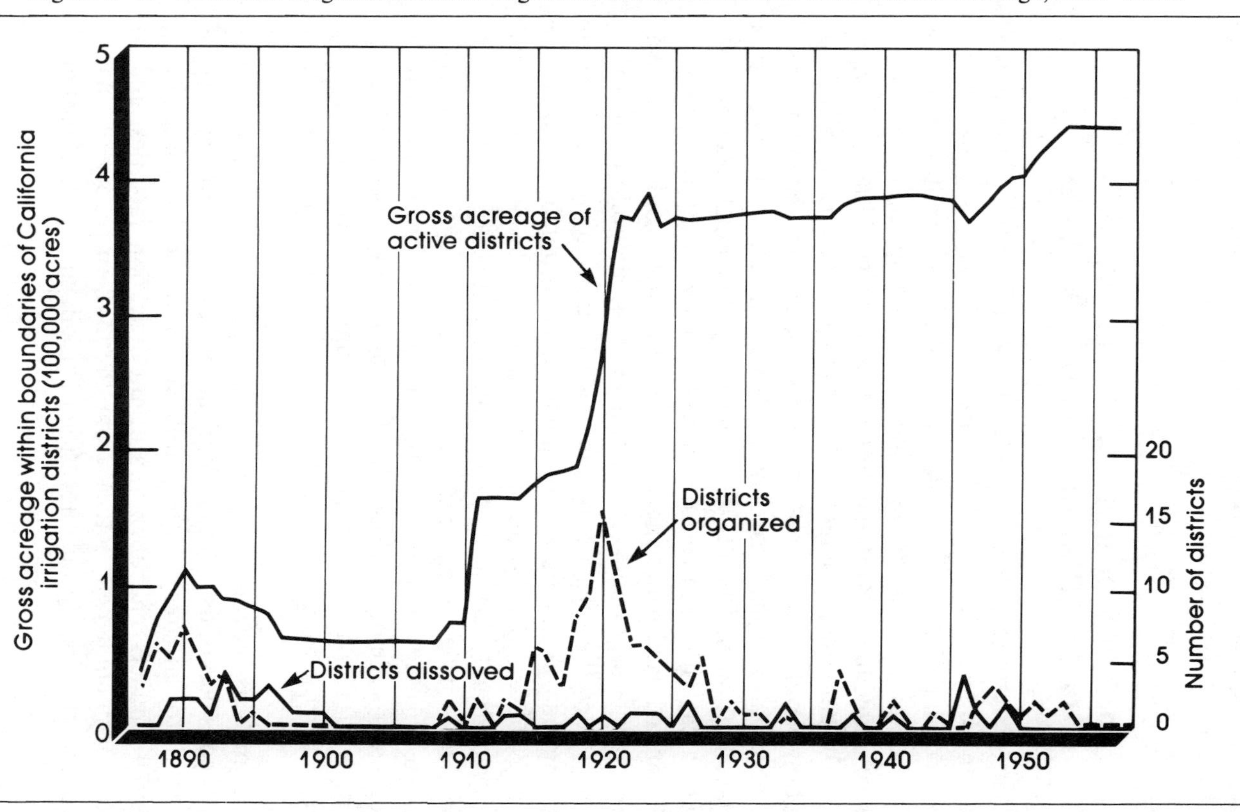

Source: Michael F. Brewer: *Water Pricing and Allocation with Particular Reference to California Irrigation Districts* (Berkeley, Calif.: California Agricultural Experiment Station, Giannini Foundation of Agricultural Economics, October 1960), Figure V.

the 1920s were the key period for determining the form of ownership by an area. Since that time, decisions about institutional choice have been relatively dormant.

A THEORY OF RESOURCE ALLOCATION UNDER MUTUAL IRRIGATION COMPANIES

Analysis of resource decisions under the contract rules of the mutual irrigation company indicates that private enterprise is quite capable of overcoming the three problems identified by traditional regulatory economics: financing, monopoly, and risk spreading. The decisions of individual, profit-maximizing farmers would allocate water efficiently among its competing uses, pursue the optimum scale of irrigation development, and efficiently allocate the economic risk. The theory also explains as an outcome of competitive market forces the fact that mutual bonds were owned by individuals residing outside the area, while mutual stock shares were owned by the farmers.

The initial landowners/developers of the area would find themselves unanimously better off from the irrigation development forthcoming under the rules of the mutual irrigation company. No compensating side payments among landowners would be required for pursuing the efficient scale of total irrigation development in the area, even if land were specialized in different types of crops employing water in varying intensities. The creation of a separate water right from land rights would increase the values of all types of land from the efficient scale of development. Thus all landowners would accept the rules of the mutual irrigation company as a wealth-enhancing strategy for the voluntary, joint development of irrigation in their area.

The analysis generating these conclusions uses three primary economic considerations: 1) the implications of competitive entry of farmers into an area, 2) the implications of competition among potential builders and operators of the irrigation facilities, and 3) some fundamental perspectives from the modern theory of finance concerning the pricing and allocation of risk in competitive markets.[7]

7. See Eugene F. Fama, *Foundations of Finance* (New York: Basic Books, 1976) for a complete introduction to the fundamental points concerning the pricing and allocation of risk-bearing activities.

The Economic Problem of Irrigation Development

Consider the situation of the initial landowners who are contemplating irrigation development. Suppose that for reasons of comparative advantage, they will not farm the land themselves. The economic attractions to farmers who will inhabit the area are the natural productivity of the land and the availability and cost of irrigation water. The original landowners are attracting farmers who are in infinitely elastic supply to the area.[8] Thus land prices in the area cannot exceed an amount, given the state of irrigation development, that provides the immigrant farmers with less than their competitively determined level of income.

The profit-maximizing landowners would adopt irrigation institutions such as the mutual irrigation company that maximize the amount farmers are willing to pay for the land in the area. The economic decisions to be made by farmers include the buying of land, purchasing water, and applying their labor in the production of crops. The farmers may also choose to purchase shares in the mutual irrigation company or rely upon the resale market for irrigation water as their source of water supply. The farmers also will bear the economic risk in their farming incomes inherent from the variable nature of the area's irrigation water supply.

Studying the nature of the resulting market equilibrium will highlight the following issues concerning the economic properties of the scale of development and the distribution of the gains from that development:

1. Contractual solutions to the potential monopoly pricing problem
2. The relations among water pricing, scale of irrigation development, and land values
3. The economic forces behind mutual debt and equity financing, with emphasis on the allocation of economic risk of project failure and variability in the value of the project resulting from fluctuations in the supply of irrigation water

8. The text assumes that all farmers are of equal ability and have numerous alternate areas where they could settle. The analysis could be generalized to include farmers of different ability, and thereby earning different levels of income, without any modifications to the key conclusions about resource allocation under private ownership.

The Monopoly Problem

The monopoly problem originated from the fact that after construction the irrigation facilities were the sole source of water supply in the area. If water from these facilities was to be sold exclusively under spot-market contracts, a bilateral monopoly problem would exist. The irrigation company could charge the monopoly price for its delivery services, thereby capturing for the owners the entire value of irrigation development. Alternatively, users could band together and force the company to sell its delivery services at short-run marginal cost, thereby expropriating the capital invested in the enterprise. The suspected unstable nature of this potential bilateral monopoly has been a source of the traditional regulatory economist's skepticism about private ownership of irrigation facilities.

Even though reliance on spot-market contacts was not feasible, a private solution can be found to this bilateral monopoly problem. Demsetz has argued that potential suppliers would bid competitively for the right to build and operate the facilities servicing the buyers.[9] The winning seller would earn only a competitive return, because the competing potential suppliers would "bid their cost curve." This process would generate a negotiated contract prior to the construction of the facilities, with the buyers committing themselves to purchase specified quantities at predetermined prices. The bilateral monopoly problem would be solved by a long-term contract.

The rules of the mutual irrigation company provided the private contractual solution to the monopoly problem. Despite the organization's exclusive right to supply the members, the organization effectively had a long-term contract with its members. The rules governing stock share rights and obligations specified both the quantity of water to be made available to each member and the costs. Purchasing of stock shares served as a voluntary long-term contract between each member and the company supplying irrigation water. There was no compulsion for farmers to become members, for they could rent water rights from members.

Klein, Crawford, and Alchian have raised questions about the long-term contract solution posed by Demsetz, arguing that after the sup-

9. Harold Demsetz, "Why Regulate Utilities?" *Journal of Law and Economics* 11 (April 1968): 55-65.

ply facility is built, the members would desire renegotiation of that contract, effectively recreating the bilateral monopoly problem.[10] In the end, the only effective method would be vertical integration between the farmers and the mutual. Once common ownership is established, the bilateral monopoly problem disappears because any opportunistic behavior would be at the expense of that common ownership's self-interest. Mutual irrigation companies accomplished this vertical integration by the water users owning the shares in the company. An alternative explanation of the vertical integration of farmers into the water supply facilities that is fully consistent with Demsetz's discussion is offered later in this discussion.

Water Pricing, Land Values, and the Scale of Irrigation Development

The following analysis ignores the uncertainty in the appropriated water supply. This procedure allows enunciation of some important aspects of the competitive equilibrium under the rules of the mutual irrigation company and generates results applicable to the case of uncertainty.

Individual Decisions of Water Use and Stock Purchases. Figure 6-2 depicts the individual farmer's demand for water as a function of the price of water on the resale market. Given the stock purchase decision, the resale price measures the opportunity cost of water use even if the farmer is a net seller on the resale market. A net seller's incremental use of irrigation water sacrifices the sale of that quantity that could produce revenue reflected in the resale price of water. If the resale price equaled P_M, the farmer in Figure 6-2 will use W units of irrigation water, a decision that is not affected by the endowment of water received from the ownership of mutual shares. The farmer's stock purchase decision, as shown in the figure, only determines his or her net trading position in the resale market. If the farmer owned S_1 shares, he or she would resell S_1W units of water; if the farmer owned S_2 shares, he or she would purchase S_2W units of water from the resale market.

10. Benjamin Klein, Robert Crawford, and Armen Alchian, "Vertical Integration, Appropriable Rents, and the Competitive Contracting Process," *Journal of Law and Economics* 21 (October 1978): 297-326.

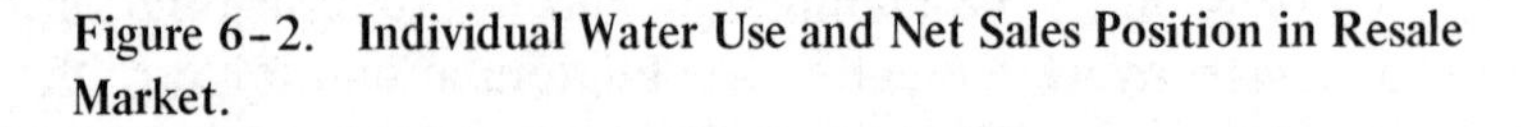

Figure 6–2. Individual Water Use and Net Sales Position in Resale Market.

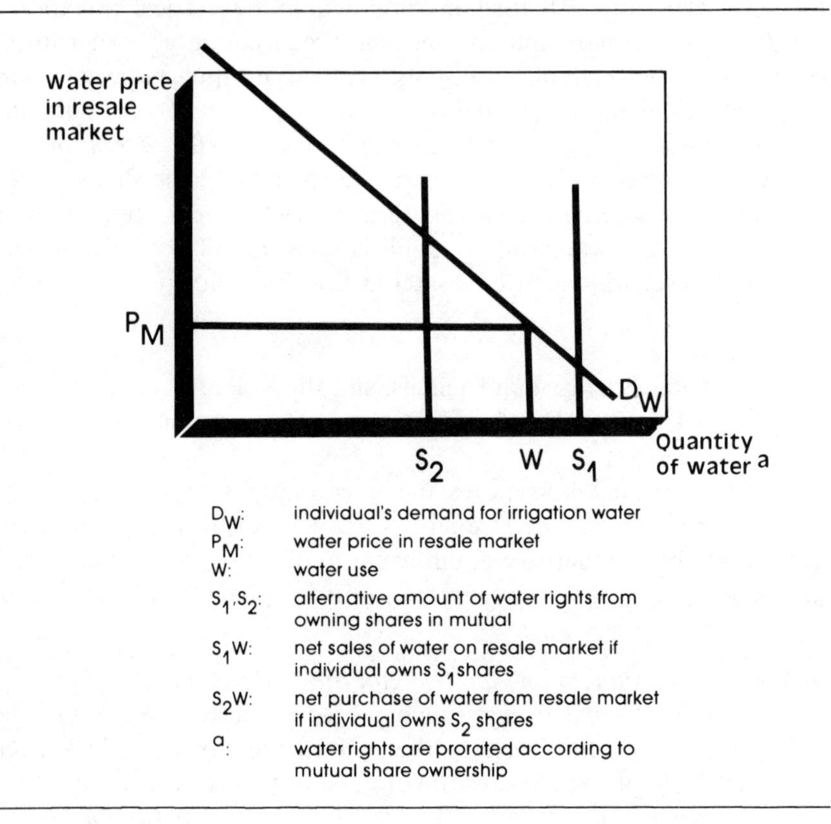

The farmer's optimal stock purchase decision depends upon the difference between the resale price of water and the financial obligations of stock ownership (hereafter called the cost of shares). If the resale price were less than the cost of shares, the farmer would rely exclusively on the resale market for the supply of irrigation water and purchase no mutual shares. If the resale price were greater than the cost of shares, the farmer would purchase (a formally) unbounded quantity of mutual shares and make a profit by reselling water rights on the resale market. This property of the demand for shares places some restriction on the equilibrium scale of irrigation investment.

Given the demand for irrigation water in an area, the scale of irrigation development cannot exceed the level W^* where the resale price of water at that quantity is less than the financial obligations of stock ownership. For if the capacity of the mutual exceeded that critical level, no individual would be willing to purchase any shares in the mutual. If the capacity of the system were less than W, everyone would be willing to purchase shares because the resale price of water would exceed the financial obligations of stock ownership. There would be an excess demand for the stock shares, and the issuing company could charge a fee for the stock issue. The equilibrium issue price would make the full price of stock ownership (the sum of the issuing fee plus the financial obligation of stock ownership) equal to the resale price of water.

In equilibrium under certainty, the distribution of shares among farmers and even outside investors would be indeterminate. The market-clearing price for the stock issue destroys the differential gain from relying on either the resale market or water rights from the mutual irrigation company. Stock ownership offers a competitive return. This indeterminancy in the ownership distribution disappears with the introduction of risk bearing.

Competitive Entry of Farmers and General Equilibrium. While the above analysis is informative about the economic forces impinging on the sale of mutual shares and retrading of irrigation water, it is incomplete because it assumes the price of land and the number of farmers inhabiting the area to be fixed. General equilibrium analysis traces how those considerations are influenced by the introduction of irrigation into the area and provides insight into who are the ultimate beneficiaries from irrigation.

Competitive entry of farmers places constraints on the allowable configuration of product and factor prices in the area. The discussion is considerably simplified by the following assumptions: (1) the area is a price taker in the markets for all of its agricultural products, and (2) land, water, and the farmer's labor are the only factors of production. The former assumption can be justified by the presumption that any one irrigation area produces only a small fraction of the nation's agricultural output. This allows the discussion to concentrate on the determination of prices for factors of production specific to the area—water and land. The effect of irrigation development can be determined by comparing two equilibria representing pre- and postirrigation development.

Prior to water development the equilibrium price for water and land will not attract new farmers to the area (see Appendix A). Now suppose that irrigation development increases the supply of water to the area. The price of land will increase for two reasons. First, the demand for land by the original farmers increases because a reduction in the price for a factor of production at constant product prices generally increases the demand for all other factors of production.[11] Second, the number of farmers increases because the lower water price, at the initial land price, increases the farmer's income above its competitively determined level. The entry of additional farmers also bids up land prices, forcing farming income back down to its equilibrium level.

Standard applied welfare analysis can be used to indicate the magnitude by which irrigation development increases the area's aggregate farming income and profits from issuing stock in the mutual (see Figure 6-3).[12] The gain in aggregate agricultural income equals the area below the general equilibrium demand for water and above the resale price of water. That income gain accrues exclusively to the original landowners, because the increased value of land equals the area $P_S^Q A P_M$ in the figure. The reasons that land captures the benefits of irrigation development are: (1) competitive entry keeps farmers' incomes at their competitively determined levels, and (2) potential competition among builders of the facilities prevents them from capturing any gains. For the scale of development indicated in the figure, stock promoters would earn profits on their stock issue equal to the area $P_M ABP_C$, because the demand for shares equals available supply when the issue price equals the difference between the resale price of water and the cost of shares.

The Equilibrium Scale of Irrigation Development. The original landowners would maximize their gain from irrigation development by selecting the capacity of the mutual where the resale price of water equalled the financial obligations of stock ownership. In Figure 6-3, the scale development represented by Q is not profit maximizing. The profits to be earned from the stock issue come at the expense of land values. Increasing the capacity of the system to point Q^* generates additional enhancement of land values represented by area ABC plus the profits earned by stock issuance at the lower scale of development. The economic source of the higher land values, of

11. See J. R. Hicks, *Value and Capital: An Inquiry Into Some Fundamental Principles of Economic Theory*, 2nd ed. (London: Oxford at the Clarendon Press, 1968), pp. 322-23.

12. See Arnold C. Harberger, "Three Basic Postulates for Applied Welfare Economics: An Interpretive Essay," *Journal of Economic Literature* 9 (1971): 785-797.

Figure 6-3. The Relation between Irrigation Development, Land Values, and Profits from Stock Issue.

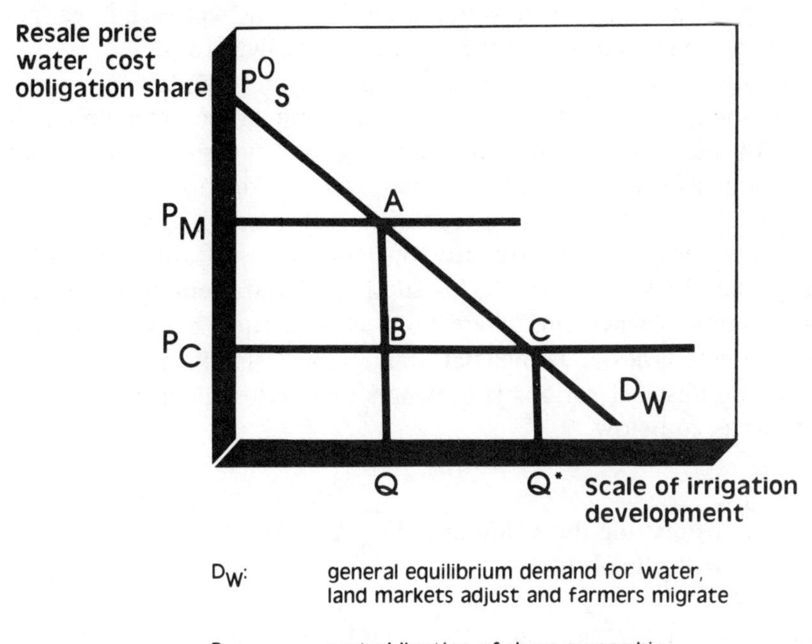

D_W: general equilibrium demand for water, land markets adjust and farmers migrate

P_C: cost obligation of share ownership

$P_M ABP_C$: stock promoter's profits at development Q

$P^0_S AP_M$: increased land values at development Q

$P^0_S CP_C$: increased land values at development Q*

course, is irrigation development Q^*, which lowered the price of irrigation water paid by farmers and enabled them to bid higher prices for the land while still earning their competitively determined level of farming income. The landowners could not successfully market the shares in a mutual with a capacity exceeding Q^* because no investor could expect a normal return from that investment. The value of the water rights (measured by the equilibrium resale price of water) would be less than the financial obligations of stock ownership.

The analysis also applies to an area with different types of land specializing in the production of different types of crops. Competitive entry of farmers guarantees that the price of each type of land is bid up to reflect the full gains from introducing irrigation to each crop. For landowners as a group, of course, their per-acre gains will differ; land used for more water-intensive crops will earn larger per-acre rents than lands used for less water-intensive crops.

Despite differences in their per-acre gains, landowners would unanimously agree on the scale of development to offer under the rules of the mutual irrigation company. All types of land become more valuable with the equilibrium level of irrigation development. At the same time, the mutual does not place responsibility for financing the enterprise directly on landowners. Rather, liability is placed on stock ownership. This situation is different from the case under public ownership, where there is separation between the ultimate beneficiaries and financial obligations of landowners. The economic interests of various landowners become fragmented in a manner discussed below.

Allocating the Economic Risk Associated with the Mutual

The financial arrangements of the mutual must confront two risk allocation problems: (1) project failure and (2) variability in the value of a successful project resulting from fluctuations in the available water supply. Modern finance theory clarifies the economic role of the contractual relations among the mutual's creditors, members, and water users. The analysis will show that the mutual's financing problems were identical to those encountered in any private business venture.

Portfolio Theory. Modern finance theory studies the pricing of assets and the equilibrium distribution of ownership in a world of risk inhabited by risk-averse individuals. Generally, individuals require a return different from the expected promised payout of an asset for them to be willing to absorb the riskiness of the promised income stream. The difference between the required return and the expected payout is called the *risk premium.* The risk premium an individual requires, however, depends upon how ownership of an asset contributes to the variability of the income stream from the individual's entire portfolio of assets and not the variability in the asset's return considered in isolation.[13] The covariability between returns from an asset and from the entire portfolio is greater (1) the larger the share of wealth represented by the particular asset and (2) the greater the covariability of returns among assets, that is, returns of different assets either move increasingly together or less in opposite directions.

In competitive capital markets, equilibrium ownership of assets is determined by those investors demanding the smallest return. Consider the example of two groups of investors bidding for bonds promising to pay $100 next year but whose actual payout is subject to uncertainty. Suppose that the first and second group require 3 and 5 percent returns respectively for holding any specified quantity of the bonds. Then the first and second groups would be willing to pay about $97 and $95 respectively for each bond purchased. Group one would outbid group two in an auction and would hold the bonds. As the expected payout of the bond was the same for each group, the differences in the groups' bids must reflect differences in their required risk premiums. Modern finance theory suggests that the analysis of pricing and ownership of the mutual's bonds and stock consider the structure of the covariability of returns from those instruments with the portfolios held by different individuals.

Bonds. The construction of irrigation facilities requires outlays prior to the use of the appropriated water. Would creditors require a risk premium for purchasing the bonds of the mutual irrigation company and being exposed to the risk of their default? Modern finance theory predicts the absence of a financing problem and offers an explanation for the pattern of bond ownership.

Outside investors could have diversified the default risk of the bonds, for the bonds' riskiness would contribute virtually nothing to the overall riskiness of the market's portfolio of assets. The value of the bonds would be a minuscule portion of market wealth. Also there would be no covariability between the returns earned on the mutual's bonds and the market portfolio, because the bonds' default risk would reflect uncertainty about the precise productivity of irrigation and its costs. The answer to these issues, of course, would be revealed with the operation experience of the mutual and not affected by short-term fluctuations in the capital market.

13. See Fama, *Foundations of Finance*, chap. 7.

The economic perspective can explain why capital investors, primarily European, purchased the bonds.[14] The area's farmers could not enjoy the risk diversification possibilities identified above, for their primary source of wealth (land) was critically affected by the eventual success of the mutual. Farmers would require a risk premium for holding the mutual's bonds. Outside investors, in contrast, would require no risk premium and would be expected to outbid the resident farmers in the bond market.

The mutual's bonds were secured by the ultimate lien on land using the water from the mutual. This collateral would be sufficiently valuable for securing outstanding debt if the project was successful, for land values would capture the economic benefits from irrigation. Thus the bond liability was self-enforcing.

There is nothing unusual about the economics of the mutual's bond financing. Modern finance theory identifies how that investment could be efficiently priced as other private assets and explains the observed ownership pattern. The traditional economic concerns about the difficulty of local areas securing financing are without theoretical foundation.

Stocks. The ownership of mutual stock can be thought of as an economic lottery. The owner pays a fixed amount per share each period, and the return is a proportionate share of the available water supply. The spot-market price of water measures the value of each unit of water received from stock ownership for any state of the mutual's water supply. Examining the covariability of return between stock ownership and the portfolios of residents and nonresidents will highlight the economic determinants of pricing and ownership of the mutual's shares.

Investors with no other assets in the area would experience a zero covariability between the returns to stock ownership and the returns on their entire portfolios. The state of the water supply of the mutual, reflecting rainfall variation, would be uncorrelated with the general return in capital markets. Thus investors would require no risk premium for holding stock in the mutual.

The situation is fundamentally different for a potential investor engaged in farming. If the short-run demand for water is price inelastic, then the value of the stock rights will be greater when there are

14. See Hutchins, *Mutual Irrigation Companies.*

shortfalls in the mutual's water supply because total value of water will be greater at lower quantities. As a higher price for water also reduces the income from farming, there will be a *negative* covariability between the return earned on stock ownership and the returns earned on the remainder of the farmer's sources of income. This covariability is more negative the less elastic the demand for water. Farmers "pay" a negative-risk premium for holding the mutual's stock because of the income insurance services represented by stock ownership.

The above nature of risk bearing implies that farmers, because they are willing to *pay* a premium for ownership, can outbid the outside investor in competition for shares in the mutual. So there are natural economic reasons for the farmers to vertically integrate into their water supply. Concerns about ex post renegotiation of the implicit long-term contracts represented by stock ownership are not required for explaining the voluntary vertical integration.

The value of this income insurance from stock ownership is an increasing function of the water intensity of the crop grown, because the income loss from a given increase in the water price is greater for the more water-intensive crops. So while all farmers in an area would be willing to pay a negative-risk premium to hold the mutual's stock shares, farmers of the more water-intensive crops would be willing to purchase more shares at any given equilibrium negative-risk premium.

The economic value of the income insurance provided by the mutual must ultimately be captured in higher land values. For if land values were not increased, farmers would be earning more than their competitively determined level of expected utility. Competitive entry would then generate decreases in the income earned by farmers, a circumstance requiring increased land prices. The magnitude of enhanced land values is greater the less elastic demand for water, the greater the water intensity of crops, and the greater the variability in the water supply.

Summary

Resource use under the rules of the mutual irrigation company possesses many desirable properties from the viewpoint of original landowners in an area. The rules guarantee the subscription of farmers to the mutual that financed construction of irrigation facilities without any elements of monopoly pricing of irrigation water. The tradable nature of water rights, and their ability to be rented during either dry or wet years, create important risk-spreading opportunities for risk-averse farmers, which improves the attractiveness of an agricultural area for settlement. The magnitude of the increased attractiveness from the use of the mutual irrigation company is greatest in areas with higher variance in the supply of appropriated water and less elastic short-run demands for water. Both of these considerations increase the productivity of stock ownership in reducing the variance in total income. The competitive entry of farmers into an area guarantees that the original landowners capture all of these benefits of pursuing irrigation development under the rules of the mutual irrigation company.

A THEORY OF RESOURCE ALLOCATION UNDER PUBLIC OWNERSHIP

Suppose an area pursues irrigation development under public ownership. What factors influence the local government's water pricing and land taxation policies? Who benefits from those fiscal policies? Who gains from the destruction of separately tradable water rights? The analysis of the decisionmaking in the public irrigation district and its economic consequences identifies why some groups benefit from the creation of public ownership.

Many of the economic forces discussed in the previous section influence the outcomes under public ownership. These include competitive entry of farmers creating an inverse relation between water pricing and land values; competition among potential builders and operators of the facilities guaranteeing them only normal returns; portfolio theory and how restricting trade in water rights affects the efficiency of the distribution of risk bearing.

The Fiscal Policy of the Public Irrigation District

The median voter model is used for analyzing the economic determinants of the district's fiscal policy. Used by economists as a way of summarizing the political determination of resource decisions, the model envisions a local political process attuned to the economic interests of the eligible voters in the public irrigation district.[15] Voters express their policy preferences by supporting candidates for the board of directors who advocate policies closest to their own preferred positions. Candidates for the district's board compete for office by selecting policy positions that enhance the possibility of their being elected. Competition for elective office prevents elected officers from straying from the equilibrium set of policies that generates the requisite plurality in elections. If a board member did deviate from that equilibrium policy, a new candidate could defeat the unresponsive member in the next election by advocating the equilibrium policy. Analysis of this process contains three parts: (1) defining the set of feasible policies, (2) examining each voter's preferred set of policies, and (3) identifying the policy position that would be sustained under competition for elective office by prospective board members.

The median voter model does not permit nonvoting modes of influence, such as monetary contributions, on the political process.[16] The added complexity of using more general models is not required for developing the themes presented below. Because the median voter model generally does not possess a unique equilibrium whenever more than two independent policy tools are at the disposal of the political process, this analysis assumes, rather than derives, that the public irrigation district builds sufficient capacity to satisfy all water demand forthcoming at its selected water-pricing and property taxation policies.[17] Appendix B presents the technical fundamentals of the model's determination of the equilibrium water subsidy and property tax.

Decisionmaking under public ownership provides the possibility for income redistribution among landowners. The median voter

15. For early use of the voting model, see Howard R. Bowen, "The Interpretation of Voting in the Allocation of Economic Resources," *The Quarterly Journal of Economics* 58 (1943): 27–48. A more extensive discussion of how voting considerations generate economically inefficient resource decisions, see James M. Buchanan and Gordon Tullock, *The Calculus of Consent: The Logical Foundations of Constitutional Democracy* (Ann Arbor, Mich.: University of Michigan Press, 1962), pp. 131–145.

16. More general models of the economics of the political sector are still in their infancy. For a discussion of models applying noncooperative game theory to the decisionmaking under public ownership, see Rodney T. Smith, "Cross-Subsidization in a (Simple) Political System" (Center for the Study of the Economy and the State, University of Chicago, May 1982).

17. See Gerald Kramer, "On A Class of Equilibrium Conditions for Majority Rule," *Econometrica* 41 (March 1973): 285–297.

model developed in Appendix B shows how the nature of the distribution of water use per acre (the degree of skewness) affects the equilibrium degree of water subsidization financed by property taxation. Landowners divide themselves into economic interests according to the relative water intensity of the crops in which they specialize. An increase in the water subsidy, by reducing the price paid for irrigation water, bids up the price of their land: the magnitude of the per-acre price increase equaling the ratio of water to land use at equilibrium water and land prices. The incidence of the property tax also falls exclusively on landowners, because of the geographical mobility of farmers and the assumed specificity of land in agriculture. Hence the district's policies affect the after-tax value of land via a tradeoff between the increasing land value due to water subsidization and decreasing land value resulting from property taxation. Landowners experience different tradeoffs because of differences in the characteristics of water demand by crops grown on their land.

The political process balances these competing interests when determining the district's fiscal policy. Under the median voter model, the preferred policy of the median voter is the only policy sustainable under electoral competition. The model offers three fundamental empirical implications. First, the median voter prefers water subsidization only if the water use per acre on his or her land exceeds that district's average use (the skewness in the district's water use distribution must be negative). Second, the median voter's preferred water subsidy rate is greater the less elastic the district's demand for water. Finally, the median voter's preferred water subsidy increases as water demand by the crop grown on his or her land becomes more elastic.

Even though majority rule will determine the fiscal policies of the irrigation district, more than 50 percent of the landowners would benefit from the subsidization. Consequently, greater pluralities of landowners would accept the creation of the public irrigation district than would support the eventual fiscal policies adopted in the district in comparison to other feasible water subsidization policies.[18]

18. In California, for example, two-thirds of the voters must approve the formation of the district, even though district policies will be dictated by a board of managers elected under majority rule. A landowner whose preferred water subsidy is less than that preferred by the median voter may decry the latter's overzealousness but still support the formation of the public irrigation district.

Destroying Separably Tradable Water Rights

In addition to the inefficiencies caused by the subsidization, public ownership also destroys tradable water rights separate from land ownership. This in turn eliminates the risk-spreading function of tradable water rights. The magnitude of the economic losses depends on the variance of the distribution of water intensity of crops grown in the area.

Figure 6-4 illustrates this inefficiency. Suppose that the equilibrium number of shares in the area's mutual irrigation company were $00'$. With two types of crops grown in the area, the shares would be divided so the marginal benefit of an additional stock share for farmers of either crop would be equalized (and in turn equal to the cost of a share of stock, P_M). A total of $0S_M$ shares would be owned by farmers of crop *A* and a total of S_M0' of shares would be owned by farmers of crop *B*. Farmers of both crops would earn their competitively determined levels of expected utility.

Now suppose that the mutual becomes a public irrigation district and thereby redistributes the water rights proportional to acreage.[19] As stock ownership in the mutual is proportionately greater for the farmers of the water intensive crop, reapportioning water rights according to acreage will shift the division of water rights to point S_P in Figure 6-4. This implicit, forced retrading in water rights carries a benefit for farmers of crop *B* from the additional risk spreading from ownership of water rights and the loss of risk-spreading benefits for the farmers of crop *A*.

The financial obligation of water rights must be considered. The costs of the system must be covered either by a direct charge on water purchases through water pricing or through the levy of a property tax for financing any water subsidization. Water charges now are effectively proportional to acreage (because water rights are), and reselling of water during normal years entails no profit because it was assumed that the market for water clears at the district water price. The property tax, which reflects the water subsidy, explicitly relates the cost of water rights in the district to property ownership. So the cost of the water right is ultimately apportioned on the basis of acreage, regardless of the mix between water tolls and property taxation.

19. The discussion assumes that just compensation is paid for the water rights, so there is no income redistribution from expropriation of private property.

Figure 6-4. The Effect of Destroying Tradable Equity Shares on Expected Utility of Farmers.

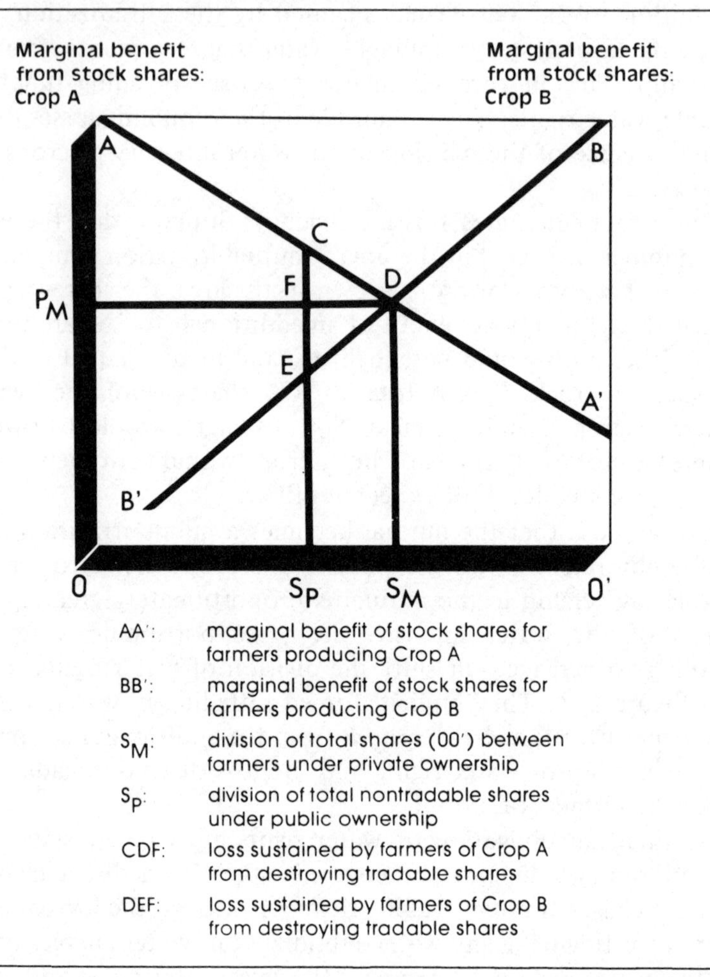

In economic terms, the forced retrading in water rights effectively specifies the quantity of water rights that each farmer must purchase at the price P_M. For farmers of the water-intensive crop A, restricting their holdings of water rights to $0S_P$ inflicts on them a loss equal to the area CDF (foregone surplus that would have been earned on the additional water rights purchased under private ownership). For farmers of the water unintensive crop B, expanding their holdings of water rights to S_P0' inflicts a loss equal to the area DEF (the amount the cost of the additional water rights exceeds their valuation for the additional risk-spreading benefits). The diagram shows that the magnitude of these losses grows with the difference between S_P and S_M. Areas with a greater variance among crops in their water intensities are likely to suffer greater economic inefficiencies, because differences in stock ownership per acre reflect differences in water intensities.

Since the division of shares under private ownership was a full equilibrium for the area, the losses in expected utility portend some exit of farmers from the area. Without exit, the residents would earn less than their competitive level of expected utility. The price of all land types would be reduced until the new configuration of land prices generated a mean and variance of total farmer income that provide the remaining residents with their competitive level of expected utility.

AN ECONOMETRIC ANALYSIS OF IRRIGATION WATER USE AND CHOICE OF OWNERSHIP IN CALIFORNIA

The econometric investigation confronts the theoretical propositions advanced in the preceding sections with evidence on the actual operation and prevalence of private and public ownership. Is there empirical support for the theory advanced in the previous section that the pricing and taxation policies of public irrigation districts stimulate the inefficient use of irrigation water? Do considerations about the effect of irrigation ownership on landowners' economic interests explain the actual choice of ownership? These questions are investigated by analysis of 1929 data on water use and choice of ownership in California.

The state of California conducted a survey on the use of water, cost of irrigation development, and acreage of 108 mutual irrigation companies and 71 public irrigation districts in 1929.[20] This sample of organizations represents almost universal sampling of public irrigation districts, but only a portion of total mutual irrigation compa-

20. State of California, *Cost of Irrigation Water in California*, Bulletin No. 36 (Sacramento, Calif.: Division of Water Resources, 1930).

nies.[21] Information is not available on the characteristics of the mutual irrigation companies excluded from the survey.

Water Use and Payment Schemes Under the Alternative Forms of Ownership

An initial examination of the payment schemes under private and public ownership creates the impression that both forms of ownership provide similar incentives for the individual farmer to conserve irrigation water.[22] One observes mutual irrigation companies using a two-part charge: (1) a direct water toll for irrigation water used and (2) an assessment on the shares of the mutual for the purpose of covering the remaining costs of the enterprise. Public irrigation districts also rely on a two-part charge—direct water tolls and property taxation. It may appear that both forms of ownership generate economic inefficiency because neither relies exclusively on water tolls.

There is no economic significance in the distinction between the two-part payment scheme used by the mutuals. Suppose that the water toll covers only the short-run cost of delivering the water to the farmer, as is often the case. The farmer will irrigate so long as the resale value of the water exceeds the short-run delivery cost. The resale value of the water will exceed the direct water toll because the original subscription to the mutual raised enough shares for financing a size of system that equated the demand for water to the full marginal cost of irrigation development (including the capital costs not reflected in the direct water toll). In other words, the resale price of water reflects both the direct water toll and an implicit water toll contained in the assessment on stock.

An important empirical implication follows: Variations in the direct water toll per acre-foot should have an identical effect on water use as variations in the indirect water charge per acre-foot represented by the assessment on stock ownership. Equation 6–1 illustrates this hypothesis.

21. The total irrigated acreage in the public districts included in the survey, 1591 thousand acres, represented 99.5 percent of the irrigated acreage in public districts reported in the U.S.D.A. *Census of Irrigation* (See Table 6–1). In contrast, the total irrigated acreage in the mutual irrigation companies contained in the survey was 362 thousand acres, or about 42 percent of the 854 thousand acres reported in Table 6–1.

22. An example of the reasoning in the text can be found in the analysis surrounding the display of the survey data in *Cost of Irrigation Water.*

$$\log (W/L)_i = a + bP_i + cSA_i + e_i \qquad (6\text{-}1)$$

where

$\log (W/L)_i$ = logarithm of water use per acre in company i

P_i = per-acre-ft. direct water toll in company i

SA_i = per-acre-ft. indirect water toll via stock assessments in company i

e_i = random error term indicating how actual water use in company i deviates from the relation summarized in the equation

a, b, c are coefficients to be estimated

The hypothesis advanced is that $b = c < 0$ because higher costs of water generate less use of irrigation water.[23]

Table 6–2 reports the results of estimating Equation 6–1 by ordinary least squares. To examine differences originating from the treatment of stock assessments associated with debt retirement, two specifications were estimated. In principle, the portion of the stock assessment reflected in the equilibrium resale price of water would be exclusive of debt retirement.[24] Unfortunately, information on debt retirement was only available for sixty-three mutual irrigation companies, all located in southern California. Therefore the two

23. Differentiation of Equation 6–1 yields:

$$\frac{\partial (W/L)_i}{\partial P_i} = b\,(W/L)_i \;; \quad \frac{\partial (W/L)_i}{\partial SA_i} = c\,(W/L)_i$$

If the direct and indirect water tolls have identical effects on water usage per acre, then the estimated coefficients b and c must be equal. The semilogarithmic functional form was chosen so that water use per acre would be finite at a zero direct or indirect water charge. A logarithmic specification does not satisfy that condition.

24. This proposition is simply a manifestation of the separation of resource decisions from financial arrangements commonly encountered in capital theory. For example, suppose there were two mutual irrigation companies identical in all respects (in terms of type of farmers, land, and so on), except that one firm issued bonds covering 50 percent of its initial capital development while the other company issued bonds for only 25 percent of its (identical) capital development. The former company would have larger stock assessments for debt retirement than the latter company, even though the resource decisions of the two mutuals would be identical. The reader may view this discussion as another application of the Modigliani-Miller Theorem of corporate finance.

Table 6-2. Regression Analysis of Water Delivered per Acre by Mutual Water Companies, Semi-Logarithmic Specification.

Sample	*Southern California Companies*	*All California Companies*
Intercept	.760 (10.25)	.913 (17.75)
Direct water charge per acre-foot	-.023 (-3.62)	-.026 (-4.43)
Indirect water charge per acre-foot, exclusive of debt retirement	-.023 (-2.62)	
Indirect water charge per acre-foot, inclusive of debt retirement		-.034 (-4.72)
R^2/F-statistic	.199/7.70	.290/20.42
Standard error of equation	.330	.358
Number of observations	63	101
t-statistic for null hypothesis: direct and indirect charges have same effects on water use	.01	.80

t-statistics in parentheses.

specifications also constitute different samples of mutual irrigation companies.

The empirical results strongly support the proposition that variations in the direct and indirect water tolls have identical effects on water use in mutual irrigation companies. In the southern California specification, the coefficients for the direct and indirect water tolls are equal to three decimal points. For the full sample, the differences in the coefficients are not statistically significant.[25] Both regressions, however, show that the level of water tolls (either direct or indirect) influence the use of water in a manner consistent with the economic theory of demand for a factor of production.[26]

Despite the same effect on water use of direct and indirect water tolls, there is an economic justification for the two-part pricing scheme. The direct water charge provides the proper economic signal

25. The number of mutuals in the full sample (101) was less than the number listed in the survey (108), because seven companies did not report water use.

26. The estimated elasticity of demand for water is considered in the next section, when the empirical analysis allows for crop differences in the demand coefficients.

for exercising water rights in any year—the resale value of water must equal or exceed the short-run costs of delivering the water. The indirect charge affects the capital investment decision by facing individuals with the cost of the individual capacities represented by their purchases of shares in the mutual.

Can a similar argument be applied to the payment schemes instituted under public ownership? That is, do variations in the indirect water charge—the property tax—affect the use of water just as effectively as variations in the direct water toll?

Bain, Caves, and Margolis have proposed a model of resource decisionmaking under public ownership that implies that all farmers would consider the full price of water use, including property taxes.[27] Their reasoning is that an individual farmer will realize that using more irrigation water, at any given direct water price, will increase the total amount of revenue necessary from property taxation. Realizing that the apparent water subsidy (the amount by which the water toll is below the marginal cost of the water supply) must be financed within the district, the farmer will consider the effect of this water use on the property tax rates.

There is a fundamental mistake in the above analysis. Each farmer's use of water influences not only his or her own property tax liabilities but also the property tax liabilities of all other landowners in the public irrigation district. Consequently, an individual's water-use decision will only consider a fraction of the total additional property tax revenues required to finance the larger water subsidy. The relevant fraction, of course, will equal the fraction of the district's total land irrigated by the individual farmer. The theoretical analysis presented earlier assumed competition in all land and water markets, implicitly asserting that each farmer's use of land and water represented such small shares of the area's totals that these fractions could be ignored.

These competing theories of resource use under public ownership can be distinguished by the following empirical test contained in Equation 6–2. Both theories expect that the coefficient for the water toll, b', will be negative.

$$\log (W/L)_i = a' + b' P_i + c' T_i + e_i' \qquad (6\text{-}2)$$

27. Joe S. Bain, Richard E. Caves, and Julius Margolis, *Northern California's Water Industry: The Comparative Efficiency of Public Enterprise in Developing A Scarce Natural Resource* (Baltimore: Johns Hopkins Press For Resources For the Future, 1966).

where

$(W/L)_i$ = logarithm of water use per acre in district i
P_i = per-acre-ft. water toll in district i
T_i = per-acre property tax levied in district i
e_i' = random term indicating how actual water use in district i deviates from the relation in equation

The theories differ, however, in their expectations about c'. The Bain-Caves-Margolis model predicts that the property tax, averaged over water use per acre, would have an effect identical to the direct water toll, making coefficients b' and c' satisfy the restriction given in Equation 6–3:[28]

$$b' = c' / \left(\frac{\overline{W}}{L}\right), \tag{6-3}$$

where $\left(\frac{\overline{W}}{L}\right)$ is the average water use per acre in the sample of irrigation districts used to estimate Equation 6–2.

The alternative theory advocated in the preceding paragraph predicts that water demand is more responsive to the direct water toll than to the property tax; the left-hand side of Equation 6–3 would be more negative than the right.[29]

28. Bain et al. posit the following demand function:

$$\log (W/L)_i = a' + b' \, [P_i + T_i / (W/L)_i]$$

Differentiating:

$$\frac{\partial (W/L)_i}{\partial P_i} = (W/L)_i \, b' \; ; \qquad \frac{\partial (W/L)_i}{\partial T_i} = b' = c'$$

The restriction is not tested by dividing T_i by $(W/L)_i$, which would result in a spurious negative relation between the transformed property tax variable with the water demand variable (the former variable has water use in the denominator). This spurious regression problem was avoided by testing the model restriction at the sample mean.

29. The direct water charge would have a stronger effect under the alternative theory because the property tax only affects water demand bv shifting the use of land. If the land supply elasticity is zero, then the effect of the property tax would equal zero. If the land supply elasticity is positive, then the property tax would reduce the amount of land cultivated in equilibrium. The effect on water use per acre depends upon whether the substitution possibilities between land or water are greater or less than those between land and other factors of production (e.g., labor and capital). In any event, those forces could not exert as much influence in water use per acre as variations in the direct water toll.

Table 6–3 reports the results from estimating Equation 6–2 by ordinary least squares. Two specifications were estimated according to the treatment of property taxation for the purpose of debt retirement. The results strongly support the theory of inefficient water use developed in the previous section. Water use is more responsive to variations in the water toll than to variations in the property tax rate. Using the theoretically preferred specification (exclusive of debt retirement), one can reject with great confidence the empirical hypothesis of Bain, Caves, and Margolis. Water-use decisions by individual farmers indeed are sensitive to pricing policies under public ownership.

The Probability of Private Ownership

Despite the economic inefficiencies of public ownership, it is plausible that the requisite number of voters may be better off pursuing irrigation development under public ownership. If so, the theory predicts that special elections would form public irrigation districts.

Table 6–3. Regression Analysis of Water Delivered per Acre by Public Irrigation Districts, Alternative Semi-Logarithmic Specifications.

Variable	*Specification 1*	*Specification 2*
Intercept	1.919 (31.92)	.930 (5.99)
Direct water charge per acre-foot	−.035 (−6.78)	−.023 (−2.63)
Property tax per acre, exclusive of debt retired	−.020 (−2.42)	
Property tax per acre, inclusive of debt retired		−.016 (−.80)
R^2/F-statistic	.538/35.53	.154/5.54
Standard error of equation	.421	.704
Number of observations	62	62
t-statistic for null hypothesis: Direct water charge and property tax (averaged over water use) have same effects on water use	−4.15	−1.30

t-statistics in parentheses.

The individual calculus behind the voting would involve the following considerations.

In principle, voters must compare two implications of that choice. First, will they benefit from the cross-subsidization of water use financed by the property taxation likely to be forthcoming under majority rule? Second, what is the magnitude of the losses caused by the fact that public ownership destroys the additional risk-spreading gains achievable under private ownership? Only if the gains from the cross-subsidization exceed the losses from sacrificed risk spreading would an individual support the formation of a public irrigation district.

Equation 6–4 illustrates the empirical strategy of testing this theory.

$$Prob = F(X1, X2) \tag{6-4}$$

The probability of observing an area organized under private ownership (*Prob*) is a function of two sets of variables: $X1$ is a vector influencing the fraction of voters benefitting from the cross-subsidization under majority rule, and $X2$ is a vector measuring the risk-spreading losses from public ownership. The greater the fraction of individuals benefitting from cross-subsidization, holding constant the losses from risk spreading, the lower the probability of private ownership. Similarly, holding constant the fraction of voters benefitting from cross-subsidization, the greater the risk-spreading losses from public ownership, the higher the probability of private ownership. The key empirical task is to identify the characteristics of an area contained in the sets of variables $X1$ and $X2$.

Recall the two characteristics of water demand in an area that influence the fraction of voters benefitting from the cross-subsidization under majority rule. First, the greater the ratio of median to average water use in the area, the greater the equilibrium water subsidy and magnitude of gains some landowners enjoy from cross-subsidization. Second, the less elastic the area's demand for water, the greater the equilibrium water subsidy, the gains of the median voter, and the fraction of voters benefitting under majority rule.

Three characteristics of an area can be identified that affect the magnitude of losses from inefficient risk-spreading due to public ownership. First, areas with greater variability in their water supply suffer larger risk-spreading losses, because they have larger demands for the risk-spreading benefits for tradable water rights separate from land rights. Second, areas with less elastic demands for water suffer greater losses from public ownership, because the gains from using water rights as a means of income insurance are greater. Third, areas with a greater variance in their distribution of water use per acre suffer greater losses, because public ownership ignores the greater diversity in the patterns of individuals' preferred ownership of water rights.

Equation 6–5 summarizes the empirical implications.

$$PROB = G(SKEW, VAR, V(S), n) \qquad (6\text{–}5)$$

The probability of private ownership depends upon four considerations: (1) the skewness of the distribution of water use per acre, $SKEW$; (2) the variance in that distribution, VAR; (3) the variability in the organization's water supply, $V(s)$; and (4) elasticity of the demand for water, n. The theory possesses unambiguous predictions about the first three variables. Increased skewness represents a lower ratio of the median to the mean water use, so the probability of private ownership increases because smaller gains will be obtained from cross-subsidization under majority rule. The probability of private ownership is increased by greater variance in water-use distribution, because embracing public ownership encounters greater losses from sacrificing demand for risk spreading accommodated by stock ownership in a mutual. Increased variability in the water supply also enhances the probability of private ownership for the same reason.

Changes in the elasticity of water demand have conflicting effects on the probability of private ownership. As demand becomes less elastic, the equilibrium amount of cross-subsidization increases under majority rule, enhancing the redistributive gains from public ownership and reducing the probability of private ownership. As demand becomes less elastic, however, the productivity of stock ownership as a means of insurance is increased. Thus the losses are increased from public ownership, destroying the risk-spreading advantages of the equity interest in the mutual. The probability of private ownership is increased. The risk-spreading considerations should be more important in areas with a greater variability in their water supply, for the losses from interfering with voluntary and efficient risk-spreading would be greater.

Severe data problems confront the estimation of the model specified in Equation 6–5. While the survey data identifies the form of ownership of the enterprise, it does not provide any indication of the remaining characteristics of the area. So all of the independent variables in the equation are missing. The research strategy adopted was to estimate each area's elasticity of demand and distribution of water use per acre and then use the imputed data in the estimation of the probability model of private ownership. The backbone of the imputation procedure is a study of how the relation between water use and water price depends upon the crop choice of an area. After presenting the results of that investigation, the imputation procedure will be discussed.

Estimating Crop-Specific Demand Characteristics. Equation 6-6 presents the specification employed in showing how the level and degree of price responsiveness of water use in a mutual irrigation company depends upon the type of crops grown in the area.

$$\log (W/L)_i = a + bFP_i + \sum_{j=1}^{5} a'_j S_{iJ} + \sum_{j=1}^{5} b'_{iJ} S_{iJ} FP_i + v_i \qquad (6\text{-}6)$$

where

FP_i is the total (direct and indirect) water charge in mutual i

S_i is the share of acreage in crop J in mutual i

v_i is a random term measuring how actual water use in mutual i differs from the relation given in equation

The terms involving the shares of acreage in different crop types capture differences in the properties of water use. The coefficients for the share variables, a'_J, measure how the logarithm of water use per acre varies at any given total (direct plus indirect) water charge according to the crops grown in the area. The coefficients for the share variables multiplied by the total water charge, b'_J, measure the differential response of the logarithm of water use per acre by crop type to variations in the total water charge.[30] For example, an area

30. The definition of share variables are:

S^1 – share acreage in citrus and orchard

S^2 – share acreage in deciduous trees and vines

S^3 – share acreage in alfalfa

S^4 – share acreage in rice

S^5 – share acreage in field crops (corn, hay, grain, cotton)

The miscellaneous crop use reported in the survey is the excluded category, which is required so that the variables in the regression will not be linearly dependent.

with all its acreage in the miscellaneous category of land use (the excluded category in the definition of the acreage share variables) would have a demand function with its logarithm of quantity intercept equal to a and its price slope equal to b. Another area with all its acreage in citrus and orchards would have a demand function with its logarithm quantity intercept equal to $a + a'_1$ and a price slope equal to $b + b'_1$. This model is estimated under the assumption that the crop share variables are exogenous. Any crop substitution created by variation in the water price involves substitutions within the categories, a justifiable procedure if the survey selected economically meaningful land-use categories.

Table 6–4 reports the results from estimating the water-use model by ordinary least squares. The summary statistics in the table include the F-tests for the important set of restrictions. For a given water price, crops employ irrigation water per acre in statistically significant different intensities, which is reflected by the joint significance of the coefficient set a'_J.[31] Similarly, the crops display statistically significant differences in their price elasticities, which is reflected by the joint significance of the coefficient set by b'_J. Finally, the set of all acreage variables, both separate and interacted with the total water charge, are statistically significant, improving the explanatory power of the model beyond that obtained by simply regressing the logarithm of water use per acre on the total water charge.

Table 6–5 reports the implied water price elasticities for the crop categories identified in the water survey. The results display considerable variability in the response of water use per acre to variations in the total water charge. Citrus and orchard, deciduous trees, miscellaneous crops, and probably alfalfa all display important price inelasticity of water demand. Consequently, producers of these crops would view the risk-spreading aspects of private ownership more highly than would the producers of rice and field crops. The standard errors of the estimated price elasticities indicate precise estimates of the magnitudes, especially for citrus and orchards, deciduous trees, and the other crop category. From an economic perspective, this means that areas having different combinations of acreage

31. The P-value of the F-test for the restriction that all a's are zero (.0003) is stronger than the P-value for the separate significance of rice's coefficient (.0008). So the other a's are themselves jointly statistically significant from zero.

Table 6-4. Regression Analysis of Water Delivered per Acre by California Mutual Water Companies, with Allowance for Crop-Specific Differences (*Semi-Logarithmic Specification*).

Variable	*Parameter Estimate*	*t-statistic*	*p-value*
Intercept (a)	.994	3.91	.0002
Direct plus indirect water charge (b)	-.056	-3.37	.0012
Share acreage in citrus and orchard:			
separate effect (a_1')	-.225	-.81	.4184
interacted with water charge (b_1')	.046	2.50	.0145
Share acreage in deciduous trees, vines:			
separate effect (a_2')	-.151	-.48	.6299
interacted with water charge (b_2')	.007	.25	.7391
Share acreage in alfalfa:			
separate effect (a_3')	.241	.50	.6157
interacted with water charge (b_3')	-.100	-1.18	.2414
Share acreage in rice:			
separate effect (a_4')	1.900	3.48	.0008
interacted with water charge (b_4')	-1.041	-2.69	.0088
Share acreage in field crops:			
separate effect (a_5')	.159	.33	.7391
interacted with water charge (b_5')	-.295	-1.16	.2505

Summary statistics:
R^2 = .571,
standard error of equation = .292,
$F(11,88)$ = 9.30,
p-value = .0001,
number of observations = 89.

F-tests of various restrictions:
(1) all separate effects of acreage shares are zero:
$F(5,93)$ = 5.46, p-value = .0003;
(2) all interactions between water charge and acreage shares are zero:
$F(5,93)$ = 5.88, p-value = .0001;
(3) all separate and interacted effects of acreage shares are zero:
$F(10,98)$ = 3.22, p-value = .0024.

Table 6–5. Implied Water Price Elasticities by Crop Type.

Crop	*Price Elasticity*[a]	*Standard Error of Estimate*
Citrus, orchard	–.067	.002
Deciduous trees	–.297	.114
Alfalfa	–.948	.475
Rice	–6.66	2.359
Field crops[b]	–2.13	1.53
Other	–.341	.101

a. Estimated by multiplying average full water price in mutual irrigation companies by estimated price slope of semilogarithmic demand function.

b. Includes corn, hay, grains.

shares in the various crop categories will have significantly different water demand elasticities.[32]

The empirical results in Table 6–4 also provide the basis for computing measures of dispersion in an area's distribution of water use per acre. As explained above, the coefficients involving the acreage share variables can be combined to obtain a crop-specific demand equation. Assuming that each acre within each crop category has the same demand function as that estimated from Table 6–4, summary statistics on the distribution of water use per acre can be computed by standard formulas.[33] These imputations are used as the indepen-

32. The formula for an area's elasticity of water demand, η_i, is: $\eta_i = \sum_j S_{ij}\eta_j$; where η_j is the elasticity of demand for water of crop j (estimated as the price slope for crop j multiplied by the area's total water charge).

33. Let w_j be water use per acre for land growing crop j in area i. Since $\log w_{ij} = a_j + b_j FP_i$, $w_{ij} = \exp\{a_j + b_j FP_i\}$. Using standard formulae:

The mean water use in area i, $\bar{w}_i = \sum_{j=1}^{6} S_{ij} w_{ij}$

The variance in the distribution, $V_i = \sum_{j=1}^{6} S_{ij} (w_{ij} - \bar{w}_i)^2$

The skewness in the distribution, $Sk_i = \sum_{j=1}^{6} S_{ij} (w_{ij} - \bar{w}_i)^3 / V_i^{1.5}$

In one crop area, the variance in the distribution is zero. The skewness was set equal to zero, for the mean and the median of a degenerate distribution are equal. Mathematically, skewness going to zero as crop variance goes to zero can be derived by noting that the numerator goes to zero at a faster rate than the denominator.

Table 6-6. Summary Statistics for Variables Entering Logistic Regression Analysis of the Probability of Private Ownership.

Variable	*Mean*	*Standard Deviation*
Demand slope: proportionate reduction in water use per acre from $1 increase in water price	-.1331	.1893
Characteristics of water demand distribution at zero subsidy:		
skewness	-.2939	2.69
variance	.5772	2.79
Cost characteristics of area water supply:		
percentage of water pumped	57.80	46.42
lift in feet	84.80	111.67

dent variables measuring dispersion in the water-use distribution of an area.

The summary statistics presented in Table 6-6 for the variables entering the study of the determinants of private ownership illustrate several important points. Considerable variability exists in the independent variables, particularly for the demand slope variable (measuring the proportionate reduction in water use from a $1 increase in the water price). On average the water demand distribution is skewed to the left, meaning that the median water intensity exceeds the mean. Within the context of the median voter model, this suggests that majority rule will support a policy of water subsidization financed by property taxation. Finally, considerable variation is displayed in the amount of pumping of water and the amount of lift. The cost of irrigation is known to be an increasing function of both of these variables.

Logistic Regression Analysis. The parts are now assembled for studying the selection of private or public ownership of irrigation facilities. Equation 6-7 presents the functional form used in logistic regression analysis, relating the probability of private ownership, *Prob*, to a vector of variables X.

$$Prob = \frac{1}{1 + e^{-XB}} \tag{6-7}$$

B is a vector of unknown coefficients to be estimated. The likelihood function (Z) for a sample of n organizations, with the fraction, q, of organizations being mutual irrigation companies is given in Equation 6-8:[34]

$$Z = \prod_{i \epsilon \text{private}} Prob\,(X) \prod_{i \epsilon \text{public}} [1 - Prob\,(X)] \qquad (6\text{-}8)$$

The coefficient vector B is estimated by maximizing the likelihood of the observed sample.[35]

Table 6-7 presents the empirical results. The estimated probability models confirm the importance of the risk-spreading motives to private ownership and the importance of income redistribution to public ownership. Consider, for example, the first specification. Areas whose water use is less responsive to the water price (that is, it has algebraically larger demand slopes) are more likely to pursue irrigation development under private ownership.[36] Risk spreading is also important in areas with greater variance in the distribution of water use per acre; these areas are more likely to embrace private ownership. As emphasized earlier, the inefficiency from the lack of separate, tradable water right depends upon the differences in stock ownership that would prevail under private ownership. Areas suffering greater losses from the destruction of the equity interest are more likely to reject public ownership. This reasoning is supported by the positive coefficient for the variance in water use.

The importance of potential income redistribution possibilities is captured by the coefficient for the variable measuring the skewness in the distribution of water use per acre. Greater skewness increases the likelihood of private ownership, an effect statistically significant at the 10 percent level.[37] Increased skewness implies a reduction in

34. The logic behind Equation 6-8 is the following. Assume that the ownership status of an organization is drawn from a binomial distribution with the probability of private ownership being given by Equation 6-7. Then the probability of private ownership is $P(X)$ and the probability of public ownership is $1 - P(X)$. The probability of independent draws from binomial distributions $P(X)$ (recall that X varies across areas) yielding the qn private companies and the $(1-q)n$ public districts is given by Equation 6-8.

35. The study used the logit routine in SAS.75.6 (Cary, N.C.: SAS Institute, Inc.).

36. Even though the theory has ambiguous expectations about the role of demand price responsiveness, there is evidence reinforcing the importance of risk spreading in promoting private ownership. States with greater rainfall variability show less presence of public and more reliance on private ownership (see Smith, "Water Districts").

37. A one-tailed test is appropriate because the alternative hypothesis to the null hypothesis of no effect has a definitive expectation of a positive coefficient.

Table 6-7. Logistic Regression Analysis of an Area's Choice of Organizational Form: The Probability of a Mutual Water Company.

Variable	*Specification 1*	*Specification 2*
Intercept	.345 [.] (4.93)	.243 [.] (2.66)
Demand slope[b]	2.462 [.563] (4.61)	2.414 [.552] (4.21)
Characteristic of water demand distribution at zero water subsidy:		
skewness[a]	.022 [.011] (1.29)	.025 [.013] (1.45)
variance[a]	.140 [.069] (2.86)	.068 [.068] (2.74)
Cost characteristics of area water supply:		
percentage of water pumped[b]		.0020 [.153] (1.32)
lift in feet[b]		.0010 [.022] (.26)
Summary-statistics:		
-2 log likelihood	174.3	171.2
Chi-square (degrees freedom)	33.77 (DF = 3)	36.80 (DF = 5)
Classification summary:		
percentage accurate	73.9	75.2
percentage classified mutual actually public	24.7	22.0
percentage classified public actually mutual	28.6	29.0
Number of observations	153	153

Note: Corresponding elasticity in brackets, *t*-statistic in parenthesis.

a. One-tail test appropriate because alternative hypothesis to no effect has a distinct expectation of sign.

b. Two-tail test appropriate because alternative hypothesis has no definite expectation about the sign of the coefficient.

the median to mean water use and a reduction in the total gains enjoyed by the median voter from water subsidization is reduced. Consequently the fraction of voters who would benefit from the formation of a public district is reduced.

The summary statistics for the estimated logistic regression indicate that the first specification identifies important distinguishing characteristics of an area that influence the selection of ownership form. Using the estimated coefficients, the model correctly classifies 74 percent of the areas according to their form of ownership. Of all the areas predicted to select private ownership, only 28.6 percent selected public ownership. Similarly, of all the areas predicted to select public ownership, only 28.6 percent selected private ownership.

Another way of illustrating the sensitivity of the probability of private ownership to variations in an area's characteristics is to compare the predicted probabilities at different levels of the explanatory variables. Table 6–8 indicates that areas with demand slopes one standard deviation above the sample mean demand slope have a probability of private ownership exceeding 81 percent. Areas with a demand slope one standard deviation below the sample mean have a probability of private ownership of about 15 percent. The probabilities of private ownership are also significantly affected by changes in the estimated variance and skewness of the distribution of water use per acre. For example, increasing skewness from one standard deviation below its mean to one standard deviation above its mean changes the predicted probability of private ownership from 49 to 61 percent.

The second specification of the logistic model in Table 6–7 expands the list of explanatory variables to include area characteristics

Table 6–8. Estimated Probabilities of Private Ownership and Changes in Area Characteristics.[a]

Variable	*One Standard Deviation Above Mean*	*One Standard Deviation Below Mean*
Demand slope	.81	.15
Skewness	.61	.49
Variance	.73	.51

a. Probability estimated by evaluating first specification of logistic model at sample means for explanatory variables except for the variable indicated in the first column.

affecting the cost of irrigation development. Areas with greater reliance on pumped water and higher lifts will experience greater costs of irrigation. Neither variable, however, is statistically significant, although their inclusion in the model improves the predictive power of the logistic model. A likelihood ratio test indicates that the cost variables taken as a set are marginally significant at the 20 percent level. So there is some evidence that areas with higher irrigation costs prefer private ownership. The inclusion of cost variables generally improves the statistical significance of the other variables.

A Revisionary Interpretation of Irrigation Development

The statistical analysis of water use and the choice of organization highlight the empirical relevance of the theory developed in this chapter. The payment schemes under the alternative forms of ownership have had predictable and important consequences for the effects of the cost of irrigation development on the pattern of water use. Public ownership, with its selected preference for water subsidization, generates an inefficient use of water. This inefficiency is economically important because of the sensitivity of water use to the water price. Many landowners may be net beneficiaries of this cross-subsidization. In fact, the key characteristic (skewness in the distribution of water use per acre) influencing the political prospects of water subsidization affects the likelihood of private ownership. Even though the welfare economist can identify areas of economic inefficiency, these income losses merely reflect predictable consequences of resource use when decisions are governed by the economic incentives prevailing under public ownership.

The empirical results clearly refute the perspective of traditional regulatory economics. If public ownership were in response to monopoly problems, then one would predict that areas with less price-elastic water demands and greater costs of irrigation development would select public ownership.[38] The ownership pattern in California showed the opposite pattern. If publicly owned enterprises insti-

38. See Richard A. Posner, *Antitrust Law: An Economic Perspective.* (Chicago: University of Chicago Press, 1976). In the appendix of this book, Posner presents a concise analysis of how the economic losses from resource misallocation under monopoly pricing depend upon the two factors mentioned in the text.

tuted efficient pricing of water, the presence of public ownership would not depend upon the vagaries of majority rule supporting income redistribution from water subsidization. In the case of California irrigation enterprises, at least, this traditional regulatory model fails to explain the functioning and pattern of ownership of irrigation enterprises.

The Prospect for Institutional Reform

The view advanced above should not be understood to imply that there are no public policy options available for encouraging institutional reform. The rules governing decisionmaking of public irrigation districts are the consequence of state legislative enabling acts. Modifying some basic rules can reduce the degree of water subsidization and even possibly influence the choice of ownership. The fiscal latitude given to public districts and rules governing voting are two areas where state enabling acts could exert economic influence.

Obviously, water subsidization cannot be financed by local districts without the fiscal tool of property taxation. At a more subtle level, the presence of prior constraints on taxation power will limit the ability of the public district to utilize its fiscal tools for income redistribution. The less latitude given, the greater the economic cost of achieving any amount of income redistribution via subsidization and thereby the less subsidization undertaken. In fact, public ownership is less prevalent in states that place prior constraints on permissible property taxation policies.[39] The likelihood is that those states also enjoy more efficient water allocation.

Second, consider the pluralities required for financing the capital development and forming an irrigation district. Greater pluralities required for approving public ownership will diminish the political viability of water subsidization and increase the efficiency of irrigation water use. Voting plurality rules have been shown to be quantitatively significant in understanding the relative growth of ownership forms in the western United States.[40] States requiring greater pluralities exhibit less prevalence of public ownership than states that require simple majorities for all political decisionmaking.

39. Smith, "Water Districts," table 6.
40. Ibid., table 7.

As irrigation becomes more valuable, there are greater economic incentives for society to embrace institutions promoting efficiency in water use and abandon the income redistribution from water subsidization. Encouraging privatization of water rights will be an integral part of the reform. The difficulty, of course, will be that existing institutions make some individuals better off than they would be under economically efficient private institutions. The growing inefficiencies of public enterprises, however, provide the opportunity for a compromise reform that protects the economic gains selected individuals garner from public ownership while producing the improved efficiency of private ownership.

APPENDIX A
THE EFFECT OF IRRIGATION DEVELOPMENT ON LAND VALUES

Figure 6–5 depicts the analysis for the case of only one type of land specialized in the production of one type of crop. Farmers must earn their competitively determined level of income from farming. Any ownership of mutual shares only provides a competitive rate of return on that investment, and the portfolio decision to purchase shares is independent of the residency decision. The price of land must be inversely related to the resale price of water, as shown by the curve *EE* that plots the factor prices consistent with the income entry condition of farmers.[41] The curve *WW* gives the combination of land and water prices that sets the area's demand for water equal to the available supply (zero) prior to irrigation development and the demand for land equal to the quantity of land in the area, which is assumed to be fixed. The land and water prices equilibrating these markets are indicated by the intersection of the curves *EE* and *WW*.

Now suppose that irrigation development increases the supply of irrigation water available in the area. The *EE* curve is unaffected

41. See Kenneth J. Arrow and F.H. Hahn, *General Competition Analysis* (San Francisco: Holden-Day, 1971) for a background discussion of the properties of a producer's income function. The key features are that any increase in a price of a factor of production (holding constant prices of other factors and the product) reduces the producers' income by an amount equal to the quantity of the factor whose price has increased. So increases in the resale price of water reduce land prices by the ratio of the quantity of water to the quantity of land demanded at initial prices for water and land.

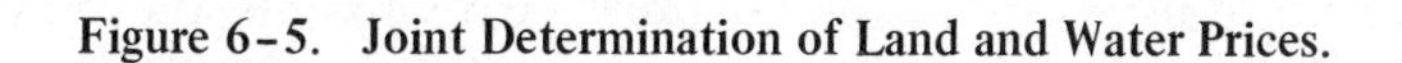

Figure 6-5. Joint Determination of Land and Water Prices.

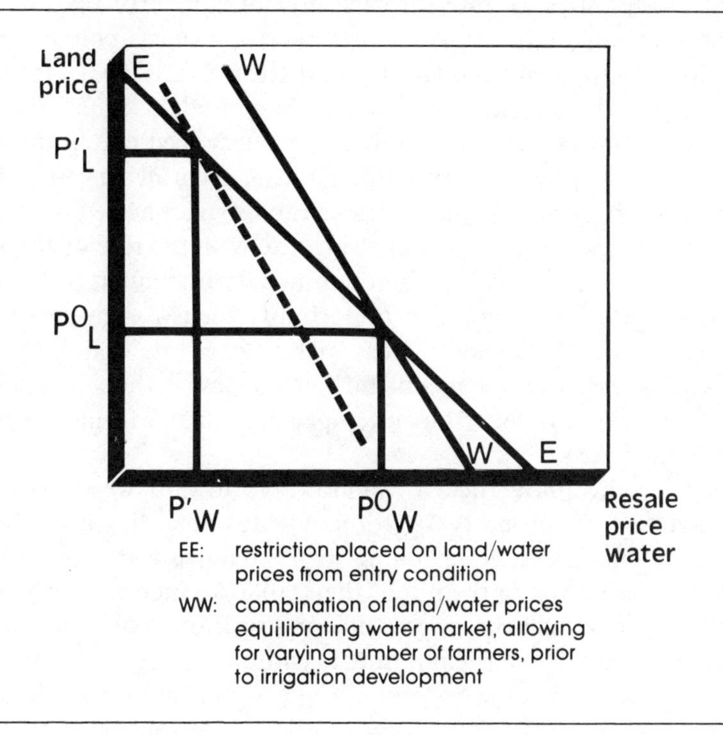

because it depends only on the level of the alternative income, prices of products, and prices of other hired factors. The *WW* curve shifts, however, because at any given land price the equilibrium resale price of water must be reduced. If the level of irrigation development shifted the *WW* curve to the dashed line in Figure 6-5, the equilibrium price for land must increase because the demand for land and the number of farmers have increased.

APPENDIX B
THE MEDIAN VOTER MODEL OF WATER SUBSIDIZATION

Because of the district's budget constraint, any water subsidy rate implies a particular property tax rate, because property tax revenues must equal the costs not covered by the revenues obtained from water rates. The locus 00′ in Figure 6–6 represents the maximum feasible water subsidy rate for each possible property tax rate. The precise location of the opportunity locus depends upon the water intensity of crops and the elasticity of the area's demand for water per acre. At the origin, the slope of the boundary equals the total use of irrigation water per acre at the unsubsidized equilibrium (the situation under private ownership). Thus areas growing more water-intensive crops have steeper slopes at the origin. The required property tax rate increases at an increasing rate with the rate of the water subsidy because, of course, water subsidization stimulates the use of irrigation water per acre. The opportunity locus for an area with a more elastic water demand increases at a faster rate than that for an area with a less elastic demand; further increasing the water subsidy requires greater property tax rates per acre in the former case (see also Figure 6–7c).

Consider the preferences of landowners toward water subsidization financed by property taxation. Landowners divide themselves into economic interests according to the relative water intensity of the crops specialized in the use of their land. An increase in the water subsidy, by reducing the price paid for irrigation water, bids up the per-acre price of their land, the magnitude of which equals the ratio of water to land use at equilibrium water and land prices. The incidence of the property tax also falls exclusively on landowners because of the geographical mobility of farmers and the assumed specificity of land in agriculture.[42] So the after-tax value of land is an increasing function of the water subsidy and a decreasing function of the property tax rate.

Consider the policy preferences of a landowner whose property is specialized in the production of the water-intensive crop. Curve 0*I* plots the combination of property tax and water subsidy rates that leave unchanged the after-tax value of the owner's land. In the neighborbood of the origin, the slope of the curve equals the amount of water used per acre of land in the unsubsidized equilibrium. By hypothesis, that water intensity exceeds the water intensity prevailing generally in the district (the slope of the feasible set of water subsidy and property tax rates). This landowner finds that there are

42. The geographical mobility of farmers is sufficient for the property tax to fall exclusively on land. So long as the water price remains fixed at a given level, the tax-inclusive price of land is constant under competition and variations in the property tax rate are fully offset by changes in the price of land.

Figure 6-6. The Relation between an Individual Landowner's Preferred Fiscal Policy and Type of Land.

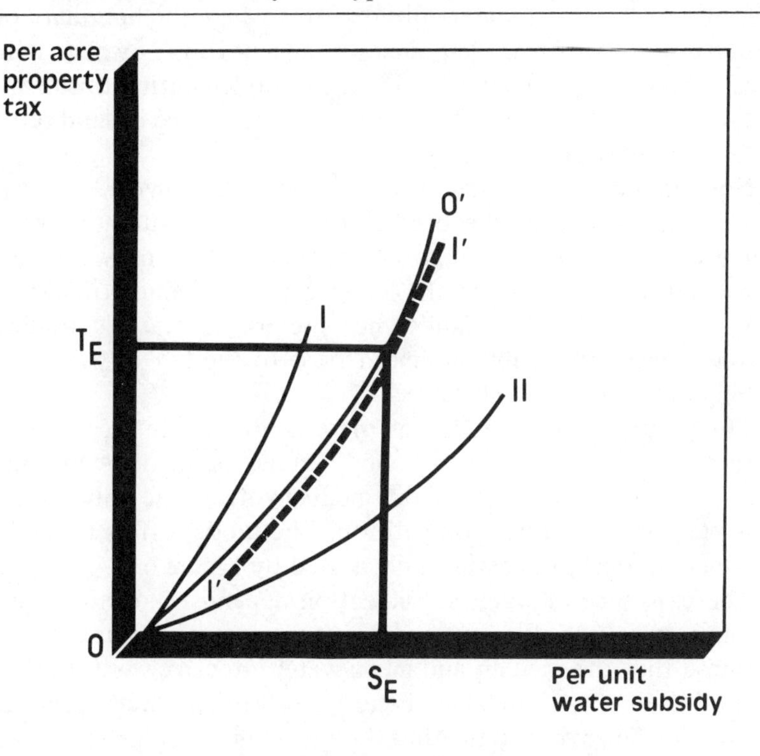

00′: locus of feasible property tax and water subsidy rates

0I: combinations of property tax/water subsidy rates that keep tax-exclusive value of land specializing in water-intensive crop at level obtained under private ownership

I′I′: combinations of property tax/water subsidy rates that provide (feasible) maximum value of land specializing in water-intensive crop

T_E, S_E: feasible property tax/water subsidy rates preferred by land specializing in water intensive crop

0II: combination of property tax/water subsidy rates that keep tax-exclusive value of land specializing in water unintensive crop at level obtained under private ownership

0: preferred feasible property tax/water subsidy rates preferred by land specializing in water unintensive crop

feasible fiscal policies (those to the right of $0I$) that increase the land's after-tax value. The owner's most preferred policy supports the property tax and water subsidy rates where the boundary of the opportunity set of feasible policies is tangent to the owner's indifference curve $0I'$. The owner's gains from implementing this most preferred policy is equal to the difference in the price of land reflected in the two indifference curves.

Now consider the policy preferences of a landowner whose property is specialized in the production of a water-unintensive crop. Curve $0II$ plots the combination of property tax and water subsidy rates that leave unchanged the land's after-tax value attained under private ownership. This landowner prefers no water subsidization because all other feasible policies (those to the left of $0II$) generate smaller after-tax land values.

The political process balances these competing interests when determining the district's fiscal policy. Under the median voter model, the most preferred policy of the median voter is the only policy sustainable under electoral competition. The model offers three fundamental empirical implications, illustrated by Figure 6–7.

The existence of water subsidization depends upon the degree of asymmetry in the distribution of water use per acre in the district. Suppose that the median and mean water intensity were equal at the unsubsidized situation, as in Figure 6–7(a). The indifference curve for the median voter, reflecting the initial price of his or her land, is tangent to the boundary of the feasible set of fiscal policies because the water intensity of the crop grown on the land equals the water intensity of the district as a whole. Note that this voter's indifference curve lies outside the boundary of the set of feasible policies. As water subsidization generates an economically inefficient use of irrigation water, the farmers could not bid up the price of the median voter's land by the full amount that the water subsidy reduced the farmer's expenditures on irrigation water per acre. Thus water subsidization would increase the median voter's price of land by less than the necessary property tax would reduce the price of the land. Difference among individual landowners in water use per acre need not portend water subsidization, because there could be a large variance of water use in this example.

The median voter only prefers water subsidization if the water use per acre on his or her land exceeds that district's average use (the skewness in the district's water use distribution must be negative).

Figure 6–7. Equilibrium Water Subsidy under Different Assumptions about Skewness in Water Use Distribution and Water Demand Elasticities.

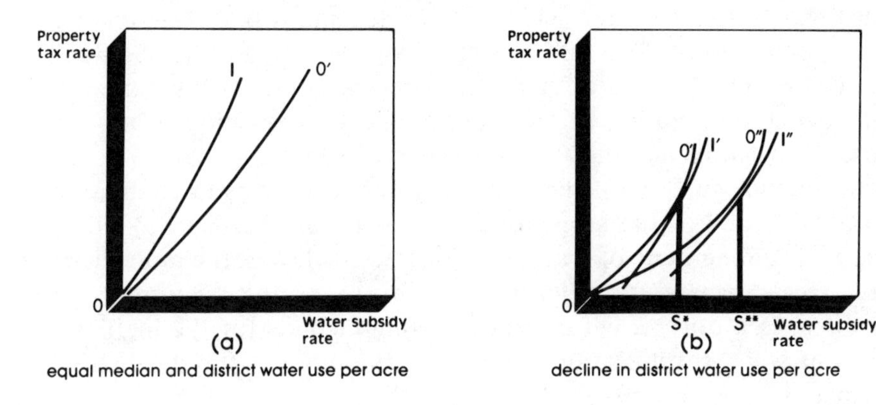

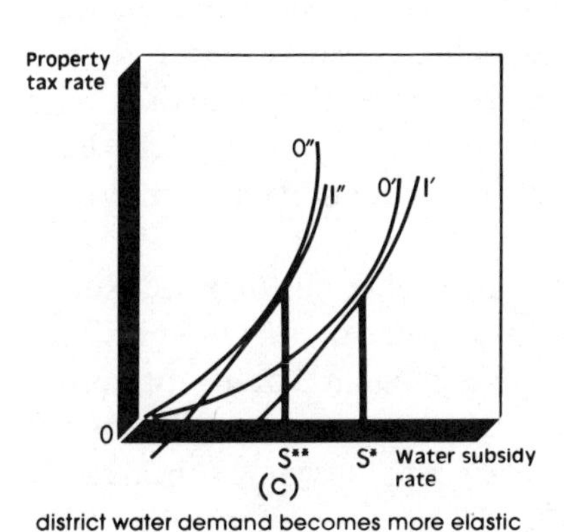

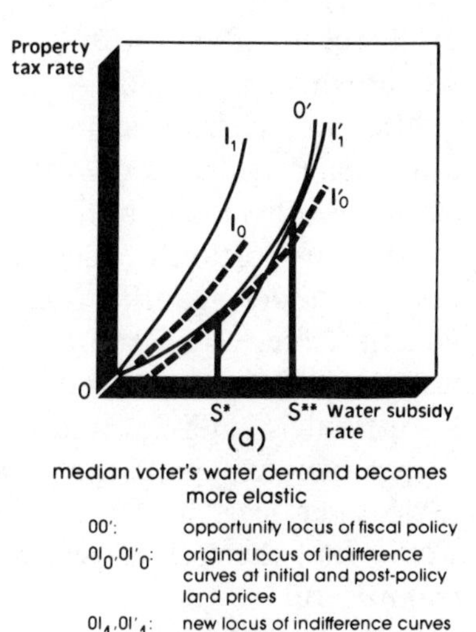

More severe (negative) skewness increases the equilibrium amount of water subsidization, as is shown in Figure 6–7(b). With no subsidy, the more severe skewness is created by a decline in the average water intensity in the district while the water intensity of the crop grown on the median voter's land remains constant. The opportunity locus shifts from $00'$ to $00''$ and the water subsidy increases from S^* to S^{**}.

The equilibrium water subsidy declines when the entire district's demand for water use per acre becomes more price elastic. As shown in Figure 6–7(c), a more elastic water demand rotates the opportunity locus from $00'$ to $00''$ because marginal increases in water subsidization require greater marginal increases in property taxation for financing the subsidy of the increasingly greater amount of water use. For simplicity, the diagram holds constant the median voter's indifference curve (and thereby the water intensity and elasticity of water demand of the crop grown on the median voter's land). So the equilibrium amount of water subsidization is lower, the more elastic the area's demand for water. In economic terms, this relation may be viewed as a price effect of redistributing income, for the inefficiencies of water subsidization are greater, the more elastic the district's demand for water.

Finally, the equilibrium water subsidy increases as water demand by the crop grown on the median voter's land becomes more elastic. As shown in Figure 6–7(d), this change makes the median voter's indifference curve system steeper, because the farmers on the land can expand their use of water at a faster rate and differentially take advantage of water subsidization.

What proportion of the voters would benefit from the water subsidization under majority rule? Figure 6–8 plots voter i's marginal net benefit from water subsidization. If the median voter's preferred water subsidy were S', voter i benefits from the water subsidization. Even though voter i would prefer an even greater water subsidy, S^*, i's net benefit equals the area $ABS'0$. All voters preferring a water subsidy at least as large as the median voter's preferred subsidy would find themselves better off with the fiscal policy generated by majority rule.

Suppose instead that the median voter prefers a water subsidy equal to S''. Then voter i can be either better or worse off from the equilibrium water subsidy, depending upon the balance between two conflicting forces: the net benefit accrued from the preferred subsidy rate (area AS^*0) versus the loss incurred because majority rule overextends water subsidization from i's point of view (area S^*CS''). Thus some voters preferring a smaller water subsidy than the median voter still enjoy net gains. If the median voter prefers a positive water

Figure 6-8. A Voter's Net Benefit from Water Subsidization under Majority Rule.

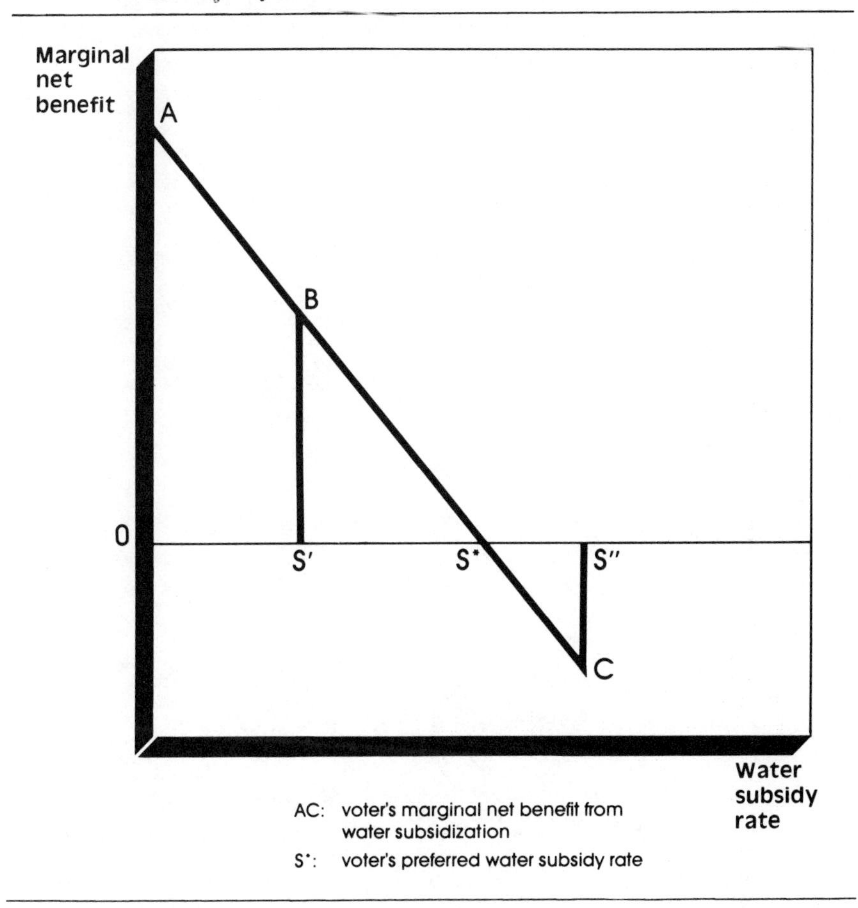

subsidy, more than 50 percent of the voters would benefit from that equilibrium water subsidization.

Generally the total gains of the beneficiaries are directly related to the economic factors increasing the equilibrium rate of water subsidy. If the marginal net benefit schedule in Figure 6-8 shifted to the right, there are increased gains from any degree of water subsidization.

SELECTED BIBLIOGRAPHY (PART II)

Buchanan, James M., and Tullock, Gordon. *The Calculus of Consent: The Logical Foundations of Constitutional Democracy.* Ann Arbor: University of Michigan Press, 1962.

Burness, H.S., and Quirk, J.P. "Water Law, Water Transfers and Economic Efficiency: The Colorado River." *Journal of Law and Economics* 23 (1) (April 1980): 111-34.

Cheung, Steven N.S. "The Structure of a Contract and the Theory of a Non-exclusive Resource." *Journal of Law and Economics* 13 (1) (April 1970): 49-70.

Demsetz, Harold. "Why Regulate Utilities?" *Journal of Law and Economics* (April 1968): 55-65.

Hartman, L.M., and Seastone, Don. *Water Transfers: Economic Efficiency and Alternative Institutions.* Baltimore: Johns Hopkins University Press, 1970, pp. 23-24.

Hirshleifer, Jack; DeHaven, James C.; and Milliman, Jerome. *Water Supply: Economics, Technology and Policy.* Chicago: University of Chicago Press, 1960.

Johnson, Ronald N.; Gisser, Micha; and Werner, Michael. "The Definition of a Surface Water Right and Transferability." *Journal of Law and Economics* 24 (October 1981): 273-88.

Long, Joseph. *A Treatise on the Law of Irrigation: Covering All States and Territories.* Denver, Colo.: W.H. Courtright, 1916.

Meyers, Charles J., and Posner, Richard A. *Market Transfers of Water Rights: Toward an Improved Market in Water Resources.* Arlington, Va.: National Water Commission, 1971.

Milliman, Jerome. "Water Law and Private Decision-Making: A Critique." *Journal of Law and Economics* 2 (1959): 41.

Seastone, D. A., and Hartman, L. M. "Alternative Institutions for Water Transfers: The Experience in Colorado and New Mexico." *Land Economics* 39 (February 1963): 31-43.

Tregarthen, Timothy D. "The Market for Property Rights in Water." In Jed P. Nanada, ed., *Water Needs for the Future: Political, Economic, Legal and Technological in a National and International Framework.* Boulder, Colo.: Westview Press, 1977, pp. 139-151.

PART III

TOWARD PRIVATIZATION

Chapter 7

PRIVATIZING GROUNDWATER BASINS
A Model and Its Application

Terry L. Anderson,
Oscar R. Burt, and
David T. Fractor

As with many other natural resources, there appear to be growing concerns that we will run out of our precious water supplies unless we can curtail the rapidly increasing demands. A 1981 *New York Times* article on the depletion of groundwater in the High Plains typifies these reports.

> In 30 years, drawing on a vast underground water formation called the Ogallala Aquifier, High Plains farmers have transformed the barren dust-bowl landscape into one of the richest agricultural regions of the world. Now, in many areas, the formation is nearly drained; everywhere the water table is dropping away from the irrigation pipes and pumps at a rate that has begun to frighten officials and farmers alike.[1]

As a result, local groundwater management districts have sprung up in an attempt to encourage conservation through educational programs and technical advice. Aid has been provided to farmers for the installation of dikes and dams to catch runoff and for other methods of increasing the supply of groundwater. Proposals have been made for interbasin transfers of water. Governor Richard D. Lamm of Colorado asserts that these large-scale technological solutions no longer are feasible. "We cannot produce our way out of a water crisis

1. "Depletion of Underground Water Foundation Imperils Vast Farming Region," *New York Times*, August 11, 1981, p. B4.

any more than we can produce our way out of an energy crisis. What we should have learned by now is that we must work on the demand side."[2]

This approach to water resources problems ignores a major economic problem—institutions. While it is true that water supplies are scarce and ultimately finite, and that demands have been increasing rapidly, it does not follow that centralized regulation is necessary. The real issue is whether the institutions provide signals and incentives that correctly reflect the scarcity, allowing resource users to respond to changing supplies and demands.

The institutions that provide signals and incentives for groundwater are various property rights and central bureaucratic agencies that dictate water allocation. Given an abundance of groundwater, the nature of these institutions made little difference until the claims came into competition with one another. Today problems with drawdown, land subsidence, salt-water intrusion, and increasing pumping cost all suggest the need for institutional reform. The competing uses for groundwater necessitate that close attention be paid to the structure of property rights if efficient allocation is to be achieved.

The purpose of this paper is to provide an agenda for institutional reform that will improve groundwater allocation. First we will survey the institutions and property rights that govern groundwater. A model elucidating the problems of allocating groundwater across time and space will be presented and used to develop a system for privatizing groundwater rights that allows for the decentralization of allocation decisions. This institutional arrangement will then be applied to the Tehachapi groundwater basin in California, comparing the results of privatization with those of existing institutions. The final section will draw implications and conclusions with respect to the future of groundwater allocation.

THE EVOLUTION OF GROUNDWATER RIGHTS

Neoclassical economists have begun to make changes in institutions and property rights endogenous in their models, just as they had with technological change. If the evolution of property rights is to be made endogenous to economic models, it is imperative that we focus

2. Ibid.

upon the economic variables that affect property rights. Professor Demsetz has suggested that "property rights arrive when it becomes economic for those affected by externalities to internalize benefits and costs."[3] Svetozar Pejovich has extended this generalization by asserting that "some important factors which govern changes in the content of property rights are . . . technological innovations and the opening of new markets, changes in relative factor scarcities, and the behavior of the state."[4] Changes in these economic variables shift the benefits and costs of defining and enforcing property rights.

The impact of these changes in benefits and costs is manifested in the evolution of groundwater rights. As long as groundwater was relatively abundant, it made little sense for the early American settlers to devote much effort to devising institutions to govern its allocation. As with many of our property institutions, the simplest rules to adopt were those from England. The English rule of absolute ownership first used to establish property rights in water, gave the overlaying landowner complete freedom to allocate groundwater without liability. Since the early English courts knew little about the hydrology of groundwater, they avoided the issue by classifying groundwater as property in the same sense as rock or mineral on or under an individual's land. "It was in the light of this scientific and judicial ignorance that the overlaying land owner was given total dominion over his 'property,' that is, a free hand to do as he pleased with the water he found within his land, without accountability for damage."[5] This form of property rights worked well as long as third-party injuries were rare: that is, as long as groundwater was not scarce.

As the demand for water grew and individuals began to compete for water and land use, the English rule of absolute ownership had to be modified. U.S. courts softened the English rule with the American rule of reasonable use, under which overlaying landowners had coequal rights to the groundwater, subject to "reasonable" use. The judicial determination of reasonableness is related to the demand of

3. Harold Demsetz, "Toward a Theory of Property Rights," *American Economic Review* 57 (May 1967): 354.

4. Svetozar Pejovich, "Toward an Economic Theory of the Creation of Property Rights," *Review of Social Economy* 30 (September 1972): 316.

5. Frank J. Trelease, "Developments on Groundwater Law," in Z. A. Saleem, ed., *Advances in Groundwater Hydrology* (Minneapolis: American Water Resources Association, 1976), p. 272.

adjacent landowners to the common supply. This aspect of the reasonable-use doctrine can create uncertainty in tenure, since the determination of reasonableness is subject to the whim of the court and can change with various economic and social conditions. As water has become more scarce, the uncertainty has increased as more uses have been challenged as unreasonable.

A third variation on the absolute-use doctrine evolved in the California courts in 1903. Since it was not possible for all overlaying users to meet their demands during drought years, conflicts arose over what were the absolute rights of the overlaying landowners. Efforts to change this doctrine resulted in the correlative rights doctrine which differed from the reasonable-use doctrine in two basic respects. First, in the event that the demand for groundwater exceeds the supply, all overlaying owners must reduce their use on a coequal basis. Second, in cases where supplies are in excess of the reasonable needs of overlaying landowners, water may be put to nonoverlaying uses.

These three doctrines are akin to the riparian rules that govern surface water. The precedent for these doctrines came from east of the hundredth meridan, where water was relatively abundant.

> Until groundwater use reached large-scale proportions it was possible even in arid states for the absolute ownership groundwater doctrine to live peaceably with the appropriation doctrine for surface water. The doctrines did not conflict because they did not meet. In fact, it was probably the insignificance of effects more than ignorance of the hydrological cycle which caused these inharmonious doctrines to be tolerated.[6]

Conflict could not be avoided, however, as population grew. The result was that in most of the western states the riparian doctrine has been explicitly repudiated and replaced with the doctrine of prior appropriation, under which water rights are acquired by use rather than tied to land ownership. Use rights, normally granted by permit through application to a public agency, are defined in terms of the quantity of water that may be withdrawn, the types of use to which water may be put, and in some cases even the dates when the water rights may be exercised. Not limited to overlaying use, appropriative

6. Edgar S. Bagley, "Water Rights Law and Public Policies Relating to Groundwater 'Mining' in the Southwestern States," *Journal of Law and Economics* 4 (October 1961): 152.

rights are established on a "first in time, first in rights" basis with preference to senior water-rights holders. This means that in times of short supply, junior rights holders may be shut out altogether.

In general the water doctrines that exist today have evolved as a result of changes in the benefits and costs of defining and enforcing property rights. The arid western states follow the appropriation doctrine with California using the correlative doctrine as well, while the more humid eastern states with their higher annual precipitation allocate groundwater according to the principle of reasonableness. Because of the abundance of groundwater in the East, there has been little incentive to modify the original legal doctrines of absolute ownership and reasonable use. It is not surprising that some eastern states have begun to modify their laws to conform more closely with those of the western states as they have experienced groundwater overdraft in recent years.

While the changing relative scarcity of groundwater has brought pressure for the establishment and revision of groundwater rights, this pressure has not resulted in an efficient institutional arrangement, that is, a set of property rights that gives water users the market incentives to put resources to their highest valued use. For this to happen, property rights must be well defined, enforced, and transferable. Definition and enforcement are necessary to give individuals the incentive to use water efficiently. In order for an exchange to take place, traders must have some idea of what rights are included. Less will be paid for rights that are not well defined and enforced, and in the extreme no trade will occur. Consider the impact of one person's pumping groundwater on another's pumping costs. If the rights being purchased cannot be exercised at the original pumping costs, the buyer will have an incentive to pump more rapidly in order to maintain his tenure. Without property definition and enforcement, all pumpers have this incentive, which can promote excessive depletion of the groundwater basin.

The transferability of property rights ensures that individuals will take into account the opportunity costs of their actions. As long as individuals are free to buy and sell water rights, market prices will emerge, making owners aware of the cost of wasting water. If rights are not transferable, however, the fact that water has more valuable alternative uses will make little difference; the owner will not be able to sell the rights and capitalize on these higher valued uses.

The property institutions that have evolved to govern groundwater are deficient both in terms of tenure certainty and transferability. California provides a case in point. To correct for problems inherent in the correlative rights doctrine, which fails to clearly define and enforce water rights, the California State Supreme Court ruled in favor of the evolving mutual prescription doctrine. Under this doctrine a basin is to be adjudicated and a safe level of extraction determined. A share of the rights are then allocated to the groundwater users in the basin on the basis of their extraction prior to adjudication. Since such a system eliminates a part of the common pool problem, it provides an institution for reducing tenure uncertainty and allowing transferability. However, in *City of Los Angeles* v. *City of San Fernando* (1975), the California Supreme Court struck a blow against the mutual prescription doctrine by partially reinstating the correlative rights doctrine. Adjudicated rights prescribed to a private pumper were transferred to the city of Los Angeles, the court arguing that rights could not be prescribed against public entities. Hence, certainty of rights was reduced. Furthermore, as we shall see later, the adjudication of the Tehachapi basin resulted in a restriction on transfer of prescriptive rights that has reduced efficient allocation in the basin. For many groundwater basins the rights have never been defined and enforced. Where riparian rights exist so that absolute or reasonable use is granted to overlaying landowners, the problems of the common pool are severe. These doctrines may work for solid minerals, but for a migratory resource like groundwater, riparian rights establish a rule of capture. Landowners have little or no incentive to conserve, for if they do not get the water, someone else will. Furthermore, under the reasonable-use doctrine the courts determine what uses are reasonable and unreasonable. The result is that tenure can change at any time and owners can lose their apparent rights in court battles without any compensation. Similarly, the prior appropriations doctrine often follows the "use it or lose it" principle; rights can be lost as a result of abandonment, which creates a disincentive for conservation.

Restrictions on transferability also exist under riparian institutions. In general riparian rights cannot be used on nonriparian land, meaning that the rights are tied to specific parcels of land and therefore cannot be transferred or allocated by a price system.[7] Where the

7. For a more complete discussion see Timothy H. Quinn, "Predicting Public Responses to the Groundwater Externality: A Proposal for Empirical Analysis" (unpublished paper, Department of Economics, University of California at Los Angeles, January 1981).

reasonable-use doctrine has allowed transfer, these alternate uses are subject to bureaucratic or judicial review. The transfer of appropriative rights also is subject to a hierarchy of uses, and in some cases, transfer of rights results in the loss of priority. While prior appropriation is suited to transferability, the doctrine as presently interpreted often places limitations that interfere with exchange. The potential exists for altering property institutions that govern groundwater allocation to make them more efficient.

A MODEL OF GROUNDWATER USE

Before turning to specific suggestions about groundwater rights, it is useful to precisely formulate the decision variables that are influenced by the institutions. The following model develops the economic conditions necessary for optimal allocation of groundwater in a basin that has both a stock and flow component. Given these conditions we ask whether the institutional setting will induce autonomous decisionmakers to achieve optimal allocation across time and space.

A simplified model of a groundwater basin is much like a tub filled with saturated coarse sand; a stream of water is flowing in (net natural recharge) and water is being pumped from the porous medium in the tub. If the incoming flow matches pumping, the level of saturation in the sand is stable; otherwise, the level is rising or falling as the difference between recharge and pumping is positive or negative, respectively. However, natural recharge to an aquifer is a random variable, and as a practical matter, the quantity pumped is frequently a random variable reflecting variations in irrigation demand caused by fluctuations in seasonal precipitation and temperature.

To explain the economic tradeoffs associated with intertemporal allocation, we present a simplified model for centralized management. If economic efficiency were the exclusive goal of controlling agencies, the results of our model might be attained. Since other criteria are part of the bureaucratic milieu, however, centralized allocation offers little hope for efficient groundwater management.

Two variables determine the economic value and allocation of groundwater over time—the annual rate of pumping and the total stock of groundwater at the beginning of the year. The role of the former is quite obvious since it determines the amount of water used per year in production. The role of stocks is two-fold. Their most direct and fundamental role is to provide the physical basis for water to be used in production, particularly under conditions where water supplies fluctuate randomly. Their second effect is on pumping costs; higher stocks imply lower pumping costs and vice versa.

Annual net economic value of production in the basin, denoted G, is a function of the annual rate of pumping, u, and the stock of groundwater, x. An inverse functional relationship exists between the stock of water, x, and pumping lift in an aquifer, which makes it possible to use either pumping lift or stocks as a variable in the economic return function. Economic value of production in the basin depends on many other variables besides u and x, but the function $G(u, x)$ is defined as a maximum with respect to these other variables for any given pair of values of u and x. Therefore, $G(u, x)$ implicitly reflects economically optimal levels of land, labor, and capital and allocation of water spatially within the basin; that is, $G(u, x)$ implies conditional optimization on all other relevant variables for given u and x.

Dynamic behavior of stocks is given by the linear equation

$$x_{t+1} - x_t = w_t - u_t, \quad t = 0, \quad 1, 2, \ldots, \qquad (7\text{-}1)$$

where t denotes the year and w is net natural recharge. Return flows from pumped water, u, are ignored for simplicity.

The appropriate criterion for efficient allocation is maximization of expected present value of net economic returns with respect to rate of pumping u_t, $t = 0, 1, 2, \ldots$, subject to the constraint of Equation 7-1 and nonnegativity of the variables, for any initial stock position x_0. Necessary conditions for the optimization problem yield the intuitive result that marginal returns from current use of water equal marginal value of groundwater stocks:

$$\partial G/\partial u = v(x) \qquad (7\text{-}2)$$

where $v(x)$ is marginal value of stocks.[8]

Of course, the entire optimization problem must be solved to derive the function $v(x)$, but at an equilibrium state in a simpli-

8. For an expanded discussion see Oscar R. Burt, "Optimal Resource Use over Time with an Application to Groundwater," *Management Science* II (1964): 80-93, and "Economic Control of Groundwater Reserves," *Journal of Farm Economics* 48 (1966): 632-647.

fied model where the random nature of recharge is ignored,

$$v(x) = (\partial G/\partial x)/r\,, \tag{7-3}$$

where r is the discount rate. Note that the variables in this equation are associated with the equilibrium state, say $u = u^*$ and $x = x^*$. The equilibrium equation for marginal value of stocks is quite intuitive in that it is the capitalization of annual marginal value of stocks in production. Annual marginal value of stocks is $\partial G/\partial x$, the value of an increment to stocks, x, while holding rate of use, u, constant. If this increment were to be received annually into perpetuity, its present value would be $(\partial G/\partial x)/r$.

While an important part of the stock value of groundwater is related to pumping costs, there are two other sources of value. First, because they are bowl-shaped, most aquifers lose part of their spatial distribution function as stocks decline. As the surface area of the water table decreases, the land surface area overlaying groundwater is reduced. Wells on the old perimeter before stocks were depleted go dry and water has to be transported to land lying near the old perimeter. Further loss of efficiency is encountered whenever the cone of depression created around the pump intersects the edge or bottom of the aquifer because pumping capacity is reduced as stocks are drawn down. This problem is especially critical for irrigated agriculture where timing of water delivery is extremely important. Since the intraseasonal storage and spatial distribution functions of the aquifer can be adversely affected as drawdown occurs, stocks have a value in addition to their direct impact on pumping costs.

Second, when recharge and irrigation demand are random variables, stocks have an insurance or contingency value. Shortages of water can cause a reduction in production to a point where water has a relatively high marginal value, creating a large opportunity value for stored water. A direct relationship exists between marginal values of stocks and variability of the random net additions to stocks in an aquifer, and the variability has more impact at low than at high levels of stocks. Under conditions of conjunctive use of ground and surface water, the variability in surface-water supplies has much the same impact as increased variability in natural recharge to groundwater.[9] As a practical matter for irrigated agriculture, the insurance value of groundwater stocks will guarantee a positive equilibrium

9. Oscar R. Burt, "The Economics of Conjunctive Use of Ground and Surface Water," *Hilgardia* 36 (1964): 31–111.

stock. Hence, the marginal value of stocks, $v(x)$, in the right-hand side of the general decision rule implied by Equation 7-2, reflects all values of stocks—pumping costs, spatial distribution, and insurance values for uncertain supplies—in all future years.

The necessary conditions for maximizing expected present value given in Equation 7-2 imply a decision rule or strategy in the context of decision theory under uncertainty. For any observed groundwater stock, x, Equation 7-2 can be solved for the rate of use, u, which makes it an implicit decision rule, denoted as:

$$u = f(x) \tag{7-4}$$

This decision rule has the property that of all functions of x, $f(x)$ yields the largest mathematical expectation of discounted returns from the groundwater basin, and in that sense, is the optimal or efficient rule.

The graph of an illustrative decision rule is given in Figure 7-1 where w^* denotes mean annual recharge. The equilibrium stock, denoted x^*, is the level of stocks approached in a probabilistic sense. Changes in stocks are governed by Equation 7-1 where w_t is treated as a random variable with mean w^*. Note that the expected change in stocks is positive and negative as $u_t < w^*$ and $u_t > w^*$, respec-

Figure 7-1. Illustrative Decision Rule.

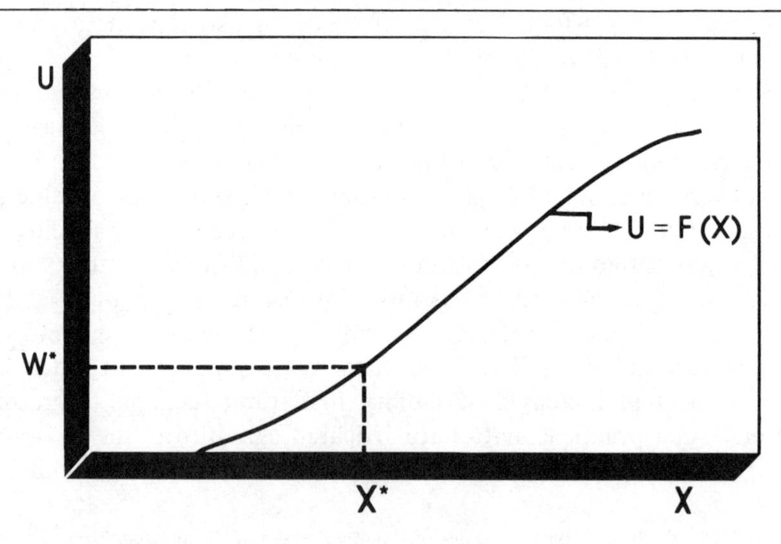

tively. Therefore, the *expected* direction of change in stocks is toward x^* from either the right or left if the decision rule in Figure 7-1 is followed.

The shape of the graph of the decision rule is dependent on the structure of the annual return function, $G(u, x)$, and the probability distribution of natural recharge, w. But $G(u, x)$, as an aggregate relationship for the entire basin, implicitly reflects the shape of the aquifer, hydrologic considerations such as specific yields of the porous media in which water is stored, pumping costs, and all aspects of the production function (productivity of various classes of land in the basin, natural climate, other sources of water such as available surface water) that generate net economic value. Under a centralized decision rule where there are no externalities, net value of the basin will be maximized.

Before turning to the discussion of privatization, it is useful to consider the implications of this model for resource waste under uncontrolled pumping. In the absence of a centralized decision rule or well-defined, enforced, and transferable property rights, externalities will arise and net value of the basin will not be maximized. Standard economic theory tells us that when there are many producing firms in the basin acting independently, each one pumping a small enough share of the total that it can economically ignore its own effect on groundwater stocks, the aggregate effect would be as if $\nu(x)$ in Equation 7-2 were zero for all levels of x. The resulting decision rule under uncontrolled pumping would equate net marginal value of water in current production to zero instead of a positive value as would occur under optimal management. Obviously, uncontrolled pumping with many firms could be very wasteful of the groundwater resource.

There are, however, some mitigating aspects to the groundwater problem not present with many other natural resources. First, water is costly to transport so that under uncontrolled pumping, the groundwater is nearly all used on land overlaying the aquifer. In effect, when groundwater is applied to a fixed land base-diminishing returns ultimately will be experienced. The structure of these diminishing returns will determine, in part, the present value of production from the basin under various groundwater allocation systems. Hence the extent of economic losses from uncontrolled pumping significantly depends on the quantitative nature of diminishing returns, that is, the structure of $G(u, x)$.

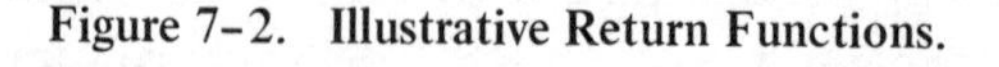
Figure 7-2. Illustrative Return Functions.

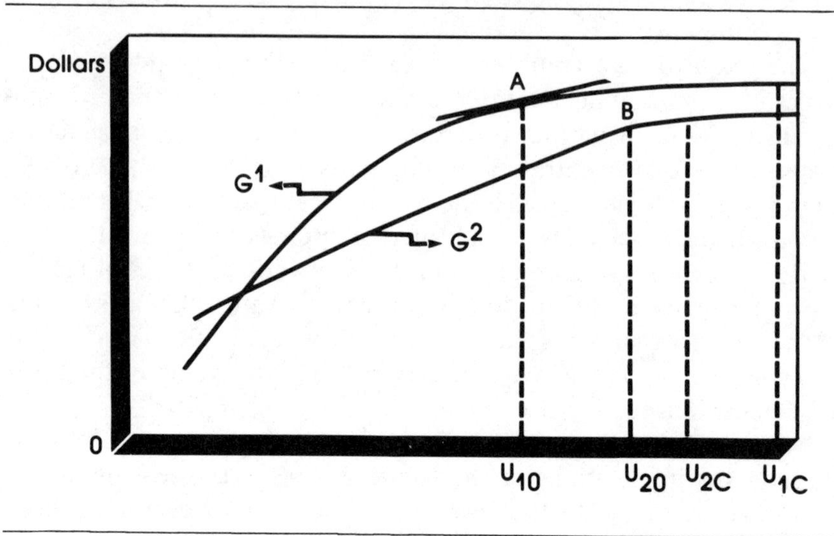

To illustrate how this aggregate return function affects resource waste, two alternative return functions with x held fixed are given in Figure 7-2. Since x is fixed, $v(x)$ is a given number that is the slope of the tangent to G^1 drawn at A. The decision rule implied by Equation 7-2 gives u_{10} as the optimal rate of use, since the slope of G^1 equals $v(x)$ at that level of u. Under competition (uncontrolled pumping), the rate of use will be increased to where marginal net returns (inclusive of pumping costs) are equal to zero since the marginal value of stocks is zero for each pumper. This implies $u = u_{1c}$ in Figure 7-2. The difference between u_{1c} and u_{10} is the wasted groundwater caused by the common pool externality. In the case of graph G^2, the counterpart of A is B for optimal rate of use, u_{20}, and uncontrolled pumping gives u_{2c}.

These return functions were constructed so that u_{2c} minus u_{20} is much less than u_{1c} minus u_{10}. In the case of G^2, a long segment of the graph is nearly linear, which could result from an abundance of homogenous land relative to applied water. On the other hand, G^1 has considerable curvature throughout and a long segment at the right-hand side with very gradual positive slope. Protracted diminishing returns exist, but they are not severe enough to drive the marginal value of water to zero until u_{1c} is reached far to the right of u_{10}.

The above analysis using Figure 7-2 measures the economic waste of a single year in units of water, but the primary consideration is a measurement in dollars at present value summed over the entire planning horizon. The opportunity cost of wasted water is the marginal value of groundwater stocks, which is $v(x)$ for the given level of x in Figure 7-2. Application of the optimal decision rule in Equation 7-4 implies a level of x for each year in the future when an initial stock is specified and the simplifying assumption is made that natural recharge is known with certainty. Each level of x implies a particular Figure 7-2, a value $v(x)$ for stock at the margin, and an amount of wasted water from the common pool problem. Therefore, a monetary value for each year is given by the product of the wasted water and $v(x)$. Each of these values is discounted to the present and the sum of these present values is total cost of the waste.

Referring back to Figure 7-2, it is seen that value of the waste depends heavily on the level of $v(x)$, which is the slope of the tangent of A (or B), as well as the quantity of water u_{1c} minus u_{10} (or u_{2c} minus u_{20}). But a third influence on value is the discount factor, which is inversely related to the distance in time from the present at which the waste occurs.

When initially developed, many groundwater basins were endowed with large stocks relative to the amount of water that could be used productively in the overlaying land area. For early years of development in such basins, common pool costs were rather modest because marginal values of stocks were low in the near future. Nevertheless, the stocks became more and more valuable at the margin as stocks were depleted. Natural recharge and sources of random variation on the demand side became a more important consideration as stocks became more scarce. Also, since pumping costs increased the externality problem became more serious. Finally, the spatial distribution function of stocks was threatened when stocks became sufficiently depleted. Present value of economic losses emanating from the common pool problem would tend to increase monotonically over time once development progressed to the point where stocks were declining.

A mitigating factor with respect to all sources of the externality is the slow movement of groundwater, particularly in some basins.[10]

10. Bruce Beattie, "Irrigated Agriculture and the Great Plains: Problems and Policy Alternatives," *Western Journal of Agriculture Economics* 6 (December 1981): 289-299.

Water must move through porous media to reach an equilibrium once disturbed by pumping activity, such as the cone of depression created around a pump. Insofar as water under land is slow to move into an area being heavily pumped, the externality is reduced. Rate of movement is proportional to the difference in levels of the two water tables and depends on various hydrologic parameters. In some basins, lateral movement a short distance under a modest head can take years.

PRIVATIZING A GROUNDWATER BASIN

As we have discussed, the key to market allocation of groundwater is well-defined, enforced, and transferable property rights. For the most part it is not enough to rely on the mitigating aspects of uncontrolled pumping to ensure efficient water allocation. Without efficient property rights or these mitigating conditions, the model developed in the preceding section describes how the actions of individual decisionmakers will diverge from those necessary for optimal allocation. Specifically, if well-defined, enforced, and transferable property rights do not exist, individual decisionmakers will ignore the benefits of foregoing water use today (conservation) in order to reduce overall costs of production in the future. In particular, they will behave as if the marginal value of stocks is near zero.

The usual reason given for a lack of efficient property rights is that transaction costs are too high. Included in this catchall phrase is everything from technological constraints on establishing rights to information and negotiation costs. The fact is, however, that geologic and hydrologic data can be obtained so that rights can be defined with sufficient accuracy to establish an operational system. Furthermore, metering systems exist that enable monitoring and enforcement of rights. Of course, the cost of this definition and enforcement may not be worth undertaking in cases where values of groundwater are low. As we shall see, however, where water is scarce these costs are not likely to be the constraints on efficient property rights.

One innovative approach to the privatization of groundwater basins was suggested by Vernon Smith.[11] The scheme would issue

11. Vernon L. Smith, "Water Deeds: A Proposed Solution to the Water Valuation Problem," *Arizona Review* 26 (January 1977): 8.

a property deed for some amount of water to each individual water user i, $i = 1, 2, \ldots n$, for n users in total. The deeds would have two components, one allowing claim to a percentage of the basin flow and the other to a percentage of the stock. The property rights would be allocated to individuals in proportion to their pumping during some base period. Using the Tuscon basin and a base year of 1975 as an example, the deeds or water rights would be determined as follows:

1. Individual proportions would be a function of total use in 1975, which was 224,600 acre-feet. Let the amount used by the ith individual be x_i acre-feet. Then the proportion of total use by individual i in 1975 would have been $x_i/224{,}600$, which is denoted p_i.
2. The flow right would be based on a fraction of long-run average net natural recharge to the basin, which has been estimated at 74.6 thousand acre-feet. Therefore, the property right of individual i to an annual flow is $r_i = 74.6\,p_i$ thousand acre-feet in perpetuity.
3. The second component would convey a right to a share of the basin's stock, which was approximately 30 million acre-feet in 1975. The share of this stock granted to individual i would also be p_i, giving a right to pump from the stock a total amount $R_i = 30\,p_i$ million acre-feet at any time in the future.

The initial allocation of water rights, which is arbitrary and primarily a question of equity, can promote waste.[12] To assign the water deed by the appropriative doctrine usually means that potential claimants must show evidence of use, and therefore users may race to the pumphouse. To avoid the incentive to waste water in establishing a priority right, the government could assign water deeds to landowners in proportion to land overlaying the aquifer. By allowing transferability, this method would ultimately achieve an economically efficient allocation.

Given some initial allocation of rights to the flow and stock components of groundwater, let us elaborate on an operational accounting system for enforcement. Pumps would be metered and each

12. See Terry L. Anderson and P. J. Hill, "Establishing Property Rights in Energy: Efficient v. Inefficient Processes," *Cato Journal* 1 (April 1981): 87–105.

owner of a right would begin with an initial stock. At the end of each year, an adjustment would be made to the stock account by subtracting the amount pumped and adding the appropriate share of aggregate natural recharge. Since the latter component is a random variable from year to year, observed stream flows or other sources of recharge would be used to estimate it. If return flows from irrigation were of consequence, these would be applied to reduce the subtraction from pumping. A method to maintain the integrity of the meters would have to be devised, and violations for pumping water in excess of the amount owned would be handled with fines.

Assigning rights to flows and stocks and allowing transferability would improve efficiency. Transferability forces private decisionmakers to consider the full opportunity costs of their actions. With this transferability it is even possible to achieve efficiency among different basins by allowing interbasin transfers. To protect third parties who benefit from incidental recharge, interbasin transfers would have to be restricted to consumptive use. For example, if consumptive use were 65 percent, as it is in the Tehachapi basin, a person who desires to transfer 130 acre-feet out of the basin would have to relinquish the right to 200 acre-feet. The remaining 70 acre-feet (35 percent) would be left in the basin to provide what would have been incidental recharge. The important point is that transferability of private rights would promote efficient allocation.

Whether this property rights system will improve efficiency by substantially reducing externality problems is another important question, one not addressed by Smith in his proposal. Perhaps a useful way to grasp the essential improvement over uncontrolled common pool pumping is to specify a simplified model where the externality is completely removed by the privatization of stocks and flows. Suppose that there are no pumping costs and that the aquifer has smooth, perpendicular sides and a perfectly flat bottom. Additionally, assume that seasonal pumping cones of depression from separate decisionmakers do not interfere with one another.

In this simplified case, uncontrolled pumping is inefficient because the water is there for capture, and one individual cannot set aside a reserve stock for future years. Each individual will pump water to a level where its net marginal value in production is zero, giving no weight to the tradeoff between current and future utilization of the stock. In the deterministic case with stocks appropriated as private property, it is well known that each firm will allocate stocks over time such that present values of marginal returns in each time period are equal.[13] If an aggregate optimization model for the entire basin is properly specified, this equality will be achieved. Therefore, the property rights system will yield the same intertemporal allocation of water as idealized central management in this simplified case.

These results can be extended to the case where natural recharge and demand for water are random variables if the objective is to maximize expected present value of economic returns. Unfortunately, an expected value criterion is quite restrictive; variability of economic returns as well as other aspects of the probability distribution become important considerations in the efficient allocation of resources. An aggregate optimization model for the basin cannot adequately represent the task faced by central management because expected value is only an approximation of economic efficiency. A more complete specification would have to take into account more than mean values of probability distributions. This tends to make the problem faced by central management intractable. On the other hand, property rights in stocks and flows look much more promising with respect to attaining economic efficiency under random conditions for recharge and demand.

An important consideration for economic efficiency where random elements exist is the availability of markets in which risks can be shared among all producers and consumers. There must be an opportunity for the relatively more risk-averse parties to exchange some risk for something else of value with the relatively less risk-averse parties. This opportunity for trade exists among all producers in the basin when stocks are privately owned. The relatively risk-averse producer will hold more stocks as a contingency against water shortage resulting from the random behavior of recharge and demand. Equilibrium price and quantities of stocks held by producers will reflect differential risk preferences among the producers.

To completely allow risk sharing with individuals outside the basin additional markets would be required. These markets might be developed through insurance schemes, but transaction costs are likely to be high. That commercial crop yield insurance is generally infeasible is evidence of the difficulty of insuring risk emanating from random weather factors. Therefore, under the simplifying assumption of zero

13. Harold Hotelling, "The Economics of Exhaustible Resources," *Journal of Political Economy* 39 (1931): 137–75.

pumping costs and absence of spatial distribution problems in the basin, privatizing groundwater provides a practical means for exchange of risk bearing within the basin. Central management schemes, which have no provision for dealing with risk sharing, are inferior to individual property rights under the simplifying assumptions.

Relaxing the simplifying assumptions so that pumping costs rise and the spatial distribution function of the aquifer deteriorates as stocks decline, the property rights system no longer completely solves the commonality problem. An individual user may have title to a certain stock of water, but conditions under which it can be obtained in the future are altered by use rates of all other users in the basin. First, rapid pumping in the aggregate will increase the relative future cost of pumping for any individual firm. Second, a firm that tends to conserve its stock of water relative to the aggregate may assume an additional risk if its location is near the perimeter of the aquifer, which might not be as deep as the center. This firm could find itself with title to a sizeable stock but no groundwater left under its land. Of course, rights in that stock could be sold, but with a declining surface area of land overlaying the remaining saturated part of the aquifer, value of the stock likely would depreciate.

To achieve efficiency given positive pumping costs, the spatial distribution externality, or both, requires a limited modification of our property rights scheme. The quantity of stocks appropriated as private property now must be determined from results of a central management model. Under an optimization model for the basin, an equilibrium stock of groundwater, x^* is implied. If the initial stock when property rights are issued, x_0 is greater than x^*, the total stock to which rights are assigned should be $x_0 - x^*$. This guarantees that stocks will not be depleted below x^*.

Estimation of equilibrium stocks, x^*, under an optimal intertemporal allocation policy poses an empirical measurement problem of both a hydrologic and economic nature. Improved information on both aspects will come forth after the initial appropriation of stocks for private property has been made, and better estimates will evolve over time. Unless dramatic changes in the economy or hydrology occur, the economic costs of errors in the choice of x^* should be relatively small. Provisions could be made to adjust the stocks made available as private property, but care must be exercised to avoid creating economically perverse incentives among owners.

Since this modification ensures that stocks cannot fall below x^*, the remaining question is how rapidly will autonomous users approach the equilibrium. Uncontrolled pumping will approach equilibrium much more rapidly than if no externalities were present and an optimal time path of use existed. However, with rights assigned to stocks and flows, there will be less of a race to the pumphouse, since individuals will be able to capture the pure stock value of the water. Groundwater will no longer be a fugitive resource governed by the rule of capture.

How closely the time path of use under privatization approximates optimality will depend in part on the interaction of firms operating under uncertainty about rates of pumping by other firms. The assignment of private rights would induce producers to pump somewhat less water than previously because stocks will have some pure inventory value. Observation of this new, more conservative behavior will generate expectations that pumping costs will increase less rapidly in the future than they did with uncontrolled pumping. This expectation will encourage conservation and precipitate a revision in expected pumping costs. The slow evolution of pumping lifts over time provides plenty of opportunity for users to compare observable evidence with their expectations and thus make appropriate revisions in their expectations. As long as pumpers follow this pattern, the time path of use under privatization will not be distorted by uncertainties about others' pumping behavior.

Furthermore, the time path of use under private property rights will be closer to the optimal path if there are restrictions in lateral movements of groundwater stocks. With such restrictions, the firm's pumping rate, as opposed to that of all other firms in the aggregate, will impinge on the firm's future pumping costs and reduce the externality.

In the final analysis, however, the actual time path will approach x^* more rapidly than is optimal to the extent that (1) each separate firm will not take full account of its actions on all firms' jointly determined future pumping costs, and (2) the spacial distribution externality remains. The amount by which the actual path diverges from the optimal path remains an empirical question. Nonetheless, in the long run the actual and the optimal time paths must ultimately converge as the equilibrium level of stocks, x^*, is approached.

While this property rights system may not be perfect, it would require far less central control than present systems. Placing decisions in private hands reduces the information requirements for central control and internalizes benefits and costs of decentralized decision-making. At least the pure inventory externality will be taken into account, and other sources of externality can be dealt with on the merits of their quantitative importance.

CASE STUDY: THE TEHACHAPI BASIN [14]

The assignment of private, transferable rights to groundwater has the potential to improve allocative efficiency, but do these potential gains justify the costs of establishing rights? If the value of groundwater is low, if the costs of defining and enforcing rights are high, or both, privatization is unlikely to occur. To date, most of the water literature has concluded that one or both of these conditions hold, making privatization impossible. In the Tehachapi basin in California, however, adjudication has resulted in a partial assignment of private rights. Hence this basin provides a case study for analyzing the property rights scheme described above. Recalling that the scheme entails the assignment of rights to stocks and flows, it is important to note that the Tehachapi adjudication only provides for flow rights. The effect of not assigning rights to stocks and of restricting transfers in the Tehachapi basin will be examined.

The Tehachapi basin (Tehachapi Valley West) is located in Kern County approximately 35 miles southeast of Bakersfield, California, and 100 miles north of Los Angeles. The 37-square-mile basin is the largest of three adjudicated basins within the area covered by the Tehachapi-Cummings County Water District.[15] Water in the basin is used primarily for agriculture, though there are municipal and industrial uses. The only source of natural recharge to the basin is precipitation in adjacent watersheds.

Groundwater use in excess of safe yield, the sum of net natural recharge and incidental recharge from applied water that returns to the basin, began in the 1930s following a steady increase in irrigated

14. The historical analysis in this section is drawn largely from Tehachapi Soil Conservation District, *Tehachapi Project Report*, 31 March 1969; John M. Gates, "Repayment and Pricing in Water Policy: A Regional Economic Analysis with Particular Reference to the Tehachapi-Cummings County Water District" (Ph.D. dissertation, University of California at Berkeley, Department of Agricultural Economics, 1969); Albert J. Lipson, *Efficient Water Use in California: The Evolution of Groundwater Management in Southern California* (Santa Monica, Calif.: The Rand Corporation, 4-2387/2-CSA/RF, November 1978). We have benefited greatly from conversations with John Otto, Assistant Manager of the Tehachapi-Cummings County Water District.

15. The other basins are Cummings Valley (13 square miles) and Brite Valley (3 square miles).

acreage. By 1960, over 60 percent of the groundwater extraction was overdraft. The water level in the overall basin dropped an average of 70 feet between 1951 and 1961, while the level around the city of Tehachapi fell 110 feet. During this period groundwater storage in the valley fell by over 61,000 acre-feet. From 1961 to 1968 the water table continued to drop an average of three feet per year.

The major consequences of this prolonged period of overdraft were that pumping costs increased dramatically and some wells ran completely dry. Fears that continued overdraft would seriously affect the agriculture-based economy brought about the formation of the Tehachapi-Cummings County Water District in 1965.

At that time a citizen advisory committee was formed to consider the options for managing the basin. The option chosen by the committee was to bring in surface water from the state water project's California Aqueduct and to adjudicate groundwater water rights in the basin. Because the basin is situated at an elevation of 4,000 feet, importation of surface water required that a pipeline lift aqueduct water over 3,400 feet. This made surface water far more costly than groundwater, which in turn made it unlikely that users would substitute away from groundwater without some additional incentive.

Adjudication of the Tehachapi basin offered the main hope for controlling overdraft. In 1966, suit was filed in Kern County Superior Court on behalf of the water district. The judgment, which was handed down five years later, followed the mutual prescription doctrine described above and limited total extraction to safe yield. The judgment determined each party's base water right as well as the safe yield for the basin. Base water rights were set at the highest average annual extraction over five consecutive years during any period after overdraft began. These rights totaled 8,250 acre-feet for the basin. Safe yield was estimated to be two-thirds of the base rights, or 5,500 acre-feet. Another provision of the judgment was that users pumping less than their allocated amount could stockpile part of this excess for up to two years. In keeping with other adjudication judgments, the amount stockpiled was limited to 25 percent of the allocation to avoid excessive stockpiling, which could impair surface drainage, and to hedge against the strain on demand if too many stockpile rights were exercised at once. The costs of adjudication totaled $300,000 for 100 users, or less than $55 per acre-foot adjudicated.

To encourage the use of imported surface water, which became available in late 1973, an exchange pool was established. The exchange pool allowed users near the surface water to be reimbursed for the difference between surface water costs and average groundwater pumping costs. For example, suppose that surface water for agricultural use was priced at $100 per acre-foot and that average groundwater pumping costs were $40 per acre-foot.[16] If an individual not adjacent to the pipeline wished to use surface water, the watermaster could authorize that user to pump groundwater in excess of his or her adjudicated right. The charge for this extra water would be $60 per acre-foot. During the same period, a user adjoining the pipeline would be required to substitute an equivalent amount of surface water for groundwater. That user would be reimbursed for the difference between surface water costs and average groundwater pumping costs, in this example $60 per acre-foot.

Before examining the impact of this adjudication it is important to note two restrictions on the exchange of groundwater rights. The first restriction results from heavy taxes on sales. The Kern County assessor has ruled that water rights severed from the land are subject to the same taxes as mineral rights. These prohibitive taxes mean that the exchange of groundwater has occurred either through sale of the overlaying land or by short-term leases.

The second restriction on exchange results from required watermaster approval for groundwater extraction at a location other than where the water right was developed. When a water right is leased by or sold to another party, the water is not physically transported but is pumped from the lessee's or buyer's well, which may be in another part of the basin. The rationale for watermaster approval is that a substantial number of transfers from one area in the basin to another could create cones of depression and increase pumping costs for some users.

Two major lessons can be learned from adjudication in the Tehachapi basin. First, it is clear that rights to groundwater can be defined and enforced. While the Tehachapi adjudication involved only rights to recharge, the fact that water can be stockpiled suggests that definition and enforcement of rights to the groundwater stock is also feasible. Second, casual observations show that major externalities in the Tehachapi basin have been eliminated through adjudication. Water levels are no longer declining, thus eliminating an upward pres-

16. Note that the average pumping costs for groundwater are determined by the watermaster and applied to all participants in the exchange pool regardless of their actual pumping costs.

sure on pumping costs. The importation of surface water has provided incidental recharge, which in turn has increased the water table in some areas. The city of Tehachapi no longer rations water as it had during some periods prior to adjudication. Rising water tables have brought previously marginal wells into production.

While limited privatization of rights to recharge has produced some improvements, further decentralization and privatization could increase efficiency even more. Problems remain due to restrictions on stockpiling of groundwater, the absence of rights to the groundwater stock, subsidies that distort the true cost of imported surface water, and constraints on the transfer of groundwater rights.

Elimination of the 25 percent limit on stockpiling would decentralize decisions and move the system toward a long-run equilibrium. One problem with this limitation is that it can generate a loss of water from the system. For example, if a farmer who is entitled to 100 acre-feet of groundwater uses only 60 acre-feet during the year, his or her allocation for the next year will be 125 acre-feet. Rights to only 25 of the 40 acre-feet not used can be retained by the farmer. While the 15 acre-feet are not lost in a physical sense, the right to use that water is lost. Line 3 of Table 7-1 shows the percentage of surplus that has been lost between 1975 and 1980. Restrictions on carry-over only make sense if the basin is at or near capacity so that stockpiling will impair surface drainage. This is not the case in the Tehachapi basin. In light of the fact that surface water is much more

Table 7-1. Groundwater Surplus and Surface Water Importation (*in acre-feet, except where noted*).

	1975	*1976*	*1977*	*1978*	*1979*	*1980*
Groundwater surplus (allocation minus use minus temporary transfers)	1,318	945	1,983	2,122	1,959	2,000
Allowable carry-over	959	771	1,268	1,397	1,141	1,193
Percentage of surplus water that is foregone	27.2%	18.4%	36.1%	34.2%	41.8%	40.4%
Imported water use						
Agricultural	4,032	2,311	1,337	1,284	1,565	2,167
Municipal and industrial	110	178	136	319	452	75

Source: Annual Reports of the Tehachapi Basin Watermaster, 1975-1980, Tehachapi-Cummings County Water District.

Table 7–2. Water Charges and Costs (*all $ values are per acre-foot*).

	1978	*1979*	*1980*	*1981*
Surface Water				
Municipal and industrial				
(no lease)	$283	$299	$394	$440
(one-year lease)	195	201	257	279
Agricultural	90	95	110	121
Groundwater				
Average groundwater pumping costs	32	32	46	59
Ratio of imported agricultural water charge to groundwater costs	2.81	2.97	2.39	2.05

Source: Personal communication with Mr. John Otto, Assistant Manager, Tehachapi-Cummings County Water District, September 1981.

costly than groundwater, there is no rationale for restricting carry-over.

The property rights framework developed in this paper calls for assignment of rights to groundwater stocks, but the Tehachapi adjudication included no such provision. It is true that the safe yield limitation eliminates externalities from drawdown. The lack of rights to the stock, however, means that valuable water will be locked up and left in the ground. While spatial distribution of wells and environmental problems probably would dictate withholding some portion of the stocks, it is difficult to justify locking up the entire resource. Just as a user is granted a perpetual right to a percentage of flow, that user could be given a perpetual right to a percentage of the stock. Table 7–2 shows that surface water for agriculture has been two or three times more expensive than groundwater, suggesting that efficiency could be improved by allowing the use of less expensive groundwater stocks.[17]

The efficiency gains implicit in the price differentials are understated to the extent that surface water delivery is heavily subsidized for most users. Although the 1981 cost of water from the state water project was approximately $18 per acre-foot, lifting the water 3,425 feet into the Tehachapi basin added over $350 to the cost per acre-

17. It would be efficient to use groundwater instead of surface water as long as the cost of surface water is greater than the sum of groundwater pumping costs and user cost, which is the imputed value of a unit change in the groundwater stock.

foot. Only municipal and industrial users without leases were required to pay the full cost. The heavy subsidy to agricultural users has induced them to use too much surface water. Eliminating this subsidy would reduce the overall demand for water, while establishing rights to pumping from the stock would encourage the use of a lower cost resource.

Finally, restrictions on transfer of water rights have reduced the efficiency of the system. Evidence in Table 7–1 indicates that users have been losing rights to surplus groundwater. It seems paradoxical that this would occur at the same time that substantial amounts of surface water are being imported into the basin at much higher costs. This paradox might be explained by high transaction costs, but the data in Table 7–3 suggest that an extensive market in water leasing does exist. The costs of marketing water rights do not appear prohibitive. A second possible explanation is that surplus water is being held for its insurance value. In a world of uncertain precipitation, irrigation requirements are not known in advance so individuals might not transfer their groundwater until they know for certain whether it will be needed. If, in the meantime, potential demanders make commitments to purchase surface water, there may be no market for the surplus groundwater. Though the water district does request advance estimates of surface water use, there is no penalty for using more or less than originally requested. Hence, uncertainty can be handled easily by purchasing surface water. Given the price differentials shown in Table 7–2, holding groundwater for insurance purposes seems expensive.

Restrictions on transfers are the most probable explanation for this paradox. Recall that water rights transfers to other locations within the basin must be approved by the watermaster. For the largest single rights holder in the basin this restriction is significant. The

Table 7–3. Temporary Transfers of Pumping Allocation (*acre-feet*).

Year	*Transfers*
1975	1,628
1976	2,022
1977	1,381
1978	834
1979	768
1980	1,026

Source: *Annual Reports of the Tehachapi Basin Watermaster*, 1975–1980, Tehachapi-Cummings County Water District.

Monolith Portland Cement Company, which held about 1,200 acre-feet of rights in 1980, has lost large quantities of water in recent years due to the carry-over limitation. Since its rights are on the far east end of the basin while agricultural demands are on the west end, watermaster approval would be necessary for transfers. This approval is not routinely granted because it is believed that large-scale transfers to one location might create cones of depression and increase pumping lifts. In light of the quantity and value of water being lost because of these transfer restrictions, it would be worthwhile to determine whether cones of depression and increased pumping costs are significant. Restrictions on transfer may prove to be an expensive solution to an unimportant problem.

CONCLUSION

Approaches to groundwater allocation traditionally have begun with central management because of the presumed infeasibility of definition and enforcement of rights. As the value of water rises, however, additional efforts will be devoted to obtaining the rental value of the water. The question is whether these efforts will be devoted to rent seeking from bureaucratic managers or to defining and enforcing rights that will encourage efficient decentralized management. Our analysis illustrates how the assignment of private rights to stocks and flows can remove nearly all externalities. The evidence from the Tehachapi basin suggests that privatization is possible at reasonable costs and that it has improved allocation; on the other hand, bureaucratic restrictions on pumping from stocks and on transfers continue to promote inefficiency. Establishing both stock and flow rights to groundwater has the potential for eliminating these inefficiencies and reducing centralized information requirements. With increasing scarcity of surface water and groundwater, privatizing the commons offers the most hope for obtaining the highest value from these resources.

Chapter 8

INSTREAM WATER USE
Public and Private Alternatives

James Huffman

For the early European settlers of the American West, the fact that water occurred for much of the year only in the often widely dispersed streams and rivers was a serious problem. They needed water to pursue the mining, and later farming, that were so critical to the success of their settlements. They constructed viaducts and ditches to get the water out of the streams, and they devised a system of water rights to make their efforts legal.[1] Although the nineteenth-century settlers were very successful in their efforts to put the limited water resources of the West to productive use, they would never have imagined the extent to which those who followed them in the twentieth century would devise methods for getting the water out of the stream. Transmountain diversions, using pipes of such enormous size that the early settlers could have driven their wagons through rather than over the mountains, are only the extreme example of an impressive array of modern technological solutions to the problem of getting the water out of the stream. The law has generally followed apace with the technology, with only the inevitable jealousies of states to establish legal barriers—barriers not to getting the water out of the stream, but to taking the water out of the state.

1. For a summary account of western American water law generally assumed to have been the product of local mining camp customs influenced by common and civil law, see Wells A. Hutchins, *Water Rights Laws in the Nineteen Western States*, Vol. I (Washington, D.C.: United States Department of Agriculture, 1971), pp. 159–175.

In the midst of this often massive effort to get the water out of the stream, there always have been a few who have sought to keep water in the stream. The federal government since its formation has been concerned with maintaining the navigability of the nation's waterways, but hydrology, topography, and the technology of modernizing transport have fortuitously kept the navigators and the out-of-stream water users from significant conflict. The navigability of the nation's streams and rivers was threatened not by those who would remove the water from the streams but by those who would place obstructions in the streams. As a result there was little reason for anyone to be concerned about a legal system designed to facilitate the task of getting the water out of the stream. By the 1970s, however, the out-of-stream water users were faced by competition from those who wanted to keep the water in the streams. The language and soon a technology of minimum flows and instream flows rapidly became as commonplace as those of diversion, consumption, and return flow in the nation's legislatures, agencies, and tribunals. The demand for the maintenance of instream flows became an important part of a revolution in American water law. The harsh realities of life on a finite planet ensured that efforts to get even more water out of the streams would coincide with a new demand to keep at least some of the water in the stream.

In a country that has relied increasingly upon government to resolve the problems of resource allocation and wealth distribution, it is not surprising that both those seeking to divert more water and those seeking to curtail diversions would look to the government for assistance. Both sides have experienced successes, in the sense that both the state and federal governments have constructed or subsidized often massive water development projects, setting aside specified flows of water to be left in the streams and rivers. In the midst of this rush to compete in the politics of water management, an occasional voice has suggested that there might be a better way. Frank Trelease, one of the few lawyers to point out that the "goddamned bureaucrats" may not have all of the answers, has argued that the system of private rights in water should not be so willingly abandoned in favor of various schemes of public water management.[2] Writing in the 1950s and 1960s, he focused on the allocation of

2. Frank J. Trelease, "The Model Water Code, The Wise Administrator and The Goddam Bureaucrat," *Natural Resources Journal* 14 (1974): 207.

water to agriculture and industry, demonstrating that Americans will derive more benefit from the available water supplies if the allocation of water to consumptive uses is left to the private market. His persuasive arguments for the restoration of private rights in water have brought many to his side. Although no doubt there is much to be gained by a privatization of rights to use water for agricultural and industrial purposes, the efficiencies of the marketplace would still be limited by the fact that most state water laws give the states the primary role in the allocation of water to instream uses. There seems to be a general assumption that water will not be allocated to most instream uses unless the state undertakes to make the allocation. In the water resource field, the allocation of water to minimum streamflow maintenance has become the archetypal case for government intervention, as Ralph Johnson observes: "In recent years it has become increasingly clear that the appropriation system, if allowed to continue unrestrained, will adversely affect and in some cases destroy valuable in-place commercial and recreational water uses."[3] This chapter will examine the validity of this presumption in favor of state intervention based upon in-depth studies of four state approaches to the allocation of water to instream flows.[4] The first section briefly examines the history and nature of people's interests in minimum streamflow maintenance. The following section examines the constraints that the private rights system has placed upon the private and public provision of instream uses and describes the basic approaches that states have used to overcome these constraints. Case studies in Idaho, Washington, and Montana then are discussed, followed by a description of Colorado's sharply contrasting approach to instream flow allocation. Finally, the prospects for the allocation of water to instream flows through a purely private system of water rights are considered.

3. R. Johnson, "Public Trust Protection for Stream Flows and Lake Levels," *U.C. Davis Law Review* 14 (1980): 256–57.

4. The information on the four-state programs is drawn from a study funded by the Office of Water Research and Technology, United States Department of Interior. James L. Huffman et al., *The Allocation of Water to Instream Flows: A Comparative Study of Policy Making and Technical Information in the States of Colorado, Idaho, Montana and Washington*, Vols. I–V (Portland, Ore.: Natural Resources Law Institute, 1980).

INSTREAM USES OF WATER

Before the nineteenth-century development of mining and agriculture in the American West, most uses of water were instream uses. In England and colonial America there was normally ample precipitation for the growing of crops, and industrial uses were limited to the use of falling water to power various types of mills. Although it was often necessary to divert water into mill ponds in order to achieve an adequate head, the diversions were ordinarily small in relation to the size of the streams, and almost all of the water was returned to the stream within a short distance of the point of diversion. Occasionally large mills were located in small streams with a resultant disruption in the streamflow, but as a general rule, industrial uses of water had very little impact on the natural flow of the stream.[5] Indeed, as Chancellor Kent observed, the English common law required that mill operators not alter the flow of the stream with respect to either the quantity or the quality of the water. "Every proprietor of lands on the banks of a river, has naturally an equal right to the use of the water which flows in the stream adjacent to his lands, as it was wont to run (*currere solebat*) without diminution or alteration."[6] The English rule that every riparian landowner has a right to the natural flow of the stream, undiminished in quantity and unaltered in quality, which proponents of instream flow protection could not improve upon, was modified very early in American jurisdictions by the qualification that the rights of riparians extend to the reasonable use of the water.[7] This modification of the English rule opened the door to consumptive uses by riparians even though they altered the flow of the stream.

Consistent with the general development of the law in the western states, the riparian doctrine of water law was imported along with the rest of the common law. In some areas, particularly western Washington and Oregon, the riparian system was suited to the climatic conditions. But most of the West was not blessed with abundant supplies of water, and settlers in these arid regions were quick to abandon the riparian doctrine in favor of the appropriation system

5. See *Mason et al.* v. *Hoyle*, 56 Conn. 255, 14 A 786 (1888).

6. Quoted in Charles J. Meyers and A. Dan Tarlock, *Water Resources Management* (Mineola, N.Y.: Foundation Press, 1971), p. 53.

7. See *Red River Roller Mills* v. *Wright*, 30 Minn. 29, 15 N.W. 167, 169 (1883).

of water rights, which recognizes water rights in those individuals who have put the water to beneficial use.[8] The appropriation system allows individuals to acquire water rights without also having title to riparian lands and permits the use of water on any lands without regard to their location in relation to the stream from which the water is diverted. The limits on water use under the appropriation system are largelv technological. Subject to the requirement that the water be put to beneficial use, water rights owners can use the water wherever they are able to transport it. The costs of water development virtually assure that any use to which water is put will be beneficial.

Unlike the English riparian rule, which assured the continued flow of watercourses, the appropriation system made it very difficult for any individual to assert a right to the flow of the stream except to deliver the water to a particular point of diversion. This situation arose in response to the need for appropriative rights holders to be able to demonstrate the existence of their rights. Under the appropriative system, water rights have priority in order of time of first use, which means that one must be able to establish the date on which the water was first applied to beneficial use. In a dispute between water rights claimants, each claimant must offer evidence of the date of first use. Given that most states did not have a system of recordation until fairly recently, the best evidence of first use is the date on which the water was physically diverted from the stream. As a result, diversion has become an essential element of any claim of an appropriative water right.[9] The water had to be taken out of the stream, but it was not a problem until the combination of changing values and diminishing water supplies brought the issue of instream flow maintenance to the public attention.

Historically, the most important reason for the protection of streamflows was navigation. In 1824, the U.S. Supreme Court determined that navigation is a form of interstate commerce, which is subject to federal control under the Constitution.[10] But the obstacles to navigation normally were physical obstructions, not inadequate flows.[11] On those streams where flow maintenance was likely to

8. See *Irwin* v. *Phillips*, 5 Cal. 140 (1855).

9. The standard elements of a valid appropriation generally include the following: intent to appropriate, notice of appropriation, compliance with state laws, diversion of water, and application to a beneficial use.

10. See *Gibbons* v. *Ogden*, 9 Wheat 1, 6 L. Ed. 23 (1824).

11. See *Wilson* v. *The Black Bird Creek Marsh Co.*, 2 Pet. 245, 7 L. Ed. 412 (1829).

be a problem, navigation was generally of little importance. Thus, although the issue of navigability has been important to recent legal disputes relating to streamflow maintenance, it is generally in the context of jurisdictional disputes between states and the federal government, and not because commercial navigation is threatened by inadequate streamflows. An exception is the recent growth of commercial services for recreational river travel, but this seldom raises constitutionally relevant issues of navigability.

The instream uses of water that have contributed to the recent pressures for instream flow protection are of three broad categories: wildlife protection, recreation, and pollution control. Perhaps the earliest legal action to ensure streamflows for wildlife, specifically fish, was in the context of federal water development projects that affected commercial fisheries. The hydroelectric dams of the Columbia River in particular had an enormous impact on the anadromous fishery that was important to the economy of the Northwest.[12] The solution, the effects of which are still being debated, was to provide "ladders" for the fish to use in their upstream migration. Of course these concerns for fish habitat protection did not stem from a scarcity of water and thus were more analagous to the earlier concerns over instream obstructions to navigation. Not until the 1950s were any significant legal actions taken to protect fish habitat from the reduction of streamflow to a level at which the fish could not survive.[13] More recently, the concern over the impact of streamflow levels on wildlife habitat has extended beyond fish to other forms of plant and animal life dependent upon the aquatic ecology.

Although wildlife habitat protection has been the primary source of concern for streamflow maintenance, recreation has been implicit in the arguments of those concerned for the fish. The biggest and most influential lobby for legal changes to protect instream flows has been promoted by organizations that represent recreational fishing. Their efforts generally have been supported by state fish and wildlife agencies, which normally depend heavily on sport fishing for political

12. For a detailed historical account see Michael C. Blumm, "Hydropower vs. Salmon: The Struggle of the Pacific Northwest's Anadromous Fish Resources for a Peaceful Coexistence with the Federal Columbia River Power System," *Environmental Law* 11 (1981): 211.

13. A 1949 Washington statute authorized state action to protect stream flows (Revised Code of Washington, 75.20.050). Oregon adopted a similar law in 1955 (Oregon Revised Statutes 536.310(7), 1977). As early as 1915 the Oregon legislature acted to preserve the flows of streams tributary to the scenic waterfalls of the Columbia River Gorge (Oregon Revised Statutes 538.200).

and financial support. Participants in other forms of outdoor recreation also have argued for instream flow protections, although at least as many forms of outdoor recreation are dependent upon the manipulation of natural streamflows as upon their maintenance.

In recent years, pollution control has emerged as yet another use for instream flows, a use that may prove to be at least as important as wildlife and recreation. Consistent with the purist orientation of the first years of the environmental movement, reducing the concentration of water pollutants through dilution was not considered a viable alternative in the early efforts to control water pollution. However, with the growing realization that zero pollution is seldom if ever a viable or defensible option,[14] agencies charged with the control of water pollution levels have increasingly looked to the effect of streamflow levels on the concentration of pollutants. Although dilution may not be the long-run solution to pollution, in the short run there can be little doubt that fresh water streams will be used to convey various types of industrial and agricultural waste, the concentration of which will be affected by streamflow levels.

APPROACHES TO INSTREAM FLOW MAINTENANCE

Wildlife habitat protection, outdoor recreation, and pollution control commonly have been viewed as public goods that will only be provided through some type of public effort. In the context of streamflow maintenance the presumption for state or federal action is fortified by the long-standing view that water is owned by the public in general and committed to private use only in the form of usufructuary rights.[15] Lawmakers and legal interpreters have been at pains to point out that under both riparian and appropriation doctrines of water law, the right holder possesses the right to use the water but does not own the water itself. The water belongs to the state, which has chosen to allocate it through a system of private rights in its use. In this context, water uses such as wildlife habitat protection, recreation, and pollution control represent the almost ironclad case for

14. See William Baxter, *People or Penguins: The Case for Optimal Pollution* (New York: Columbia University Press, 1974).

15. Water rights owners are held to possess a right to use the water, but they do not own the water itself.

public action. To the extent that there is a justification for the provision of water to these uses, it has been generally assumed that it will only be achieved through state or federal action.

Because other water users had been successful for many years in inducing the state and federal governments to subsidize consumptive water uses, those advocating government action to keep water in the streams were faced by opponents experienced in the politics of public water policy formation. The existing law of private water rights posed some unexpected obstacles to the implementation of instream flow legislation. The most common approach of the new legislation was to authorize the state, through one of its agencies, to appropriate water to maintain minimum streamflows. Some states proceeded to appropriate water for instream flows only to be told by the courts that the absence of a central feature of the appropriative doctrine—diversion—prevented such appropriations.[16] Further, it was not always clear that the instream water uses were beneficial under existing law, nor was it easy to determine when the state had ceased using the water for instream flows and thus abandoned its right. To the extent that these constraints were statutory, it was an easy matter for the state legislatures to change the law, assuming a favorable political climate. But in some states the elements of an appropriative water right were claimed to be a part of the constitutional law, which made change more difficult.

That these factors impeded government appropriations of water for instream flows to a large extent was simply a product of inadequate legislation and the lawyer's eye for legal loopholes. If the states really wanted to get involved in protecting stream flows, there was no doubt that the law would eventually be adapted to the achievement of that end. The more significant aspect of these constraints was that they were, and still are in most states, part of the system of private rights in water. Until it was proposed that the state appropriate water for streamflow protection, the appropriation system was widely believed to exist exclusively for the acquisition of private rights. Because it is generally assumed that instream flows will only be protected through state action, those aspects of water law that initially prohibited the states from appropriating water for instream flows still operate to prohibit individuals from making such appro-

16. See *Colorado River Water Conservation District* v. *Rocky Mountain Power Company*, 158 Colo. 331, 406 P. 2d 798 (1965).

priations or from acquiring existing water rights for instream flow purposes.

Regulation

Perhaps the most obvious form for government action to protect instream flows is regulation. The states' expansive police powers presumably can be used for regulating the use of water as easily as for regulating the use of land. For complex historical reasons, political constraints on state regulation of water use in the West are more severe than on the regulation of land use. There is no reason to assume, however, that the legal powers of the states are significantly different in the case of water than they are for land. Pursuant to the states' police powers, instream flows might be preserved by actions analagous to zoning regulations, which would limit private water rights holders to actions that would not be detrimental to the public interest in maintaining streamflows to reduce pollutant concentrations. Even without the justification of protecting the citizens' health and welfare, however, there is ample precedent for state actions designed to preserve aesthetic and other noneconomic values.[17] Barring significant change in the judicial interpretation of constitutional limits on the states' ability to promulgate regulations that limit private property rights, it would seem that the only serious constraint on state regulation to require instream flows is the political climate in which water rights owners have substantial influence.

Conditional Rights

A second alternative for state action to preserve instream flows is the imposition of conditions on newly acquired or transferred water rights. Like regulation, the state's power to impose conditions arguably derives from the police power, but unlike regulation many states already possess statutory authorization that can be interpreted to give the state the power to issue conditional rights. Most state laws provide that the state can apply a public interest standard in the recognition of new appropriative rights or in the transfer of existing

17. See *Berman* v. *Parker*, 348 U.S. 26 (1954).

rights. Pursuant to this power the relevant state agency could refuse to approve a new right or a transfer of right because it is contrary to the public interest in instream flows or could recognize the right on the condition that it be revoked if streamflows are negatively affected. As in the case of regulation, the political climate no doubt operates as a constraint on such state action, but under existing law it appears that the state has the power to recognize rights made conditional on minimum streamflow maintenance. The principal disadvantage of the approach from the point of view of the state is that it can only be applied to new appropriations or to water rights transfers, whereas regulation presumably could apply to all existing rights.

Reservation

A third approach the state might employ is to reserve unappropriated water from future appropriation. This approach resembles the reservation process employed by the federal government to exclude portions of the public domain from availability for private acquisition under the homestead and other land disposition laws. Because the state is the owner of the water and has chosen to make that water available for private rights in its use, there is no legal reason why the states cannot decide to reserve all or some of the unappropriated water from future appropriation. Although it has been argued in some states that there is a private constitutional right to appropriate unappropriated water, there is no indication that the claim will be upheld.[18]

State Acquisition of Water Rights

As was indicated above, the most common approach to the state protection of instream flows has been state acquisition of water rights. This can be accomplished in three basic ways: appropriation, purchase, and eminent domain. Legislative authorization for a state

18. In Colorado the claim has been specifically rejected. In The Matter of the Application for Water Rights of the Colorado Water Conservation Board in the Roaring Fork River and Its Tributaries, District Court for Water Division No. 5, Findings of Fact, Conclusions of Law, and Order for Entry of Judgment (26 June 1978), pp. 13–14.

agency to appropriate unappropriated waters for minimum flows has the political advantage of avoiding conflicts between the state and holders of existing water rights. However, the approach severely limits the opportunity for the state to protect streamflows because it can act only on those streams that are not fully appropriated and normally will result in the acquisition of very junior rights, which may be ineffective in maintaining adequate minimum flows. Authorization for the state to purchase existing rights will permit the state to acquire more senior rights and thus more adequately protect streamflows. The same end can be accomplished through eminent domain if the method is a legal form of state action to protect streamflows.

Public Trust

A final approach to the states' protection of instream flows is reliance on the public trust doctrine. Pursuant to this approach, the state might claim or be assigned a responsibility to protect instream flows pursuant to its role as trustee of a public right in the maintenance of streamflows. The public trust theory, which has historical roots in common law, has been variously revived in recent years for the purpose of asserting rights or duties of state action in the public interest.[19] The basic concept holds that the public, or all individuals in common, have a right to certain natural conditions—in this case, minimum streamflows—that supersedes any private rights in the use of the natural resource, and that the state has a responsibility to assure that those private rights do not infringe upon the public right.[20]

CASE STUDIES OF STATE INSTREAM FLOW PROGRAMS

Idaho—Setting Flows by Statute

In 1977 a group of Idaho citizens sought by initiative petition to get the Hydro-Power Protection and Water Conservation Act on the

19. See J. Sax, "The Public Trust Doctrine in Natural Resource Law: Effective Judicial Intervention, 68 *Mich. L. Rev.* 471 (1970); J. Sax, "Liberating the Public Trust Doctrine from Its Historical Shackles," 14 *U. C. Davis L. Rev.* 185 (1980).

20. See Johnson, "Public Trust Protection."

November 1978 ballot. The proposed law would have set minimum streamflows on all Idaho rivers and streams with unappropriated waters while recognizing the validity of all existing water rights. Prior to that time the only Idaho law relating to minimum streamflows was an authorization for state officials to appropriate water for the maintenance of water levels in designated lakes and flows in designated springs.[21] The constitutionality of this law had been upheld in 1974 in the face of claims that the state constitution prohibited the state from appropriating water, excluded minimum flows from the definition of beneficial use, and required an actual diversion of water for an appropriation to be valid.[22] The 1977 initiative drive was abandoned when the 1978 Idaho legislature adopted a statute that established three specific base flows on the Snake River and authorized the Idaho Water Resources Board to appropriate waters for the purpose of maintaining instream flows, subject to the approval of the state legislature.[23]

Under the 1978 statute the Water Resources Board may apply to the director of the Department of Water Resources for a permit to appropriate water for instream flows on its own initiative or in response to a request for such action by any private party. For an application to be approved by the director it must (1) not interfere with any vested water rights; (2) be in the public interest; (3) be necessary for the preservation of fish and wildlife habitat, aquatic life, recreation, aesthetic beauty, navigation, transportation, or water quality; (4) be a minimum rather than an ideal or desirable flow; (5) be capable of being maintained as indicated by past flow records. In addition, the application, like all other applications to appropriate water, must not conflict with the local public interest.

Although a decision on the application is dependent upon technical information relative to streamflows, existing rights, and minimum flows necessary for various purposes, the director has considerable discretion in the application of the two public interest standards. It was presumably in recognition of that discretion that the legislature required that all approved applications for permits to appropriate water for instream flows be submitted to the legislature within

21. Idaho Code, 67-4031 to 67-4311 (1971).

22. *State Department of Parks* v. *Idaho Department of Water Administration*, 96 Idaho 440, 530 P. 2d 924 (1974).

23. Idaho Code, 41-1503 et seq.

five days of the beginning of the legislative session. The legislature then may either approve or disapprove the director's determinations; a failure of the legislature to take any action is understood to be an approval of the application.

Because the system is relatively new and because the Water Resources Board has proceeded cautiously, it is too early to determine the impacts of the law. Some minimum flows have been established in addition to the base flows set by the legislature in the original legislation. However, these have generally been in noncontroversial areas where competing demands for water are minimal. Because the system is so closely linked to the political process by the requirement for legislative approval, it is extremely unlikely that the Water Resources Board will take any actions that are contrary to the interests of any politically influential group in the state. Agricultural and mineral interests, both heavy users of water in Idaho, are very influential in the state legislature. Hence it is unlikely that the Idaho approach to instream flow preservation will result in the protection of flows in the more populous and developed areas of the state. If such streams are protected, it will be a result of the ability of those valuing instream water uses to garner the necessary political power in the state legislature.

Washington—Setting Flows by Bureaucratic Expertise

Washington had one of the earliest state laws designed to give the state a role in maintaining instream flows. The power to deny or make conditional appropriation permit applications was granted explicitly in a 1949 amendment to the Washington appropriative permit law.[24] The director of the Department of Ecology (DOE) is required to notify the Departments of Fisheries and Game of pending applications for appropriation permits. Based upon the recommendations of those two departments and the DOE's assessment, the director can either deny permits or make their granting conditional on the maintenance of minimum streamflows. Pursuant to this power about 250 Washington streams have been effectively closed to any future consumptive appropriations.

24. Revised Code of Washington, 75.20.050.

In 1969 the Washington legislature authorized the Department of Ecology on its own initiative or at the request of the Departments of Fisheries or Game to establish minimum streamflows for wildlife habitat maintenance, recreation, aquatic life protection, other environmental values, and water-quality control.[25] As of 1980 the DOE had received twenty-six requests for the setting of minimum flows, one of which had been established.[26] The lack of action under the 1969 law was largely due to the 1971 adoption of another statute that authorized the DOE to set base flows defined as the flow sustained in a stream during extended periods without precipitation. Pursuant to that statute the department launched two major programs for setting base flows, one for western Washington and one for the Columbia River and its tributaries. The principal difference between the two statutes is that the DOE is required to establish base flows for all perennial rivers and streams, while the setting of minimum flows is entirely discretionary. Thus the task of setting base flows, given the department's interpretation of the law, is highly technical.

The DOE has established a five-step process for setting base flows.[27] The first step is a stream system analysis, which involves the collection and analysis of historical streamflow data. Then the various streams are rated on the basis of their value for the various instream uses outlined in the statute. Hydrographs are developed to determine the percentage of time flow duration and the discharge duration for each of the streams in question. The stream rating system then is used to determine what the base flow for each stream should be. Except for the task of rating the streams, the process is strictly technical. Although no doubt there are professional disputes about appropriate methodology, the task is simply to chart the volume and nature of the flow on an annual, seasonal, and daily basis. Once this is accomplished a formula is applied to each stream depending upon its rating, yielding a base flow.

The Washington system is heavily dependent upon the work of technical experts in the fields of hydrology and fish and wildlife biology. Although public participation is encouraged at various stages in the process, the technical nature of the DOE approach makes it difficult for people other than technical experts to become involved. Be-

25. Revised Code of Washington, 90.22.010 to 90.22.040.
26. Huffman, *Allocation of Water to Instream Flows*, Vol. V, p. 17.
27. Ibid., p. 21.

cause the stream rating system, the heart of the policy, comes early in the process, it is easily lost in the debate over technical questions. The stream ratings result from consultation among various state officials, who are subject to political pressures, in contrast to the Idaho approach, in which the state legislature has the final say. The Washington system allows the DOE to waive base flow requirements if hydro-power water use is threatened in low flow years and requires a reassessment every five years. It would appear, however, that the reassessment is likely to take the form of refinement of technical data rather than reevaluation of the water allocations resulting from the base flow program.

Montana – Setting Flows by Reservation

Montana has assumed by far the most aggressive state role in the setting of minimum streamflows. Although a reservation statute exists in the state of Washington, it has been of no importance to the maintenance of instream flows.[28] However, Montana's reservation law has made the state the dominant allocator of the state's water resources. Prior to 1973 when the reservation law was adopted, both the Department of Fish and Game and the predecessors of the Department of Natural Resources and Conservation (DNRC) had authority to appropriate water for public purposes.[29] Although it is not clear whether DNRC can appropriate for minimum streamflows, the Fish and Game statute was enacted specifically for that purpose and the department made twelve appropriations under the law prior to its repeal in 1973.[30] Both departments also have the power to acquire water rights by purchase, condemnation, exchange, and lease, although neither has been in a financial or political position to use that authority for the acquisition of instream flow rights.[31]

The 1973 Water Use Act was adopted pursuant to the legislature's 1972 constitutional mandate to "provide for the administration, control, and regulation of water rights."[32] The act authorizes the United States, the state, and its political subdivisions to apply for

28. Revised Code of Washington, 90.54.050.

29. Montana Code Annotated, 89-801 (1947) and 85-1-209 (1979).

30. Huffman, *Allocation of Water to Instream Flows*, Vol. IV, pp. 17-18.

31. Montana Code Annotated, 87-1-209 and 85-1-204(1) (1979).

32. Montana Code Annotated, Constitution, Article IX, Section 3 (1979). Pursuant to that provision the 1973 act was adopted. Montana Laws, Chapter 452, Section 2 (1973).

water reservations for existing or future beneficial uses or to maintain minimum flows, levels, or quality of water. Reservation applications, like ordinary applications to appropriate water, are to be made to the Department of Natural Resources and Conservation with approval to come from the Board of Natural Resources and Conservation, consisting of seven members appointed by the governor for staggered terms. In the context of western water law, the Montana reservation law is a striking change of direction in that it permits the acquisition by government agencies of prospective water rights. There was some precedent for government appropriation of water rights, but the concept of rights in future use is contrary to the history of a water law system that granted rights on the basis of use and took them away on the basis of nonuse.[33]

Although the statute does not require that the reservations on any particular stream be considered in a single proceeding, the circumstance of pending applications for significant appropriative rights on the Yellowstone River led the DNRC to organize a single massive proceeding to consider all reservation applications on that river and its tributaries.[34] The result was a protracted process of application, hearing, and debate leading to allocation of all of the unappropriated water in the Yellowstone River. Because private water users could not apply for reservations, the board sought to assure that the reservations that it granted did not tie up all of the water and thus prohibit any future private development of water. However, the variable nature of the streamflow and the inadequacy of much of the data available to the board raises some doubt about the prospects for future private water development.

Proponents of minimum streamflows fared extremely well in the Yellowstone reservation proceeding. The Department of Fish and Game applied for a reservation of 8.2 million acre-feet per year for fish habitat maintenance, an amount that in some years would exceed the total annual flow of the river. The Department of Health and Environmental Sciences applied for an instream reservation of

33. See *Utt* v. *Frey*, 106 Cal. 392, 39 P. 807 (1895).

34. In 1974 the Montana legislature adopted a moratorium on water appropriations on the Yellowstone River for a three-year period pending completion by the DNRC of the reservation proceedings. Montana Code Annotated 85-2-601 to 608 (1979). In 1977 the legislature extended the moratorium, which was further extended by action of the Montana Supreme Court. Montana Laws, Chapter 26, Section 1 (1977). See Huffman, *Allocation of Water to Instream Flows*, Vol. IV, pp. 25-29.

6.4 million acre-feet. The board eventually granted a reservation of 5.4 million acre-feet to Fish and Game near where the river leaves the state and numerous other flows at various points on the river and its tributaries.[35] The Department of Health was granted the same reservation at the downstream boundary of the state. Of course the board granted numerous other reservations for consumptive water uses by municipalities and agriculturalists, but by far the lion's share of the water was reserved for instream flows.

It is difficult to determine which factors played an important role in the board's decision. There is little doubt that the board was heavily dependent upon the information supplied by the various state departments in their applications, particularly the DNRC's environmental impact assessment and recommendations. The enormous volume of data that the board had to assess was technically complex. Although the members of the board are political appointees, they have been relatively free of political pressure, at least in the Yellowstone proceeding, and thus have been able to exercise their personal judgment about what decision is in the best interests of the people of the state. Under the provisions of the reservation statute, the board is required to review its reservation decisions at least once every ten years, but there is not likely to be significant change with respect to the instream reservations since the basis for reassessment is whether the amount of water reserved is necessary for the intended use. In the case of instream water use that issue will be very difficult to evaluate, except on the basis of information supplied by the departments of state government that hold the reservation right.

Implications of the Three State Programs

The instream flow programs of Idaho, Washington, and Montana involve two general approaches. The more dominant approach in all three states is to change the fundamental basis for the initial assignment of rights in water to permit the state to exclude certain waters from availability for private appropriation. Although the Idaho law speaks in terms of the state's acquisition of appropriative rights, the fact that the legislature must agree to every state appropriation for minimum flows differentiates the state's appropriative rights from

35. Huffman, *Allocation of Water to Instream Flows*, Vol. IV, pp. 72–74.

private water rights. For example, it is most unlikely that these minimum flow rights can be abandoned or transferred to private parties, at least not without specific authorization from the legislature. The terminology of appropriative water rights is applied to the state's regulatory actions as a convenience to facilitate their integration with the existing law, rather than to establish the state on a par with private water rights holders. The Montana legislature repealed a statute that authorized the state to acquire appropriative rights, and Washington has never employed the terminology of appropriation to describe the state's role in allocating water to instream flows. Thus, although only the Montana approach is self-described as a reservation system, the practical effect of both the Idaho and Washington approaches is to reserve water from availability for private acquisition.

The second general approach in the three states has been the direct regulation of existing private rights. In fact this approach exists far more in theory than it does in practice. In all three states the relevant administrative agency may refuse to approve water rights transfers that are found to be contrary to the public interest, which presumably includes the maintenance of minimum streamflows. All three states also have authority to deny appropriation permits on the basis of the public interest, but the exercise of this power will have the same effect as the reservation of water from private appropriation. The regulatory approach has been little used in any of the three states, in part because of the widespread political power of vested private water rights holders. However, the increasing urbanization in all three states and the resultant disassociation of individual economic welfare from the legal mechanisms for water allocation are likely to improve the political viability of the regulatory approach. Certainly all three states are well imbued in the regulatory philosophy and legal mechanics of land-use regulation, which could be readily applied to water-use regulation.

Some variation on reservation has been the dominant approach to date, the impact of which on the allocation of water in a particular state depends largely upon the existing conditions in that state. In Montana, where there is an abundance of unappropriated water, the reservation approach to instream flow protection will give the state a dominant role in water-use decisionmaking. In states where most water has been appropriated by private users prior to the implementation of a state reservation program, the state's role in water allocation will be far less significant. Those states will not achieve a dominant role in water allocation without resorting to regulation similar to that common in land-use decisions.

One implication of the reservation approach to instream flow maintenance is that there is no logically valid public-trust principle under which such flows are to be maintained. A public-trust duty by the states to maintain streamflows theoretically predates any private rights and can be implemented by the simple denial, suspension, or cancellation of appropriation permits that would result in the violation of the public trust. The affirmative reservation of water from future appropriation implies that the water would otherwise be available for appropriation. Of course, the existence of a public-trust duty on the part of the state may be little different from the power that the state may assert pursuant to its police powers, except that the state has discretion in implementing the latter. If the states recognized a trustee duty they could easily base their streamflow protection actions on the existence of the public trust and would not be constrained to protecting flows on streams that are not yet fully appropriated.

Given the theoretical foundation of western water law, which recognizes that the states have authority to grant private rights of use in publicly owned water supplies, there is little doubt that the states have the authority to pursue the reservation approach to instream flow protection. The reluctance of the states to resort to regulatory approaches must be attributed to political rather than legal constraints, particularly considering past experience with land-use regulation. Thus it is important to consider the policy arguments that might be invoked to justify future resort to regulation.

The assertion that minimum streamflows are a public good that will not be provided without state intervention is based on the assumption that no private individual or corporate entity will provide for instream flows because they will be unable to profit from the necessary investment. The inability of investors in instream flows to gain an adequate return on their investment is attributed to the fact that many individuals experience external benefits for which they cannot be forced to pay because of an assortment of transactions costs and the existence of free riders. In other words, it is argued that water resources will be inefficiently allocated unless the state intervenes to ensure that a sufficient amount of water is allocated to instream flows.

Whether state intervention can actually improve upon efficiency is an empirical issue that cannot be resolved on the basis of existing data. There is reason, nevertheless, to resist this theory. It is possible that the costs of state transactions will be as high or higher than the costs of private transactions. But more importantly, it may well be found that existing inefficiencies in water allocation result from deficiencies in the private rights system rather than from alleged market failures. The existing water law seriously limits private acquisition of instream flow rights, so we cannot be sure from experience that the initial public-good assumption is accurate. And even if we accept the public-good assumption with respect to streamflow maintenance, there are alternative approaches to state involvement that are far more likely to approach the goal of efficient water allocation than the systems being employed in Idaho, Washington, and Montana. The state of Colorado has implemented one such alternative.

Before considering the Colorado approach, it will be useful to briefly detail the reasons for urging caution in the further implementation of the existing instream flow laws. The question of what water should be reserved from future private appropriations, whether addressed in the context of a particular situation or an entire water basin or political jurisdiction, turns on whether the people of the state will benefit more from the allocation of particular waters to instream flow maintenance or to private acquisition of some other use. To the extent that water reservations are generally stated, the allocational problem will be delegated to an agency bureaucrat, legislator, or board member, depending on the context. An examination of the instream flow programs in Idaho, Washington, and Montana suggests that the designated public officials are in no position to make such allocational decisions with respect to the objective of allocational efficiency. Whether in the context of stream rating under Washington law or water reservation under Montana law, the decisionmakers have very little information about the relative values of the water for the competing uses. If one could equate a democratic result with an efficient one, the Idaho approach might be defensible on an efficiency basis, but the hard truth of the matter is that the delegation of any issue such as water use to a state agency will result in a decision based upon distributional rather than allocational considerations. Particularly in a democracy, public officials will decide on the basis of who benefits from water use rather than on which water uses will produce the most net benefits.

In Idaho, where the popularly elected representatives have an opportunity for a direct say on every instream flow allocation, the processes of political compromise and log rolling will be most obvious. In the case of local streams, local interests are likely to dominate. In the case of major rivers like the Snake, the instream flow issue will be subject to the same political factors as any other decision of statewide importance. In Montana, the political process will determine the outcome in the long run, since those board members whose views lead them to unpopular decisions will be replaced by others whose views conform to those of the current governor. Even if the governor and the board members free themselves from any political considerations, the board will be faced by the incomprehensible task of allocating the waters of an entire river basin with only their own sense of what is in the interest of the people of the state. As a result they will tend to look to state agencies for counsel, and the decision may not differ from that which the agencies would have arrived at on their own. In Washington, the difficulty of coping with the value questions leads the decisionmaking agencies to focus on the technical issues. The stream rating system employed by Washington's Department of Ecology, although not arbitrary, does not reflect the efficient allocation of water in the particular streams. The fact that a stream is a good habitat for trout in no way is determinative of whether the stream should be maintained as trout habitat. That issue can only be resolved in the context of the possible alternative uses of the water in the particular streams at a particular time.

The impossibility of deciding the optimal use of a given quantity or flow of water leads public officials to establish water-use priorities or standards, which are as difficult to challenge as they are to justify, and then focus on the technical problems of meeting the established standards. It is clear in both Montana and Washington that these technical problems play the dominant role in the instream flow deliberations. When a resolution is finally reached there is a tendency to believe that the allocational issue has somehow been resolved. In reality, however, the allocational efficiency of the resultant instream flow reservation depends entirely upon the efficiency of the initial standards that defined the technical problem. The technical expert can provide evidence on how much water is required to maintain a trout habitat but has only personal opinion to offer on the issue of whether the state should preserve that trout habitat. The reservation processes do not begin to provide a solution to the allocation problem; rather, they provide a mechanism for particular interests to guarantee that their preferences will be controlling.

COLORADO – STATE PARTICIPATION IN THE MARKET

In 1963, the Colorado legislature authorized the Colorado River Conservation District to appropriate water of any natural stream sufficient to maintain the fish habitat for public use.[36] The district's implementation of the instream appropriation power was challenged, and the Colorado Supreme Court found "no support in the law of this state for the proposition that a minimum flow of water may be 'appropriated' in a natural stream for piscatorial purposes without diversion of any portion of the water 'appropriated' from the natural course of the stream."[37] A 1973 amendment to the 1969 Water Rights and Administration Act eliminated the statutory diversion requirement, which had been the basis of the Supreme Court's decision on the 1963 law, and broadened the definition of beneficial use to include minimum streamflows "to preserve the natural environment to a reasonable degree."[38] Again the power of the state to allocate water to instream flows was challenged, this time on constitutional grounds. In 1979 the Colorado Supreme Court held that the 1973 amendment did not deprive Colorado citizens of their constitutional right to appropriate water and that the constitution did not require a diversion of water for a valid appropriation.[39]

On the surface the Colorado law appears to be very similar to the authority of other states to appropriate unappropriated waters, an approach that effectively reserves waters from future private appropriation. However, two characteristics of the Colorado law make it significantly different. The Colorado Water Conservation Board has authority to acquire instream flow rights by means other than appropriation. The law is not specific on how the board may acquire instream flow rights, but certainly purchase of existing rights is the

36. Colorado Revised Statutes Annotated, 37–46–107 (j).

37. *Colorado River Water Conservation District* v. *Rocky Mountain Power Company*, 158 Colo. 331, 406 P. 2d 798, 800 (1965).

38. Colorado Revised Statutes Annotated, 37–92–103 (3).

39. *Colorado River Water Conservation District* v. *Colorado Water Conservation Board, Colo.*, 594 P. 2d 570 (1979).

most obvious approach the board might take. The statute also specifically forbids the acquisition of instream flow rights by eminent domain, the clear intent of which is that the state, acting through the Water Conservation Board, is to participate in the water rights acquisition system on the same terms as any other prospective water rights owner. Obviously the state's potentially deep pocket can give it a significant competitive advantage against most private parties, but the prohibition on resort to eminent domain assures that state instream flow rights will only be acquired from willing sellers.

A committee consisting of officials from several state and federal agencies was formed in 1973 to identify priorities for the appropriation of instream flows.[40] Although faced with the same difficulties in setting priorities that Washington officials face in classifying streams under their rating system, Colorado officials encounter serious constraints on which instream rights they can actually acquire, while Washington's DOE is required to set base flows on every perennial stream in the state. The two constraints faced by the Colorado board both have characteristics of market influences. Because the board must satisfy the same requirements for an appropriation as anyone acquiring a private water right, the resources of the implementing agencies limit the number of appropriation permit applications the board can file. More importantly, any rights that the state acquires by purchase will be acquired at the going market rate, thus forcing the board to carefully order its priorities. In Washington and Montana the state officials may have access to water rights market information, but they are required to reserve water for instream purposes, and there are no direct incentives to take into account the relative market values of various water uses. The Colorado system removes the inevitability of instream flow action by the state while forcing the state to deal with the realities of the water rights market.

Of course the Colorado system is not neutral with respect to the market allocation of water rights. The state does have enormous potential resources to draw upon, but taxpayers are likely to be far more cautious about public expenditures when they are able to identify the specific returns on those expenditures, as they are with the public school systems. The Colorado requirement that the board obtain specific legislative appropriations for the acquisition of instream rights gives taxpayers a similar sense of where their money is going.

40. Huffman, *Allocation of Water to Instream Flows*, Vol. II, p. 53.

Under the reservation systems the costs of instream flow maintenance are impossibly obscured because the states do not compete in the private market and the reserved waters have values in alternative uses that will be known only in the context of future markets. The appropriative part of the Colorado system suffers from the same problem in theory, but the realities of Colorado's water situation greatly diminish its significance in that state. Unlike Montana, where nearly four million acre-feet of water per year are reserved to instream flows where the Yellowstone flows through Billings, the state's largest city, the appropriated instream flow rights in Colorado are all on very small segments of high alpine streams. Thus, for significant minimum flows to be established in the populated areas of the state, it will be necessary for the board to acquire instream flow rights in the water rights market rather than through appropriation.

The Colorado system offers no magical solution to the problem of determining what level of streamflows will be in the public interest. Although the Colorado system restricts the state to what it can afford, instream flow preservation is only one of a multitude of budget items for the state. There is probably a tendency to rely on technical experts within the bureaucracy, as is the case in other states where financial constraints are largely absent. The Water Conservation Board relies on the Division of Wildlife in the determination of where instream flow rights should be required and how much flow should be maintained.[41] Because that agency's personnel are only competent to estimate how much flow will be necessary for a particular purpose, their recommendations are relevant only after the state has determined the priority of purposes it will pursue. The difficulty of that task will no doubt lead the priority question to be submerged in the data of the technical issues of fish habitat maintenance.

These problems notwithstanding, the Colorado approach offers promise as a means for the state to participate in water allocation decisions without totally distorting or ignoring the value information that the water rights market provides. In the context of land-use regulation, constitutional provisions requiring compensation by the state to parties whose property rights are taken, if enforced, can help to preserve some market influences on government action. However, water presents a different problem in states such as Montana where a

41. Ibid., p. 54.

significant amount of water is unowned and the state can reserve water as if it had no value or a different value from water privately controlled. It is not surprising that water-short Colorado would turn to the market approach while water-rich Montana would turn to the reservation approach.[42] It is relatively easy to tie up water that thus far has been insufficiently valuable to justify its acquisition. However, the value of water will only rise with increasing demands, and without political changes the reserved waters of Montana and Washington will be unavailable even if the instream uses are worth far less than alternative uses.

It is not clear whether the Water Conservation Board has the authority to dispose of as well as acquire instream flow rights. The law does not specify that the state may exchange its appropriated rights for other rights that might have greater instream value, but if the purpose of the Colorado approach is to take advantage of the allocative advantages of the market, it is essential that such transfers of state-owned water rights be permitted. Indeed, most of the market advantages that justify requiring the state to purchase instream rights without resorting to eminent domain would be lost if the state cannot in turn sell those rights if subsequent market values warrant such an action. The state's holding instream rights in perpetuity, even if those rights were purchased, will have the same long-run allocative consequences as if the state initially had acquired the rights by eminent domain, reservation, or regulation.

PRIVATE RIGHTS TO INSTREAM FLOWS

It is a virtual certainty that the possibility of private provision of instream flows was not even considered by state legislators when instream flow programs were adopted. Yet it may well be possible to provide for instream water uses through the existing systems of private rights in water. No doubt the presumption in favor of public action is in part a consequence of the relative paucity of private rights in instream flows, but it does not follow that the only way to provide for minimum streamflows is by state action. Three factors have contributed to the paucity of private rights in instream flows.

42. James L. Huffman, "Water and Public Control," in *New Directions in Water Policy* (Corvallis, Ore.: Oregon State University Press, 1980).

It has been widely believed that water is a common-pool resource and therefore not amenable to allocation to many uses through a system of private rights. As a consequence, private rights systems have not been designed to accommodate instream flow rights, and governments have undertaken often massive programs to provide uses that supposedly cannot be provided privately. The following discussion assesses the validity of the common-pool argument as applied to water resources, and examines the existing law of private water rights and the extensive involvement of government in the provision of consumptive water uses. It should be clear from the discussion that instream water uses can be privately supplied if private rights in water are clearly defined, enforced, and transferable through appropriate institutional changes.

The Common-Pool Problem

The notion that water is a common-pool resource that cannot be privately allocated may have had some historic validity. The traditional argument has taken the following form. Almost all surface water contributes to the flow of water in drainage basins, which increase in size from the peaks of the mountains to the shores of the continent. Indeed much of the groundwater is tributary to these surface flows, which themselves are part of the earth's complex hydrologic cycle. Because of the migratory and integrated nature of the water resource, it is generally assumed that the problem of defining private rights in water is far more complicated than the definition of private rights in land. More closely analagous is the problem of assigning property rights in oil and gas resources, the history of which is replete with inefficiencies and wasted resources. The solution in oil and gas law has been voluntary or state-imposed pooling and unitization. The solution in water law has been the appropriation doctrine, which assigns rights with temporal rather than geographic points of reference. When dealing with migratory resources such as water, we cannot put up a fence to mark the boundaries of private property. When the use of migratory resources is consumptive, rights can have volume as a parameter, but when the resource is in its natural migratory environment it is not possible to define with adequate precision the content of any particular right. The best solution is a rule of capture, which, though adequate for a society of hunters and gatherers, provides none of the certainty necessary to resource development in a modern society. The temporal priority scheme of appropriation doctrine works well when the water is diverted and can be measured, but when the water is left in the stream it is impossible for private rights holders to enforce their rights. The owner of a private right to a minimum streamflow will not know the right has been violated until the flow is too low and the fish are dead.

Although the definition of private rights in water is generally more difficult than the definition of private rights in land, and instream rights definition may not have been possible during the nineteenth century when appropriation doctrine was developed, the argument summarized in the preceding paragraph is not convincing in the context of instream flow protection in the 1980s. Sophisticated technologies of streamflow monitoring can serve the law of instream flow rights just as the technology of barbed wire served the nineteenth-century law of private rights in grazing land. Defining the parameters of a right to instream flows is no more difficult than defining the parameters of a right to divert water for agriculture or industry. Indeed, if the states have any expectation of enforcing minimum streamflows, they must surely recognize that the common-pool arguments are no longer a justification for precluding private instream rights, at least in terms of rights definition and enforcement.

A few private rights to instream flows exist despite the institutional obstacles. The Nature Conservancy owns an instream flow right on Boulder Creek near the city of Boulder, Colorado. Individuals in Montana own rights to spring creeks of the Yellowstone Valley, and people willingly pay for the opportunity to fish in those creeks. Private investors have proposed the purchase of lands bordering the lower Deschutes River in Oregon, access rights to which they would market on a membership or temporary-use basis in order to protect the stream for sport fishing. Arizona appears to authorize private acquisition of instream rights.[43] The most persuasive evidence of the private willingness to invest in instream flow water uses is the enormous support of the efforts of the many organizations that seek to influence the public allocation of water resources. Through lobbying

43. Arizona Revised Statutes 45-141(A) (Supp. 1978). For a discussion of the prospects for private instream rights in Arizona see Tom Scribner, "Arizona Water Law: The Problem of Instream Appropriation for Environmental Use by Private Appropriators," *Arizona Law Review* 21 (1979): 1095.

and litigation, organizations such as the Sierra Club and the National Wildlife Federation have spent millions of dollars to influence the enactment and assure the implementation of legislation allocating water to instream flows. That people clearly value instream water uses, even in the face of enormous institutional obstacles, occasionally has been demonstrated through the acquisition and retention of private rights.

The valuation of water for instream uses does not have to be a mysterious process. Certainly instream uses are not of infinite value, although the reservation approach to state provision of instream flows seems to assume that no other uses will ever be sufficiently valuable to justify state abandonment of instream flows. Those who would claim that minimum streamflows should be provided no matter what other demands for water may exist are preservationists in the tradition of the national park and wilderness advocates of generations past. Few would not feel the loss if Old Faithful were plugged with a power generator, or the cliffs of Yosemite were dynamited for their minerals. But we deceive ourselves if we contend that humans will choose to perish from a lack of resources in preference to destroying the aesthetic wonders of our national parks. Fortunately we seldom, if ever, will face those extreme choices because of the expanding availability of substitutes for scarce resources. Instream water uses also have their value, which may be sufficiently high that we are depriving ourselves of certain benefits by relying on the government to provide the desired flows. An inevitable consequence of government actions that overproduce certain benefits is that other benefits must be underproduced. To the extent that the government may be overproducing certain water uses through subsidization, society will experience the underproduction of other water uses.

As a general rule the value of a particular volume or flow of water is a function of the temporal priority of the associated right and of the location of the diversion or instream use. Normally greater seniority will give the right greater value, and downstream rights will be more valuable than upstream rights because of the numerous geographic advantages of locating most productive activities downstream. The value of an instream water use, like any other water use, will depend upon the values of alternative uses of the water. As a general rule, then, the more alternative uses foregone because of a particular instream use, the higher the value of that instream use must be to justify the lost opportunities.

Instream water uses, like all other water uses, have values that can be translated into private investment in water rights. Whether or not a private entity will choose to invest in an instream water use depends upon the value of that use in relation to other water uses, and upon the legal possibilities of owning instream water rights. Once an institutional framework that permits and does not discriminate against private ownership of instream water rights is implemented, the existence of instream water rights will depend upon the values that people place on instream uses. Aside from the few examples of private instream rights that exist despite the extant institutional obstacles, there is no conclusive evidence that private instream rights will in fact be acquired when the institutional obstacles are removed. However, through a hypothetical example it can be demonstrated that such rights can and will be acquired if they are sufficiently valued.

To make an appropriation of water for an instream flow, assuming no institutional obstacles, private party *X* needs only to value that use in excess of the costs of making the appropriation. Those costs will be relatively low since no diversion is required, and *X* simply needs to comply with the existing state procedures for an appropriation. Once *X* has the instream right, assuming no obstacles to rights transfers, other parties may propose to purchase the right so that the water can be used in some other way. Although *X* may place a very high value on the instream use, *X* will be willing to sell the right to *Y* if *Y* offers to pay an amount that will allow *X* to acquire even larger instream values at some other location. If *X* values the instream use more highly than *Y* or any other prospective purchaser, *X* will retain the right, and the water to which *X* is entitled will remain instream.

In many areas of the United States the preceding hypothetical scenario is not a real possibility because many streams are fully appropriated during the low flow seasons of the year. That *X* will not be able to appropriate an instream flow during the dry season when instream flow maintenance is a problem does not alter *X*'s ability to acquire and retain instream rights if *X* values the instream use of particular waters more than the party presently owning the relevant water right. If *Y* has a right to use 20 cubic feet per second (cfs) of water during the months of June, July, and August and produces $2,000 of additional net income by using that water for irrigation, *Y* will be willing to sell the right to use that water during the summer to *X* for some price in excess of $2,000. *X* might make optimal use of its resources by thus leasing water in years of unusually low flow, or *X* might purchase the water right if the value of the permanent maintenance of that 20-cfs flow exceeds the value of the right to *Y*. As with other water uses, the value placed on an instream use will have to be higher in some situations than in others if an instream right is to be acquired and retained. But there is nothing about instream uses that prevents their being provided privately. If the instream use is valued more highly than uses that would be foregone, the instream use will be provided.

Legal Obstacles

As the earlier discussion of state approaches to instream flow maintenance indicated, the private water rights system, designed to facilitate consumptive water use, has erected numerous obstacles to the acquisition of instream water rights. Although many state laws have been changed to permit state acquisition of instream water rights, most do not permit private acquisition of instream rights. In some states it is not yet clear whether the changes will be found to apply to private acquisition of instream flow rights. Five specific aspects of appropriation doctrine pose obstacles to the private acquisition of instream rights.

The diversion requirement, which prohibited Colorado's first instream flow appropriations, still may be a major obstacle to private rights in instream flows. As was indicated previously, the central purpose of the diversion requirement is to facilitate determining the temporal order of appropriations and measuring the amount of water being used. The earliest unit of water measurement commonly used in the West, the miner's inch, was based upon the diversion mechanisms employed by the early miners. Obviously an instream water user has no need or desire to divert water, and the requirement is no longer of any value with respect to consumptive rights, since records establish evidence of priority and modern measuring methods have long made the miner's inch an historical curiosity. The diversion requirement must be repealed if private instream rights are to exist.

Two legal obstacles to private instream flow rights, the beneficial-use requirement and the rules of abandonment or nonuse, have similar historical roots. The beneficial-use requirement is an outgrowth of the same judicial reasoning used to justify the reasonable-use requirement of American riparian doctrine. However, where the reasonable-use rule was essential to the consumptive use of water under a riparian system, the beneficial-use rule had no similar purpose under the appropriation system, the whole purpose of which was to allow consumptive water use. While the beneficial-use rule made it clear that the state would permit only socially meritorious water uses, a reading of the case law will reveal that the rule has seldom been invoked as a restraint on the appropriation of water. Beneficial uses have always been designated in general terms such as industry and agriculture with the implicit recognition that any water use worth investing in is beneficial to the public. Occasionally the law has required specific amendment, as in the case of recreation, and excluded specific activities such as coal slurry from the definition of beneficial use.[44] In general, however, the economics of water use assure that water will not be applied to nonbeneficial uses.

The beneficial-use standard is linked with the law relating to abandonment and nonuse, by the nineteenth-century bias against speculation in the future values of resources. By requiring rights claimants to demonstrate that they were putting the water to a beneficial use, the state was able to preclude individuals from diverting water and then not using it in anticipation that they or others might be able to use it in the future. In this respect the water law system was far more effective in discouraging speculation than the public land disposal laws, which were consistently violated for speculative purposes. Although the law of abandonment generally was justified on the logical premise that a right acquired by use is lost by nonuse, its purpose was clearly to prevent speculation. It was argued that not only were idle resources unproductive, an anathema to growth-conscious westerners, but permitting one individual to hold water rights without using the water allowed that individual to profit from the future increased demand and higher value of water that would inevitably come with western development. Although speculation has distributive consequences that may have seemed undesirable to nineteenth-century judges and legislators, it has no negative impact on the efficiency of water resource allocation.

Both the beneficial-use standard and the law of abandonment are current obstacles to private acquisition of rights in instream flows.

44. See Hutchins, *Water Rights Laws*, pp. 542–544; Montana Code Annotated 85–2–102(2) (1979).

The beneficial-use standard can either be amended to include instream uses or repealed without any harm to efficient water allocation. The rules of abandonment can be easily adjusted to recognize that the fact that water remains in the stream does not mean that the water is not being used. The legitimate purpose of abandonment law, to ensure that water is not excluded from productive use by uncertainties about title claims, will decrease in importance as recording of water rights becomes the rule rather than the exception.

Another legal obstacle, restraints on the transfer of existing water rights, often makes it difficult for water rights to be shifted from one use to another. Assuming the legal recognition of private instream rights, the efficient level of instream water use will not be achieved unless instream water users are able to purchase or otherwise acquire water rights now being applied to other uses. In many areas of the West, streams are fully appropriated and instream benefits cannot be realized without the acquisition of existing rights. In addition, it must also be possible to change the point of diversion of a right on a particular stream or basin. Often, the instream user's water rights will not be strategically located on the stream, and there should be no arbitrary restriction on changing the place of use of the water. Of course such changes or rights transfers must not negatively affect other water rights, but many legal restrictions are not for the purpose of protecting vested rights. Often it will be possible to transfer a water right from a consumptive user to an instream user without affecting the total consumptive use of water on the stream. If the stream right extends over only a segment of a stream, additional water will be made available for consumptive use downstream. The law should be structured so that instream right holders can transfer the consumptive components of their acquired rights to downstream water users and thus finance a part of the costs of the acquired rights, provided the sale does not negatively affect third-party rights.

If instream uses are put on the same legal footing as all other water uses, and if the water rights system is generally improved to allow for a free market in water rights, it will be possible for instream values to be realized through strictly private actions. However, even if the legal obstacles are eliminated, a major obstacle to private rights will remain. Ironically, that obstacle, employed to justify public action to protect instream flows, is a function of public actions in support of competing water uses.

Government Subsidization of Competing Water Uses

One need only travel the major river basins of the West to appreciate the dominant role of federal and state government in the allocation of water. Rivers and many small streams are "regulated" with dams, the vast majority of which have been built at public expense. The water from these dams is used to irrigate hundreds of thousands of acres, generally at far below market cost to farmers. Electricity is generated and sold at less than market prices. The state of California is a spider's web of publicly funded canals and pipelines, all of which subsidize certain water uses. The state of Montana has implemented a water reservation system that excludes the reservation of water for industrial use but allows state agencies to tie up water for agricultural, municipal, and instream uses. Sometimes, as in Montana, the instream uses receive a far bigger slice of the pie than they would get in a private market.

The vast bulk of government subsidies, however, benefit consumptive water users. So long as the existing system of government subsidization of consumptive water use continues, it is unlikely that instream water users will be able to afford to compete in a private rights market. Their only alternative is to seek government subsidies themselves, which is precisely what they have been doing. It is very likely that many of the critically low flows that are now the rule on most western rivers and streams during the late summer months would not exist but for government subsidization of competing water uses. Of course, the late summer flows of some streams are made possible by those government projects, but that fact only underscores the disruptive impact of existing government water programs on the water market.

It has long been argued that government subsidization is necessary to water development because of the enormous costs of large dams and massive water transfer projects. But private capital has been aggregated in amounts far exceeding the cost of any existing or proposed public water project. If the large water development promises an adequate rate of return, private resources can bear the cost, unless, of course, the government is willing to do it. As long as competing uses continue to be subsidized, repairs to the legal system clearly are not sufficient for the privitization of rights in instream water uses.

CONCLUSION

For most of America's history, instream water uses have been supplied because of abundant water sources, the proximity of human activities to those water sources, and relatively little demand for consumptive water uses. People now live in the once foreboding deserts and use water for an array of activities never contemplated a century ago. Instream water uses are no longer free goods. The uniform response in the western United States, where water problems are most serious, has been to resort to various types of state action designed to protect and maintain minimum streamflow levels. The effects of these programs largely reflect the scarcity of water in particular streams and rivers. The reservation approach, sometimes achieved in the name of appropriation, places the entire burden of determining the proper allocation of water to instream uses on state officials, whose decisions are apt to reflect the relative power of the various water-user lobbies. The valuation issue is often lost in technical argument over how much water is necessary for a particular purpose, which may have been chosen without any consideration of allocative efficiency. In states with abundant water, instream users will probably do well, at least until water scarcity forces a reassessment. In water-scarce states, instream users must compete with other water-user groups with considerable experience in water politics.

Assuming that public officials are concerned about the efficiency of their water allocation decisions, the unavoidable problem, whether water is abundant or scarce, is to determine what allocation will serve the best interests of the people of the state. Where regulations and subsidies distort market information on the relative values of competing water uses, the prospects for an efficient allocation are dim indeed. The only solution is the privatization of water allocation decisions through the existing or altered systems of private rights in water. With specific changes in the existing law of property rights in water and extensive alteration of the role of government in water allocation, significant instream water use should result from private action. The achievement of that objective could take years. In the interim states should consider the Colorado approach, which potentially involves the state in the water rights market and thus promises that state actions will be at least marginally informed on the issues that are critical to efficient allocation of water.

Chapter 9

BUILDING MARKETS FOR TRADABLE POLLUTION RIGHTS

M. T. Maloney and Bruce Yandle

INTRODUCTION

An examination of the property rights structure for natural resources reveals a series of puzzling questions. Why do some natural resources—for example, land—seem to have well-structured property rights and smoothly functioning markets in which those rights are exchanged? What economic forces explain the evolution of property rights and the timing of the emergence of trading those rights? If tradable rights are so efficient, why does it take so long for those legal devices to supplant other apparently less efficient systems for allocating resources?

Each of these questions is relevant to an analysis of property rights to the use of rivers and streams for the discharge of industrial wastes. Whereas industrial plants have for centuries used the natural environment as a receiver of wastes, property rights to pollute and a market for trading those rights have begun to develop only recently in the United States.[1] Previously, the disposal capacity of rivers was allocated by various command and control schemes. The typical alloca-

1. A market for trading of pollution permits was announced formally by the Wisconsin Department of Natural Resources for the Fox River in March 1981; see William O'Neil, Martin David, Christina Moore, and Erhard Joeres, "Transferable Discharge Permits and Economic Efficiency," Report no. 8107 (Madison: Social Science Research Institute, University of Wisconsin, May 1981).

tive system defines standards of control at each source of pollution, allowing only a limited amount of discretion on the part of the user.

The purpose of this study is to explain the development of water quality control in the United States while focusing on the emergence of tradable rights. Since federal involvement in this area first appeared in 1948, evolution of the allocative institutions has been a tedious process. The model we use to explain this history will offer insight for the future of water-quality regulation.

Our model is a mixture of the theories of property rights and special-interest groups as a force in government. An understanding of property rights reveals that the cost of monitoring use is a crucial factor in shaping the institutions of environmental quality control. A special-interest theory of government regulations leads us to examine possible coalitions between various special-interest groups.

From this combination theory we draw three main conclusions. First, monitoring of water quality is a difficult problem because each of the many permutations of water users within a particular system yields a unique distribution of water quality. Given this monitoring problem, it is costly to allow a discharger of wastes at one site to sell pollution rights to a discharger at another location. Second, the potential gains from such transfers are reduced, since rights to environmental use have been vested in each site permitted for pollution. While confined to specific locations, these rights are alienable through the transfer of land. Finally, special-interest groups can delay the evolution of tradable rights and snuff out markets with regulations. Even so, there is little evidence that this has happened in water-quality regulation. The most prominent special-interest effect in the law has been the enormous federal subsidy for municipal sewage treatment facilities.

This study develops a rudimentary theory of property rights, followed by a discussion of how the rent-seeking behavior of special-interest groups may distort the development of property rights. The next four sections relate the history of water-quality regulation from the early, prefederal period through the most recent developments. The most important and revealing aspects of this experience are summarized in terms of the theory presented earlier. The paper concludes with some thoughts on the future of water-quality control.

A THEORY OF ALIENABILITY

The force driving the actions of economic agents, which manifest themselves in markets and the price mechanism, is a search for the wealth created by the scarcity problem. Markets are based on a system of property rights to scarce resources and goods. The rights to property allow the owner to exclude users, husband resources and enhance wealth. However, there is no private market activity unless property rights can be transferred. Thus, the presence of private transferability distinguishes the market solution from other methods of allocating scarce resources.

Property rights theories have had considerable success in explaining the development of markets and other institutional arrangements across a broad range of situations.[2] Two fundamental principles can be distilled from this work.

1. *As property becomes more valuable, more effort will be devoted to property rights definition and protection.*[3] Demsetz shows that Canadian Indians developed property rights for hunting ground as the value of beaver pelts increased due to an emerging fur trade. Anderson and Hill extend this idea by applying their theory of the supply and demand for property rights activities to western cattle ranching. They point out that as the value of land and horses (a determinant of the demand for the associated property rights) rose and fell, there was a corresponding rise and fall in the expenditure of resources on property rights definition and enforcement. Similarly, as the cost of property rights to land fell with the introduction of barbed wire, more fencing was used to define and enforce property rights.

2. A succinct statement and interesting application of the fundamental principles can be found in Harold Demsetz, "Toward a Theory of Property Rights," *American Economic Review* 57 (May 1967): 347-359; Terry Anderson and P. J. Hill, "The Evolution of Property Rights: A Study of the American West," *Journal of Law and Economics* 18 (April 1975): 163-180; John Umbeck, "A Theory of Contract Choice and the California Gold Rush," *Journal of Law and Economics* 20 (October 1977): 421-437; Benjamin Klein, Robert G. Crawford, and Armen A. Alchian, "Vertical Integration, Appropriable Rents, and the Competitive Contracting Process," *Journal of Law and Economics* 21 (October 1978): 279-328.

3. Implicit in our statement of this theorem is a property rights enforcement supply function that has a slope larger than the demand for enforcement.

2. *Contract enforcement costs are a function of the structure of the contract.* We expect a (constrained) minimization of these costs by economic agents. Thus, as enforcement costs are higher due to exogenous forces, contract provisions that lower these should be invoked more frequently. Umbeck shows that during the California gold rush, the earlier contract choice of sharing the product of a claim was abandoned as the mining population (and stealing) increased and thereby increased the cost of enforcing this type of agreement.[4]

It is useful to extend these two principles by drawing a distinction between the definition and enforcement of property rights. Enforcement costs refer to protection of property rights, whereas the contract structure is analogous to their definition. From this we can state a third proposition:

3. *Increasing the generality of property rights definition—that is, increasing the flexibility, discretion, or expansion of the rights' transferability by the holder or contracting parties—causes the cost of definition and enforcement to rise.*

This proposition is well exemplified in terms of contract performance. Highly technical, elaborate, sophisticated contracts limit the discretion of the contracting parties, restricting their rights and reducing their alienable or transferable interests. While more costly to write and enforce, complex contracts reduce the potential for post-contractual opportunistic behavior, that is, reneging on the terms of the contract, by restricting the parties' flexibility and discretion.[5] In Umbeck's example of gold mining, we expect that the sharing contracts had inalienable interests because the cost of monitoring theft and work rules would have been higher had transferability been allowed. However, once land allotments replaced sharing agreements because of the massive population increase, transferability became

4. Population increases caused the costs of preventing stealing and of enforcing work rules to escalate. Sharing contracts were abandoned in favor of land allotments. With land allotted, smaller groups many times resumed the sharing agreements. See Umbeck, "Theory of Contract Choice," p. 437.

5. An enlightening discussion of this type of opportunistic behavior is found in Klein, Crawford, and Alchian, "Vertical Integration." We argue here that such opportunistic behavior only occurs if the contracting parties have alienable interests. Hence, contracts are written to limit this activity, or corporate integration occurs so that both parties share an incentive to maximize the value of the firm.

acceptable because its cost fell.[6] As another example, university instructors generally cannot subcontract their classroom responsibilities, although they can do so with their research activities. Because monitoring contract performance is more severe in the former case, transferability is proscribed.[7] In terms of contract performance and transferability, the cost of monitoring by the other parties to the contract increases as transferability becomes more flexible.

The case also can be stated in terms of property rights protection. As property transfer becomes easier, the linkage between possession and ownership becomes blurred.[8] Opportunities for theft and misuse expand. If *A* possesses *B*'s nontradable property, this fact can be considered prima facie evidence that *A* misappropriated it. This would not be true if the transferability of *B*'s property were not restricted, for a good-faith trade may have occurred.[9] That is to say, there is a monitoring cost to property rights. Property can be stolen or used in ways not authorized by the property rights holder. The holder attempts to restrict this undesirable activity and hence incurs positive costs, which can be reduced by restricting transferability.

Our discussion of contract restrictions relates to *alienability*, the ability to use discretion in the exercise of a property right. The more the property right definition is constrained by government sanctions or private contract enforcement mechanisms, the less alienable it becomes. A restriction in the ownership of cattle that forbids branding during a certain time of the year is a less alienable property right than one that allows branding year-round.[10] On the price axis of the

6. The rules governing transferability were still restrictive—the bill of sale and transfer of consideration had to be witnessed by two disinterested parties. See Umbeck, "Theory of Contract Choice," p. 436.

7. Other examples of limited alienability include the case of the Chrysler Corp., which is trying to sell its tank division to General Dynamics. In the *Wall Street Journal* (28 January 1982, p. 2), John Kotter and Walter Mossberg report that under federal law weapons contracts cannot be transferred by the companies holding them unless approved by the Pentagon. Mortgage contracts and insurance contracts have similar provisions against transferability.

8. For a detailed discussion of this point, see M. T. Maloney and R. E. McCormick, "A Positive Theory of Environmental Quality Regulation," *Journal of Law and Economics* 25 (April 1982): 99–124.

9. Consider the case of Continental Can, which had a patent on a machine. The firm did not allow the machine to be sold and the leasee agreement did not allow for transferability. Hence, anyone using the machine without a lease was guilty of theft.

10. Anderson and Hill, "Evolution of Property Rights," p. 175, relate this example in the context of proposition one.

supply function of alienability is the cost of supporting each level of alienability. These are the marginal costs of the resources spent to monitor and enforce property rights.

The following proposition is offered with respect to the demand for alienability:

4. *The more alienability included in property rights, the more valuable they become, but at a decreasing rate.* The well-known gains from transferability are labeled, appropriately enough, as gains from trade. The interesting aspect of this phenomenon is that resources move from users with the lowest value to those with the highest. Rights to the property allow the holder to husband use optimally both before and after the move to the highest valued user. The demand for alienability will be determined by the extent to which property rights distribution diverges from optimality before trade commences.

The more transferability allowed under the aegis of the property rights enforcement agency, the lower the benefit of additional transferability. A scheme that restricts trading slightly will exclude only a few of the high-valued users from gaining possession of the asset. Similarly, if the initial distribution of the resource is such that only the highest valued users hold the rights, the marginal benefit of alienability will derive only from expected future shifts in supply or demand. Hence, a second determinant of the demand for alienability is the variance in the determinants of supply and demand for the asset.

Thus far, we have examined two opposing forces acting on the definition of property rights. Looked at in only these terms, the equilibrium for alienable rights—that is, the intersection of the supply and demand for tradability—could fall anywhere along the spectrum from zero transferability to fee-simple rights, which are completely transferable. If technology, population, income, and the supply of other resources are very stable, nontradable rights to water quality could be allocated on a perpetual basis with no loss in efficiency. Indeed, there might be a net cost if trading were allowed and the cost of monitoring were not imposed on the trading parties. Alternatively, the opposite case can be easily envisioned. For instance, the right to use water from a river may be specified in such a way that a precise amount must be withdrawn each day and used only in a certain fashion. Such a right has nearly zero alienability.

Failure to perform the identified tasks causes loss of the right.[11] In another case, the right might be vested so that an amount of water must be withdrawn but can be used in any way so long as the quantity and quality return characteristics meet a certain standard. This right embodies some alienability because any operation that meets the return standards can profitably exercise the use right. At the fee-simple extreme, water rights might be issued to a specified amount of potential water withdrawal without regard to the return characteristics. This right is perfectly alienable, as the definition of the right itself precludes sale to no one.[12]

Institutions and Water Quality

The tradability of property rights, a focal point in the regulation of water quality, is just one of several aspects of property rights institutions as they relate to environmental resources. Broadly stated, these include (1) common access without scarcity, (2) common property, (3) public property, and (4) private property.[13] This outline is ordered on the basis of less to more transferability of rights. In the first stage, there is no scarcity, and hence, common access is not an allocative device. In the common property stage, common access rations the resource, excluding some users. In the public property stage, exclusionary rules akin to use privileges develop in conjunction with some enforcement procedure. Private property is the stage characterized by fully tradable, fee-simple rights.

As property becomes scarce, common access allocation ceases to be efficient. Competing users vie for the resource. The first come, first served process ultimately excludes some, and the curtailments are not likely to be optimal.[14] As a result, potential gains from trade

11. The right as stated could be sold to another who wanted to use the water asset in the same way. Sometimes assets lack even this aspect of alienability. For instance, the rights to oyster in the marsh areas of South Carolina identify the precise method of production and cannot be sold.

12. However, the cost of such a fee-simple right is high, as the water-use benefits of all downstream users are threatened by each sale. Thus, it is hard to imagine that the demand for transferability could be great enough to cause the intersection of supply and demand to occur at this level of alienability.

13. See M. T. Maloney and Bruce Yandle, "Rent Seeking and the Development of Property Rights in Air Quality, mimeographed (Clemson, S.C.: Department of Economics, Clemson University, 1980).

14. They may be, however, if the optimal allocation is one of relocation and the users with the lowest relocation costs are the ones driven away.

generate a demand for an entrepreneurial activity that we will call rent seeking. Scarcity implies rent, yet previously free resources typically do not have defined ownership. Hence, economic agents attempt to gain these rents by creating institutions that define and protect the rights to the newly scarce property. Just who obtains the rights is ambiguous.

The Coase theorem tells us that the distribution of the property rights will make no difference concerning the use of the resource.[15] This argument is predicated on two assumptions. First, the resource must be freely tradable. Second, income effects must be negligible. Since environmental scarcity is normally associated with locational scarcity, land rents cause the income effects to be unimportant. In other words, property rights definitions will cause environmental wealth to be vested in one or the other landlord but will leave the actual allocation of the property unchanged.[16] As developed above in the discussion of the supply and demand of alienability, when the costs and benefits of the property rights institution are considered, fully tradable private property rights may not emerge, which will affect the distribution and use of environmental assets. If pollution rights are not tradable, the party that gains the rights must use them, and hence property will be allocated to production based on this distribution.

In the case of water quality, the movement from common access to common property occurs when the assimilative capacity of rivers, streams, and lakes is overwhelmed by discharge. Water quality deteriorates until certain users and uses are precluded. Aesthetic enjoyment, swimming, drinking, and health are impaired, while industrial and municipal discharges continue unabated in this initial stage of scarcity.

As predicted by proposition one, increased scarcity of water quality creates a demand for property rights to cure the inefficiency of common access. However, proposition three predicts that the rights will embody little transferability because of the cost of measuring and monitoring the desired water quality characteristic. Water quality is a multifaceted resource requiring measurement in many dimen-

15. See R.H. Coase, "The Problem of Social Costs," *Journal of Law and Economics* 3 (October 1960): 1–44.

16. See M.T. Maloney, "The Coase Theorem and Industry Equilibrium," *Quarterly Review of Economics and Business* 17 (Winter 1977): 113–118.

sions. In the early stages of increased scarcity the measurement and monitoring capacity simply will not be available. A corollary to proposition three is that the longer market participants cope with scarcity, *ceteris paribus*, the more transferability will be built into the property rights to the scarce assets. Knowledge about the asset, a resource affecting property rights at each instant, is costly to change rapidly. Hence, water-quality rights are predicted to begin as use rights with discharge requirements and rigid locational assignments. Transfer of these rights will be proscribed.

Moreover, to the extent that the early assignments of use privileges merely prevent common access in discharge from eroding the rents to a scarce resource, the demand for transferability among dischargers is low because the highest valued users are assigned the assets (see proposition four). Increased scarcity increases the demand for transferability as the old assignments diverge from optimality. As increased scarcity occurs over time the cost of transferability falls.[17] Growing scarcity steps up the property rights definition and enforcement activity on more facets of water quality and increases the transferability embodied in the rights concerning the older dimensions of the asset.

Effects of Special-Interest Groups

The development of water-quality rights may occur through private action or government intervention.[18] As scarcity increases and discharge affects larger geographical regions, government intervention becomes more prominent. Theoretically, government exists as a property rights institution because of a comparative cost advantage in protecting property.[19] Collective action in this activity, while cheaper than individual action, does have a cost, which at the ex-

17. To say that water-quality rights take on more transferability over time is not a particularly valid scientific prediction because we do not know exactly when the change will occur. However, the argument has some appeal as a theoretical development in reference to special-interest-group rent seeking, which is developed in the next section.

18. Coase ("Problem of Social Costs") discusses wny one or the other of these outcomes will prevail. Anderson and Hill ("Evolution of Property Rights," p. 177) discuss the private collective action of western miners prior to government regulation of water rights.

19. See Douglass North, "A Framework for Analyzing the State in Economic History," *Explorations in Economic History* 16 (July 1979): 249-259, especially section III, p. 252.

treme is a function either of decisionmaking (unanimity rule) or lost individual freedom (dictatorship). We can imagine a political market equilibrium that falls between these extremes. The importance for our study of water-quality property rights is that the institutions of government provide a mechanism through which economic agents can pursue rent-seeking behavior, adjusting the property rights rules to enhance their wealth positions.

Special-interest groups may demand nontransferability of property rights in order to create a monopoly position for the property they hold. It is obvious that if property is inefficiently distributed and nontransferable, that which, by chance or otherwise, falls into the valued use will be more valuable. If 500,000 acres of land producing minerals would be efficient and only 300,000 are so allocated, the rent per acre will be higher. By restricting transferability such monopoly situations may be created. However, regulatory rules that specify limited tradability cannot be branded a priori as cartel devices, even though restrictive rules can have precisely this effect. As developed in the last section, limited transferability, at least in the early stages of water-quality regulation, is expected based on property-right enforcement considerations.

Several theories have been profered to elucidate special-interest-group government. Its behavior may follow the pattern of industry-wide regulation as analyzed by Stigler and Peltzman, or it may be better explained by the coalition formation theories of political scientists.[20] A confluence of the two suggests that regional regulation of specialized resources will be the predicted response of the political process.[21] Our approach explains water-quality regulation based on property rights considerations, with special interests posed as an alternative when a property rights approach does not fit the pattern of regulation. Beyond this simple approach we can look to changes in the political determinants of rent-seeking behavior by special-interest groups to explain changes in the institutions. These

20. George Stigler, "The Theory of Economic Regulation," *Bell Journal of Economics and Management Science* 2 (Spring 1971): 3-21; Sam Peltzman, "Toward a More General Theory of Regulation," *Journal of Law and Economics* 19 (August 1976): 211-240; Barry Weingast, Kenneth Shepsle, and Christopher Johnson, "The Political Economy of Benefits and Costs: A Neoclassical Approach to Distributive Politics," *Journal of Political Economy* 89 (August 1981): 642-664.

21. Empirical evidence on this point can be found in M. T. Maloney, R. E. McCormick, and R.D. Tollison, "Exporting Economic Regulation" (working paper, Blacksburg, Va.: Center for Study of Public Choice, Virginia Tech, 1981).

determinants include group size, dispersion, homogeneity (diversity of interests outside of a particular issue), regional political power and political characteristics (structure and size of state legislatures), and regional specialized resources (which can be profitably cartelized).

In summary, property rights definition and enforcement activities vary directly with the value of the asset over which the rights are being defined. The property rights structure will be chosen with the cost of definition and enforcement in mind. The tradability of property rights evolves based on three forces: (1) the cost of defining and enforcing rights, (2) changes in market equilibria for the property, and (3) the rent-seeking behavior of special-interest groups. Keeping these in mind we will review the evolution of water-quality property rights in the United States.

EARLY POLLUTION CONTROL EFFORTS

Grappling with Scarcity

Water pollution in the United States was caused more frequently by the discharge of untreated sewage than by industrial discharge.

> In 1900 municipal wastes reaching streams had a pollution effect equivalent to the raw untreated sewage from a population of about 24 million. . . . pollution from organic industrial waste (of animal or vegetable origin such as food processing, textiles, paper) being discharged to streams had a population equivalent of 15 million persons.[22]

There were some industrial pollution problems in selected areas, but industry typically was caught in the regulatory net cast out to control municipal sewage.[23] Industry was understandably opposed to regulation, since from a property rights perspective their use of water for waste disposal was not often hampered by declining water quality. Lieber relates the case of a soft drink bottler in Mississippi

22. Murray Stein, "Problems and Programs in Water Pollution," *Natural Resources Journal* 2 (December 1962): 395-396.

23. Pollution from paper mills in the Puget Sound is such a case. Between 1958 and 1962 twenty special commission sessions were held to study the problem and in 1962 the Governor called a federal-state conference. Some modicum of pollution control was achieved. See Harvey Lieber, *Federalism and Clean Waters* (Lexington, Mass.: Lexington Books, 1975).

that lobbied for pollution control because of its obvious need for intake water quality.[24]

Moreover, even if a water user, industrial or municipal, requires high water quality at the intake, pollution abatement at the outfall has no value if the discharger is located along a flowing water source. In this sense, property rights to water quality are like parking restrictions: Everyone wants them imposed on others, but there is no direct benefit when they are imposed on oneself. As a consequence, efforts to define property rights to water use have often been thwarted until human health became threatened. When environmental use brings disease and epidemics, common access allocation is replaced by public property control. This empirical observation is consistent with proposition one in our theory section. Because wastes flow away, the demand for property rights activities is lower than if each discharger's wastes imposed some costs on that discharger. At the same time, the cost of property rights activities is high because, to be beneficial, they must be defined and enforced on other, geographically remote economic agents.

Since municipal discharge was the main culprit, the property rights institutions developed for industrial polluters were rudimentary use permits loosely enforced. The intersection of demand and supply for industrial property rights to pollution discharge and for alienability in those rights had moved only slightly from the zero point on the horizontal axis. As for the cost of defining and enforcing these property rights, the nature of many industrial pollutants made effective control institutions hard to formulate. A few examples of the pre-federal period illustrate these points.

The ORANSCO Approach

The Ohio River Valley Water Sanitation Commission (ORANSCO) was a compact established in 1948 that eventually included the states of Illinois, Indiana, Kentucky, New York, Ohio, Pennsylvania, Virginia, and West Virginia.[25] ORANSCO's origin can be traced back to 1935 when the Chamber of Commerce of Cincinnati began to push

24. Ibid.

25. This discussion is based on Edward J. Cleary, *The ORANSCO Story,* Resources For the Future (Baltimore: Johns Hopkins Press, 1967).

for pollution control both in their city and throughout the entire Ohio River basin. Located at the lower end of the Ohio River, Cincinnati was the receiver of water into which the wastes of 19 million people and some of the largest industrial plants in the world were discharged.

While Cincinnati, like most cities of the era, lacked municipal sewage treatment facilities, its problem was really the pollution received from upstream. In 1931 a long period of low water flow brought an epidemic of gastroenteritis among cities along the Ohio River. That, and an outbreak of typhoid in 1936, provided the impetus for the affected states to change the river's status as a common access resource. Cincinnati took the lead in 1938 when the citizens passed a $1 million bond issue for the construction of a sewage treatment plant. Less success had been achieved in persuading industrial dischargers to alter their behavior, possibly because their waste was then less harmful to human health than that of the cities, possibly because of the competitive ramifications. For example, an industrialist who opposed the Pennsylvania legislature's water pollution control bill in 1935 told a committee, "We are in sympathy with the lofty purpose of this bill, but its adoption would place Pennsylvania at an unfair competitive disadvantage. If drastic pollution legislation is to be fair, it must be national in scope to provide uniformity." The argument for uniform treatment of industrial discharges was to become a prevalent theme when Congress finally supported federal water pollution control legislation in 1948.[26]

The eight states that formed the ORANSCO compact eventually set the pace for progressive pollution control programs. By 1960 ORANSCO had robot monitors on streams giving automatic readings to headquarters of ten different water-quality measures. In 1965 the monitoring system was complete. By 1967, some 90 percent of the 1,700 direct dischargers into the Ohio River had complied with ORANSCO minimum treatment guidelines; 94 percent of the population in the basin connected to sewers were served by municipal treatment plants, compared to less than 1 percent in 1948. Capital expenditures for sewage treatment facilities totaled $1 billion, of which 90 percent was locally financed.

26. Ibid., pp. 42–43.

Industrial Pollution Standards: Rights to Discharge

ORANSCO's initial attempt to grapple with the complex problem of developing waste treatment requirements for industry was to set discharge standards for salt wastes.[27] Staff reports to the commission pointed out that the salt pollution problem was one of concentration and hence depended on the amount of discharge relative to streamflow. Chloride salts do not die away, and high concentrations necessitate downstream clean-up for both industrial and drinking water purposes.[28] The staff report indicated that downstream clean-up was substantially more costly than upstream dilution. Upstream discharge could be varied based on streamflow and thereby acceptable concentrations could be maintained. Variations in discharge could be achieved by building storage lagoons or by adjusting production when streamflows fell below the level that would yield the recommended concentration.

The basic problem, of course, was to determine at which point along the river and its tributaries the concentration would be measured. If concentration is measured at the outfall, the polluter is constrained by the pollution level of the stream above its plant and by the water flow of the stream. However, as the measurement station is moved downstream the polluter receives the additional diluting effects of tributaries entering along the way. The property rights question becomes, Does a polluter have any rights to a discharge/flow ratio at its outfall that yields concentration levels downstream? If there is no control on the entry of new firms either upstream from it or on another tributary the firm has no enforceable property right. This was a major concern of the existing firms in response to the staff report.

Essentially divesting existing polluters of their rights, the report called for measurement of concentration at a point on the main stream where concentrations reached the highest level before downstream use. Each polluter's rights were to be prorated by the flow of

27. Underground accumulations of brine, which date back to prehistoric times when the sea covered the Ohio valley and are rich in chloride compounds of sodium, calcium, and magnesium, are pumped to the surface where the desired elements are extracted. The remaining saline liquid must be disposed of and is a major source of industrial pollution.

28. Indeed, the federal drinking water standard in effect at the time was 250 parts per million, whereas 50–175 ppm was considered to be of doubtful quality for industrial use.

the tributary on which it was located. When concentrations were expected to exceed the quality standard at the measurement point, discharge limitations would be set on the tributary-flow prorated basis. Entry, which was not restricted by the proposed rules either upstream or on another tributary, would reduce a plant's permissible discharge. The largest polluters, who were generally exceeding the quality standard at their outfalls, were to be the first to reduce discharge when the quality standards were exceeded at the measurement point. These reductions were to continue until their discharge concentrations at the point where their tributaries reached the main stream were the same on a prorated basis as all others. Industry spokesmen pointed out that discharge restrictions for existing facilities would simply invite entry by new firms on less productive lands adjacent to unpolluted tributaries. Moreover, such new discharge would increase the restrictions on the old plants and accelerate the entry of new firms.

The reconciliation of the dispute basically granted the old sources nontransferable, site-specific property rights to their existing discharge levels, albeit averaged for water flow in the system. The commission required that the discharge of all new sources and most old sources be monitored but did not restrict entry. These weak property rights, granted by fiat through the inaction of the commission, were able to control common access, protecting the water-use value of existing polluters and downstream users, until the advent of federal regulation. Controlling the variation in discharges and not reducing output enough to induce entry of new firms improved overall water quality.

Though the existing firms won a major battle, it is not clear how they would have fared before the commission in the face of increased scarcity. The commission showed no signs of understanding even the simplest property rights issues. Indeed, the salt discharge standards promulgated by the Environmental Protection Agency (EPA) in 1974 made a property rights leap that ORANSCO was unwilling to take.

The EPA set a 150-parts-per-million outfall standard for existing firms and a zero discharge standard for new firms.[29] While the

29. See Environmental Protection Agency, *Development Document for Effluent Limitations Guidelines and New Source Performance Standards for the Major Inorganic Products Segment of the Inorganic Chemicals Manufacturing Point Source Category* (Washington, D.C., March 1974).

150-ppm standard is more strict than the ORANSCO action, the property vested by the new/old distinction is similarly more valuable. Because no new sources can compete for discharge rights, restrictions of pollution by existing firms will restrict output, raise prices, and enhance profits, all as evidence of the environmental asset's value.

The nontransferable EPA standard is an entry barrier for new firms. However, based on our theory of property rights, we are hard pressed to argue that this is inefficient. Certainly the EPA standard is superior to the ORANSCO approach. To the extent that the demand for water quality requires a reduction in mining-related salt discharge, setting standards for the most productive existing mines and prohibition of pollution for any new mines is efficient, at least until the productive capacity of the old mines falls. In other words, because the initial assignment of rights was optimal, there was no need for the rights to be alienable.

Discharge Management in Other Regions

Although the state of New York passed its first pollution control legislation in 1903, not until 1949 was legislation passed in that state that had an impact on pollution problems.[30] The 1949 law established a permit system and required approval of new or modified sources. Old sources escaped attention and likely gained rents by avoiding costs imposed on competitors. In any case, New York's pollution problems, like those of the states along the Ohio River, was primarily caused by municipalities, not industry, and the municipalities were less than cooperative with the state regulatory authorities until the state provided funding in 1965 when the Pure Water Program was launched. Voters approved a $1 billion bond issue for municipal treatment plants, and sewage treatment plants began to spring up across the state. Turning to the industrial pollution problem, the state established a permit procedure based on water-quality standards, and by 1973 had 364 monitoring stations, one for every 200 miles of river water, giving continuous readings of water quality.

In 1961 the Texas Water Pollution Control Board came into existence. Included in the required membership of the board were the representatives of three special-interest groups—agriculture, oil and

30. Lieber, *Federalism and Clean Waters*, pp. 151–152.

gas, and manufacturing. Between 1961 and 1967 not a single violation was filed by the Texas Water Pollution Control Board. Texas adopted new legislation in 1967, apparently in anticipation of or because of pending federal legislation. The new law tightened the pollution control system, removed special-interest dominance of the board, and established an effective water pollution control program based on permits and water quality standards. Indeed, in 1973 Lieber described the state's program as so good that nothing would be gained by the implementation of the 1972 federal legislation.[31]

The development of water-quality regulation in the state of Massachusetts, particularly along the Merrimack River, serves as a final illustration of state and local pollution control activity.[32] Activities at the state level began in 1887 when water pollution control legislation focusing on public health concerns was passed. As a result of that action, all rivers in Massachusetts were classified as to industrial or recreational use, with rivers in the latter category to be maintained as trout streams. The Merrimack, Blackstone, and Neponset rivers were classified as industrial streams. They were in effect waste disposal systems for industrial plants and were not to be used under any circumstance for drinking water or recreation.

The classification system seemed to work. In 1936 a special Massachusetts health commission reviewed the earlier decisions and reported that the industrial streams were

> of great industrial value and their use for this purpose has contributed to the prosperity of the Commonwealth. Although the Commission does not wish to condone willful defilement of any stream, it believes that the most that can be expected in such cases is that the manufacturers use all practicable means to prevent pollution.[33]

From the post-World War II period to the middle 1960s, residents in cities along the Merrimack expressed strong preferences for keeping the industrial status of their river. There were no health problems. Drinking water was available from other sources, and industry, which was in a state of decline in the region, was able to operate longer without incurring high water treatment costs. Referenda for

31. Ibid., p. 170.

32. George T. Downey, *The Significance of Government Policies and Attitudes in Water Pollution Control: A Case Study of the Merrimack River Valley*, dissertation for Clark University (Ann Arbor, Mich.: University Microfilms, 1969).

33. Ibid., p. 125.

bond issues to fund improved waste treatment facilities were always defeated. It was not until the federal government became involved in water quality that Massachusetts revised its management of the Merrimack. Even then there were serious questions about the need for improved quality. In effect, the river had been able to assimilate wastes and meet the preferences of the population in its basin.

Industrial Discharge Before 1972

In a congressional hearing in 1945, Warren N. Watson, secretary of the Manufacturers Chemists Association, argued that only new firms should be affected by pollution laws.

> In the problem of pollution, . . . industry must be recognized as having some proprietary rights to our watercourses. Its right of discovery or priority demands that it must not be forced to bear an unfair burden because of later happenings. . . .
>
> No regulatory scheme should be imposed that would force an old established industry to close down because of too rigid pollution standards where there is no technically satisfactory or economically operable system available for treatment of this particular waste. In the establishment of any new facility on any watercourse, a local authority should be provided before which the proposed industry can lay its project and obtain approval of its waste disposal scheme. Such permit might be a necessary requirement before starting construction.[34]

While such positions, typical of industry at that time, arguably reflect only the rent-seeking concerns of special interests, they are not completely without merit in a property rights framework as revealed in the discussion of ORANSCO's salt discharge regulation. The nonmarketable regional permit systems of this period were in large part responsible for the scarcity of water quality that resulted from industrial discharge and the high costs of monitoring water quality and, hence, defining alienable rights.

34. U.S. Congress, House, *Hearings Before the Committee on Rivers and Harbors*, 79th Cong., 13, 14 November 1945, p. 312. The bills were H.R. 519, 587, and H.R. 4070.

THE FEDERAL WATER POLLUTION CONTROL ACT OF 1972: DEFINING PROPERTY RIGHTS

The first federal water-quality legislation was the Water Pollution Control Act of 1948, followed by amendments in 1956, 1961, 1965, 1966, and 1970.[35] In 1970 President Nixon turned the Rivers and Harbors Act of 1899 into the Refuse Act by using it to issue permits for industrial discharge.[36] All of these laws show a progression of federal involvement in water-quality control. However, the 1972 amendments brought an abrupt change to the basic pattern of pollution control regulation embodied in the 1948–1970 laws. Enacted over President Nixon's veto, the amendments gave federal authorities a major role in pollution control, establishing a National Pollution Discharge Elimination System (NPDES) to issue permits. In effect, the act tightened the property dimensions of the right to pollute, and similarly, the right to some level of water quality.

In addition to nationalizing the pollution of the nation's rivers and streams, setting up an accounting system for their use, and giving authority to monitor use and gain data, the 1972 law required the administrator of the EPA to establish effluent limitations at industrial point sources based on the best practicable technology (BPT). Permits were to be issued on the basis of the limitations, which were to be in place and operating throughout industry by July 1, 1977. Tighter standards based on the best available technology (BAT) were

35. The Oil Pollution Act of 1924, while clearly related to water pollution, dealt only with discharge from ocean vessels (see 33 U.S.C. 604). The summary of water pollution control legislation is based on: Richard H. Bachmann, "The Application of Effluent Limitations and Effluent Guidelines to Industrial Polluters: An Administrative Nightmare," *Houston Law Review* 13 (1976): 304; Jan T. Brown and Wallace L. Duncan, "Legal Aspects of a Federal Water Quality Surveillance System," *Michigan Law Review* 68 (1970): 1131–1165; Frank J. Barry, "The Evolution of the Enforcement Provisions of the Federal Water Pollution Control Act: A Study of the Difficulty in Developing Effective Legislation," *Michigan Law Review* 68 (1970): 1103–1154; Jerome S. Kalur, "Will Judicial Error Allow Industrial Point Sources to Avoid BPT and Perhaps BAT Later? A Story of Bad Dictum, and Ugly Consequence," *Ecology Law Quarterly* 7 (1979): 955–988; Patrick A. Parenteau and Nancy Tauman, "The Effluent Limitations Controversy: Will Careless Draftsmanship Foil the Objectives of the Federal Water Pollution Control Act Amendments of 1972?" *Ecology Law Quarterly* 6 (1976): 1–59.

36. See "Statement on Signing Executive Order Establishing A Water Quality Enforcement Program," No. 473, *Public Papers of the President, Richard Nixon, 1970* (Washington, D.C.: Government Printing Office, 1971). This use of the 1899 legislation was short-lived due to court rulings.

to be in place by July 1, 1983, and all new sources of pollution were required to apply BAT or new-source performance standards, which in general would exceed BPT.

The 1972 law preempted state standard setting and enforcement of water quality that were more lax than the federal requirements. It also imposed uniform standards for all the nation's rivers and streams, foreclosing the use of abundant water quality or citizen preferences for pollution relative to other variables such as the competition of states for new industrial plants. Firms could no longer shop for "cheap" water into which they would dump their waste. One could say that all water-using industries were organized in a loose cartel in that restrictions on water use did not follow the course of natural scarcity. The point was summarized in the conference report on the legislation:

> [T]he intent of Congress is that effluent limitations applicable to industrial plant sources within a given category or class be as uniform as possible. The Administrator is expected to be precise in his guidelines, so as to assure that similar point sources with similar characteristics, regardless of their location or the nature of the water into which the discharge is made, will meet similar effluent limitations.[37]

While satisfying those who wanted cleaner water, strictly enforced effluent limitations could achieve the goals of an output-restricting cartel.

A number of industry suits contended that the EPA should identify factors such as costs of technology, plant age and process, and energy requirements to be considered by state permit-issuing authorities when setting conditions for individual polluters.[38] The EPA was unwilling to go so far but already had adopted the notion of variances, which allowed a source to operate legally in violation of BPT.[39] The variance procedure had to be approved by the agency's

37. Bachmann, "Application of Effluent Limitations," p. 304.

38. Parenteau and Tauman, "Effluent Limitations Controversy," pp. 3-5.

39. C. James Koch and Robert A. Leone, "The Clean Water Act: Unexpected Impacts on Industries," *Harvard Environmental Law Review* 3 (1979): 84-111. argue that with variances granted to weaker existing firms, the shutdown of marginal plants was reduced and market price and therefore profits for lower cost plants increased. This argument is vacuous. To receive a variance must be more profitable than not to, especially if all other competitors don't. But standards imposed on all firms in an industry, even if entry of new firms is not restricted, may cause profits of low-cost firms to go up if they can meet the standard more cheaply than high-cost firms. See Maloney and McCormick, "Positive Theory of Environmental Regulation."

administrator and thus was outside the discretionary control of the states.[40]

The result of the legal skirmishes was that uniform standards of water quality were interpreted to mean uniform point-source standards, and variances became a means by which politically powerful firms avoided these standards. Because discretion was not a prerogative of the states, barriers to competition that might be created could not be torn down by interstate rivalries. Moreover, the source of political power was not related to regional water quality. The EPA rulings resulted in a significant increase in the *potential* for rent seeking by special-interest groups at the federal level. However, it is not clear that this potential has ever been exercised.

Existing Versus New Sources

Section 306 of the 1972 act defined standards of performance for new sources that were stricter than those for existing sources. The new-source standards would apply to any source, "the construction of which is commenced after the publication of proposed regulations prescribing a standard of performance . . . which will be applicable [to that category of sources]."[41] The standard defined for new sources would require BAT or better-performing technology, while existing polluters would face the less strict BPT standards until 1983. While language identifying just when a modified existing source became new was deleted from the draft version of the 1972 act, the EPA adopted the principle that reconstruction involving 10 percent or more of an existing source would invoke new-source standards. Thus existing sources had obtained high-entry barriers affecting new competition.[42] In a landmark case, *E.I. duPont de Nemours & Co.* v. *Train* (1976), the Supreme Court approved the EPA's variance procedure for BPT but not for BAT.[43] In other words, an existing

40. Though the wording in this paragraph is convenient, we do not think of the EPA or its administrators as autonomous economic agents. Rather, we treat the agency as an arm of the president and Congress.

41. Quoted in Bachmann, "Application of Effluent Limitations," p. 365.

42. The slow pace followed by the EPA in writing BPT permits contributed significantly to the stronger position of existing firms versus new firms and probably extended even longer the deadline for BAT requirements. See Kalur, "Will Judicial Error Allow Sources to Avoid BPT and BAT?" p. 958.

43. Ibid., pp. 967–968.

plant's problems in meeting BPT could be considered and adjustments made when developing its permit. This was not the case for new plants: The Court ruled specifically that variances were not allowed for new sources.

> [T]he Supreme Court, referring to the statutory language that makes it unlawful for any owner of any new source to operate or discharge in violation of the standard set by the Administrator, ruled that Congress intended the standards to be an *absolute prohibition.*[44] (emphasis added)

The 1972 Clean Water Act in Review

Table 9-1 describes the property rights elements of the 1972 act as interpreted and implemented by the EPA. As shown, there are three property elements derived from the act: (1) the goals of the legislation are to deliver public property in the form of uniform national baseline levels of water quality; (2) existing polluters are given private property in the form of allowable amounts of effluent discharge compatible with the limitations and control technologies defined by the EPA, the amount of property obtained shifting if BPT is translated to BAT; and (3) new sources obtain limited entitlements when they are built, in an amount compatible with BAT limitations.

In their summary of pre-1977 clean water legislation, Kneese and Schultze cite as its major deficiency the failure to provide institu-

Table 9-1. Property Rights Characteristics of the 1972 Clean Water Act.

Physical system: All national waters
Enforcement mechanism: State-operated NPDES permit system
Monitoring capability: Existence of control technologies at each source and monitoring of stream water quality

Defined property: Baseline of quality described by effluent limitations
Implied owner: Federal government

Defined property: BAT level of pollution with variances until 1983; BPT with variances after 1985
Implied owner: Existing polluters

Defined property: BPT level of pollution on permissible waters
Implied owner: New polluters

44. Ibid., p. 973.

tional arrangement for efficient management of water quality on the basis of river basins:

> In the longer perspective—especially in light of the relationship between management of water quality on the one hand and the need to develop programs for control of the residuals from nonpoint sources on the other—the failure to build institutions that could undertake efficient region-wide management was perhaps the most profound deficiency of the entire approach.[45]

Upon examining that period from a longer perspective, we are inclined to disagree. Certainly, nationwide uniformity is not desirable from a property rights perspective and admits only of ignorance or rent seeking by special-interest groups. That variances were issued not on the basis of existing water quality where there were no competing users, but instead on the basis of "need" is the handiwork of old-fashioned, pork-barrel politics. However, regional management by a federal agency could not develop until property arrangements were better defined and monitoring capabilities improved. The 1972 legislation did create these institutions: NPDES permits are property definitions and the BPT and BAT source standards are the monitoring device. The alienability characteristics thus established were crude, but apparently there was not sufficient demand for more sophistication from 1972 to 1977, a point discussed in the next section.

Paradoxically, the 1972 act did create a property rights protection device—new-source performance standards. By making BAT stricter than BPT and not allowing variances for BAT, the act vested rights to pollute in existing firms. These rights, though inalienable in a spacial context, were a protected environmental asset. The BPT standards made the right to pollute valuable and the stricter BAT standards prevented erosion of this value by entry of new firms. Thus, a first step was achieved in the movement to markets for water quality. Even so, had the EPA devoted more resources to measuring and monitoring pollution during the period, it is possible that markets for pollution would have emerged prior to 1977.

45. Allen V. Kneese and Charles L. Schultze, *Pollution, Prices, and Public Policy* (Washington, D.C.: The Brookings Institution, 1975), p. 45.

THE 1977 CLEAN WATER AMENDMENTS: IMAGES OF A MARKET

As with earlier amendments to water pollution control legislation, the 1977 amendments internalized some of the legal and institutional developments that resulted from the 1972 law. A key problem to be addressed was that the statutory deadlines included in the 1972 legislation had either passed or were rapidly approaching, with little or no hope of achievement. Congress had proven to be incapable of forecasting compliance calendars with any degree of accuracy. Further, the real cost of installing BPT and BAT had been identified, as had the realities of economic hardship associated with plant shutdowns and the resulting dislocations.

In terms of the model presented in the first section this evidence can be interpreted to mean that the value of the property defined by the 1972 act was not as great as had been anticipated. The reduction in property right enforcement activities predicted by the theory in fact did occur. Technology-based standards were maintained as the primary device for managing water quality. However, the deadline for achieving BPT was extended to April 1, 1979, and the BAT deadline was extended one year to July 1, 1984. Yet a third category of control technologies was introduced and applied to so-called conventional pollutants, those normally treated in publicly owned treatment works. The less severe BCT (best conventional pollutant control technology) requirements replaced BAT, except where toxic pollutants were concerned.

The NPDES permits based on BPT, BCT, or BAT were property rights to use water as a discharge medium up to some level or intensity, as well as rights to a degree of water quality for downstream users. Thus, the permits were a kind of contract between upstream and downstream water users. The inalienability built into the permits was a necessary component of the contract because the downstream users were silent partners. Alternative institutions that took more direct account of the downstream users might have been constructed in lieu of the 1972 legislation. It is possible that the NPDES system was not optimal, all costs and benefits considered, that the ineptitudes of the law were designed intentionally to bestow monopoly rewards on some at the expense of others. However, as pointed out in the previous section, the NPDES system may have been the best approach based on monitoring and enforcement costs.

If the value of water quality had been overestimated in the 1972 act, proposition two implies that the contract structure was chosen improperly also. Enforcement was overemphasized relative to definition of property rights. Reallocation of the water-quality asset and redefinition of the rights to it can be analyzed as an efficient margin of substitution in the face of the shortfall in water quality value. In fact, a number of avenues were pursued in the 1977 amendments: (1) regional rather than national water-quality standards were used as a basis for permitting; (2) intraplant transferability of permits was considered; and (3) transfer of permits among plants was approved on a limited basis.

Regional Definition of Water Quality

While the 1977 law preserved the paradoxical separation of point-source effluent limitations and ambient water-quality standards, it acknowledged the relationship of water quality to point-source standards. Until the 1977 amendments, the EPA and the states had two, not necessarily related, standards to achieve. Industrial effluent guidelines were uniform across categories of industries (e.g., specialty steel manufacturing), yet the water quality in receiving streams was not uniform.

The achievement of BPT by every plant along every river or stream did not create uniform ambient stream standards, for those streams that were less polluted at the start would inevitably be cleaner than others that might never achieve the ambient water-quality standards. To deal with the dirty streams, the EPA could require stricter BPT permits for plants. But what about the streams that exceeded the desired water-quality standards? Could an industrial discharger relax its treatment of wastes if the effect did not reduce the quality of a receiving stream or the required level of control for a neighboring plant?

This question was answered affirmatively in section 301(g) of the 1977 amendments. A discharger of conventional pollutants could receive a modified BAT limitation if the effect would: (1) result in at least BPT compliance, (2) not adversely affect water quality so as to cause additional clean-up requirements for other dischargers into the same body of water, and (3) not prevent attainment of the fishable and swimmable goal or impose a health hazard.[46] Thus, the regional uniformity of standards in the 1972 act that Kneese and Schultze criticized was changing, and a kind of interregional transfer of rights was developing.

This section of the law also acknowledged emerging property rights that could be traded among dischargers who used the same receiving waters. If a discharger could reduce its treatment without adversely affecting water quality, certain questions emerge: Which polluter among a group would gain that privilege? Would it not make sense to allow the high-cost polluter to be the first to modify its actions? And suppose another polluter could increase its level of treatment to facilitate such actions—should one polluter be allowed to pay another for that activity?

Intraplant Transfers: The Evolving Bubble Concept

Protected from unbridled entry of new competition by the BPT/BAT distinction, existing plants had struggled all along to reduce further the cost of meeting specific plant-level effluent limitations. The EPA's permit procedure was essentially based on a pipe-by-pipe analysis, with each point of effluent subject to specified BPT minimum pollutant loadings and flows. Under a strict interpretation of the law, the firm's discharge rights were assigned legally to each point. Once a permit was issued, the firm had a contract. But the rights endowed to each point were not alienable—they could not be traded, even among similar sources within the same plant.[47] In other words, if a plant were discharging chromium-laden effluent from two sources having different abatement cost characteristics, the firm could not reduce treatment at the higher cost source, increase treatment at the lower cost one, and meet the same total effluent discharge at a lower total cost. There was simply a no-trade situation. In some cases, EPA regional administrators took it upon themselves

46. Kalur, "Will Judicial Error Allow Sources to Avoid BPT and BAT?" pp. 983–984.

47. While adjustments or tradeoffs cannot be executed within a plant, the individual permits themselves are limited property rights and can be transferred to a new plant owner. See 43 *Federal Register* 37079, 21 August 1978.

to allow plants to equate marginal costs among sources, but the approach was not institutionalized and therefore was outside the law.[48]

Cost-minimizing issues had surfaced in suits contesting the EPA's procedures under the 1972 amendments. In *American Iron and Steel Institute* v. *EPA* (1977), the industry charged that the EPA had not considered adequately the combined treatment of waste sources, reducing possibilities for economies of scale in the treatment of similar wastes.[49] Yet while the Court agreed with some of the industry's complaints, it merely remanded the iron and steel regulations back to the EPA for minor revisions.

Plants in some industries such as pulp and paper were allowed to choose their own methods of achieving overall effluent reduction targets, an advantage denied to firms in such industries as iron and steel. Some regions allowed in-plant trading and combined treatment for any plant that wanted it; other regions toed the line and wrote permits on a pipe-by-pipe basis; and some industries, no matter where their plants were located, were allowed to minimize costs.

The simple notion of in-plant discharge adjustments became known as the "bubble concept," implying that the regulator would treat an entire plant as if it were encased in a bubble.[50] Of concern was the total discharge from the bubble into receiving waters; what went on under the bubble was beside the point. In the case of water quality, the bubble concept is a type of plumbing problem. Collecting the wastes of many sources and treating them at one point as one source might be cheaper than the individual source approach generally used when the EPA wrote the permits.

48. According to Booz, Allen & Hamilton, EPA Regions II and X operated in this fashion. The same report indicated the EPA had allowed in-plant trading for the pulp and paper industry. See Booz, Allen & Hamilton, "The Water Bubble Concept As An Alternative Effluent Limitations Approach" (paper prepared for the Environmental Protection Agency, Bethesda, Md., 25 November 1980), pp. 8-9.

49. Water Quality Committee, "Annual Review of Significant Activities–1977," *Natural Resources Lawyer* XI (1977): 238-239. A similar concern was raised by the same industry in 1979, with a specific request for permission to use the bubble. See "Current Developments," *Environmental Reporter*, 7 March 1980, p. 2087.

50. The use of the word "bubble" is more appropriate for air pollution, but the actual practice is the same for both pollutants. See M. T. Maloney and Bruce Yandle, "Bubbles and Efficiency," *Regulation* (May/June 1980). A thorough discussion of the bubble approach is given in Jack L. Landau, "Economic Dream or Environmental Nightmare? The Legality of the Bubble Concept in Air and Water Pollution Control," *Environmental Affairs* 8 (1980): 741-781.

In 1978 the EPA began to investigate vigorously the possibilities of recognizing the bubble concept as a part of revisions in the NPDES permit program.[51] The agency contracted with Booz, Allen & Hamilton to study the practicality of the approach and to identify potential cost savings if allowed.[52] While the idea was clearly sound from the standpoint of in-plant economies, the EPA had to consider the administrative costs of monitoring a more complex, case-by-case procedure that might be called for if bubbles were allowed. For instance, if many sources could be collected to form one source without redefinition of the BPT and BAT guidelines, the regulatory administrative costs would be relatively low. On the other hand, if the bubbling brought together diverse sources for which new standards had to be written, the administrative costs might be extreme. Harking back to our theory, the question turns on the cost of alienability relative to its demand.

Booz, Allen & Hamilton investigated the approach under rather restrictive assumptions mandated by the EPA, concluding that

> In the context of industry's current and anticipated practices, EPA's effluent guidelines, and the interpretation of these guidelines in the writing of NPDES permits, there are relatively few direct discharging plants to which the bubble concept can be applied where any cost savings will result.[53]

However, one exception to this otherwise pessimistic conclusion about the prospects for the bubble was identified—the iron and steel industry, the same industry that earlier sued the EPA in search of cost-minimizing control opportunities.

While the study identified places where the bubble concept had been applied all along and suggested other potential opportunities, the operating assumptions imposed on the study, which were integrated into EPA policy, restricted the bubble to existing plants that had achieved BPT control.[54] The bubble would be used to assist these firms in achieving BAT levels of effluent limitation. In addition, no single-point source would be allowed to discharge more

51. See 43 *Federal Register* 37080, 21 August 1978, and Landau "Economic Dream," pp. 772-778.

52. Booz, Allen & Hamilton, "Water Bubble Concept."

53. Ibid., p. 3. Direct dischargers are opposed to indirect dischargers, which release their wastes into municipal water treatment plants.

54. The requirements are spelled out in the announcement for iron and steel effluent limitations. See 48 *Federal Register*, 7 June 1981, p. 1870.

waste than accepted for BPT permits.[55] But in some limited circumstances the new regulation allowed permits to be rewritten so that wastes could be collected and treated.

Marketable Property Rights: The Cost Savings

As indicated by the Booz, Allen & Hamilton study, certain EPA regional administrators had already taken it upon themselves to implement the bubble for existing firms in their regions. Other entities went even further, turning the image of a market in the 1977 amendments into reality. While at the national level debate still raged over the theoretical possibilities for applying the bubble at the plant level, the state of Wisconsin was demonstrating the cost savings that could accrue when property rights were defined, enforced, and traded among different firms on the same river basin. In March 1981, the Wisconsin Department of Natural Resources announced regulations that allow certain dischargers to transfer pollution rights by approved contracts.[56] The Fox River basin thus became the first body of water in the United States to become subject to a market-determined reallocation of pollution property rights among different plants at different sites. The Fox River receives BPT discharge from ten paper mills and four municipalities along a 22-mile reach of the river. The common pollutant is biochemical oxygen-demanding waste (BOD), which can be measured and monitored.

Fortunately, a recently completed analysis of the resulting permit market provides a clear indication of the cost savings to be anticipated when firms and municipalities begin to exchange permits. The analysis by O'Neil, David, Moore, and Joeres estimated the level of incremental cost being registered by each of seven different dischargers under EPA pipe-by-pipe regulations. As shown in Table 9-2, the abatement cost to source 1 for removing the last unit of BOD (.001 mg/liter) is $72, while the cost for source 5 is $11; the gain obtained

55. The point was made emphatically, though not as final policy, by Edward Kraut, EPA attorney-advisor, in a memorandum to the EPA administrator (12-5-78): "For the bubble concept to allow averaging of point sources to achieve a composite effluent limitation for a plant is to ignore the intent of Congress that when technology is available the law requires that the discharge of all pollutants be eliminated." (See *Environmental Reporter*, 5 January 1979, p. 1662.)

56. O'Neil, David, Moore, and Joeres, "Transferable Discharge Permits."

Table 9-2. Incremental Abatement Costs: Fox River Study.

Discharger	*Incremental Cost ($/unit)*
1	72
2	11
3	5
4	14
5	11
6	37
7	27

Source: O'Neil, David, Moore, and Joeres, "Transferable Discharge Permits," p. 13, Table 2.

by trading one less unit treated at source 1 and treating one more unit at source 7 is $61.

Table 9-3 reports the annual total cost for five levels of water quality under either a system of marketable permits or uniform end-of-pipe regulation. As indicated, the potential savings in annual cost for managing BOD in the Fox River ranges from $4.5 to $6.8 million. Similar results have been found in analyses of the control of BOD for the Willamette River and the control of phosphorus discharged into Lake Michigan, both programs under the auspices of the Wisconsin Department of Natural Resources.[57] In the case of BOD, the marketable property rights approach saved $1,300 in treatment costs per day, while the savings for phosphorus treatment was $960 per day.

As in the intraplant situation, the equilibrium for transferability depends on both benefits and costs. While the benefits of trade are aptly demonstrated by the Wisconsin experiences, the costs are less obvious. The property rights institution founded on the NPDES permits does not vest water-quality demanders directly. Hence, their interests must be protected by the regulatory procedure for permitting discharge. Trading of rights as occurred along the Fox River might violate the rights of some of these hidden property rightshold-

57. See Randolph M. Lyons, "Auctions and Alternative Procedures for Public Allocation with Application to the Distribution of Pollution Rights," Report no. 1, National Science Foundation Award PRA 79-13131 (Urbana: Department of Civil Engineering and Institute for Environmental Studies, University of Illinois-Urbana, March 1981); and Martin David, Erhard Joeres, and J. Wayland Eheart, "Distribution Methods for Transferable Discharge Permits," *Water Resources Research* 16 (1980): 833-843.

Table 9-3. Comparative Total Cost: Market versus Uniform Regulation at Outfall.

	Annual Cost (in millions of dollars)	
Quality Level[a]	*Marketable Rights*	*Regulation*
I	$ 5.4	$11.1
II	10.3	16.1
III	16.8	23.6

a. Quality levels are based on dissolved oxyen level in streams – 2.0, 4.0, and 6.2 ppm, respectively, for the same flow/temperature.

Source: O'Neil, David, Moore, and Joeres, "Transferable Discharge Permits," p. 14, Table 3.

ers. While there may have been few of these users in the Lower Fox River area, just as there were few along the Merrimack River in the prefederal days, whether this is generally true requires further study.

Indirect Dischargers

At the beginning of the federal involvement in water pollution control, most industrial effluent was being discharged into municipal treatment plants, thus indirectly, into the nation's rivers and streams. Even in 1973, the Council on Environmental Quality reported that roughly one-half of all industrial plants were discharging indirectly.[58] Thus it seems logical that much of the early federal activity would be related to the funding of expansions for publicly owned treatment works (POTWs). The 1948 legislation, for example, authorized $22.5 million annually in fiscal 1949 through 1953 for loans to states for the construction of POTWs. The 1956 amendments authorized $50 million in matching grants. Funding was increased to $80 million in 1962, $90 million in 1963, and $100 million annually in 1964–1967. With the 1972 legislation, the federal government authorized $2.75 billion and increased the matching level to 75 percent of construction costs.[59]

58. Council on Environmental Quality, *Environmental Quality–1973* (Washington: Government Printing Office, September 1973), p. 170.

59. *Congressional Quarterly Almanac* (Washington, D.C.: Congressional Quarterly Publishing Co., 1948), p. 152; Ibid., 1956, p. 570; Ibid., 1965, p. 745; Ibid., 1972, p. 709.

Indirect dischargers were not subject to the BPT/BAT-based NPDES permits, which instead were imposed on the municipal POTWs into which they discharged. The 1972 legislation only required that states impose pretreatment standards where indirect discharge might interfere with typical POTW processes. States were required to establish user charges for indirect dischargers to recover the costs imposed by industry. However, the details of full-cost recovery were not specified. Average cost pricing would bring one result, marginal cost another. Furthermore, since land and other costs for municipal plants were not usually based on the same costs faced by private firms when building pollution control facilities, there was still a differential effect between direct and indirect dischargers.[60] Koch and Leone observed that "local governments were also reluctant to enforce the cost-sharing provisions. Despite EPA efforts . . . , three years after the Act was passed not one single cost-sharing program was operational."[61] The advantage that might have existed for a textile plant, for example, discharging into a POTW rather than directly into the stream created the kind of local special-interest-group pressures that had been eliminated by the rest of the 1972 act. Fees could vary from city to city, as could pretreatment standards. Ultimately, the political forces operating the POTWs had no incentive to make them work, just as they had no incentive to construct them in the first place.

These problems began to be solved with the 1977 amendments. National pretreatment standards were set for indirect dischargers, but small sources of industrial waste (less than 25,000 gallons per day) were exempted from industrial cost recovery so long as their waste did not damage a POTW. While national pretreatment standards would enforce uniform output restrictions on firms in the same industry, in our property rights framework they can be viewed as the only way the downstream municipal and industrial water users could ensure effective operation of the POTWs for which they shared in the construction costs through the federal subsidy program.

Thus, the indirect-discharge issue is a microcosm of the entire water-quality regulatory experience. The institutional approach has yielded both special-interest effects and relatively efficient property rights activities.

60. Kneese and Schultze, "Pollution, Prices, and Policy," pp. 92–93.
61. Koch and Leone, "Clean Water Act," p. 103.

WILL MORE MARKETS DEVELOP?

Buried in the complex maze of water pollution control laws and regulations written since 1948 are the necessary foundation stones for a system of marketable property rights to the use of the environment. Yet even the crudest of open markets has just begun to surface. The pregnant institutional framework now includes:

1. A definition of the system to be controlled. The boundary conditions for the market are defined.
2. A system of entitlements to specific discharge privileges. Permits stating the precise amount of environmental use are in place.
3. An overall system of public property. Ambient water-quality standards have been set, and fences are in place marking off the amount of the environmental pasture to be used for industrial purposes.
4. Legally enforceable contracts. State enforcement programs and discharge permits must be enforceable in court in order to gain the EPA's approval.
5. Bioassay techniques and other forms of discharge monitoring. Those who cheat and invade the property of others can be identified.

So why have markets for discharge permits not generally emerged?

This failure can be explained in several ways. First, one can argue that regulators are ignorant of the efficiency gains offered by markets, or that they are informed but have no incentive to release the allocative powers of the market. In other words, the regulators' incentive structure may work against their incurring the costs of organizing markets.

Anticompetitive Special-Interest Regulation

A second explanation turns on arguments about rent-seeking behavior on the part of all major factions involved in pollution control. Industrial firms arguably gain protection from new competition, thereby enjoying increased profits, when regulators impose strictly enforced new-source standards on aspiring competitors. The regulators then operate as if they were cartel managers, policing existing firms to make certain that they observe uniform effluent guidelines, which restrict output. A full-blown, unregulated market might destroy the regulators' cartel powers, leave entry of competitors to the whims of local or regional permit markets, and eliminate any rents gained by artificially contrived environmental scarcity.

Environmentalists fit neatly into this rent-seeking model. Their arguments for cleaner water, rapid and strict enforcement of the law, and the inability of raw markets to deliver a guaranteed level of water quality throughout the United States assist the government-managed cartel. The environmental law firms assist in maintaining the barriers to entry and disciplining existing firms and the EPA for lax enforcement of the cartel agreement. Elected officials gain from the command and control scheme by simultaneously satisfying the environmentalists and existing industry, so long as the rules do not impose excessive costs on existing firms.

Property Rights Considerations

The cartel explanation of the retarded growth of markets, while generally valid, overlooks an important aspect of water-quality control. A market for discharge rights does exist in that pollution permits can be transferred from one owner to another at the same location. While the interesting aspect of the Fox River market is that pollution can be spatially relocated, the necessary conditions for this type of market may occur infrequently because (1) the ability to transfer the site permit to another firm by selling the site reduces the demand for transfer across sites, and (2) the cost of alienability across sites is very high.

A permit market is simultaneously a market for water quality. To let pollution permits move upstream between two sources is to reduce the water quality for all existing and potential users in between. The discharge rights identified by the NPDES permitting system are limited to a small zone or point. At the same time, a larger zone of a water course is affected collectively by each plant's discharge. Industrial wastes from an upstream plant reduce the quality of water at the intake of other plants, so quality must be monitored there. To sort out whose waste is whose, to enforce property rights, requires complex monitoring capabilities that add high costs to the supply of transferability between points. These monitoring costs fall when a number of firms discharging similar wastes are located on a water course with few if any major tributaries or other types of users. As expected, transferability has emerged first in such settings.

There is no mechanism for protecting users who value quality but do not discharge if permits are allowed to move spatially. Evidently, this problem was overcome informally on the Lower Fox River, but progress in this direction has been slow elsewhere. Clearly, legally enforceable rules for such a process would be hard to promulgate at the national level.

The POTW Issue

One might suggest that the demand for and existence of national regulation is itself a product of special-interest pressures. Uniform national control of individual industries is a tried-and-true method of government cartelization. However, this argument disregards a crucial piece of the history of water-quality regulation. The major emphasis of the legislative history has been focused not on direct industrial discharge but on municipal sewage treatment into which a growing amount of indirect industrial discharge has gone. The fact that indirect industrial discharge was ignored by federal action for so long makes the cartel explanation of water-quality regulation less credible, particularly since the 1972 amendments omitted regulation of indirect dischargers across all industries.

The question of who will pay for municipal sewage treatment has generated pressure for a higher level of government to subsidize the cleanup. While water-borne disease can travel upstream as well as down, water pollution due to municipal discharge normally has no direct negative effects on the upstream polluter, with the full negative impact reaching the downstream receiver. The natural distribution of property rights based on common access vests upstream cities and divests those downstream. The natural alternative to this allocation scheme—downstream cities bargaining with upstream cities and financing their water treatment facilities—has not occurred. Instead, pollution-control regulation has migrated to higher levels of government, mandating clean-up programs upstream and down and financing them from the general tax coffers. This process occurs at the national as well as the state and regional levels.[62] Instead of a rent distribution associated with the natural flow of discharge, such schemes effectively reverse the ownership of the environmental asset.

From a political economy perspective, we hypothesize that these schemes resulted from downstream cities being more politically powerful than those upstream. A coalition of downstream users is stronger because only a few cities are upstream to all users. The law of gravity would transfer downstream land rents to the ultimate upstream environmental owners, regardless of the actual geographical distribution of expenditures on sewage treatment. Thus the political process has simply reordered the natural distribution of land rents.

From a property rights perspective, the migration of regulation to the higher governmental authorities with general taxing authority can be explained by monitoring costs. Overseeing municipal water treatment requires legal institutions that have jurisdiction over all the affected parties. For instance, if Cincinnati were to give money to Pittsburgh for a water treatment facility, what guarantee does it have of performance? The legal machinery available to enforce performance ex post is hard to imagine. In other words, the rigidity of judiciary markets contributes to the forces pushing toward national control. The experience of indirect dischargers further supports this argument. Indirect dischargers were omitted from regulatory action at first; the individual POTWs were supposed to define and impose their own standards and charges. However, because the POTWs had no incentive to do so, the EPA was forced to promulgate pretreatment standards in order to ensure proper operation of the federally financed POTWs.

Some Final Thoughts

Though water-quality control begins and ends with municipal discharge, institutions have developed along the way that define and enforce property rights to water quality for all, promoting a market-like reallocation of discharge rights. Tighter controls required of municipal treatment works in their monitoring of and charging for

62. Recall that ORANSCO and New York State both implemented sewage treatment plans wherein there were no cross-payments from downstream to upstream polluters.

treatment of industrial wastes has in a sense closed the last loophole for the uneconomic discharge of industrial effluent. Dischargers of industrial waste will now confront scarcity at every turn—controls are applied when these firms seek to discharge directly into rivers and streams, and publicly owned treatment works require pretreatment of industrial wastes and payments to defray the cost of handling approved discharge into their plants. Although rent-seeking activities will still lead industrial firms to support stricter standards for new sources and to lobby for technology-based standards to be applied to existing polluters, the growing scarcity of pollution privileges will ultimately bring pressures for trading. The mechanisms now in place will support the expected emerging markets. But national markets for pollution rights are not apt to develop.

As noted earlier, spatially tradable pollution rights are expected to develop first where dischargers of the same waste are located along streams that do not have large tributaries and where a high level of water quality is not desired for aesthetic reasons. In such locations, which lend themselves to lower cost monitoring and the internalization of benefits gained by efficient environmental use, industrial dischargers will have an incentive to trade and will not face the attenuation of property rights to pollution created when dischargers upstream or consumers of environmental quality in mid-stream expand their demand for water use.

Since the EPA presently encourages states to experiment with markets for pollution rights, it will be up to local citizens, environmental control agencies, and industrial dischargers to identify those locations where markets might work based on the physical characteristics of the environment and the composition of industrial dischargers. Local agencies then must define the particular effluents that can be made subject to a market mechanism. The existing level of discharge for present users must then be measured, along with the ambient water quality that emerges when all dischargers operate. Given this information, along with knowledge of streamflow and peak loads, the agency can then endow to existing users a level of discharge that allows a targeted level of water quality to be maintained.

If an effective market is to emerge, the endowment of rights must take on all the legal characteristics of a deed to real property, which can be recorded, transferred, and enforced. This system will require an acceptable monitoring mechanism to which trading parties will adhere when disputes about water use are settled. Of course, each discharger will have an incentive to monitor the activities of other users, just as landowners police their property and prosecute trespassers. In any case, an official monitoring agency will be required, even though private parties will assist in the protection of the property rights.

As additional pollutants are considered as candidates for a market system, even where the noted physical arrangements are ideally suited, it is possible that some will emerge in the market and others will be reserved for regulatory control. The cost of monitoring use will play a significant role in this final determination. That is, the extent to which transferability is allowed is functionally related to the cost of monitoring use and the benefits of extensive trading.

Because of the importance of monitoring to both the operation of rent-seeking cartels and efficient trading, we suggest that the EPA devote significant resources toward the improvement of its monitoring capabilities. The ability to measure and monitor pollution is fundamental to the protection of property rights, whether or not they are traded. That capability is crucial when trade begins. Indeed, trade may never begin in some locations until the agreeing parties are convinced that they are indeed buying and selling a defined entity.

Although some public policy analysts might be inclined to urge unfettered markets upon all water-quality users, we are more inclined to argue for caution. Our concern has nothing to do with doubts about the efficiency characteristics of markets. Indeed, our concern is that those characteristics be given a chance to emerge, that markets not be forced prematurely, that administrative costs, monitoring systems, and the other legal devices necessary to support and enhance trade be recognized and internalized by all trading parties. If these costs are not recognized and borne by those who gain directly from trade, those who bear the costs may bring an early end to experimental markets, which otherwise could have flourished.

We close this chapter on a note of optimism about the prospects for marketable rights to pollute. Our society now stands at a threshold of markets that has taken a decade to construct. As we push to step through the door, we must recognize the costs and benefits found when we enter the world of markets. In our opinion, the benefits can be large, so long as the institutional threshold is stout. But property rights are meaningless in a world where monitoring does not exist, where transferability carries more cost than potential traders are willing to bear.

SELECTED BIBLIOGRAPHY (PART III)

Anderson, Terry, and Hill, P. J. "The Evolution of Property Rights: A Study of the American West." *Journal of Law and Economics* 18 (April 1975): 163-80.

Bagley, Edgar S. "Water Rights Law and Public Policies Relating to Groundwater 'Mining' in the Southwestern States." *Journal of Law and Economics* 4 (October 1961): 152.

Beattie, Bruce. "Irrigated Agriculture and the Great Plains: Problems and Policy Alternatives." *Western Journal of Agricultural Economics* 6 (December 1981).

Huffman, James L. "Water and Public Control." In Pete Klingeman, ed., *New Directions in Water Policy.* Corvallis: Oregon State University, 1980.

Huffman, James L., et al. In *The Allocation of Water to Instream Flows: A Comparative Study of Policy Making and Technical Information in the States of Colorado, Idaho, Montana and Washington*, vols. 1-5. Portland, Ore.: Natural Resources Law Institute, 1980.

Klein, Benjamin; Crawford, Robert G.; and Alchian, Armen. "Vertical Integration, Appropriable Rents, and the Competitive Contracting Process." *Journal of Law and Economics* 21 (October 1978): 279-328.

Maloney, M. T., and McCormick, R. E. "A Positive Theory of Environmental Quality Regulation." *Journal of Law and Economics* 25 (April 1982): 99-123.

Maloney, M. T., and Yandle, Bruce. "Bubbles and Efficiency." *Regulation* (May/June 1980): 49-52.

Scribner, Tom. "Arizona Water Law: The Problem of Instream Appropriation for Environmental Use by Private Appropriators." *Arizona Law Review* 21 (1979): 1095.

Smith, Vernon L. "Water Deeds: A Proposed Solution to the Water Valuation Problem." *Arizona Review* 26 (January 1977): 8.

Tarlock, Dan. "Appropriation for Instream Flow Maintenance: A Progress Report on 'New' Public Western Water Rights." *Utah Law Review* (1978): 211.

Trelease, Frank J. "The Model Water Code, the Wise Administrator and the Goddam Bureaucrat." *Natural Resources Journal* 14 (1974): 207-29.

Umbeck, John. "A Theory of Contract Choice and the California Gold Rush." *Journal of Law and Economics* 20 (October 1977): 421-37.

INDEX

ABOUT THE EDITOR

Terry L. Anderson received his B.S. (*cum laude*) in business administration from the University of Montana and his M.S. and Ph.D. in economics from the University of Washington. He is Professor of Economics at Montana State University, has taught at Seattle University (1971) and the University of Washington (1971–72), and has lectured at the University of Birmingham, England (1982) and Oxford University (1982–83). He has been a Research Assistant, Graduate School Research Fund (1968); National Fellow, National Science Foundation (1969–71); Research Fellow, U.S. Small Business Administration (1980); and National Fellow, Hoover Institution (1980).

Dr. Anderson is the author of *The Economic Growth of Seventeenth-Century New England* (1972), *The Birth of a Transfer Society* (with P. J. Hill, 1980), *The Water Crisis: Averting the Policy Drought* (1983), and *Growth and Welfare in the American Past* (with Douglass North and P. J. Hill, 1983).

He has contributed to *Frontiers of Economics* (G. Tullock, ed., 1976), *Managing the Commons* (G. Hardin and J. Baden, eds., 1977), *Bureaucracy vs. Environment* (J. Baden and R. Stroup, eds., 1981), and *Explorations in the New Economic History: Essays in Honor of Douglass North* (R. Ransom, R. Sutch, and G. Walton, eds., 1982). His articles and reviews have appeared in *American Journal of Agricultural Economics, Cato Journal, Economic History Review, Explorations in Economic History, Journal of Economic History, Journal of Law Economics, Journal of Libertarian Studies*, and *Western Wildlands.*

ABOUT THE CONTRIBUTORS

Oscar R. Burt is Professor of Agricultural Economics at Montana State University and has been Assistant Professor, University of California, Davis (1961–1964), Associate Professor, University of Missouri (1964–1968), and Visiting Professor, University of California, Davis (1972–1973). He received his B.S. in agricultural economics from the University of Nebraska, and both his M.A. in statistics and Ph.D. in agricultural economics from the University of California, Berkeley.

Specializing in the areas of agricultural production economics and natural resources economics, Dr. Burt has written numerous technical papers and research monographs, and was a contributor to *Advances in Groundwater Hydrology* (Z. Saleem, ed.). His articles have appeared in such professional journals as *Accounting Research, Agronomy Journal, American Economic Review, American Journal of Agricultural Economics, Econometrica, Land Economics, Management Science, Operations Research, Society for Industrial and Applied Mathematics Review, Southwest Social Science Quarterly, Western Journal of Agricultural Economics, and Water Resources Research.*

Alfred G. Cuzán received his B.A. in government and economics from the University of Miami and his M.A. and Ph.D. in political science with an emphasis in economics from Indiana University. Presently, he is Associate Professor of political science at the University of West Florida in Pensacola and previously has taught at New Mexico State University. He was the recipient of a Woodrow Wilson Fellowship (1969), a National Defense Educational Act Fellowship (1969–72), and a National Institute of Mental Health Fellowship (1973, 1974).

Dr. Cuzán's primary research interests focus on natural resource policies, political economy, public administration, taxation and budgeting, and comparative government. He has written numerous articles for *American Journal of Economics and Sociology, Behavioral Science, Coastal Zone Management Journal, Idaho Journal of Politics, Journal of Libertarian Studies, Latin American Research Review, Public Choice, Western Political Quarterly*, and other journals.

Price V. Fishback is currently Assistant Professor of Economics at the University of Georgia. He received his B.A. from Butler University and his M.A. and Ph.D. from the University of Washington. Dr. Fishback has taught at the University of Washington and has conducted economic research and forecasting in the private sector. His additional research interests include economic history, labor economics, and applied microeconomics and econometrics, with a current emphasis on employment conditions for blacks in the coal-mining industry.

David T. Fractor is Adjunct Assistant Professor at the Department of Agricultural Economics and Economics, Montana State University. He received his B.A. in economics from the University of California, Los Angeles, and his M.S. and Ph.D. from the University of Oregon, where he previously taught economics. He has conducted research projects on a variety of economic subjects, including natural resources, property rights, macroeconomics, and labor economics. He is a contributor to *Natural Resources* (with J. Baden and R. Stroup), and his articles have appeared in *Journal of Leisure Research.*

B. Delworth Gardner is Professor of Agricultural Economics at the University of California, Davis. He received his B.S. and M.S. from the University of Wyoming and his Ph.D. from the University of Chicago.

Dr. Gardner has been Professor and Head, Department of Economics, Utah State University (1962–76); Visiting Professor, University of California, Berkeley (1965); Visiting Scholar, Resources for the Future (1968-69); President, Western Agricultural Economic Association (1971); member, Task Force on Energy and Mechanization, National Academy of Science (1976); and Chairman, Committee on Rangeland Management, National Academy of Science (1979–82).

Dr. Gardner's articles have appeared in *American Journal of Agricultural Economics, California Agriculture, Economic and Social Issues, Journal of Range Management, Land Economics, Natural Resources Journal, Revista Paraguaya de Sociologia, Southern Journal of Agricultural Economics, Water Resources Research, Western Economics Journal, Western Journal of Agricultural Economics*, and other scholarly and trade publications.

Micha Gisser is Professor of Economics at the University of New Mexico, Albuquerque. Following his studies at the School of Law and Economics in Tel Aviv, where he earned his B.S., he received his M.A. and Ph.D. at the University of Chicago.

A former Fellow of the Ford Foundation, Dr. Gisser has been Assistant Professor, Roosevelt University (1962–64); Economic Advisor, Ministry of Agriculture, Israel (1964–66); Visiting Lecturer, Hebrew University, Israel (1964–66); and Associate Professor, Ohio State University (1966–67).

He is the author of *Intermediate Price Theory*, and his many articles on natural resources and agricultural problems have appeared in *American Journal of Agricultural Economics, Econometrica, International Journal of Control, Journal of Law and Economics, Journal of Political Economy, Land Economics, Natural Resources Journal*, and *Water Resources Research*.

James L. Huffman is Professor of Law at the Lewis and Clark Law School and Director of the Natural Resources Law Institute. He received his B.A. from Montana State University, his M.A. from Tufts University, and his J.D. from the University of Chicago. In addition to serving as an Intern to the United States Agency for International Development (1968) and as Consultant to the Council of State Governments (1978–79) and the U.S. Fish and Wildlife Service (1977–80), Dr. Huffman has been a Raymond Fellow, University of Chicago Law School (1972–73); Visiting Professor, University of Auckland, New Zealand (1980–81); and Fellow, Institute for Humane Studies (1981). His articles and reviews have appeared in *Environmental Law, Idaho Law Review, InSite, Journal of Legal Education, Land and Water Law Review*, and *Natural Resources Journal.*

Ronald N. Johnson, Associate Professor of Economics at Montana State University, has previously taught at the University of Washington and the University of New Mexico. He received his B.S. in economics from Utah State University, his M.A. from California State University, Long Beach, and his Ph.D. from the University of Washington.

A contributor to *Bureaucracy vs. Environment* (J. Baden and R. Stroup, eds., 1981), Dr. Johnson has written articles and reviews for *American Economic Review, American Journal of Agricultural Economics, Annals of the American Academy of Political and Social Sciences, Economic Inquiry, Explorations in Economic History, Journal of Economic History, Journal of Labor Research, Journal of Law and Economics, Journal of Political Economy, Land Economics, Natural Resources Journal*, and *Southern Economic Journal.*

Michael T. Maloney, Associate Professor of Economics at Clemson University, received his B.A. from Lewis College, his M.A. from Western Illinois University, and his Ph.D. from Louisiana State University and has previously taught at Emory University. He has engaged in research for the Environmental Protection Agency, Water Resources Research Institute, and the Law Enforcement Assistance Administration. His articles have appeared in *Journal of Business, Journal of Econometrics, Journal of Law and Economics, Quarterly Review of Economics and Business, Regulation*, and *Southern Economic Journal.*

Randal R. Rucker is a Ph.D. candidate in the Department of Economics at the University of Washington. He received both his B.S. and M.S. from Montana State University and has been a Research Associate in the University's Department of Agricultural Economics and Economics. He has also taught in the Department of Economics and has been Research Assistant in the Department of Demographics at the University of Washington.

Rodney T. Smith is presently Visiting Assistant Professor of Economics and Associate Director for the Center for the Study of the Economy and the State at the University of Chicago. He received his B.A. from the University of California, Los Angeles, and his Ph.D. from the University of Chicago. Dr. Smith, who has been Visiting Assistant Professor of Property Rights, Claremont McKenna College (1977–78), Research Economist at Rand Corporation (1974–78), and Staff Economist for the Presidential Commission on Housing Policy (1973), has written and lectured extensively on the economics of public regulation. His past research has concentrated on energy regulation, taxation, private and public ownership of utilities, and U.S. grain reserve policy. His publications have included articles in *American Economic Review, Journal of Business*, and *Journal of Law and Economics.*

Timothy D. Tregarthen, author of *Food, Fuel, and Shelter* and *Dictionary of Concepts in Economics* (with N. Sidener), is Professor of Economics and Department Chairman at the University of Colorado, Colorado Springs. He received his M.A. and Ph.D. from the University of California, Davis, and has been a Visiting Fellow at Glacier Institute of Management, England (1967); Woodrow Wilson National Fellow (1967–68); National Defense Educational Act Fellow (1968–69); Lecturer, University of California, Davis (1970–71), and Visiting Professor, Colorado College (1980–present).

In addition to serving as consultant to the Wright-Ingraham Institute and numerous private companies, Dr. Tregarthen has written articles and reviews for *Denver Journal of International Law and Policy, Environment and Planning, Geographical Review, Scandinavian Journal of Economics,* and *Social Science Quarterly.*

Bruce Yandle, a former Senior Economist for the President's Council on Wage and Price Stability (1976–77), is currently Executive Director of the Federal Trade Commission. He is also Professor of Economics at Clemson University, having earned an M.B.A. and a Ph.D. in economics from Georgia State University.

Dr. Yandle has served as codirector for numerous housing market studies projects and as coinvestigator for Clemson's Water Resources Research Institute. His publications include *Environmental Use and the Market* (with H.H. Macaulay), *Managing Personal Finance* (with H.H. Ulbrich), *Benefit-Cost Analyses of Social Regulation* (with James C. Miller, III), and *Labor and Property Rights in California Agriculture* (with R.L. Cottle and H.H. Macaulay) and articles and reviews in *American Journal of Economics and Sociology, Business, Industrial Organization Review, Journal of the Academy of Marketing Science, Journal of Economic Issues, Journal of Financial and Quantitative Analysis, Journal of Labor Research, Land Economics, Policy Analysis, Public Choice, Public Finance, Public Finance Quarterly, Quarterly Review of Economics and Business, Reason, Regulation, Social Science Quarterly*, and *Southern Economic Journal.*